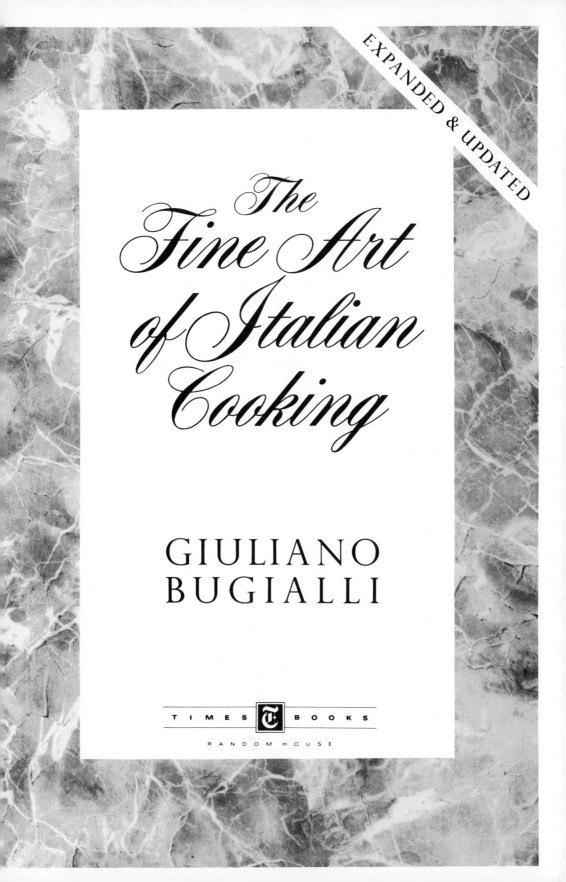

EXPANDED & UPDATED

The Fine Art of Italian Cooking

GIULIANO BUGIALLI

TIMES BOOKS

RANDOM HOUSE

Library of Congress Cataloging-
in-Publication Data
Bugialli, Giuliano.
The fine art of Italian cooking/Giuliano Bugialli.—
Expanded and updated.
p.   cm.
Includes index.
ISBN 0-8129-1838-X
1. Cookery, Italian.   I. Title.
TX723.B76   1989
641.5945—dc20   89-40182

ILLUSTRATIONS BY MICHAEL IVENITSKY
DESIGNED BY BARBARA MARKS
ART DIRECTION BY NAOMI OSNOS

Manufactured in the United States of America

9   8   7   6   5   4   3   2

First Edition

TO MY MOTHER,

WHO WAS THE WORST COOK

IN THE FAMILY,

BUT THE BEST EVERYTHING ELSE

I would like to thank Henry Weinberg, without whom this new edition of the book could not have been done, and both him and Audrey Berman for their help with the first edition.

For individual recipes I thank Avv. Fabrizio Vitaletti of Florence, and, for advice on the Genoese recipes, Mrs. Carla Sanguineti Weinberg.

For permission to reproduce manuscript material, we are deeply grateful to Biblioteca Casanatense (#255), Biblioteca Universitaria di Bologna (#158), and the Library of Congress (Medieval #153).

Contents

Preface
to the Second Edition

*T*he *Fine Art of Italian Cooking* is celebrating its twelfth birthday with a new edition. The original appeared in 1977 in a quite different environment regarding Italian cooking. The importance of Tuscan *cucina* for Italy as a whole was not widely understood outside the home country, and so I felt it important to clarify this point. Some joked about my so-called chauvinism, but the laughter was sympathetic. Tuscan *cucina* is now much better known, and I hope you can pardon my satisfaction for the role that this book played in that evolution.

The other main purpose of the original was to show that Italian was a fully developed "cuisine," to be taken as seriously as any, not merely another ethnic food. In order to do this I traced its history back to the Renaissance and perhaps created some incredulity to my claims that many "haute cuisine" dishes had an Italian, indeed a Florentine, origin. Again it is satisfying that these claims now seem to be taken for granted and are not considered at all "chauvinistic."

And so, these aims accomplished, let us go on to a new, somewhat expanded version that fills in a few lacunae in the original. I have corrected the relative lack of veal and of dried pasta dishes. The historical background section of the introduction, which many seemed to enjoy, is expanded to include an account of the famous wedding of

Maria de' Medici to Henry of Navarre, soon to be King of France. Discussion of ingredients has required revisions. Olive oil availability has changed drastically, for both gastronomic and health reasons; extra-virgin olive oil has changed from an esoteric term to a household phrase. *Pancetta,* porcini mushrooms, a great variety of Italian cheeses, fresh herbs, radicchio, are all so generally available that one need no longer suggest substitutions.

To make a more fully rounded picture of Tuscan cooking, I have added almost thirty additional recipes. And so, this, the first of my children, has gotten a little taller but is still recognizable. I hope you like what has been added.

GB

Preface to the First Edition

*I*f you have traveled in Italy or known Italians abroad, you quickly realized that a Roman is different from a Florentine, a Neapolitan from a Milanese. These differences are even stronger in Italy than in most other countries, because each of its areas had both a long history and a developed culture before it became part of the unified Italy of recent times. In customs and in language, there are dialects—and there are dialects in food as well.

All the Italian cookbooks I have seen abroad are written from the point of view of some "dialect," which then extends outward to include food from the other regions. Recently, there have been books written from the viewpoints of Naples, Sicily, and Emilia-Romagna. My book starts with a Tuscan, even a Florentine, point of view. But, just as one speaks dialect or vernacular in the home, with the family, so home cooking tends to exaggerate regional differences. And very rarely does one region restrict its cooking to those dishes which are "alla" that region. *Cotoletta alla milanese* is made all over Italy, as is *Pizza alla napoletana.*

In examining many Italian cookbooks abroad, particularly those that stress northern Italian, one finds an inordinate number of Tuscan recipes. Probably the most immediate reason for this is that the most influential cookbook of modern times in Italy was that of Pellegrino Artusi, a Florentine of the last century. He established Tuscan cooking as the standard of *buona, sana cucina,* "good, healthy cooking." There is a further reason, however, of which most people are still unaware. Just as in the midst of a peninsula of different dialects the genius of Dante, Boccaccio, and Petrarch was able to establish Tuscan as the Italian language, so at the same time, in the fourteenth century, Florentine cooks began to codify the cooking of the emerging Renaissance. The Florentine manuscript of the early 1300s was copied twenty-five years later by the Bolognese, fifty years later by the Venetians. By 1450 this tradition had expanded to and developed in the north of Italy and even France, and probably other countries influenced by the Italian Renaissance.

It is interesting to trace this tradition through the oldest extant manuscripts up to the early nineteenth century. They yield much valuable material that confirms the antiquity of many classic Italian dishes and help in arriving at authentic versions.

It must now be obvious that my attempt here is something more ambitious than telling you about the recipes I learned at my mother's knee. Aside from the fact that my mother hates to cook, I find that an inadequate approach for conveying the range and richness of Italian cooking.

If not in Mama's simple kitchen, where does one look for such cooking? Not in the trattorie. Essentially, trattorie are unpretentious places, generally of working-class origin, that produce dialect food, sometimes of very high quality but within a limited framework. In Florence and elsewhere in Italy, people of all walks of life enjoy the trattoria food for its honesty and simplicity, when it is genuine. The problem arises when trattorie attempt to become *ristoranti,* and they decide to add a touch of the "continental," or what they think is French cooking. Then they cease to be honest.

The fine cooking in Italy, that which indeed retains the old Italian gastronomy, takes place in the homes of certain old Italian families, who have taken the trouble to preserve their traditions. One starts with these recipes. It is then very important to verify both the antiquity and the correctness of these recipes through ancient manuscripts and old printed books. By scrupulously comparing one's own experience with that of the old families, as well as with old manuscripts and early books, it is possible to arrive at generalizations about techniques, spicing, and so on, and to produce authentic recipes that remain gastronomically very valid indeed.

Dear reader, don't let me scare you off. This book is also a basic Italian cookbook, containing many recipes that are not too time consuming as well as some that are of more recent vintage. (I am not, for example, going to avoid dried pasta because it has formed a part of the Italian menu only for the last hundred and fifty years.) It is just that the book includes techniques, for sauces, aspics, pastry, breads, and so on, that truly belong to Italian cooking.

With the aid of illustrations, I have attempted to help the reader acquire the basic culinary techniques that are necessary for the finer Italian *cucina,* techniques that go beyond the procedure for a single recipe. These include boning poultry and fish; tying and larding meats; making stuffings, forcemeats, and sausages, broths and aspics, pastries and breads; ways of chopping and cutting; and, something about presentation.

It was not possible to do everything in this book that one could in a more specialized one, but I hope at least to provide an introduction to the technical side of the art of Italian cooking.*

I strongly feel that a northern Italian cookbook, from a Tuscan, even a Florentine, point of view is very much needed abroad. As I previously mentioned, in northern Italian cookbooks quite a large percentage of the recipes are Tuscan. I hope my colleagues will forgive me if I now say, as a native Tuscan and Florentine, that for the most part their Tuscan recipes are unrecognizable to me. It would be pointless, even ungracious, for me to give specific examples of some of the gaffes in these recipes, for they could easily enough be traced to specific books and authors, some current ones justly held in high esteem for those areas closer to home in which they are indeed expert. In sum, while I don't want to criticize anyone, one simply cannot allow these completely inauthentic versions of Tuscan dishes to circulate with authority.

*This is more fully developed in my *Classic Techniques of Italian Cooking.*

In closing this preface, I would like to discuss two books of the last century, one in English and the other in Italian. These are Janet Ross's *Leaves from My Tuscan Kitchen* from the 1890s and Artusi's *The Art of Eating Well*.

Artusi's book, a classic and charming to read as well, is extremely valuable historically. It gave Italians in the last century the impetus to keep to their own cooking, and had a very positive influence. However, it still retains a lot of Austrian and French influence. (We must remember that when he wrote a Hapsburg was still sitting on the Tuscan throne.) For example, much as we all love sour cream, it just isn't Italian, and Artusi has recipes using it. Another problem is that Artusi's book, like most cookbooks in Italian, does not always give specific quantities and is vague on procedure. It is a book for those who already know the dishes.

The purpose of Janet Ross's book was probably to stimulate her fellow English to use more vegetables in their diet. But, while she took her recipes from the cooks in her Florentine villa, they must have been doing continental cuisine. Vegetables that are staples of the Tuscan repertory like rape and kale do not appear, while not-really-Italian vegetables such as Jerusalem artichokes and red cabbage do. And many of the recipes are overtly French. The book, then, is more an interesting historical document of what the international set who had Florentine villas ate in the late nineteenth century.

So now, after all this, perhaps you can understand why I feel that an Italian cookbook, in English, from a Tuscan point of view is necessary.

Page of an early fourteenth-century Florentine manuscript showing recipe for *savore per paparo,* a type of foie gras.

A fourteenth-century Venetian copy of a Florentine cookbook showing a recipe for *torta di latte,* a type of quiche. This manuscript also contains the recipe for *quinquinelle,* the original quenelles.

Some Historical Background

Visitors who spend a long time in Italy, especially those who come to know the language, often tell me that what they are most struck by is the uninterrupted historical continuity of Italian life and customs. The normal architecture of house and garden seems to be much the same as one sees in the paintings rescued from Pompeii and other places destroyed by the eruption of Vesuvius almost two thousand years ago.

There are also recipes that survive from that world of several thousand years ago. And why not? Many of the basic ingredients of Italian cooking were there—wine, olive oil, flour, and grains, most of the same species of game, meat, and fish, even some of the same cooking utensils in terra-cotta and copper. And today we find traces of two kinds of cooking. While Apicius's book gives us the elaborate dishes of the upper class of the Empire, there was a simpler cooking, which ordinary people ate every day, and this, like many aspects of Roman culture, came from the Etruscans, the people who inhabited Tuscany and whose descendants still live there.

We know that the upper classes in the Middle Ages ate in a way that was related to the way the ancient Romans did, and that a probable by-product of wars and campaigns of that period, such as the Crusades, was the protection of trade routes that brought back the important spices and other ingredients necessary for that elaborate cooking. (It seems probable that in these centuries the tradition of "high" gastronomy best survived at Constantinople, capital of the surviving Roman Empire untl 1453, and possibly in Moorish Spain.) Polenta and fish-in-soup dishes survived from the food of the common man.

Modern gastronomy, like most of modern culture, begins in Italy about 1300. The first cookbook manuscripts, Florentine in origin, date from that period. (France's Taillevent was almost a century later.) And it is not merely the date of these manuscripts, but also the attitude contained in them, that is important, for they look toward the future rather than the past. The manuscripts are contemporary with Giotto, the founder of modern painting, with Boccaccio and Petrarch, and with Landini, the first great Renaissance composer, all of whom were Florentines who, we hope, ate the cooking of "Anonimo Toscano," the first modern cookbook writer. Butter, unknown in Roman times, had been discovered (ironic for those who think that Florentine cooking uses olive oil but no butter), and thickening with flour was known to "Toscano," while still unknown in France; so was a sauce quite close to the modern *maionese* and "milk pies" related to the modern quiche.

The non-Italian world tends to think that Italian cooking began with the mid-fifteenth-century writer Platina, and with the recipes of his friend, the great chef Maestro Martino. This is because Platina was lucky enough to benefit from the invention of printing and because his book, translated into French and German, was an important medium for carrying Italian cooking into those countries. But there were manuscripts long before Platina, manuscripts that have come to be studied only recently, and that I have studied for this book. (It was in one of the manuscripts, from the fourteenth century, that I found the term *quinquinelle* describing a sausage-shaped forcemeat, without skin or pastry covering—the origin of quenelles.) There is a tendency also to rely on *Larousse Gastronomique* for historical information, and this is not always accurate. For one thing, *Larousse,* I believe, relies completely on secondary sources, such as the books of Carême from the early nineteenth century, as well as histories that are not aware of manuscripts before Platina.

It is only when we realize the extent of Renaissance Italian influence on France, Germany, England, Poland, and other European countries in other cultural fields that it is possible to believe just how great was the gastronomic influence. There are many dishes we now do not consider Italian that probably originated there, or at least we can say they are present in sixteenth-century Italian cookbooks. These include cherry soup, which we now associate with Hungary; turtle soup, now thought of as English and American; fruit pies, again English and American; stuffed cabbage, Eastern European, and so many dishes now thought to be French that it is not possible to list them.*

In this vein, we can safely say that Italian gastronomic supremacy was not challenged until the time of Louis XIV, a ruler who, ironically, was grandson of a Medici, whose theater was called *Theâtres des Italiens,* and whose court composer and ballet master was the Florentine Lulli. It was a long time, however, before this challenge succeeded to any great extent. For one thing, while La Varenne's book was influential in Italy from about 1690 on, it was so principally because it listed actual amounts with the ingredients, not because its culinary approach was basically different from that of the Italians. Also, the *potacci* and fricassèe found in La Varenne already existed in sixteenth-century Italian books. In the eighteenth century, some Italian dishes were given French names, but the dishes were basically the same. And as late as the second half of the eighteenth century, Catherine the Great of Russia still had an Italian rather than a French chef.

---

*It is worth noting just how the discovery of America affected first Italian and then other European food. The Spanish first brought back tomato and potato plants, but only for ornamental purposes. Again, it was the curious Florentines who started to eat them, in the sixteenth century. Tomatoes were eaten green, either breaded and fried or in *frittate*. Green tomatoes are eaten in both these ways to this day, and the recipes are included in this book. (The spread of the red, ripe tomato did not come until centuries later, going from Naples all over Italy.) Potatoes were widely eaten in Florence two centuries before Parmentier, and deep-fried potato strips, so-called French-fried potatoes, are doubly Florentine, since both the potato and deep-frying were taken to France from Florence. Cannellini beans, sometimes called Tuscan beans in modern times, are white kidney beans and come from America. It is doubly ironic when Italian cookbooks in America tell you to substitute Great Northern beans for Tuscan beans, since the latter are even more American than Tuscan. Turkey was quickly adopted by the Italians in the sixteenth century, to substitute for peacock, that most prestigious bird. Americans, who rightfully consider the turkey their own, are generally surprised to discover for how many centuries it has been an intrinsic part of the Italian menu.

My purpose in giving this survey is to make the reader radically rethink what he regards as Italian cooking and its proper limits. And I can only conclude it by recounting a recent experience of my own. I was amused to see an advertisement for a cooking school in Paris that stated that it was including in its curriculum of classic French dishes pastas and *risotti,* because "after all, they are among the world's great dishes." If culinary history continues the way it has gone, a hundred years from now pasta and *risotti* will be considered French dishes, possibly with French names.

"LA BUONA, SANA CUCINA"

*D*uring the sixteenth and seventeenth centuries, Italian cooking reached an incredible degree of complication and elaborateness, not only in the cooking of the dishes, but also in their presentation, compared to which even nineteenth-century presentation is pale. That was the era in which butter, ice, and sugar sculpture, still enduring today as the acme of complex presentation, reached their height. Meat was served in such a way that the animal still appeared to be alive, and the feathers of birds were put back on after the birds were cooked. The supposed living creatures were then presented in a simulated natural environment, perhaps sculpted from sugar or marzipan. Fish were served on ice "brooks" or "rivers." Famous sculptors and architects were employed to do their work in sugar or butter for important banquets, and the sculptor Canova was discovered as a twelve-year-old cook's assistant—doing the butter sculpture.* It is difficult for the modern temperament to think of works by important artists disappearing in the course of one evening's entertainment.

But the sixteenth century was also the beginning of a revolt against unhealthy and complicated cooking. Good sense was not dead, even

---

*For detailed discussion of this, see *Giuliano Bugialli's Classic Techniques of Italian Cooking*, pages 19–29 and 34–37 for presenting the "live" pheasant.

then. Many revolted against the excesses described above, just as many are today turning against all the overrichness—all the butter and cream, the foie gras, and so on—that flourished in the schools of chefs like Escoffier. In the sixteenth century the Florentines started their search for the lightest possible, the most healthy, the most elegantly simple cooking—a search that has continued to the present day.

This centuries-long search for a food that expressed the Florentine Renaissance point of view has arrived at a synthesis that stresses freshness, genuineness, and high quality of ingredients (in opposition to the view that covers up weak ingredients with spices and sauces); a classic simplification in approach to herbs and spices; and an abhorrence of heaviness, overrichness, and excessive use of fat. To this end, many spices, butter, cream, fat, and heavy sauces were removed from repertory dishes.

This is all in perfect accord with today's health preoccupations, and perhaps tells us why there is a new appreciation of Italian cooking and its natural attitude toward food.

A SIXTEENTH-CENTURY FLORENTINE DINNER

A Florentine nobleman of the sixteenth century did us the great favor of writing down the menus of every meal eaten in one of the great houses during the year 1546. Some of the dishes eaten are still associated with international gastronomy, and it is a surprise to find that they were already established at that time in Florence. The renaissance of cooking that took place in Florence starting in the fourteenth century may have been given impetus by the arrival there of the Byzantines fleeing Constantinople when it fell to the Turks. Caviar was a standard item in this Florentine household, and while we know that sturgeon existed in northern Italy at that time, even in the Arno itself (it had been the favored fish even of the ancient Romans), caviar is referred to as a dish for which the Greeks (that is, the Byzantines) had a great taste.

And it is possible, as we have suggested previously, that Constantinople was the center of gastronomy before Florence. It was at this time in Florence that the practice of dressing salad with oil and vinegar was established.

This listing of menus is particularly interesting because it shows that, for the first time in the modern West, there was a fixed order of courses and many defined conventions for formal dining. The strange thing to us is that fish and meat were never eaten on the same day. There were either many fish dishes or many meat dishes. (Eggs, mushrooms, cheese, of course, could be included with one or the other.) Indeed, the modern order of courses with fish before meat was established only relatively recently. La Varenne in 1650 and Brillat-Savarin in the early 1800s were still following the order of courses established in Florence in the sixteenth century.

The first course, called even then antipasto, was a series of appetizers quite different from what the term brings to most people's minds today. Since the pasta course was not introduced until the middle of the 1800s, the word antipasto could not have meant "before the pasta," but "before the pasto" (or meal).

The second course was the boiled course. This never varied, whether the third course was fried or roasted dishes.

The fourth, or fruit, course included both fruit and vegetables and sometimes *frutta di mare,* like oysters.* (This may be how *frutti di mare* got its name, by being included in the fruit course.) If included, cheese was most generally eaten with this course. When, however, it was cooked in a special way, such as fried or in a pastry, it could be served with the antipasti.

Pastries themselves could belong to any course, depending on what was in them. Again, it was the Florentines who tended to localize sweet dishes at the end of the meal. Honey and sugar had been used in many kinds of dishes before this time, and since cane sugar was newly available and a popular luxury in the sixteenth century, it was not possible to

---

*It was to the Florentines that we must give the credit for firmly including fruit, and especially vegetables, as a standard part of every meal. Other parts of Europe and America have lagged behind in this, even to the present day.

localize sweet dishes totally; there was, however, a great push in that direction.

Let us start with a day in Lent, March 17, 1546. We can expect a fish day. But though some of the dishes eaten hardly connote sackcloth and ashes, the meal is still simpler and contains fewer courses than would a feast-day meal.

Antipasti

Schiacciatine (little schiacciate or pizzas) with ground rosemary, olive oil, and pepper (see page 55)
White endive–dandelion salad
Tarts of pesci ignudi (a type of fish no longer available)
Fettunta, Tuscan garlic bread, with pignoli (see page 119)
Rombi (slices of turbot) fried with slices of glazed citron

The Boiled Course

Poached sturgeon (using the whole large middle section)
Little sturgeon balls, polpe, poached in a spicy fish soup
Lentil soup served with caviar
Savor bianco di Amandole, spicy almond sauce (probably to accompany the poached sturgeon)
(A great variety of sauces and savori were used to accompany these boiled and poached dishes, some of the recipes for which are given later in this book.)

The Fried Course

Fried broccoli with bitter-orange sauce and pepper
Fried tench (a freshwater fish from the Bisenzio River near Florence)
Deep-fried whole little fish from the Arno (pesciolini), squid, and little shrimp, garnished with lemon slices and olives

Fruit

Tart or pie of pureed chick-peas, with red apples (matching colors were
    important)
Ground almond pudding with sugar
Hearts of palm
Fennel

On the evening of the same day, everyone supped lightly:

Salad of mint, lettuce, field salad with flowers and capers
Spinach *alla fiorentina,* probably then as now with *balsamella* and Parmi-
    giano (see page 547)
Little pastries, some each of artichokes, cardoons, and fennel

This really was a typical day. I did not choose one that had such
rarified dishes as breasts of quail treated in some elaborate way, or
peacock tongues, or sturgeon livers. The feast days included at least two
more elaborate courses, as well as more dishes in each course. A roast
could be substituted for the fried course, but it was not usual to have
both. Game was widely used on the meat days, and since everything
was eaten in what was regarded as its best season, there was no special
single period for game.

THE MARRIAGE FEAST OF
MARIA DE' MEDICI

*T*he feast was the center of Renaissance social and artistic life.
    Theaters were revived only in the late sixteenth century, and
most entertainment took place as part of the dinner, between the
courses. Comedies, intermezzi, ballets, operas, madrigals, with sets done
by the leading artists of the time and elaborate stage machinery, all took
place at dinner. Table decoration was developed at this time, and it was
designed by major artists as a part of the staging. The feast generally

had several hundred guests seated at a huge horseshoe table, within which the spectacle took place. It was dining as theater, and, indeed, sometimes noble and royal hosts would set up stands so that the populace could sit and watch the diners as well as the entertainment.

Service of the courses was a ceremony, with a long line of waiters carrying large canisters with many courses to be placed on a credenza, if at room temperature, or on the table, if hot. The job of organizing the dinners was so important that the chief of the household, called *scalco,* was always an important nobleman himself. And some of the most popular of the first books printed were manuals for the *scalco* or *maestro di casa* or *maggiordomo,* instructing how to organize a large household for these dinners and entertainments.

The table settings had napkins that had to be folded into fantasy objects, fruit, and animals, which worked in the themes of the theatrical presentations. The art of napkin folding was so highly developed and complicated that what has passed down to us, even at its most showy, is just a shadow of the high art of that time when major sculptors designed the figures into which the napkins were to be folded, and specialists spent days or even longer in the folding techniques.

Courses were arranged as *serviti,* of which there were at least four. For each *servito,* a line of waiters would carry in large canisters containing from four to as many as thirty courses.

The first was a group of *antipasti* or appetizers, and that Italian term was used even then. The first, room temperature ones, were placed on the credenza, or were already in place when the guests sat down. (Sometimes the guests danced in another decorated salon before sitting down to table.) An example of the simplest antipasto group, on a day of Lent, served to a small group in a Florentine household in the 1540s, contained a pie of fresh caviar, a pâté in crust of wild *prugnoli* mushrooms, stuffed crabs, small fish in marinade, and *bottarga,* a dish made from salting and pressing mullet eggs, and finally, a large spicy salad. For a large feast, such as the marriage of Maria de' Medici described below, there were twenty-four dishes in the *servito.* Large feasts could include a group of hot *antipasti* as well.

The next group, called *alesso,* was made of boiled and poached dishes, and also included soups and *minestre.* Italian cooking at that time had many dishes involving meat or fish made into ravioli or *gnocchi* served in one of a large number of spicy broths, which were somewhere between a modern broth and a sauce.

For example, the large middle section of a sturgeon would be poached whole, while the meat from the other sections could be made into these dumplings, to be cooked in a classic *ginestrata* broth.* At this same Lenten meal, the boiled course contained poached tench (related to carp), small poulps (octopus or cuttlefish) in a sauce, and a *minestra,* really a soup, of asparagus and salted eel. The modern soup or *minestra* course is a holdover from this more elaborate combination of dishes.

The next *servito,* corresponding to our main course, would be the fried or roasted one. Occasionally, at a really large *convito* or feast, both might be served.

A large feast would also include a *servito* of prepared desserts, pastries, creams, aspics, pies. But the fruit course was always the last and included fresh and prepared fruits, raw vegetables, and sometimes cheese, truffles, and shellfish such as oysters.

As previously stated, the order of dishes was quite strict, though different from ours. Cooked vegetables appeared in pies or tarts or in other forms, as part of the *antipasto* or fruit courses, but not as a separate *servito.* Fish and meat were never served on the same day.

The Renaissance feast reached its climax in 1600 when Maria de' Medici became the second Queen of France from Florence's ruling family. As the guests entered the splendid Sala dei Cinquecento of the Palazzo Vecchio, frescoed by Michelangelo, Leonardo da Vinci, and Vasari, they were greeted by two large fountains spouting the liqueurs that would be served later. As mentioned before, the huge tables were arranged in a horseshoe so that the elaborate theatrical, musical, and ballet entertainments could be presented inside the table arrangement, between courses. The table settings were intimately connected with the staging of the works and were designed by the great architect Bernardo Buontalenti, also famous for his ice sculpture. The sugar sculpture was made by two of the greatest sculptors of the day, Giambologna and Pietro Tacca. It took them four months to make the sugar sculptures

*See previous section.

alone. Buontalenti also did the sets and painted the backdrops. To connect the table setting with the spectacle, Buontalenti shaped the napkins into different animals. Often a live animal such as a bird would be inside, ready to fly out when it was opened. The feasts for this wedding were also historic musically. At another dinner two days later held in the Pitti Palace, the very first opera ever written, Peri's *Euridice,* was presented within the horseshoe, one act between each two *serviti.* At the Palazzo Vecchio feast, the music was by the celebrated court composer, Cavalieri.

Servito 1: Cold Dishes

The first *servito* consisted of twenty-four cold dishes. Most of these had spectacular presentations. There was a group in which creatures were disguised to appear alive in their natural habitats. Cooked peacock was redressed in its feathers and shown eating fruit in a simulated wood. (When done for a less-than-royal feast, pheasant was commonly used.) A cooked swan, also redressed, was shown swimming on a lake of wine. A pastry fortress was made, with "live" birds perched on the turrets. Swimming "live" fish were covered by an aspic bell. An even larger group of dishes consisted of foods disguised to look like graceful animals or fantastic creatures. The turkey was made up as a hydra, the prosciutto carved into a cock, and castles were made of salami. Little dogs of *mangiar bianco (blancmange)* paraded across the table.

There was a group of pâtés in crust, their original Italian name being *pasticci.* These consisted of capon in the form of a crane, veal made to resemble a unicorn, wild boar in the form of a swan, and another of meat which looked like a dragon.

A huge butter sculpture also adorned the table, and there were bowls made out of lettuce. A large *turbante* (later given the French name *"vol au vent")* with animals perched on it, and filled pastry tarts represented Florence's own puff pastry.

Small figures of sugar were joined by fantastically carved fruits, such as citrons, made into figures, flowers, and animals.

Cooks, sculptors, and architects designed all of this fantasy as a collaborative effort and coordinated it with the scenic effects of the spectacle. At one point, for example, two clouds descended from the ceiling and hovered over the tables, revealing two singers representing Athena and Juno in chariots.

Servitos 2 and 3: Hot Dishes

The next *servito* was the first of the hot ones. It consisted of eighteen dishes including eight types of fowl: ortolans on toast, quails on a pastry crust, squab, turkey, pheasant, chicken, boned capon cooked in a spicy broth and covered with ravioli or *gnocchi* of capon meat, and hot squab pâté in crust made to resemble rocks for the scenery. Others included hare and rabbit larded with *pancetta* (bacon) and a hot pastry pie of brains and sweetbreads. The edible decorations were biscuits in the form of roses, another pâté shaped like a fish, and ears or *orecchioni* of pasta (which are still made in Italy as *orecchiette*).

After each *servito,* there was an act of a comedy and one act of an opera or intermezzo which had madrigals, ballets, and generally a mythological plot. It is interesting that the five-act comedies and operas were alternated with each other as well as with the *serviti* of dishes.

The second hot *servito,* of ten dishes, featured small game birds: thrushes with thrush sausages, doves on a crust with their pâté, and white partridge. Especially decorative were a stuffed suckling pig and a large multi-layered *torta* or *pastello*. A pie of small tart peaches accompanied the meats.

Servitos 3 and 4: Desserts; Cheese and Fruit

The nine desserts, arranged on the credenza, consisted mainly of elaborate cakes and pastries. One contained a surprise. When its crust was opened, live rabbits leaped out. This was a novel variant of the Medieval and Renaissance delight in making closed pies containing live birds which flew away when they were opened. The "four and twenty blackbirds baked in a pie" was a reality at feasts of this time.

The cheese and fruit were served together, fourteen dishes in all, the old Etruscan March cheese *(Marzolino)* and the creamy soft *Raviggiuoli* among them. The quince in aspic and the *mele* (apples) were glacéed.

What seems strange to us is that fennel, artichokes, and other vegetables were served together with strawberries, peaches in wine, and other uncooked fruit.

Since it is documented that at this time fifty-two different wines were shipped into Rome regularly, we can assume that for an extraordinary event like this there was an even wider assortment of wines to accompany these dishes.

This feast made a great impression on its guests, for there are many detailed accounts of it in letters and diaries of the period, the most famous of which is that of Michelangelo Buonarotti, the younger (poet and grandnephew of the great Michelangelo). Maria de' Medici went on to Paris to continue the tradition of great dining there, which owed so much to her predecessor, Queen Caterina de' Medici, and which she passed on to her own grandson, Louis XIV. We have a vivid picture of Maria from Rubens's celebrated series, "The Triumphs of Maria de' Medici." The last Medici, Anna Maria Luisa, died in Florence in 1741, leaving no descendants.* But the traditions of the family in art and in food still dominate the Florentine consciousness and remain a bond between Florence and France.

A FORMAL DINNER IN ITALY

*M*ost people generally prefer to dine informally, but once in a while they like to "pull out all the stops." In serving a formal Italian dinner, it is fun to do it in the real Italian manner, which is different from that of England or France.

Before dinner, *aperitivi* are served. Among the best known are dry or sweet vermouths such as Martini, Cinzano or Punt e Mes, or nonvermouths such as Campari, Cynar, or Aperol. Food is not served with aperitifs, except for some light salted thing, like almonds.

An Italian table is set with the service plate and all the silver and

---

*Many named Medici claim descent, but this is spurious.

glasses that will be used during the meal. Each course is brought on a plate, which is placed on the service dish and removed at the end of the course; the service plate is never removed during the meal. The silver used for a course is removed after that course, but since all the silver needed for the entire meal is already on the table at the beginning, no new silver is added during the meal. The same is true of glasses; a glass is removed when the wine changes, but new glasses are never added.

Bottles of wine are never kept on the table. If there are no waiters, the head of the house, if male, generally fills the glasses and keeps the bottles on a credenza until refilling is in order. If the head of the house is a woman, she either fills the glasses herself or asks her escort or the youngest male guest to do it for her.

When everyone is seated, the antipasto is served at the table. The kind of wine served depends on the dish, whether it is hot or cold. Generally, wines accompanying antipasti are on the light side, and the least serious wine of the evening.

It is with the so-called first course, or *primo piatto,* that true Italian convention departs from much overseas usage. Wine is *never* served with pasta at a fine dinner, a fact that never fails to shock my non-Italian friends. But so it is. With soups, there is more flexibility. If the soup contains wine, none is drunk to accompany it. If the soup does not contain wine, generally the wine of the antipasto course may be continued, but a serious new wine is not introduced. In an elaborate dinner, there is sometimes a course—the *piatto di mezzo,* or in-between course —between the first and second. This is usually an elaborate treatment of a vegetable, a *sformato* or some other complex dish. A typical example would be a *sformato* of vegetables with sweetbreads and brains in a sauce of *balsamella* and Parmigiano. The vegetable used should not be too closely related to the vegetable used to accompany the second course. The accompanying wine is usually the same as that of the second course, which follows.

The serious wine of the evening is usually served with the second course, *secondo piatto.* Usually one vegetable accompanies this course, served in a separate dish. The only exception to this is in those dishes of which the vegetable is an integral part, such as *arista* with *rape,* in which the vegetable should be served on the same dish as the meat.

Bread is always served with the second course, but is never accompanied by butter. The bread is brought in whole and then cut on the credenza, *not* on the table, in the presence of guests. It is then passed around in a basket. The bread is not put on the plate with the main dish, but is usually left to rest on the table next to the dish. However, lately little silver bread dishes have been introduced.

In general, Italians, not liking to confuse a dinner with a wine tasting, do not use more than three wines plus *aperitivo* in a single meal. In any case, never serve more than one wine with the same course.

A salad may be served in lieu of the vegetable accompanying the second course. The dressing is always oil, salt, and either wine vinegar or lemon juice. Herbs, cheeses, croutons, and similar additions to a dressing are never used. If a cooked vegetable accompanies the second course, no salad is served. There is no separate salad course.

Next there is a fruit or cheese course—one or the other, not both. The well-known cheese-pear combination would not be used in a formal dinner. A mild cheese is served, such as Taleggio, a soft pecorino, or even a factory cheese such as Bel Paese. A strong cheese such as Gorgonzola, Parmigiano, provolone or even an aged pecorino would not be appropriate. If cheese is served, the wine of the previous course is continued. If fresh fruit is served instead, it would not be accompanied by wine. If the fruit is cooked or embellished, as, for instance, strawberries or raspberries with whipped cream or in wine, it would be a combined fruit and dessert course. Except when the fruit is in wine, a fruit dessert may be accompanied by a sweet wine.

The dessert course is accompanied by a sweet wine or by a dry or sweet spumante or champagne. (Just as the French under English influence made champagne drier in the late nineteenth century, the Italians have now made some of their spumante dry.)

Espresso coffee, always black, is served after dinner, in another room. It is not served at the dinner table. Brandy and cordials are not really in order at a formal dinner in Italy.

Obviously, Italians do not dine formally every night. But it may amuse you to try it when you're planning a "big" night with an ambitious Italian menu.

Some Basic Ingredients

HERBS AND SPICES

*T*he basic herbs of Tuscan cooking are rosemary *(rosmarino* or *ramerino)*, parsley *(prezzemolo)*, sage *(salvia)*, and basil *(basilico)*. Tarragon *(dragoncello)* is a specialty of Siena, and marjoram and thyme are called for in special dishes. Oregano *(origano)* is rarely used in the north of Italy.

The omnipresent spices of Tuscany are nutmeg *(noce moscata)* and, of course, black pepper. White and hot red pepper are sometimes called for, and a great variety of spices is used in the older recipes—cinnamon, ginger, cardamom, coriander, and cumin. Saffron was once used as much as salt and pepper are today; fennel seed and aniseed are used in special dishes.

Basil

Fresh basil is a joy and a necessity to many Italian dishes. Since it is not available all year, a number of ways have grown up over the centuries of preserving it. For me the least satisfactory of these are freezing and drying, since they both cause the essential flavor to be much diminished.

The two better ways to preserve fresh basil are in coarse salt or under olive oil.

Bay Leaves or Laurel

Fresh bay leaves of course are best. In areas where they are not available, commercial dried ones must be substituted. Look for leaves that retain a fresh green color.

Parsley

Use the flat large-leaved, so-called Italian parsley. Fortunately, it is available throughout the year. Do not confuse it with cilantro, used in Chinese and Mexican cooking.

Rosemary

Commerical dried rosemary leaves are perfectly fine to use, though they should not be so old that they have lost their flavor. They should be blanched in boiling water for a few seconds to soften before using. Even better, of course, is fresh rosemary. The plants grow well indoors in pots, as well as outside. The rosemary plant does most of its growing in the winter, so if it is kept indoors, it should be placed near a window that can be kept partially open in winter. The reason many indoor rosemary plants don't thrive is because they don't get enough air and light. Try to have enough plants to enable you to put an entire sprig inside a roast fish or fowl.

Quantities in the recipes which follow are for fresh, blanched, dried, or rosemary preserved in salt. Use the same amount of any of the three.

Sage

Much dried sage seems to come from the Balkans and has a flavor that is not appropriate to Italian cooking. It is best to take the trouble to buy fresh sage in season and to preserve it in salt. Fresh American sage is the same as Italian.

Tarragon

Dried tarragon usually comes from France. It is perfectly adequate, though fresh tarragon is of course preferable when it is in season. Be careful when you buy fresh tarragon when it is out of season in your area: Some hothouse versions are completely flavorless and usually, to compound the insult, very expensive.

PRESERVING HERBS IN SALT

In a Mason jar with a lid that closes tightly, place a layer of coarse-grained or kosher salt. Make a layer of fresh leaves of the herb you wish to preserve (basil, sage, rosemary). Before using, wipe the leaves with paper towels, but do not wash them.

Alternate layers of salt and leaves until the jar is full. Cover the top layer with a layer of salt.

Basil preserved in this way loses some of its green color, but preserves all of its flavor. Dishes based on really fresh basil such as *pasta alla puttanesca* (see page 181) would not be possible, but almost all others are with this substitution. Keep the jar in the refrigerator, tightly closed. The color and flavor of other herbs is preserved.

Or preserve basil leaves covered with olive oil. This type of preserved basil is best for making pesto, as it keeps its green color rather well. However, it is not useful for dishes that do not have an olive oil taste.

Herbs preserved in salt are washed only before using for cooking.

OLIVE OIL

*E*ach December in Italy, olives are passed through a press, usually made of heavy stone, to obtain their oil. The fruit is pressed three times. The first pressing produces extra-virgin olive oil, which must always meet certain standards of acidity, color, and aroma to qualify for that classification. The cult of olive oil in Italy and critical refinement about it equals the fanaticism of wine expertise. The olives must be hand gathered to qualify for the extra-virgin label and the acidity, the percentage of oleic acid, must not exceed 1 percent of weight. The less the oleic acid, the better the flavor. The two lesser classifications, virgin and pure olive oil both must not exceed 2 percent weight in acid. Otherwise virgin oil retains the high standards of extra-virgin, while pure olive oil is subjected to alkaline and physical processing and is mixed with some extra-virgin oil to obtain an acceptable result.

Flavor varies according to climate and soil and the more than sixty olive varieties grown for oil production. The darker oils may or may not have a richer flavor; it depends on region and the mode of production.

The best olive oil is produced on farms, often connected with vineyards. Ideally it is best to use oil from a particular region for dishes of that area. Those sections of Italy which do not produce olive oil rarely have regional dishes that utilize it. The lighter but rich and flavorful oil of Liguria is perfect for its recipes, that of Puglia and Calabria for the wonderful Southern repertory. Tuscany has celebrated oil, but one must be careful as the demand for it has now exceeded the supply and the farms producing it now import some oil from other regions to bottle under their labels. Taste the oil to be sure.

Extra-virgin olive oil from most regions of Italy is now widely exported and available in other countries. Get familiar with the wide range of it as you would with wines. For the mostly central Italian recipes, use oil from Lazio and Umbria as well as Tuscan. An extra bonus has been granted us in recent years: This delicious oil is now considered to be extremely healthful. Use it and enjoy it.

BUTTER AND "COOKING OIL"

hough Renaissance cookbooks have sections on how to make different kinds of *butiro,* the old word for "butter," Italy does not produce outstanding butter compared to Denmark, France, or the United States. Italian butter is lower in fat, which could be good, but it is also less tasty. Parma, the home of Parmigiano cheese, produces some of the best Italian butter.

Butter as a spread is almost unused in Italy, except with caviar; cooking with butter is characteristic of the regions north of Tuscany. Sauces based on butter, flour, and milk (as, for instance, *balsamella*) very probably originated in Florentine cooking of the Renaissance, but today it is Emilia-Romagna, with Bologna (which Italians call "Bologna the fat"), that stresses, and perhaps overuses, butter and cream, like some old-style French cooking. In Bologna, a good festive meal could very well have a buttery and/or creamy base to every course. This is not typically Italian, not very healthy, and really just as limited as having a tomato base to every course. However, used with proper balance and sparingly, butter- and cream-based dishes have an important place.

The cooking oil most used in Italy—light and really completely tasteless—is a mixed-seed oil called, generically, *olio di semi*. Outside of Italy, this mixture may be approximated with ⅔ corn oil and ⅓ sunflower (not safflower) oil. Peanut oil is rarely used in Italy. Olive oil is no longer common for frying in Italy; in certain dishes, a little is sometimes added for its flavor to vegetable oil.

PROSCIUTTO, SALAMI, AND PANCETTA

*I*taly produces a boiled ham *(prosciutto cotto)* quite similar to that produced in other countries, so when it is called for in a dish, there are no problems at all.

But it is the uncooked, unsmoked ham cured in salt that is the most characteristic kind of Italian ham. When we say "prosciutto" abroad, we refer to this kind of ham, though properly it is *prosciutto crudo,* or uncooked ham.

Prosciutto varies a great deal in Italy according to region. The celebrated prosciutto of Parma from Langhirano is sweet, and if it is possible to say such a thing, it is almost like a "dessert" prosciutto. It is this prosciutto that goes so well with fresh figs or melon as an antipasto. (More salty prosciutti are less appropriate.) San Daniele prosciutto from the far north of Italy is equally celebrated and less sweet.

Tuscan prosciutto, salty and more countrified, is used with salami for antipasto, accompanied by good Tuscan bread without salt.

Making your own prosciutto is not difficult if you have an unheated outdoor shed behind the house, but I am not suggesting it here.

Italians rarely smoke meats, and smoked prosciutto or *pancetta* (which would be bacon) would totally ruin most Italian dishes. However, in the extreme North of Italy, a smoked prosciutto called *speck* is used as well as a smoked *pancetta,* but these are appropriate only to dishes of the Alpine region.

Factory-made Genoese and Milanese salamis and mortadella, the original bologna from Bologna, are sometimes useful for regional dishes. The Bolognese keep the recipe for real mortadella a secret, though it is made mainly from pork.

Tuscan salamis are celebrated in Italy, but again are made on farms and vineyards rather uncommercially. The fennel-flavored *finocchiona* is especially appropriate to eat with figs and melon as antipasto. When in Italy, be sure to try both of these.

Pancetta, the same cut of pork as bacon but salted rather than smoked, is very important to Italian cooking. It is generally found in a rolled-up form, resembling a salami. If *pancetta* is not available, substitute fatty prosciutto.

WINE FOR COOKING

*G*ood-quality wine should be used for cooking. In fact, in dishes in which the wine is a main element, such as pears cooked in Chianti and port or fresh strawberries in wine, I would say that the right wine is essential to the dish.

Tuscan dishes taste more authentic when a Tuscan wine, such as imported Chianti, is used.

WINE VINEGAR

*I*n Italy, vinegar means wine vinegar. It is probably most practical to think of obtaining a "mother" and making vinegar with Italian wine.* Commercial balsamic vinegar is good but appropriate only for a limited number of dishes. The better the quality of the wine, the better the vinegar.

COARSE-GRAINED SALT

*T*his type of salt, also available as kosher salt, is much to be preferred for some purposes. In the recipes it is specifically called for when needed; otherwise use ordinary salt.

MUSHROOMS

*W*hite, cultivated mushrooms, so-called *champignons de Paris,* are not popular in Italy. There is still a wide acquaintanceship with wild mushrooms, of which the most popular is the large-capped brown *porcino* mushroom. *Porcini* grow best under the chestnut trees in Tuscany and elsewhere. They often reach great size, and the caps are broiled and eaten as a main dish. In season, they are widely available in markets there, along with several other species. The incredible flavor of *porcini* is preserved and in some ways even intensified by drying. Fortunately, dried *porcini* are available in Italian markets and gourmet shops outside of Italy. Though dried *porcini* are expensive, very small quantities go a long way, and they are worth the price. Other types of wild mushrooms are used for specific dishes in different localities, but *porcini*

*For the technique of making wine vinegar, see *Giuliano Bugialli's Classic Techniques of Italian Cooking,* page 45.

are used all over. Dried *porcini,* soaked and cleaned, impart their strong flavor to milder fresh mushrooms; the combination is useful. Soak the *porcini* in lukewarm water for a half hour, then clean off all sand attached to the stems before using.

The soaking water has a strong *porcini* flavor. It may be used for cooking after being strained through several layers of paper towels to remove sand. This water may be frozen in ice cube trays for future use in sauces.

TRUFFLES

*T*he main truffle areas of Europe are Alba and Norcia in Italy and Périgord in France. The first produces white truffles and the last two black ones: the Italians prize the white ones above the black for their great fragrance and flavor. Though they are not commercially exploited, there are also white truffles in parts of Tuscany, and a few other regions, generally gathered by local people who keep their location a well-guarded secret. No truffles have yet been discovered in the Western Hemisphere, though some knowledgeable people feel that parts of California should have them, as the countryside is similar in places to areas where they are found in Europe.* Truffles are available in cans, but exported fresh ones are increasingly available.

Many feel the fall season, with its game and truffles, is the best time to see what Italian cooking is capable of.

ALMONDS

*O*nce almonds were to European cookery what butter and cream are to French today, or tomatoes to southern Italian. Almond trees grew (and still do, in lesser numbers) all over the lands and islands

*Experiments in cultivating them are going on.

of the Mediterranean, and the trade in their nuts was a major industry. Ground up, they were used as the basic thickening and as the base of the dishes of the "white" category (remember the color categories of early cooking), such as *savor bianco* and *bianco mangiare*. Present research points to Catalonia in northern Spain as the key area for the origin of these dishes rather than France, as scholars used to automatically assume. Almond milk was also widely used, and effectively disappeared only recently.

The almond was for centuries one of the most important artistic and religious symbols of Europe. It was the symbol of fecundity. Tables for feasts were often almond shaped, and all of the paintings and early dramas about the Annunciation are full of almond shapes.

Almond trees are the first to bloom, usually in February, and to see a Mediterranean island covered with their white flowers and remarkable aroma is never to forget the experience.

BITTER ALMONDS

*A*side from the normal almond tree, there is another species that produces a nut of a totally different taste. These almonds, bitter almonds, are used extensively in Italian, Hungarian, and other types of cooking. The characteristic taste is that which predominates in the type of Italian cookie called *amaretti,* widely exported.

The real bitter almond is increasingly difficult to obtain. Even apricot pits, once substituted for their similar taste, are no longer commercially available. The nearest substitution is unblanched almonds, the skin imparting some bitterness.

ANCHOVIES

*A*nchovies are preserved in two ways: (1) in oil, filleted and lightly salted; (2) in salt, unfilleted. The first type is much more readily available and more convenient. However, the second type is preferred by good Italian cooks for their taste. They can be found occasionally in barrels, especially in Italy, but more often in large tins. It is worth the extra trouble if you can find them.

Do not hesitate to open a large can, as the anchovies can still be preserved in their salt after the can is opened. The heads of the fish are already removed, but it is necessary to fillet them—that is, to open them and remove the central bone.

Anchovy paste is a commercial preparation sold in a tube. It is, of course, inferior to a freshly prepared paste, but is sometimes useful. It substitutes only for the anchovies; other ingredients must be added to it, depending on the recipe.

CHEESE FOR COOKING

Parmigiano

What can one say in praise of Parmigiano? Not only Italian cooking, but French cooking as well could not exist without it. It comes from the zone of Parma, as the name suggests, and of Reggio Emilia. Made from cow's milk, it is aged for two or three years. The existence of Parmigiano has been documented for about two thousand years.

The word *grana* is a generic term for this kind of large wheel, hard rind cheese, developed by the Etruscans and probably the first type of cheese specifically meant for long aging and distant travel. Good *Grana Padano* is also available. The best is from the Piacenza area and is indeed called Piacentino. On these large wheels the rind often has either *Parmigiano-Reggiano, Grana Padano,* or *Grana* printed all over it.

The drier outer part of the cheese is best for grating. If the inside is still rather soft, it is better for eating. The already grated cheeses sold under the name of Parmigiano should not be considered, unless you have no other choice. In cooking, remember that these cheeses should not be allowed to brown, as they become bitter. This is dealt with in the individual recipes.

Pecorino (sheep's cheese)

Italy produces a wide variety of sheep's cheeses. Some, aged a few months, are eaten as a dessert or as snacks. When aged longer, they are used for grating. Tuscany is famous for its pecorinos, the most celebrated being those of the Siena area. These cheeses, aged a relatively short time, are increasingly available outside Italy.

The Italian pecorinos most known abroad are the aged ones used for grating, such as *Romano* and *Sardo,* from the areas of Rome and Sardinia. These usually play the same role as Parmigiano in the dishes of their areas, and are sometimes used in combination with Parmigiano. Sardo has come to be increasingly used for Genoese dishes as the local pecorinos of that area are disappearing. Romano is of course most suitable for Roman dishes or for southern Italian dishes requiring grated pecorino. For those Tuscan dishes which specifically call for pecorino, one may use substititions; such as *ricotta salata* of sheep's milk.

When buying Romano or Sardo, be careful to see that it comes from a large form of imported cheese. Local imitations should not be used unless there is no alternative.

Groviera

In the border area of Switzerland, Italy, and France a cheese is produced (of the type often called "Swiss cheese") called in Switzerland and France "Gruyère" and in Italy "Groviera," the name coming from the Swiss town of Gruyère. The French and Italian versions are not imitations since they really come from the same area. Groviera is widely used in Italy, both for eating and, grated, for cooking. If Groviera is not available, this is no problem, use Switzerland Swiss cheese or French Gruyère.

Gorgonzola

Italians don't generally like moldy cheeses with a strong smell, but Gorgonzola is the exception. It comes from Lombardy, outside of Milan. Try to get the *dolce,* or sweet, type rather than the salty. Only substitute blue cheese if you absolutely must; Gorgonzola is sweeter and milder.

Mozzarella

The best mozzarella comes from the *bufaline* (water buffaloes) of Italy, not from cows. It is not widely available. We find imported and domestic cow's milk versions in many countries. The *bufalina* cheese is too fine, in any case, to use in cooking and is reserved for eating. Part-skim mozzarella is available and produces a lighter result.

Ricotta

Ricotta is not considered a cheese in Italy, any more than yogurt would be.* Non-Italians tend to class it with cheeses because it outwardly resembles freshly made cheese. The best Italian ricotta is dry and made from sheep's or water buffalo's milk. Most ricotta found outside of Italy is made from whole or part-skim milk and is a first curd, really like a fresh cheese and is more watery. In the recipes I have compensated for this in various ways (though not by adding flour when it is not called for). If you like, squeeze out the ricotta in a cheesecloth to make it drier. Part-skim ricotta also produces a result closer to the original.

BEANS

*C*annellini beans are picked in June and eaten fresh at that time. They are then preserved by drying. Commercial methods of drying seem to have changed in recent years. I have noticed from my own experience that cooking times seem to be drastically shorter than in the past, though even these times vary considerably. Variation depends on the source of the beans and the time of year they are used. If dried in early autumn, they further dry throughout the year. For these reasons it is best to test the beans from time to time to be sure the suggested time is correct for that particular batch. Also bear in mind that Italians like beans a little firm, even a bit al dente.

*Real ricotta is made from the "whey" or second curd.

If you wish to speed up the soaking process, a tablespoon of flour added to the water introduces some fermentation, which hastens the softening a bit.

RICE *(see page 244)*

TOMATOES (POMODORI)

*I*n Italy, plum tomatoes are used for sauces. Cherry tomatoes, never eaten in salad in Italy, are preserved through the winter by keeping them on a layer of straw in a cool, high place; a few are added to cook in the broth. The larger tomatoes are used for salad, and are generally eaten greener than they are abroad.

Tomatoes were brought to Europe from South America by the Spanish, who used them for decoration, never to eat. It was the Florentines who, in the sixteenth century, first ate them, as we have already mentioned, but the real spread of the tomato in Italy and France began only in the late 1700s.

One must join in the tragic chorus of those complaining about the decline of tomato quality due to mass marketing. Mealy tomatoes with thick, difficult-to-bruise skin are promoted because they can travel; the tender-skinned varieties (close in quality and texture to the San Marzano type) are less available. Also, like other fruit, tomatoes are picked unripened in order to make them last longer; they ripen artificially and lose their flavor. The great advantage is supposed to be that we can have fresh tomatoes all year long if they can travel long distances.

For sauces, fresh, very ripe plum tomatoes are best. But, because of their sporadic availability, the quality of canned tomatoes becomes an important matter. We recommend, in the following order of preference:

1. San Marzano tomatoes (from the Naples area). Abroad, the can should say "imported from Italy." Be particularly careful to check that the label says "imported from *Italy*."

2. Domestic plum tomatoes. In some countries they are often less ripe when canned, so they must be cooked at least fifteen minutes longer than the Italian ones. They also tend to be more watery, but the extra cooking will also take care of that, since it reduces the liquid. Do not add sugar in an attempt to duplicate the taste of the sweeter San Marzanos. It creates an artificial, unpleasant taste. Better less sweet but natural.
3. Imported (not Italian). Some brands distribute some cans that say "imported," but in small print you can read that it is from another country, not Italy.

Tomato Paste

Tomato paste is not a substitute for tomatoes, but an ingredient in its own right, with its own taste. Some imported brands are packaged in tubes, so you can use a little at a time and not waste what remains. Encourage your stores to stock these tubes.

A Note on Equipment

SEASONING NEW POTS

*T*o initiate aluminum or stainless steel pots, the only thing you have to do is carefully clean them. But you must be very careful to season other types of pots in the right way.

For Terra-cotta Pots (glazed or unglazed)

Place the pots in cold water for 24 hours. Remove the pots from the water, fill them with more cold water, and let stand for 24 hours more.

Remove the water from the pot and carefully rub it, to be sure that any remaining surface dust is removed. The terra-cotta pot is now ready to be used, with the following cautions: Always put the pot on a "flame tamer." Start with a low heat until the pot is well warmed, then turn up the heat.

Terra-cotta pots are used a lot, not only because they retain heat evenly but because they give the food a particular "soft" taste that is not possible to reproduce with a different pot. In Italy I think there is no family without a very old terra-cotta casserole or saucepan in which meat sauce is made year after year.

In the old times, terra-cotta pots were seasoned not only by placing them in water but also by rubbing them with garlic cloves afterward. This was done to avoid the formation of mold on unglazed terra-cotta, which can happen with seasonal changes. The garlic-seasoned pot, called *la pentola all' aglio,* could be used to make meat sauce adding little or no garlic.

For Iron Frying Pans or Skillets

Iron pots are the most difficult to maintain because they must be kept well seasoned to prevent rust from forming.

Quickly wash in cold water, then dry with paper towels. Freely oil the inside of the pan, all over. Sprinkle the inside part of the pan with salt, then place the pan on a low flame, and with some paper towels rub the salt-oil mixture all over inside. Keep doing this until the salt becomes dark in color and the pan very hot.

Remove the pan from the flame, discard the salt, and wipe the pan off with paper towels.

Repeat procedure with the oil and salt. In order to have a very well-seasoned pan you must repeat the procedure at least three times.

Copper pots do not have to be seasoned.

BAGNO MARIA AND DOUBLE-BOILER TECHNIQUE

*I*n the sixteenth century, a Florentine lady, Maria de' Cleofa, invented these techniques. The French term *bain-marie* is simply a translation of *bagno maria, "maria"* referring to the lady mentioned above.

In both *bagno maria* and double boiler, you are using gentle, *moist* heat to cook slowly. In the *bagno maria,* which in Italy is used to cook, not merely to keep things warm, the large pot or container that holds the food is put into a large pot of water. The flame heats the water, which then transmits its heat to what is cooking. (*Fagioli al fiasco,* see page 516, is a special form of *bagno maria* cooking.)

In the double boiler, one pot fits atop the other. The water in the bottom pot does not actually touch the upper pot; its steam, strong because enclosed, produces the necessary heat. (See page 518 for an illustration of a double boiler.)

Pastry creams and cream custards are among the things which require the double-boiler technique. When egg yolks are mixed with sugar and heated, a slight chemical change, as well as a change in color, takes place at a critical moment. The heat must be of the special sort produced by a double-boiler technique so the eggs heat but do not cook.

These devices involving a scientific principle, however modest, were typical of the Florentine mind when the *bagno maria* was invented, roughly the period of Leonardo da Vinci.

CHOPPING WITH THE MEZZALUNA

The mezzaluna or half-moon is the usual implement for hand chopping in Italy. Cleavers and large knives are used in France but not in Italy. The rolling back-and-forth motion of the mezzaluna is perhaps less tiring because the implement does not have to be lifted off with each stroke. And when mastered it is also quicker for the same reason. If you are used to other implements, they may be substituted, but do get acquainted with the mezzaluna and see if you prefer it as do almost all Italians.

Breads and Pizzas

~

BREAD

*T*uscan "country" bread is one of the main accomplishments of Tuscan cooking. It is extremely light and yeasty, having three rather than two risings, and it contains no fat. It ranges from almost white to slightly dark and even very dark, almost completely whole wheat. Its extreme versatility comes not only from its lightness and crustiness, but also from the fact that it contains virtually no salt. For this reason, it is easier at first to appreciate the superiority of this bread when it is accompanied by olive oil and condiments, such as in the dish called *fettunta;* or when covered by a game spread, such as in the dish called *crostini;* or when it is used in hearty soups or as the basis for homemade bread crumbs. Florentines say that the Tuscan bread is not meant to be eaten alone, but rather as an accompaniment to food or as an ingredient in a dish. But eventually addiction sets in; non-Tuscans adjust to the saltlessness and go on to appreciate the bread for its own sake. For this reason, local versions of it are sold in many parts of Italy. In Bologna or Milan, one can find what the natives call "Tuscan" bread in the stores. Once attuned to it, one finds some other breads, previously admired, now too heavy or too greasy. Forgive my paean, but I am trying to convey just how passionate even the most sophisticated and traveled Florentines are about their bread.

It is possible to make completely authentic Tuscan bread outside of Italy. First of all, a brick oven can be improvised in your own oven (to be explained later). Then for the white bread, all-purpose unbleached flour is perfectly adequate. For darker bread, however, even *pane integrale,* a little more "elbow grease" is necessary, since a small amount of whole-wheat flour may have to be ground by hand, pulverized whole-wheat flour being ground differently from Italian. But the result is worth the 10 minutes or so of extra work.

Tuscan cooking includes a goodly number of dishes made with bread, more than any other Italian region, many of them dating back to a time before dried pasta was used in central Italy as a standard part of the diet. One can jump to the conclusion that these bread dishes are "peasant," or country, food, but this would be incorrect. Bread was an expensive, even luxury item until recent centuries—probably because the flour for bread had to be ground very fine. More standard, inexpensive staples were made from coarsely ground meal, from the *puls* that was the standard staple of the ancient Roman populace to the polenta of modern times. These Tuscan bread dishes come from a period when bread was a food of the rich.

We include recipes for the standard light Tuscan country bread; the dark bread *pane scuro,* which has some chaff in it; and the real whole-wheat, or *pane integrale.* In addition, there are recipes for bread with olives, bread with sausage, and the famous ancient *pan di ramerino* (bread made with rosemary and olive oil), mentioned by Boccaccio. We include as well *pane co' Santi* made with nuts, and *buccellato,* the famous sweet bread of Lucca.

After breads, there are recipes for pizzas and their Tuscan relatives, *schiacciate.* Then we discuss how to make good homemade bread crumbs, so important in Italian cooking, and little fried *crostini* (croutons) for soup.

Throughout the book there are recipes for a few of the Tuscan standby dishes that are made from bread. This saltless bread is versatile enough to form the basis for both "salted" and "sweet" dishes.

Yeast

FRESH COMPRESSED YEAST

Compressed yeast is found in cakes of just over ½ ounce, which are comparable to single packets of active dry yeast, or in 2-ounce cakes. With the resurgence of interest in home-baked bread, compressed yeast is found in more and more stores and supermarkets. This yeast should be dissolved in lukewarm water (about 85 degrees). Watch the expiration date on the wrapper to be sure that the yeast is fresh.

ACTIVE DRY YEAST

Packets of active dry yeast are found almost everywhere. Each packet is comparable to a cake of compressed yeast just over ½ ounce in weight, but may take slightly longer than compressed yeast to rise to the desired lightness. Two packets are generally necessary for each of the loaves of bread described here. This yeast must be dissolved in hot water (about 115 degrees); be sure that you use it within the cut-off date on the packet.

Absolutely do *not* proof the active dry yeast with sugar. It will ruin the taste of Tuscan bread.

Flour and Wheat

WHITE FLOUR

Unbleached all-purpose flour works well for Tuscan bread; no special or imported flours are necessary. Do not sift the flour before using. One cup of flour weighs 4 ounces.

DARK FLOUR

To make both the dark bread and the whole-wheat bread, a little extra work is necessary, for it is not possible to use most already ground dark flour. Wheat is ground with a cylindrical grinder in Italy, instead of the rotary type used in some places, and the result is a completely different type of dark flour, in which the chaff is not pulverized but remains in larger pieces. There is, however, an easy solution to this. The old-fashioned wooden hand coffee-grinders are still used and widely available. Using the hand coffee-grinder and winter-wheat berries, widely available in health food stores and elsewhere, you can grind, in about 10 minutes, the small amount of dark flour necessary to mix with the white flour for *pane scuro,* the dark bread.

Improvising a Brick Oven

The taste of bread varies a lot depending on how it is baked. The optimum for taste and for consistency of crust is obtained by baking bread in a brick oven, heated by burning oak branches mixed with a few walnut branches, and then swept out with a broom of olive branches dampened with rain water. This is the old way of baking bread, and the result is superb. The bread has a perfume that is impossible to forget, and the crust has a crispness obtainable only by baking in a brick oven. While we may not be able to duplicate the flavor produced by oak, walnut, and olive, we can easily produce a brick oven.

To improvise a brick oven in any stove, just cover the middle shelf of the oven with a layer of ovenproof unglazed terra-cotta bricks or tiles from ½ inch to 1 inch thick. It is only the bottom surface that must be of brick in order to get the effect of a brick oven.

Be sure to light the oven at least 10 minutes before the usual time, because bricks need extra time to warm up.

Pane toscano

TUSCAN COUNTRY BREAD

MAKES 1 LOAF

*T*o make the basic white bread, use unbleached all-purpose flour. First, the yeast is dissolved and mixed with a little flour and allowed to rise, then the risen "sponge" is mixed with the rest of the flour and the dough allowed to rise again. Finally, the dough, which is not placed in any pan or container, is put into the oven, directly upon the bricks. Though the dough is not actually punched down when carried to the oven, it does fall, and has to rise a third time in the oven. This third rising, once much used but now rare, produces a very light bread.

Begin to make the bread at least 6 hours before you need it, as it requires at least 2 hours for the two risings, 55 minutes in the oven, and 3 hours to cool. (A little leeway should be left in case the yeast rises more slowly than usual.) Remember, concentrated yeast should be dissolved in lukewarm water, active dry yeast in hot water. The latter may take a little longer to rise to the required lightness. (The illustration on page 42 shows the use of the hands and movements for kneading.)

(continued)

PANE TOSCANO *(continued)*

Bread is always served with the second course in an Italian meal, and with cheese if there is a cheese course. As we have seen, it is also used for a good many other things. Tuscan white bread has no oil, but can still keep for some days wrapped in a cotton towel—not in plastic or foil, as it will become soggy. It can also be frozen.* Naturally, this bread has an affinity for Chiantis and other Tuscan wines. (Tuscan cheeses complete the trinity.)

Tuscan bread is not eaten with butter at meals. The main exception is in *crostini* with butter and caviar, as an antipasto. Bread and butter is sometimes eaten as a snack, particularly by children.

FOR THE "SPONGE" (FIRST RISING)

1 ounce (2 cakes) compressed fresh yeast or 2 packages active dry yeast

½ cup lukewarm or hot water, depending on the yeast

½ cup plus 1 tablespoon unbleached all-purpose flour

FOR THE DOUGH (SECOND RISING)

5 cups unbleached all-purpose flour

1¾ cups lukewarm water

Pinch of salt

DISSOLVE the yeast in the water in a small bowl, stirring with a wooden spoon.

Place the ½ cup flour in a large bowl, add the dissolved yeast, and mix with the wooden spoon until all the flour is incorporated. Sprinkle the additional tablespoon of flour over, then cover the bowl with a cotton dishtowel and put it in a warm place away from drafts. Let stand until the sponge has doubled in size, about 1 hour.

Arrange the 5 cups of flour in a mound on a pasta board, then make a well. Place the sponge from the first rising in the well, along with the salt and ½ cup of the lukewarm water.

With a wooden spoon, carefully mix together all the ingredients in

*Freezing does not affect the crust, but the inside becomes more crumbly. The bread works perfectly for cooking and toasting, but perhaps should not be served as is.

the well, then add the remaining water and start mixing with your hands, absorbing the flour from the inside rim of the well little by little (see the illustration below).

Keep mixing until all but ½ cup of the flour is incorporated (about 15 minutes), then knead the dough with the palms of your hands, in a folding motion, until it is homogenous and smooth (about 20 minutes), incorporating the remaining flour, if necessary, to keep the dough from being sticky (see the illustration at the top of page 42).

Give the dough the shape you prefer (a long or round loaf), then place in a floured cotton dishtowel (see the illustration on page 42). Wrap the dough tightly in the towel and again put it in a warm place, away from drafts, and let stand until doubled in size, about 1 hour. The time varies a bit, depending on the weather.

Preheat the oven to 400 degrees. Be sure the bricks in your oven are free from dust. When the dough in the second rising has doubled in size, quickly remove from the towel and place immediately in the oven.

Bake the bread for about 55 minutes. Do not open the oven for 30 minutes after you have placed the dough in the oven.

(continued)

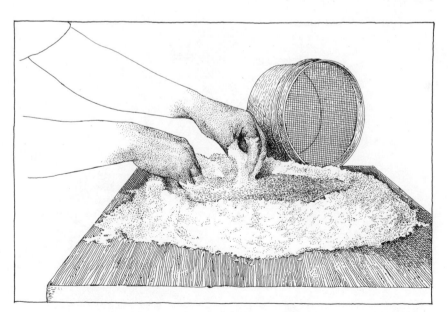

Tuscan Country Bread: Combine the flour and "sponge" (first rising).

Knead the dough.

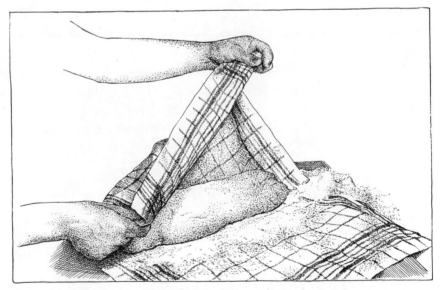

Cover the shaped dough with a towel for the second rising.

COOLING THE BREAD

When the bread is finished, remove it from the oven and place it on a pasta board, standing on one of its sides, not lying flat. The bread must cool for at least 3 hours before it is at its best for eating, and the room where the bread cools must be very airy.

Pane scuro

TUSCAN DARK BREAD

MAKES 1 LOAF

*D*arker Tuscan breads are as common as ordinary "country" bread in Florence and the rest of Tuscany. They are made in the same way, with the three risings and the brick oven. The major difference is that the darker flour is coarser and requires more yeast in order to rise.

The darker breads last longer than the white bread, as they do not dry out as fast. For dishes such as the salad *panzanella* (see page 113) or the bread soup, they are preferable to the lighter bread.

Using a hand coffee-grinder, grind ¼ pound of winter-wheat berries, and mix all of it, wheat and chaff, with 5 cups unbleached all-purpose flour. The ratio 1 to 5 dark to white gives a good dark bread.

Follow the directions for *pane toscano* on page 39, but using 1½ ounces (3 cakes) of compressed fresh yeast (or 3 packages active dry yeast) for the "sponge" and 1 cup (¼ pound) whole-wheat flour, ground as described above, plus 5 cups unbleached all-purpose flour, instead of all-white flour, for the second rising.

Pane integrale

TUSCAN WHOLE-WHEAT BREAD

MAKES 1 LOAF

*F*ollow the directions for *pane toscano* on pages 39–43, but using 2 ounces (4 cakes) compressed fresh yeast (or 4 packages active dry yeast) for the "sponge" and 2 cups (½ pound) whole-wheat flour,

(continued)

PANE INTEGRALE *(continued)*
ground as described on page 38, plus 4 cups unbleached all-purpose flour, instead of the all-white flour, for the second rising.

Pane con salsicce

SAUSAGE BREAD

MAKES 1 LOAF

*T*he sausage bread described below and the bread with olives on page 45 are both snacks rather than bread to be eaten with a meal. In the country, especially in the vineyards and villas, bread was usually baked in large quantities, and one of each of these would be included for *merenda,* or "snack." Because the sausages or olives make the dough heavier, and more difficult to rise, extra yeast is added.

The sausage bread is also deliciously flavored with sage.

½ pound sweet Italian sausages without fennel seeds (preferably Tuscan, see page 449)

2 tablespoons olive oil

FOR THE "SPONGE" (FIRST RISING)
1½ ounces (3 cakes) of compressed fresh yeast or 3 packages dry active yeast
¼ cup lukewarm or hot water, depending on yeast

½ cup plus 1 tablespoon unbleached all-purpose flour

FOR THE DOUGH (SECOND RISING)
5 cups unbleached all-purpose flour
1¾ cups lukewarm water
Pinch of salt

4 or 5 sage leaves, fresh or preserved in salt (see page 19), torn in thirds
2 teaspoons olive oil

CUT the sausages into 1-inch pieces, then put, along with the olive oil, into a saucepan and sauté very gently for 10 minutes. Remove from the flame and set aside until needed.

Using the ingredients listed, make the "sponge" and dough according to the directions for *pane toscano* on pages 40–41, through the kneading of the dough.

Add the sausage pieces and the sage leaves to the dough and knead gently for 5 minutes more.

Lightly oil a 10-inch springform pan using the olive oil. Place the dough in the pan, cover with a cotton dishtowel, and put in a warm place, away from drafts. Let the dough stand until doubled in size (about 1 hour); the time will vary a bit, depending on the weather.

Preheat the oven to 400 degrees.

When the dough has doubled in size, remove the towel and immediately place the springform pan in the oven. Bake the bread for about 60 minutes; do not open the oven for 30 minutes after you have placed it in the oven.

Remove the pan from oven, allow to cool for 5 minutes, then open it and transfer the bread to a pasta board.

To cool the bread, follow the directions on page 42.

Pane con olive

BREAD WITH OLIVES

MAKES 1 LOAF

*L*arge olives are used in olive bread. In Tuscany, small olives are used to make the marvelous oil, but large ones were cultivated for eating. This type, so-called Greek olives, are now even being imported into Tuscany, as the cultivation of olives for eating is disappearing there, along with the ancient agriculture. The olives are usually baked into the bread with their pits, but since we are no longer used to this, I advise you to pit the olives first—since someone might just bite too hard and lose a tooth.

PANE con olive is made exactly the same as *pane con salsicce,* except that ½ pound pitted black olives are kneaded into the dough instead of the sautéed sausages, and the sage is left out of the ingredients for the second rising. See pages 44–45 for instructions.

Pan di ramerino

ROSEMARY BREAD

MAKES 1 LOAF

*T*he earliest known source for the *pan di ramerino* recipe is a sixteenth-century manuscript that belonged to the Medici family, but the dish is even older. In certain earlier periods it was associated with Thursday of Easter week, when it was customary to visit seven churches. During the period of these visits, vendors at stands outside the churches would sell little *panini di ramerino* with crosses on top, much like the English hot cross buns. The hawkers would shout one of the best-known Florentine street cries, *"Pan di ramerino all'olio."* Our recipe is for the older version, the large single *pane,* without religious association, and said to have been used to place food on, in lieu of dishes, before such conveniences were common. Nowadays, *pan di ramerino* is eaten all year round, and is one of the favorite snacks of Florentine schoolchildren.

Despite its additional ingredients—rosemary, olive oil, and raisins —the technique of making *pan di ramerino* is the same as that of making Tuscan bread. The same can also be said for the following recipes with special ingredients, *buccellato* (see page 48) and *pane co' santi* (see page 50).

FOR THE "SPONGE" (FIRST RISING)
1 ounce (2 cakes) compressed fresh yeast or 2 packages active dry yeast

1/2 cup lukewarm or hot water, depending on the yeast
1 cup unbleached all-purpose flour

FOR THE DOUGH (SECOND RISING)
4 1/2 ounces raisins
1/2 cup plus 2 tablespoons olive oil
2 heaping tablespoons rosemary leaves, fresh or preserved in salt or dried and blanched

1/2 cup lukewarm water
3 cups less 2 tablespoons unbleached all-purpose flour

DISSOLVE the yeast in the ½ cup lukewarm or hot water. Put the cup of flour in a bowl and add the dissolved yeast. Mix until thoroughly combined, then cover the bowl with a cotton dishtowel and let stand in a warm, draft-free place until doubled in size (35 minutes to 1 hour, depending on the freshness of the yeast).

Meanwhile, in another bowl, soak the raisins in lukewarm water to cover for 15 to 20 minutes.

Place the ½ cup olive oil in a saucepan with 1 heaping tablespoon of the rosemary and sauté very lightly, until the rosemary turns golden. Allow to cool (about 15 minutes). When the "sponge" is ready, mix the olive oil containing the rosemary into it with a wooden spoon.

Drain the raisins and add to the "sponge"-rosemary mixture, along with a pinch of salt and ½ cup lukewarm water. Mix everything together with a wooden spoon, and then, when thoroughly combined, add the remaining rosemary, uncooked. Incorporate 1 cup of flour, little by little, continuously mixing with the wooden spoon.

Sprinkle the remaining flour (almost 2 cups) on a pasta board and place the dough on it. Knead the dough until all the flour is incorporated, then oil your hands and continue to knead for 8 to 9 minutes more. Repeat, oiling your hands again and kneading for a final 8 or 9 minutes.

Oil an 8½-inch springform pan. Place the dough in springform pan and let rise in a warm, draft-free place, covered with a cotton dishtowel, until doubled in size (about 40 to 55 minutes).

Preheat the oven to 425 degrees.

Bake the bread for 40 to 50 minutes, until the crust is brown and the bottom sounds hollow when rapped with the knuckles.

Pan di ramerino may be eaten warm after 15 or 20 minutes, or cold.

Buccellato

MAKES 1 LOAF

A sweet bread from the old walled town of Lucca, it is eaten as a snack or with strawberries as a dessert (see page 603), and can be made in a regular loaf shape or as a ring. Because of the glacéed fruit, raisins, and other extra ingredients, it requires more yeast than ordinary bread.

You can't stroll through Lucca's marvelous old piazzas without seeing someone eating *buccellato.*

FOR THE "SPONGE" (FIRST RISING)

1 cup milk
2 ounces (4 cakes) compressed
fresh yeast or 4 packages
active dry yeast

2 cups unbleached all-purpose
flour
Pinch of salt

FOR THE DOUGH (SECOND RISING)

5 ounces raisins and mixed
glacéed fruit, combined
2 cups lukewarm milk
1 large orange with thick skin
10 tablespoons (5 ounces) sweet
butter
5¾ cups unbleached all-purpose
flour

1 cup less 1 tablespoon
granulated sugar
2 tablespoons light rum
5 extra-large eggs
⅓ cup dry Marsala
1½ tablespoons aniseed

To make the "sponge," heat the milk in a saucepan to lukewarm or hot, depending on the yeast you are using. Dissolve the yeast in the milk in a small bowl.

Place the 2 cups flour in a large bowl and make a well in it. Pour the dissolved yeast into the well, along with a pinch of salt. With a wooden spoon, gradually incorporate all the flour into the liquid yeast. When all the flour is incorporated, cover the bowl with a cotton dishtowel and leave to rise in a warm place, away from drafts, until the yeast has doubled in size (about 1 to 1½ hours).

Soak the raisins and glacéed fruit in a bowl with 1 cup of the lukewarm milk for 20 to 25 minutes. Grate the orange and let stand until needed. Melt 8 tablespoons of the butter in a small saucepan set over boiling water and set aside.

When the "sponge" has risen, place the 5¾ cups flour on a pasta board. Make a well in it and place the "sponge" in the well. Add the sugar and mix well with a wooden spoon, and when all the sugar is incorporated, add the warm melted butter, rum, 4 of the eggs, the Marsala, and aniseed. Mix with the wooden spoon until all the ingredients are well combined.

Start adding the remaining warm milk, little by little, incorporating some of the flour from the inside rim of the well. Keep mixing until three-fourths of the flour is incorporated, then add the grated orange peel and start kneading the dough. Knead until all but 2 tablespoons of the flour are incorporated and the dough is smooth (about 20 minutes).

Drain the raisins and glacéed fruits, add to the dough, and knead for 5 minutes more incorporating the leftover flour. Shape the dough into a ring.

Butter and flour a baking sheet. Place the dough on it, cover with a cotton dishtowel, and let rise in a warm place, away from drafts, until it has doubled in size (from 1 to 1½ hours).

Preheat the oven to 400 degrees.

Place baking sheet in the oven for 35 minutes, then beat the remaining egg in a bowl and quickly remove the baking sheet from the oven. Brush the top of the *buccellato* with the beaten egg and return it to the oven for 20 to 25 minutes more.

Remove the *buccellato* from the oven and let stand until cold (2 to 3 hours) before serving.

Pane co' santi

NUT BREAD FOR ALL SAINTS' DAY

MAKES 1 LOAF

*P*ane co' santi or *dei santi* is, as the name suggests, originally for All Saints' Day, November 1 (American Halloween is All Saints' Eve). This bread exists in a nonsweet version, given here, but is also made with sugar as a dessert. Made with both walnuts and almonds, its fascinating combination of ingredients, combining flavors associated with sweets, such as anise, with a shocker like black pepper, reveals the medieval palate. *Pane co' santi* is, however, still very much alive.

FOR THE "SPONGE" (FIRST RISING)

2 ounces (4 cakes) compressed fresh yeast or 4 packages active dry yeast

1 cup lukewarm or hot water, depending on the yeast

1 ½ cups unbleached all-purpose flour

FOR THE DOUGH (SECOND RISING)

4 ounces raisins
4 ounces walnuts, shelled and blanched
1 cup olive oil
2 tablespoons (1 ounce) lard or sweet butter
2 ounces almonds, blanched
6 cups unbleached all-purpose flour

Pinch of salt
Grated peel of ½ orange
1 teaspoon aniseed
1 teaspoon freshly ground black pepper
¾ cup lukewarm water

PREPARE *pane co' santi* with the ingredients listed, according to the directions for sweet bread for All Saints' Day on page 608.

Piccoli crostini fritti

ITALIAN CROUTONS

SERVES 4

*W*ith soups of the *passati* and *minestre* types, homemade croutons are often served. A few float on top with the grated Parmigiano. Versatile Tuscan bread, left over, even some days old, is cut into little squares, which are then fried in olive oil until quite crisp. These add their own delicious flavor and crispness to the soup.

2 large slices Tuscan bread, several days old	*½ cup olive oil* *Salt*

THE bread should be some days old, but not completely hard. Cut the bread into pieces about ½ inch square. Prepare a serving dish with paper towels on bottom.

Heat the olive oil over medium flame in a frying pan. When the oil is hot, put in the bread pieces and let them fry until golden all over (about 4 minutes), then remove from the pan with a strainer-skimmer and place on the prepared serving dish. Sprinkle with a little salt.

Place about 1 heaping tablespoon of *crostini* in each individual bowl and pour the *passato* or *minestra* over them just before serving.

Pizza alla napoletana

PIZZA, NEAPOLITAN STYLE

SERVES 4

$\mathcal{T}$his is the classic pizza, made with a yeast dough.

FOR THE DOUGH

½ ounce (1 cake) compressed fresh yeast or 1 package active dry yeast

Slightly less than 1 cup lukewarm or hot water

2 cups unbleached all-purpose flour

Pinch of salt

1 tablespoon olive oil

FOR THE TOPPING (ALLA NAPOLETANA)

2½ tablespoons olive oil

3 large ripe tomatoes, peeled, or 6 canned plum tomatoes, preferably imported Italian, approximately (to make 10 tablespoons pureed tomatoes)

4 ounces mozzarella

3 whole anchovies in salt or 6 anchovy fillets in oil, drained

1 heaping tablespoon capers in wine vinegar, drained

Salt, freshly ground black pepper, and Italian oregano to taste

DISSOLVE the yeast in the lukewarm or hot water.

Arrange the flour in a mound on a pasta board and make a well in it, then pour the dissolved yeast, salt, and the olive oil into the well.

With a fork, slowly work the flour from the inside wall of the well into the liquid.

When the mixture becomes solid enough to resemble a dough, work in the rest of the flour with a folding motion of your hands, leaving about 1 tablespoon of flour unincorporated. Place the dough in a bowl, sprinkle with the leftover flour, and cover with a cotton dishtowel. Let rest until doubled in size (about 1 hour at warm room temperature, away from drafts).

Meanwhile, using 3 fresh tomatoes or 6 whole tomatoes from the can, but none of the liquid, pass the tomatoes through a food mill, using the disc with smallest holes, into a small bowl. Using the large holes of a cheese grater, coarsely grate the mozzarella; set aside. If whole salted anchovies are used, clean them, removing the bones under cold running water; place the fillets in a small dish.

Preheat the oven to 450 degrees.

When the dough is ready, place a sheet of heavy aluminum foil (about 16 × 18 inches) on a board. Oil it with 1 tablespoon of olive oil, then place the dough on the foil. Spread the dough (using the tips of your fingers, not a rolling pin) until you have a sheet of dough about 16½ × 14 inches.

Spread the pureed tomatoes over the surface of the dough. Distribute the grated mozzarella evenly over the tomatoes, then the anchovy fillets and capers. Add salt, pepper, and oregano to taste and pour the remaining 1½ tablespoons olive oil over everything.

Slide the pizza and the foil directly onto the middle shelf of the oven and back in the preheated oven for about 35 minutes, or until crisp. Remove, slice, and serve.

Pizza may be made in an improvised brick oven, stretching dough on paddle (without oiling) and placing it directly on bricks with the paddle.

Pizza con cipolle

PIZZA WITH ONIONS

SERVES 4

*T*his pizza is made exactly the same as the pizza in the previous recipe, but 3 large red onions, cut up and sautéed in 4 tablespoons of butter until soft (about 30 minutes), are spread over the pizza instead of the tomatoes, mozzarella, anchovies, and capers. The seasonings remain the same, but the amount of oil poured over before baking is increased to 2 tablespoons. Bake as previously directed.

Special pizza

SERVES 4

*T*his is a pizza dough that substitutes potato for yeast as a fermenting agent. It takes longer to rise, but the dough can be made thinner, for a finer, crisper pizza. The pizza will also keep longer and reheats well. The dough probably represents the influence of the southern Italian *torta di patate* upon the Neapolitan pizza.

FOR THE DOUGH
1 potato (about 4 ounces)
½ cup cold milk
½ cup cold water

2½ cups unbleached all-purpose flour
1 tablespoon olive oil
½ level teaspoon salt

FOR THE TOPPING
Either of the toppings (alla napoletana *or* con cipolle) *on pages 52–53*

BOIL the potato for about 25 minutes, then cool, peel, and put through a ricer. Measure ½ cup of riced potatoes and set aside.

Combine the milk and water and heat to lukewarm.

Arrange the flour in a mound on a pasta board and make a well in it. Place the riced potato in the well and add the olive oil and salt. With your left hand, slowly pour the watered milk into the well; at the same time, with a fork, slowly work the flour from the inside rim of the well into the potato. Take care always to leave some flour under the potato-flour mixture so it does not stick to the board.

When the mixture becomes solid enough to resemble a dough, work in the rest of the flour with a folding motion of your hands, leaving about 1 tablespoon of flour unincorporated. Flour the ball of dough with the remaining flour and place it in small bowl. Cover the bowl with a cotton dishtowel and set aside for 3 hours at warm room temperature, away from drafts. (Do not expect the dough to double in size; it will rise only a little.)

When the rising time for the dough is almost up, preheat the oven to 450 degrees and prepare the filling of your choice. Proceed with forming and baking the pizza as directed on page 53.

Schiacciata con ramerino

"PIZZA" WITH ROSEMARY

SERVES 6

*T*he pizzalike *schiacciate* of yeast dough have been made in Florence at least since the sixteenth century and are mentioned in the 1546 dinner discussed on page 7. In the most famous Neapolitan cookbook of the eighteenth century the only reference to pizza is to *pizzette alla fiorentina*. The typical Florentine *schiacciata* is flavored with rosemary or sage and olive oil on top, and does not use tomatoes like the various Neapolitan *pizze*.

½ ounce (1 cake) compressed fresh yeast or 1 package active dry yeast
1 cup lukewarm or hot water, depending on the yeast
2¼ cups unbleached all-purpose flour

Salt
3 tablespoons olive oil
1 heaping tablespoon of rosemary leaves, fresh or preserved in salt or dried and blanched
Freshly ground black pepper

IN a small bowl, dissolve the yeast in the lukewarm or hot water.

Place the flour in a mound on a pasta board. Make a well in the flour and pour in the dissolved yeast and a pinch of salt, and then, using a fork, slowly incorporate all but 3 or 4 tablespoons of the flour from the inside rim of the well. At that point the dough should be firm. Knead it for 15 minutes more.

Sprinkle the dough with the remaining flour and cover it with a cotton dishtowel; let stand in a warm place until doubled in size (about 1½ to 2 hours).

(continued)

SCHIACCIATA CON RAMERINO *(continued)*

When the dough has risen, oil a 15 × 10½ × 1-inch jelly-roll pan with a tablespoon of the oil. Place dough in the pan and spread it out with your fingers until it covers the bottom. Sprinkle on the rosemary, salt, lots of freshly ground pepper, and the remaining oil, then cover with plastic wrap and let stand until the dough has risen again to almost double in size (about 1 hour).

Preheat the oven to 450 degrees.

Bake the *schiacciata* for about 40 to 45 minutes, until crisp, then remove from the oven and serve immediately from the pan, cutting it across into slices.

Focaccia al ramerino e aglio

FOCACCIA WITH ROSEMARY AND GARLIC

SERVES 12 AS AN APPETIZER

*T*he thinnest of the flat breads is pizza, then comes *schiacciata* and finally the highest, *focaccia*. The dough is arranged in a baking pan so that it comes out a bit higher than a *schiacciata*. The *focaccia* is made in a heavily oiled pan whereas *schiacciata* has a minimum of oil. Most *focacce* have lard or butter in the dough itself. This *focaccia* has its main herb, rosemary, inside the dough as well as sprinkled on top. As with most dishes traditionally made with lard, butter is most often the present day replacement. But try it with lard once, just to taste the original and know the difference that the butter makes. Here the garlic is finely chopped and spread over the top, rather than being in whole cloves as it is in some other versions.

FOR THE SPONGE

2 cups plus 1 tablespoon unbleached all-purpose flour

½ ounce fresh compressed yeast or 1 package active dry yeast

1¼ cups lukewarm or hot water, depending on the yeast

Pinch of salt

FOR THE DOUGH

1½ cups unbleached all-purpose
*   flour*
4 tablespoons (2 ounces) lard or
*   sweet butter, at room*
*   temperature*
2 tablespoons rosemary leaves,
*   fresh or preserved in salt or*
*   dried and blanched, finely*
*   chopped*

Salt to taste
Abundant freshly ground black
*   pepper*

TO BAKE THE FOCACCIA

6 tablespoons olive oil
Coarse-grained salt
2 tablespoons rosemary leaves,
*   fresh or preserved in salt or*
*   dried and blanched, finely*
*   chopped*

2 medium cloves garlic, peeled
*   and finely chopped*

TO SERVE

2 tablespoons olive oil

Freshly ground black pepper

PREPARE the sponge. Place the 2 cups flour in a large bowl and make a well in it. Dissolve the yeast in the water, then pour it into the well with the salt. Use a wooden spoon to incorporate the flour, little by little, until it is all used. Sprinkle a tablespoon of flour over, cover bowl with a cotton dishtowel, and let rest until the sponge has doubled in size (about 1 hour). When the sponge is ready, spread out the 1½ cups of flour on board and place the sponge in it. Add the butter, rosemary, salt, and pepper and start incorporating them into the sponge, kneading in a folding motion until all the flour is incorporated and the dough is elastic and smooth.

Use a rolling pin to roll out a large enough sheet of dough to fit a jelly-roll pan. With 2 tablespoons of the oil, grease the pan. Place dough in pan, spreading it out to reach the sides. Sprinkle the coarse-grained salt over, then drip the remaining olive oil to cover the entire surface.

Mix the chopped rosemary and garlic together and with your finger

(continued)

FOCACCIA AL RAMERINO E AGLIO *(continued)*

push the mixture into the dough at several points over the surface. Prick dough all over with a fork, then cover pan with plastic wrap and let rest in a warm place, away from drafts, until doubled in size (about 1 hour).

Preheat the oven to 400 degrees. When the dough is ready, bake it for 25 minutes or until golden all over. Remove from oven, slice, and serve hot, dripping the 2 tablespoons of oil over the surface and sprinkling with freshly ground black pepper.

Pangrattato

HOMEMADE BREAD CRUMBS

*W*hen you have some Tuscan bread left over, allow it to become hard and make it into bread crumbs. You will see what a difference there is in flavor when you use bread crumbs made from good homemade bread.

CUT leftover Tuscan bread (see page 39) into small pieces and place on a cookie sheet. Put the sheet into an oven preheated to 250 degrees and bake the bread pieces for about 45 minutes, until golden brown and very crisp.

Remove the sheet with the toasted bread from oven and let stand until completely cool (about 2 hours), then transfer the bread pieces to a food processor or blender and grind until very fine.

Remove the bread crumbs from the food processor and place them in a jar. Close the jar tightly and store it in a place that gets a good bit of light; do not refrigerate.

These bread crumbs may last, without losing their flavor, for as long as 6 months.

Sauces

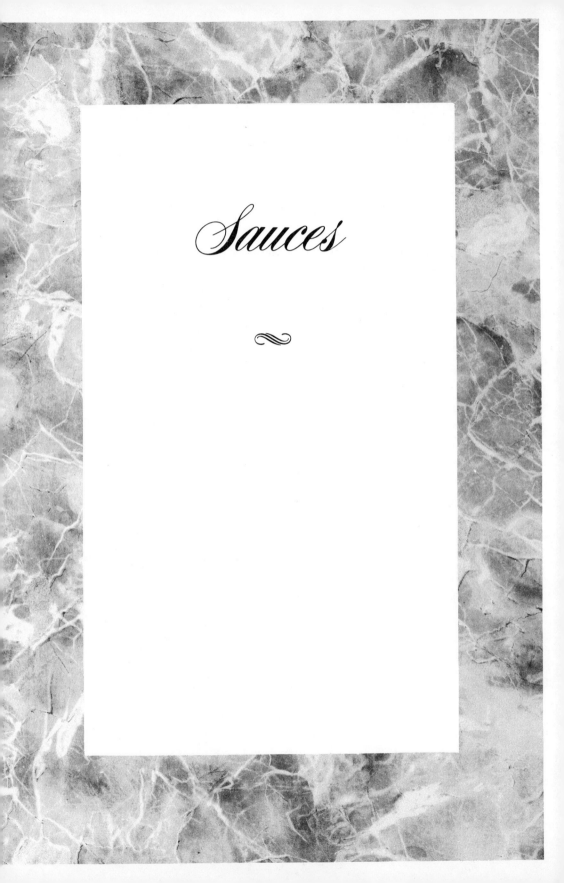

*G*ood Italian cooking avoids the overuse of sauces. If one or two courses have a sauce, usually the others do not. Meats and vegetables are often cooked to bring out only their own flavors, and these flavors are not covered with sauces.

A new school of French cooking has recently adopted this attitude in reaction to what many now consider the overuse of sauces in that cuisine in recent centuries. This same reaction took place in Italian cooking some centuries ago, for sixteenth-century Italian cooking had many, many sauces, some called "savors," of which a number served as bases for later French sauces. However, it would be a mistake to think that present-day Italian cooking does not retain a great variety of sauces, though they may be used sparingly.

In the Renaissance, sauces were often placed in categories according to color: *ginestrate,* or yellow sauces, the color of broom flower, often containing saffron; white sauces based on ground almonds and dried bread; green sauces based on herbs, and red sauces on wine or kermes. The substances that created these colors were often the same that produced vegetable dyes for fresco painting or fabric dyeing; it is no accident that chefs belonged to the same guild as painters and pharmacists, the latter using spices for medicines. Many of these sauces remain. The egg- and oil-based sauces, mayonnaises and so forth, likely emerged within the same Florentine guild, as the techniques are not unrelated to those of making paints from vegetable dyes for fresco and oil painting (see *savore di gamberi,* page 77). Those sauces based on hot oil or butter thickened with flour and mixed with milk or broth, such as *balsamella* (béchamel) or *salsa bianca* (white sauce), probably originated in Italy, as thickening with flour was known in Italy for some time before it was known in France.

The best-known Italian sauces are those used with pasta, some including tomatoes and some without them. We have included about an equal number of each. A sauce such as *carbonara* really exists only in the context of its pasta dish and is included under pasta. We have attempted to clarify some misconceptions about the three basic types of meatless tomato sauce, and to give a variety of types containing meat and fish. However, as we feel that often tomato sauces are overused, we offer an equal number of sauces for pasta that do not contain tomatoes.

Aside from pasta, Italians use sauces mainly on meat, fowl, and fish. Deep-fried dishes, with or without batter, are almost never served with sauce, and sautéed meats most often have their own sauces, already part of the dish. Roasted and poached or boiled meat dishes are most often accompanied by a sauce, but by no means always. A Florentine would never adulterate the purity of the Chianina steer meat in a *bistecca alla fiorentina*. (A châteaubriand with béarnaise sauce would probably shock him.) The most he might add is a few drops of lemon juice after the steak is cooked.

In sum, when sauces are used on freshly cooked or cold roasted and boiled meats and fish, by far the majority will be uncooked and based on fresh herbs, garlic, olive oil, nuts, wine vinegar or lemon, or *maionese*. There is quite a goodly variety of these, and we include a large sampling. Most fulfill the requirements of our health-conscious age. Even the cooked ones are rather light.

There are a few vegetables that are sometimes served with sauce, such as cauliflower with anchovy sauce or with shrimp sauce.

Some of the sauces we include have such an interesting and surprisingly long history that we have added some historical notes. We hope you will find them entertaining; we are sure you will be surprised about the origins of some.

BASIC SAUCES

Balsamella

BÉCHAMEL

MAKES 2 TO 2½ CUPS

*T*hough this sauce was given the name béchamel by the French in the eighteenth century, it probably existed long before that in Italy. The fifteenth-century recipe for *crema di miglio fritta* starts with a technique very close to this.

Balsamella is a basic sauce used in making many dishes. It is placed on top in some, used as a base inside of others, and ties together the ingredients of still others. It also serves as the base for several other sauces.

4 tablespoons (2 ounces) sweet butter

¼ cup unbleached all-purpose flour

1½ to 2 cups milk, depending on thickness desired

Salt to taste

MELT the butter in a heavy saucepan over a low heat. (It is important to use a heavy pan and low heat so the sauce will thicken without burning.) When the butter has reached the frothing point, add the flour. Mix very well with a wooden spoon, then let cook until the color is golden brown or lighter according to the recipe. Remove the pan from the heat and let rest for 10 to 15 minutes.

While the butter-flour mixture is resting, heat the milk in another pan until it is very close to the boiling point. Put the first saucepan back on the heat and very quickly add all of the hot milk. Be careful not to pour the milk in slowly; that can create lumps in the sauce. Begin mixing with a wooden spoon while you pour and keep mixing, always stirring in the same direction, to prevent lumps from forming.

When the sauce reaches the boiling point, add the salt and continue to stir gently while the sauce cooks slowly. Remove from the heat; the sauce is ready to use.

If sauce is allowed to cool, transfer it to a crockery or glass bowl and in order to prevent a skin from forming, press a sheet of buttered wax paper immediately on top of the sauce.

Salsa bianca

WHITE SAUCE

*I*talian cooking shares with French not only *balsamella,* called béchamel in France, but also the basic sauce called *salsa bianca,* in which broth substitutes for the milk of *balsamella.* Florentine scholars count these sauces among the simple *colle,* or binders, that Caterina de Medici's cooks took to France. Certainly Pantanelli, one of Caterina's cooks who arrived in France in 1533, knew the technique of what the French call the roux, because he brought it with him in the *pasta soffiata* (page 572) or as the French later called it, *pâte à chaud.*

In any case, *salsa bianca* is the base for three sauces included here: *salsa di capperi* (caper sauce; see page 78), *salsa di funghi* (mushroom sauce; see page 79), and *savore di gamberi* (shrimp sauce; see page 77). If the butter is left light, the *salsa bianca* is called *bionda;* if the butter is allowed to turn brown, *salsa scura.*

There is no need to give a separate recipe for *salsa bianca,* as the technique is incorporated into the three recipes mentioned above.

Maionese

MAYONNAISE, THE "GOOD OLD WAY"

MAKES MORE THAN 2 CUPS

I talian *maionese* differs from some other types. It employs green virgin olive oil and egg yolks rather than whole egg, and is flavored only with lemon juice. Good virgin olive oil is basic to the sauce; therefore the color of the sauce will be a rich green, not a light yellow. And all the other ingredients must be of top quality—very fresh eggs, freshly squeezed lemon juice—as they have no place to hide. The *maionese* should have an almost solid texture.

Maionese can be made with a blender or electric beater, but the result is not the texture of the typical Italian *maionese* and the taste is a bit metallic. Making it by hand is a little more work, but with some practice it can be done in 10 or 15 minutes.

Regions of Italy that do not have good olive oil, such as Emilia-Romagna, sometimes substitute vegetable oil, but we do not recommend it.

It is not the Italian practice to keep *maionese* very long. In Italy it is almost always made just a few hours in advance. We do not recommend keeping it in the refrigerator for several days.

The written sources for *maionese* and mayonnaise are both quite late ones, and the French one is a little older. The name is probably of French origin. However, let us put forward some reasons supporting a probable Italian origin for the technique itself: (1) the fourteenth-century Italian recipe for *savore di gamberi* (see page 77) uses a mixture of egg yolk, oil, and lemon juice, though it is flavored with other things and perhaps was lightly cooked; (2) the Italian recipe is simpler and more basic; (3) much of the olive oil region of France belonged to Italy until quite recently; (4) egg yolk emulsion in oil is related to Florentine painting techniques. Remember, painters and chefs in Florence belonged to the same guild.

2 extra-large egg yolks, very fresh, at room temperature	*1 tablespoon freshly squeezed lemon juice*
Scant 2 cups virgin olive oil	*Salt to taste*

THE egg yolks must be at room temperature; if the eggs are refrigerated remove them 1 hour in advance. Squeeze the lemon juice.

Place the egg yolks in a crockery bowl. Mix them slowly, using a wooden spoon and always stirring in the same direction.

When the yolks are well mixed, add the first drop of olive oil and stir slowly until it is absorbed. Continuing to stir slowly, always in the same direction, add more oil, a drop at a time, only adding new oil when that already present is well absorbed.

As the emulsion begins to thicken, add several drops of oil at a time, but be careful not to add too much oil too soon. At this point it should begin to resist as you stir.

In the later stage, when the emulsion begins to resemble *maionese* in thickness, the oil may be added in slightly larger amounts. *This can be a danger point.* Be sure not to add too much oil before that already present is well absorbed, or the emulsion can separate—in Italian *impazzire,* "go crazy." Don't get overconfident.

Be sure to mix in the last oil thoroughly, then place the lemon juice and salt in a tablespoon, mixing with a fork until the salt is somewhat dissolved. Cautiously add 1 drop of juice to the *maionese* (this is the danger point for curdling). When the danger of curdling is past, put in the rest of the lemon juice and salt, mixing well.

If the mixture curdles, begin again with a new egg yolk and oil, and when the emulsion succeeds, mix in the curdled one, little by little, thus saving it.

SAUCES FOR MEAT OR CHICKEN

Maionese

MAYONNAISE

PLAIN *maionese* is the most basic sauce for boiled meat or chicken. For the recipe, see page 64.

Salsa verde

GREEN SAUCE

MAKES 1½ TO 2 CUPS

*G*reen sauces were an entire category centuries ago. They could be based on many types of green herbs, which were ground together with other ingredients in the all-purpose grinder of that time, the mortar and pestle. Thyme, marjoram, and tarragon were among the herbs that could be used. The modern pesto, now associated with Genoa, could be considered a type of *salsa verde*.

These green sauces are generally uncooked, and are piquant accompaniments to boiled and poached dishes. The basic, most usual type used today is given below. It can be varied by adding anchovies and/or capers to taste.

1 slice Tuscan bread (see page 39) or white bread, if Tuscan bread is not available
Red wine vinegar to cover
About 25 sprigs Italian parsley, leaves only

2 medium cloves garlic, peeled
1 hard-cooked extra-large egg, cold
1 cup olive oil, approximately (enough for a creamy texture)
Salt and freshly ground black pepper to taste

SOAK the bread in wine vinegar for 20 minutes.

Place the parsley leaves and garlic on a chopping board and chop very, very fine; then transfer to a crockery bowl, add the cold egg yolk, discarding the white, and mix very well with a wooden spoon. Squeeze the soaked bread dry and place it in the bowl.

Little by little add the olive oil, always stirring; mix thoroughly until the sauce has a creamy texture. Add the salt and pepper, then stir again until the salt and pepper are very well incorporated.

Place the sauce, covered, in the refrigerator for 1 hour before serving.

Salsa verde del Chianti

GREEN SAUCE WITH WALNUTS

MAKES 1½ TO 2 CUPS

*T*his recipe and the following one are centuries old, and I have been able to verify their antiquity in Renaissance cookbooks. They are among the many uncooked, piquant sauces that are used with boiled meats and fowl or poached fish.

This differs from *salsa verde* in its use of ground walnuts.

6 ounces walnuts, shelled
15 sprigs Italian parsley, leaves
* only*
4 leaves of basil, fresh or
* preserved in salt (see*
* page 18)*
2 medium cloves garlic, peeled

Salt, freshly ground black
* pepper, and cayenne pepper*
* to taste*
2 hard-cooked extra-large egg
* yolks*
1 cup olive oil

PLACE the walnuts on a chopping board and chop them very fine. Transfer to a crockery bowl.

Place the parsley, basil, and garlic on the board and chop very fine, then transfer to the crockery bowl with the walnuts. Season with salt, freshly ground black pepper, and cayenne pepper and mix very well with a wooden spoon.

Continuously stirring, add the first egg yolk, then the second, discarding the whites, and finally the olive oil, tablespoon by tablespoon. Keep stirring until the sauce is smooth and homogenous.

Taste for salt and pepper, then cover the bowl and refrigerate for 1 hour before serving.

Salsa rossa del Chianti

RED SAUCE

MAKES ABOUT 1½ CUPS

*T*his sauce is found among the old families of the Chianti. Though the tomato paste was added in recent centuries, it was probably a substitution for some other ingredient that intensified the red color of the Chianti vinegar; we know that color was very important in Renaissance food.

The crumb of the bread, mashed with mortar and pestle, was a very characteristic binding element in sauces and soups of that time. (It is interesting that in English we don't even have a word for the inside of the bread to correspond with the Italian *mollica di pane.*) Probably bread crumbs, which are widely used in modern times, at some point substituted for *mollica* in many recipes.

2 large slices Tuscan bread (see page 39)
1 cup red wine vinegar
10 sprigs Italian parsley, leaves only
15 leaves fresh basil

2 tablespoons tomato paste, preferably imported Italian
½ cup olive oil, approximately (enough for a smooth texture)
Salt and freshly ground black pepper

REMOVE the crust from the bread slices and soak the slices in the wine vinegar for 20 minutes.

Meanwhile, chop the parsley and basil leaves very fine and place in a crockery bowl.

Squeeze the liquid out of the bread and put it in the bowl with the herbs, then add the tomato paste and start stirring with a wooden spoon. Add, little by little and stirring constantly, enough olive oil to make a smooth cream.

Taste for salt and pepper. Let the sauce rest, covered, in the refrigerator for 1 hour before serving.

Salsa rossa forte

SPICY RED SAUCE

MAKES ABOUT 1 CUP

*T*his colorful sauce gets its color and its name from the fresh sweet red bell peppers that are so easy to find in Italy. If they cannot be found, fresh pimientos or, as a last resort, sweet green peppers may be substituted. The flavor remains excellent, but the color changes and gives lie to the sauce's name.

1 slice white bread
½ cup red wine vinegar,
  approximately
2 large red, green, or yellow
  bell peppers, or pimientos
1 large clove garlic, peeled

½ teaspoon hot red pepper
  flakes or cayenne pepper
Scant ½ cup olive oil,
  approximately (enough to
  obtain a smooth sauce)
Salt and freshly ground black
  pepper

SOAK the white bread in the wine vinegar for 20 minutes.

Place a pot of boiling water on a burner; next to that burner place the peppers, so they get singed by the heat. (The singeing makes it easy to peel the skin from the peppers; the steam from the boiling water keeps the singed peppers from drying out.) Keep turning the peppers in order to singe them all over. Remove the peppers from the heat and place them in cold water, then remove the skin, seeds, stems, and hard top sections.

Squeeze the soaked bread dry, then combine with the peppers and garlic and either chop very fine or blend in the blender or food processor.

Transfer everything to a crockery bowl and add the olive oil, little by little, stirring constantly with a wooden spoon, until all the oil is incorporated and the sauce is very smooth. Add red pepper, taste for salt and pepper, then refrigerate, covered, for 1 hour before serving.

Savore di noci

MAKES ABOUT 1½ CUPS

*A*nother Renaissance herb sauce, based, like *salsa verde del Chianti,* on crushed walnuts, but flavored with parsley and *agresto* or lemon juice. It contains no garlic. Use on boiled and unspiced roasted meats and fowl.

2 ounces walnuts, shelled
10 sprigs Italian parsley, leaves only
3 tablespoons agresto *(see page 72), or juice of ½ lemon and peel of ¼ lemon*

Salt and freshly ground black pepper to taste
Scant ½ cup olive oil, approximately (enough to obtain a smooth sauce)

PUT the walnuts and parsley in a mortar, along with the *agresto* (or lemon juice and lemon peel), and grind very fine. Transfer it to a crockery or glass bowl, then taste for salt and pepper. Add olive oil, little by little and stirring constantly with a wooden spoon (always in the same direction, as when you make *maionese*).

When you have obtained a smooth and homogeneous sauce, cover the bowl, and refrigerate for 1 hour before serving.

NOTE: You can also make this sauce using a blender or food processor. If you do so, put all the ingredients except half the olive oil into the blender container and blend until smooth and homogeneous. Remove from the blender, pour into a crockery bowl, then add the remaining olive oil, little by little and stirring as described above.

Salsa primavera di magro

SPRING VEGETABLE SAUCE

MAKES ABOUT 1½ CUPS

A red sauce for the season when the vegetables, especially toma-toes, are fresh. It comes from Grosseto, near the Tuscany seaside. The name evokes the springtime quality of fresh uncooked vegetables newly in season. *Salsa primavera* is used mainly with roasted and boiled meats and fowl, not with fish.

1 small red onion, cleaned

*1 large, ripe tomato or 2
    canned tomatoes, preferably
    imported Italian, drained*

1 large clove garlic, peeled

*3 basil leaves, fresh or preserved
    in salt (see page 18)*

*½ slice white bread, crust
    removed*

*Pinch of hot red pepper flakes
    or cayenne pepper*

1 tablespoon red wine vinegar

¼ cup olive oil

*Salt and freshly ground black
    pepper*

CUT up the onion and tomato, then place in a mortar with the garlic, basil leaves, bread, and red pepper. Grind very well, until homogeneous, then transfer to a crockery bowl and add the olive oil, little by little and stirring very well with a wooden spoon. Taste for salt and pepper (the sauce should be very peppery), then add the wine vinegar, stirring until very well incorporated.

Transfer the sauce to a sauceboat and refrigerate, covered, for 1 hour before serving.

Salsa d'agresto

AGRESTO SAUCE

MAKES 1½ TO 2 CUPS

*A*lthough this sauce has disappeared from regular use, it is delicious. I discovered it in a Renaissance cookbook, and much to my surprise my mother remembered eating it in a country village before the First World War. It survived until that recently.

Agresto is the juice of grapes that are not yet ripe, and in olden times it was used more often than vinegar or lemon juice.

Since unripe grapes are available for only about one month a year, it was a very special seasonal dish. My mother remembers that in that village, with its little tenth-century Romanesque church, the inhabitants would peel each grape by hand before crushing them in the mortar. The *agresto* could also be preserved by cooking it with herbs and spices to make an aromatic vinegar. (A fourteenth-century cookbook gives a recipe for making *agresto* from the sediment in the wine kegs. This was also cooked to preserve it.)

Unless you have a grape arbor and the month is July or August, substitute lemon juice for the *agresto* in this sauce. It is still very good.

2 handfuls **agresto,** *or juice of 1 lemon and peel of ½ lemon*
9 walnuts, shelled
2 ounces almonds, blanched
½ small red onion, cleaned
10 sprigs Italian parsley, leaves only
1 medium clove garlic, peeled
2 slices white bread, crust removed

1 teaspoon granulated sugar
Salt and freshly ground black pepper to taste
½ cup lukewarm chicken or meat broth, approximately (enough for a smooth sauce), preferably homemade

GRIND the *agresto* (or lemon juice and peel), shelled walnuts, and blanched almonds in a mortar or blend in the blender or food processor.

Chop up the onion, parsley, and garlic. Add to the contents of the mortar or blender, along with the bread. Blend until very thoroughly mixed, then season with sugar, salt, and pepper. Add enough lukewarm broth to obtain a smooth sauce.

Pass the sauce through a food mill, using the disc with the smallest holes, into a medium saucepan, then cook over low heat for 2 minutes; do not allow it to boil. Transfer the sauce to a sauceboat and allow it to cool before serving.

NOTE: This sauce can be preserved in a jar by covering over with a thin layer of olive oil.

Acciugata

ANCHOVY SAUCE

MAKES ABOUT 1 CUP

A very simple sauce in which the anchovies are crushed and mixed into hot olive oil, this is also widely versatile, being equally at home with dried pasta, a vegetable such as cauliflower, or with leftover cold veal cutlets *alla milanese* or *braciole fritte*.

(See the recipes for *spaghetti all' acciugata* on page 183, *cavolfiore con acciugata* on page 534, and *braciole fritte con acciugata* on page 348.)

5 whole anchovies in salt or 10 anchovy fillets in oil, drained	*1 cup olive oil* *Freshly ground black pepper* *Salt, if necessary*

IF anchovies under salt are available, fillet them while holding them under cold running water to remove excess salt. Drain on paper towels. Heat the olive oil in a heavy saucepan over low heat. When the oil is very hot, almost sizzling, remove the pan from the heat. Immediately add the filleted anchovies and mash them into the oil, using a fork, until they make a paste.

Sprinkle with pepper, then taste for salt and add it if necessary. (If the anchovies have been preserved in salt, it probably will not be.) Serve very hot.

Salsa al dragoncello

TARRAGON SAUCE FROM SIENA

MAKES ABOUT 1 CUP

*T*he old city of Siena, sitting proudly on its hill, is full of ancient dwellings, each with window boxes full of flowers—and tarragon. This herb is still called there by its antique name, *dragoncello,* and its flavor fills many of its old dishes—including this sauce, which is still very much alive in its native city.

The combination of the tarragon and red wine vinegar, best when made from old Chianti, makes this a pungent sauce for roasted or boiled meats and fowl. Naturally, fresh tarragon works best, but good dried tarragon that has retained its flavor also works well. The vinegar should be from a good-quality wine, if Chianti vinegar is not available.

2 slices white bread, crusts removed
¼ cup red wine vinegar
3 cloves garlic, peeled
1 heaping tablespoon tarragon leaves, fresh, or 1 scant tablespoon tarragon leaves, dried

2 to 3 tablespoons olive oil
Salt and freshly ground black pepper to taste

SOAK the bread in ¼ cup of wine vinegar for 20 minutes.

Chop the garlic and tarragon leaves finely, or else grind finely in a mortar. Transfer to the bowl containing the bread and wine vinegar and mix very well with a wooden spoon, so that the bread comes apart and combines smoothly with the other ingredients.

Using the wooden spoon, stir continuously for 10 to 12 minutes, adding the olive oil in the process. Years ago, a type of ridged wooden spoon called a *frullino,* which had the effect of a wooden hand blender, was used at this point. Alas, it has almost disappeared. Taste for salt and pepper, then stir for 10 minutes longer.

Cover the bowl and refrigerate for 1 hour before serving.

SAUCES FOR FISH

Maionese

MAYONNAISE

PLAIN *maionese* is the most basic sauce for poached fish. For the recipe, see page 64.

Maionese al prezzemolo

PARSLEY MAYONNAISE

SERVES 6

*A*nother variant of mayonnaise used for poached or deep-fried fish.

Maionese *(see page 64)*
10 sprigs Italian parsley, leaves
  only

1½ teaspoons very finely
  chopped, cooked spinach
  (optional)

MAKE the *maionese,* mixing it a little longer at the end so that it will be even more solid (the parsley will liquify it somewhat).

Chop the parsley very fine. Wait until a few minutes before you serve the sauce before adding the chopped parsley to mayonnaise. Combine thoroughly. (If you prefer a very green color, add the optional cooked spinach.) Taste for salt, as the addition of the parsley may require a little more.

NOTE: The mayonnaise may be made several hours before and kept in the refrigerator, but the parsley must be added only immediately before serving.

Maionese con gamberetti

SHRIMP MAYONNAISE

SERVES 6

A variant of *maionese* used for poached or deep-fried fish.

Maionese (*see page 64*)   **3 or 4 drops white wine vinegar**
5 medium shrimp, unshelled   **Salt to taste**

MAKE the *maionese*. Leave it in the crockery bowl in which it was made.

Cook the unshelled shrimp for 4 to 5 minutes in boiling water to which the wine vinegar and salt have been added, then shell and chop coarsely.

Wait until just before serving to mix the chopped shrimp into the *maionese*.

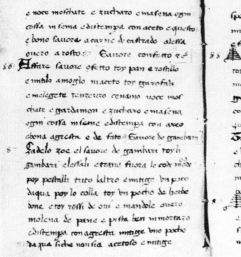

Page of another fourteenth-century manuscript, a Venetian copy of the Florentine original, showing the recipe for *savore di gambari,* a shrimp *maionese,* the recipe for which appears opposite.

Savore di gamberi

*C*ertain Florentine dishes of the fourteenth century were more highly spiced than most Italian cooking of the present day and relate more to various types of curry. Cooking the sauce is optional. I prefer it uncooked, both for taste and because the connection to later sauces is clearer that way.

The mixture of egg yolks, oil, and *agresto* (here, lemon juice) makes it an early version of *maionese,* one that works beautifully with a light fish, poached or roasted. For the sweet and strong spices, we have selected, with much historical justification, the ones used below.

1 slice white bread, crusts removed	*½ teaspoon ground coriander*
½ cup cold milk	*Pinch of freshly grated nutmeg*
8 medium shrimp, unshelled	*Pinch of ground ginger*
5 almonds, blanched	*Pinch of cayenne pepper*
2 extra-large egg yolks	*Salt and freshly ground black*
½ cup olive oil	*pepper to taste*
	2 tablespoons lemon juice

SOAK the bread in the milk for 15 to 20 minutes.

Boil the shrimp for 15 minutes in salted water. Remove the shells; cut off the tails about ½ inch from the ends and save them.

Place the shrimp and almonds in a mortar or blender and grind or blend very thoroughly, then transfer to a crockery bowl. Squeeze the bread dry and add it to the bowl. Mix well with a wooden spoon, so the bread comes apart and combines smoothly with the other ingredients.

Add the egg yolks, one at a time, and incorporate them, always stirring in the same direction. Add the olive oil, little by little, stirring constantly but very gently. Add the spices; mix them in very well.

Add the lemon juice, little by little, always stirring with the wooden spoon, and add the shrimp tails, mixing them in very gently.

Transfer the sauce to a sauceboat and serve.

Salsa di capperi

CAPER SAUCE

SERVES 4

A light caper sauce, made from a base of *salsa bianca,* that is, with broth. The caper sauce is placed over the fish dish after each is cooked separately. It is not to be confused with the technique of cooking the capers together with the fish as used in the dish *pesce ai capperi.* Used best with roasted fish, but also with poached.

4 ounces capers in wine vinegar
6 tablespoons (3 ounces) sweet
  butter
¼ cup unbleached all-purpose
  flour

1¼ cups meat broth, preferably
  homemade
Salt and freshly ground black
  pepper to taste

DRAIN the capers and chop them coarsely. Set aside. Heat the meat broth to boiling in saucepan.

Meanwhile, melt the butter in a heavy saucepan over low heat. When the butter is completely melted and very hot, add the flour and mix it in with a wooden spoon. Stir for 1 or 2 minutes, then pour all the hot meat broth into the pan at one time and stir for 1 or 2 minutes, to prevent lumps from forming.

Add the chopped capers; taste for salt and pepper. Let the sauce simmer for 10 to 15 minutes, then transfer it to a sauceboat and serve hot.

Salsa di funghi

MUSHROOM SAUCE

SERVES 6

A light sauce of dried wild mushrooms, on a *salsa bianca* base, this is used for roasted meat and fish and for poached fish. It depends on the strong flavor of *porcini* mushrooms, imported from Italy.

1 ounce dried porcini
   mushrooms
1 1/2 cups lukewarm water
4 tablespoons (2 ounces) sweet
   butter

1/4 cup unbleached all-purpose
   flour
Salt and freshly ground black
   pepper to taste

SOAK the dried mushrooms in the lukewarm water for 20 minutes, then drain, but save the water. Rinse mushrooms, removing sand attached to the stems. Place the mushrooms on a board and chop them coarsely. Set aside.

Strain mushroom water several times through paper towels to re-move sand, then pour into a heavy enameled saucepan. Use this water as the basis for the sauce. Heat until the water is close to the boiling point. Put the butter in another heavy saucepan and place it over low heat. When the butter is melted and quite hot, add the flour and stir with a wooden spoon. When flour is all incorporated and begins to sizzle, pour all the hot mushroom water in at one time. Stir continuously for 3 to 4 minutes, to prevent lumps from forming.

Add the chopped mushrooms; taste for salt and pepper. Simmer for 12 to 15 minutes more, stirring every so often, then transfer to a sauceboat and serve hot.

Page of a fifteenth-century manuscript, including the recipe for *crema di miglio fritta,* showing the early Italian use of flour for thickening and the technique of roux and *balsamella.*

SAUCES FOR PASTA, RICE, AND SOUPS

Balsamella con parmigiano

BÉCHAMEL WITH PARMIGIANO CHEESE

MAKES 2 TO 2½ CUPS

*B*alsamella mixed with Parmigiano cheese is used so often that it merits separate consideration. Indeed, the French give it a separate name, *Mornay sauce*. Needless to say, however, the sauce is of Italian origin.

This sauce is used over pasta dishes, some of which include a second sauce as well.

2 to 2½ cups balsamella (see   **¼ cup freshly grated**
 page 62)   **Parmigiano**

WHEN the *balsamella* is removed from the flame, still hot, add the Parmigiano and mix through very well with a wooden spoon. (The cheese should be incorporated only *after* the sauce has been removed from the flame.) If sauce is allowed to cool, transfer it to a crockery or glass bowl and in order to prevent a skin from forming, press a sheet of buttered wax paper immediately on top of the sauce.

Sugo di pomodoro fresco

FRESH TOMATO SAUCE

MAKES ABOUT 2 CUPS

*T*his simple sauce, which really deserves the adjective "classic," is perhaps the best recipe to demonstrate the basic point of view of Florentine cooking—that it is enough to combine absolutely necessary ingredients, of high quality and in the classic proportions, in order to produce the best cooking. It is antithetical to the Florentine point of

(continued)

SUGO DI POMODORO FRESCO *(continued)*

view to "improve" a dish by adding one's favorite herbs, cooked butter or cream, for these additions destroy the classical proportions of the dish and obscure the fundamental combination of flavors, each of which must be tasted.

We also feel that this version of fresh tomato sauce brings out the flavor of the tomato better than versions that add onion and/or sugar.

The basil is used not primarily for its own flavor, but because it is the best thing to bring out the flavor of the tomato itself. When fresh basil is available, it is not even cooked with the tomatoes. If basil preserved under salt must be substituted, the leaves are cooked with the tomatoes for only about 2 minutes and then removed.

This sauce is used with fresh and dried pasta, *topini di patate,* and with rice. It is also the base for the sauce of fresh mint used for *tortelli alla menta* (see page 196).

2 pounds fresh, very ripe plum tomatoes or 2 pounds canned tomatoes, preferably imported Italian, undrained	**Salt to taste** **10 leaves basil, fresh, or preserved in salt (see page 18)**

IF the tomatoes are fresh, cut them in half and place them in a high-sided saucepan; do not add anything else. Simmer slowly for about 1 hour. (If canned tomatoes are used, use the entire contents of the can, including the liquid, and cook for only about 20 minutes.) After cooking, pass the tomatoes through a food mill using the disc with smallest holes, then place back in the pan and add salt to taste. If fresh basil is not available, place the preserved basil leaves in the pan. Simmer for 2 or more minutes, then remove the basil leaves, if present.

When fresh basil is available, tear the leaves in two or three pieces and place them on the bottom of the serving dish. Place freshly cooked pasta over them, then place the sauce over.

NOTE: To serve, add a little uncooked olive oil or butter, freshly ground pepper, and freshly grated Parmigiano cheese to pasta and sauce. (Notice that olive oil or butter are added uncooked. This typical Tuscan usage is consistent with modern ideas of healthy cooking.)

Pommarola

SUMMER TOMATO SAUCE

SERVES 6

*T*his is the type of tomato sauce in which the *odori* (the aromatic vegetables) are simmered together with the tomatoes rather than sautéed first. We feel that the classic *odori* should include garlic, and we do not recommend that sugar be added to fresh or canned tomatoes to sweeten them; the result is artificial.

Pommarola is used as the summer tomato sauce, and should really be made strictly with fresh tomatoes. If only canned tomatoes are available, it is better to make *sugo scappato* (or *di magro*), in which the *odori* are sautéed. Simmering the *odori* with canned tomatoes does not produce a very convincing result.

In some parts of Italy, people eat a small portion of pasta as much as once a day, so *pommarola* is usually made in large quantities, to last four or five days. The following recipe is for only one meal for 6 people.

2½ pounds fresh, very ripe plum tomatoes
1 medium red onion, cleaned
1 large carrot, scraped
1 celery rib
1 small clove garlic, peeled

5 sprigs Italian parsley, leaves only
3 basil leaves, fresh or preserved in salt (see page 18)
Salt to taste

CUT the tomatoes in half. Cut the onion, carrot, and celery into small pieces; do not chop them.

Place all the ingredients in a stock pot; do not add oil or water. Simmer, covered, very slowly for 1½ to 2 hours, then pass everything through a food mill using the disc with the smallest holes. (If the sauce is to be stored, do so at this point without adding anything else.)

Reheat the sauce (whether freshly made or stored), adding salt.

NOTE: Pommarola may be eaten with fresh or dried pasta, rice or with *topini*. Only after the sauce is placed on these freshly cooked dishes should you add uncooked olive oil or butter and fresh pepper. On pasta or *topini* you also add freshly grated Parmigiano.

Sugo scappato (o di magro)

WINTER TOMATO SAUCE

SERVES 6

*I*n the winter, when canned tomatoes generally form the basis of the tomato sauce, the sauce changes accordingly. The *odori* (aromatic vegetables) are chopped and sautéed. Wine and broth are added. It is really like a meat sauce without the meat, and so the name *scappato* means the meat has "escaped." (The alternate general term *di magro* also usually means without meat.)

This recipe is enough for 6 portions of dried pasta.

2 carrots, scraped

1 large red onion, cleaned

2 celery ribs

1 large clove garlic, peeled

5 or 6 sprigs Italian parsley,
*   leaves only*

2 or 3 leaves basil, fresh or
*   preserved in salt (see page*
*   18)*

Salt and freshly ground black
*   pepper to taste*

5 tablespoons olive oil

¾ cup dry red wine

1 cup hot meat or chicken
*   broth, preferably homemade*

1 pound fresh, ripe tomatoes,
*   skin and seeds removed, or*
*   1 pound canned tomatoes,*
*   preferably imported Italian,*
*   drained*

CHOP the carrots, onion, celery, garlic, parsley, and basil very fine, heat oil in a flameproof saucepan (preferably terra-cotta, but a heavy enameled one will do), then add chopped ingredients along with the salt and pepper. Heat over low heat and sauté very gently until golden (about 12 minutes).

Add the wine and let it evaporate; then, stirring very well with a wooden spoon, pour in the hot broth and reduce on low heat for about 15 minutes. Add the tomatoes and simmer very slowly for about 20 minutes until they are completely cooked and the sauce is homogenous.

Taste for salt and pepper. If more salt is needed, add an extra ½ cup of lukewarm water also, in order to integrate the additional salt, and reduce.

Sugo di "cipolle"

SAUCE OF CHICKEN GIZZARDS

SERVES 6

A really fine sauce that has a flavor related to game. The concentration of chicken gizzards gives a taste you might not predict, one that is close to that of pheasant or other game birds.

Use with spaghetti and other dried pasta.

1 medium red onion, cleaned
½ celery rib
1 large clove garlic, peeled
10 sprigs Italian parsley, leaves only
¼ cup olive oil
Salt and freshly ground black pepper

1 pound chicken gizzards, cleaned, but left whole
1 cup dry red wine
¼ cup tomato paste, preferably imported Italian
2 cups of hot chicken or meat broth, preferably homemade

FINELY chop, by hand, the onion, celery, garlic, and parsley, heat oil in a flameproof terra-cotta or enameled saucepan, then add chopped ingredients. Add salt and pepper and sauté very gently, over low heat, until golden (about 30 minutes). Add the chicken gizzards and sauté, still over low heat, for at least 35 to 40 minutes.

Add wine and simmer until it evaporates, then add the tomato paste and stir very well. When the tomato paste is all incorporated, pour in ½ cup of the hot broth. Simmer for 1 hour longer, adding ½ cup more of broth, little by little as needed.

Remove the chicken gizzards and chop them extremely fine, either by hand or with food processor. Put back in the casserole and add the remaining cup of broth. Taste for salt and pepper and simmer very slowly until all the liquid is incorporated; the sauce should be quite thick and smooth.

Sugo di carne

MEAT SAUCE

MAKES 2 TO 2½ CUPS

*T*his type of meat sauce for pasta is Tuscan, and is probably the type most commonly used throughout northern Italy. Many people mistakenly believe that any meat sauce means "Bolognese." There are three types of meat sauces used in the Bologna region, of which only one is *salsa bolognese,* the others being two types of *ragù,* one of which uses milk or cream and omits wine.*

The excellence of the Tuscan meat sauce comes from the famous Chianina beef, the red Chianti wine, and the *porcini* mushrooms of the area. Little more need be added to come up with a fine sauce, and the simplest possible one for the purpose.

*1 ounce dried porcini
    mushrooms
1 carrot, scraped
1 celery rib
1 medium red onion, cleaned
8 sprigs Italian parsley, leaves
    only
1 large clove garlic, peeled
Small piece of lemon peel
¼ cup olive oil
½ pound beef sirloin, in one
    piece*

*½ cup dry red wine
Salt and freshly ground black
    pepper to taste
1 pound canned plum tomatoes,
    preferably imported Italian,
    drained
1 tablespoon tomato paste,
    preferably imported Italian
2 cups hot meat or chicken
    broth, preferably homemade*

SOAK the mushrooms in 2 cups of lukewarm water for 20 minutes.

Finely chop the carrot, celery, onion, parsley, garlic, and lemon peel, heat oil in a flameproof casserole (preferably terra-cotta), then add chopped ingredients. Sauté very gently until golden (about 15 to 20 minutes).

---

*Salsa bolognese has garlic and a number of other ingredients that are different from Bolognese *ragù.*

With scissors, snip the meat into tiny pieces and add to the contents of the casserole. (The authentic meat sauce uses snipped pieces of meat rather than ground meat; this way the pieces retain their identity and flavor instead of amalgamating into a homogenous mixture.) Sauté the meat pieces for 12 to 15 minutes, then add the wine and cook until it evaporates (15 to 20 minutes).

Taste for salt and pepper, then add the tomatoes and tomato paste and let cook very slowly for 20 to 25 minutes.

Drain the soaked mushrooms, reserving the soaking liquid. Rinse mushrooms, removing sand attached to the stems. Strain mushroom water several times through paper towels to remove sand. Add the mushrooms to the sauce and simmer very slowly for at least 1½ hours, adding hot broth and the mushroom water as liquid is needed, until all the broth and mushroom water have been added. (The sauce should be of medium thickness, neither too liquid nor too dense.)

Salsa di tonno

TUNA SAUCE

SERVES 4

A good winter sauce for dried pasta. Fresh tomatoes and tuna are not necessary; the result is excellent with canned ingredients. This is used all over Italy for all kinds of dried pasta. As with any sauce made with fish, do not add Parmigiano or other grated cheese.

1 small red onion, cleaned
¼ cup olive oil
1 cup canned tomatoes,
*   preferably imported Italian,*
*   drained and seeded*

1 can (3½ ounces) tuna in olive
*   oil*
Salt and freshly ground black
*   pepper*

CHOP the onion very fine, heat oil in a flameproof terra-cotta or enameled saucepan, then add onion. Sauté very gently, over low heat, until golden. Add the tomatoes and simmer until the liquid is evaporated.

Drain the tuna and transfer directly from can to pan, breaking the tuna up with a fork and mixing it in with the tomatoes.

Taste for salt and pepper.

After 8 to 10 minutes, remove the pan from flame; the tuna should be well incorporated.

Cibreo

SAUCE OF CHICKEN LIVERS, CRESTS, AND WATTLES

MAKES 2 TO 2½ CUPS

C ibreo, the sauce of chicken livers, crests, wattles, and the little yellow unborn eggs, was so beloved of that legendary *buona forchetta* ("a good fork," as the Italians call a good eater) Caterina de' Medici, that she literally almost ate herself to death on it. She ate so much *cibreo* one evening that she took violently ill and barely survived.

If eaten in moderation, however, those results do not follow, and especially if you can find the crests and eggs (get to know a chicken farmer), you may understand why Caterina went to such extremes.

Coarse-grained salt	**¾ pound chicken livers**
¼ pound chicken crests,	**(including some cut up veal**
wattles, and unlaid eggs	**kidneys, optional)**
½ small red onion, cleaned	**1 cup dry white wine**
5 or 6 sprigs Italian parsley,	**½ cup meat or chicken broth,**
leaves only	**preferably homemade**
3 tablespoons (1½ ounces)	**1 extra-large egg yolk**
sweet butter	**Salt and freshly ground black**
1 tablespoon unbleached all-	**pepper to taste**
purpose flour	

HEAT 2 cups of salted water in a saucepan. When the water reaches the boiling point, put in the crests and wattles (setting aside the unlaid eggs) and cook them for about 5 minutes. Drain the crests and wattles and cool them under running water.

Chop the onion and parsley finely.

Heat the butter in a saucepan over medium heat, and when it is hot, mix in the flour with wooden spoon and sauté for 1 minute. Then add chopped onion and parsley and sauté, stirring constantly for 3 or 4 minutes more. Add the whole chicken livers and the boiled crests and wattles, and then, after 3 or 4 minutes, the wine. Lower the heat and allow the wine to evaporate very slowly (about 5 or 6 minutes).

While the wine is evaporating, heat the broth in a second saucepan. When lukewarm (and no warmer), remove the broth from the flame and mix in the egg yolk.

When the wine has evaporated, taste for salt and pepper. Add the broth with the egg yolk and the unlaid eggs and stir very well. Let simmer for 2 to 3 minutes more, until the chicken livers, crests, and wattles are soft.

Remove the saucepan from the flame and serve very hot.

NOTE: The sauce is used both for fresh pasta (*tagliatelle con cibreo*, page 172) or for a main dish (*ciambella con cibreo*, page 468).

Salsa di fegatini

CHICKEN LIVER SAUCE

SERVES 6

A sauce, based on chicken livers, white wine, and broth, that is superb with delicate fresh pasta. Butter is used with the olive oil, unusual in a Tuscan recipe. There is no tomato, and Parmigiano should not be added.

1 medium white onion, cleaned
3 tablespoons (1½ ounces)
*   sweet butter*
2 tablespoons olive oil
8 chicken livers, cleaned
Unbleached all-purpose flour
*   for dredging*

¾ cup dry white wine
Salt and freshly ground black
*   pepper*
1 cup hot meat or chicken
*   broth, preferably homemade*

CHOP the onion very fine, then place in a heavy saucepan with the butter and olive oil and sauté very gently until golden.

Cut the chicken livers in quarters and flour them lightly, then add to the pan and sauté for 2 to 3 minutes. Add the wine and let the livers cook in it very slowly until the wine evaporates.

Taste for salt and pepper, then add the hot broth, mix very well, and simmer for 10 minutes, at which point the sauce should be cooked and homogenous.

NOTE: You can use this sauce for fresh pasta (*tagliatelle con fegatini,* see page 173) or as accompaniment to *riso in bianco* (buttered rice).

Agliata

GARLIC SAUCE

SERVES 6

A white sauce, uncooked, creamy, and only mildly spicy. The cold sauce is placed on hot, cooked dried pasta or rice *in bianco,* that is, with uncooked butter melted over it. Rather widely used in northern Italy today, *agliata* appears in the first known Italian recipe book, from Florence in the 1300s. Half the garlic was left raw, and the other half cooked under hot wood ash. As in most white sauces of that time, almonds provided the binding ingredient and the color. The recent versions of the sauce, currently used in northern Italy, use all raw garlic and *mollica,* the inside part of the bread, in place of almonds.

This will dress 1 pound of dried pasta or 2 cups of raw rice.

4 slices Tuscan bread (see page 39) or white bread, if Tuscan bread is not available

1½ cups cold milk

4 ounces walnuts, shelled

2 large cloves garlic, peeled

Salt and freshly ground white pepper to taste

REMOVE the crust from the bread slices. Soak the bread in the cold milk for 20 minutes in a crockery bowl.

Place the shelled walnuts and garlic in a stone mortar and grind very fine with a wooden pestle, then transfer to the bowl containing the bread and milk.

Stir continuously with wooden spoon; after 2 or 3 minutes, taste for salt and pepper.

Stir for 10 minutes more in order to break up the bread and make a homogenous sauce, then cover the bowl and place it in the refrigerator for 1 hour. Serve the sauce in a sauceboat.

Agliata may also be made by placing all ingredients together in a blender or food processor.

Pesto (Battuto alla genovese)

BASIL SAUCE

MAKES 4 TO 5 CUPS

*P*esto, an uncooked sauce, is one of the most typical products of Genoese cooking, and contributes much to the distinction of that fine *cucina*. It is used with pasta such as *trenette* or lasagne, with soups such as minestrone, or *zuppa di pesce,* and with boiled potatoes. It is also known as *battuto alla genovese*. Genoese friends of mine like to point to a recipe in Virgil as the oldest known version of pesto. It is also related to the many types of *salse verdi* that one finds in old Renaissance cookbooks.

The name pesto of course refers to the pestle, as the grinding was originally done with that implement and a mortar. It is no exaggeration that every Genoese family has a mortar and pestle that is actually used. Centuries ago, all over Italy these implements were used to grind everything. The name "mortadella," which now refers to a Bolognese sausage, originally referred to any kind of forcemeat made with mortar and pestle. The Genoese are wonderfully conservative about food, so that medieval and Renaissance dishes that have disappeared elsewhere still hang on in Genoa.* Therefore the making of pesto in Genoa is a rite and must be done with mortar and pestle.

In other parts of Italy it is rare to find pesto still made with mortar and pestle. Though the Genoese would be scandalized, in Tuscany we make it with a *mezzaluna,* like other *battuti.* Much less laborious than doing it the Genoese way, it still results in a texture close to the original. It is also possible to make pesto in the blender or food processor, but this should be the third choice, as the texture is more liquid and the taste somewhat different. All three ways of making it are described.

Biancomangiare is an example. It is a dish probably of Catalan rather than Provencal origin that was very important in medieval and Renaissance Italy. It was the main dish of the *bianco* or white category.

It was made with rice pulverized into flour, hens, almonds, and spices. It was not originally a sweet like the French *blancmange* that derives from it. It survived in close to its original form in Genoa until quite recently.

Recipes for pesto vary widely in detail. I know that in Florence there are Tuscan touches to it. I have found that these go back to a period when many kinds of green sauces based on herbs were used in Tuscany, including one based on basil. Probably this merged with the famous Genoese one at some point. I think, however, that this Tuscan pesto should not be regarded merely as an inauthentic version, since it probably has its own claims to validity.

I have had some lively discussions with several Genoese friends in order to arrive at the "true" Genoese pesto:

1. Basil, garlic, olive oil, and grated cheese are basic to all the recipes.
2. Nuts exist in the older recipes; they were not a later addition. We should not be surprised, as nuts were commonly used in all green sauces of the Renaissance. Pignoli or walnuts or both may be used.
3. Cheese: The older Ligurian recipes used sheep's cheese, such as the local pecorino or pecorino Sardo. Local pecorino is difficult to find now in Liguria, so Sardo is used, mixed with Parmigiano, which is made from cow's milk. Other aged pecorino, such as Romano, is often substituted for Sardo, particularly outside of Liguria.
4. Many modern published recipes mix a little butter into the ingredients to be ground. Even many of the old Genoese families have adopted this.
5. The basil stays somewhat greener when crushed with mortar and pestle than with other methods. However, even in Genoa, a little parsley is sometimes added to keep the color greener.

As for Tuscan pesto:

1. Both walnuts *and* pignoli are used.
2. Since pecorino is still widely available in Tuscany, we grate local aged pecorino and mix it with Parmigiano.
3. *Pancetta* is used in place of butter.
4. Since pesto is made with a *mezzaluna* in Tuscany, something must be added to keep the green color. A little cooked spinach is used instead of parsley.

(continued)

Pesto (Battuto alla genovese) *(continued)*

Whichever method you use, 1½ cups of olive oil will produce quite a thick pesto. It is best to start with a thick sauce. Additional liquid is added in the pasta recipes that use it, and, of course, in the soups.

To preserve pesto, it is not necessary to freeze it, nor even strictly necessary to refrigerate it. Omit the cheese and add enough olive oil to come about ½ inch above the pesto. This is the way pesto has been preserved through the winter for centuries, a method that retains more of the original taste than when frozen. Mix in the cheese before serving whatever amount of pesto you wish to use.

MAKING PESTO WITH MORTAR AND PESTLE

12 walnuts, shelled
2 tablespoons pignoli
1 teaspoon coarse-grained salt
5 black peppercorns
3 medium cloves garlic, peeled
4 tablespoons (2 ounces) sweet butter
6 handfuls fresh basil leaves (about 3 cups)*

4 ounces freshly grated Parmigiano
4 ounces freshly grated Sardo, Romano, or additional Parmigiano
1½ cups of olive oil, approximately

PLACE the walnuts, pignoli, salt, peppercorns, and garlic in a stone mortar, along with the butter. Use a wooden pestle, not to crush, but rather to push the ingredients in a circular motion against the stone, which will grind them.

Add the basil leaves and grind until well integrated, then add the grated cheeses and grind the mixture a bit more. (Originally the cheese was cut into pieces and also ground in the mortar. I know of no one who still does this.)

Transfer the mixture to a bowl. Add the olive oil, little by little, mixing with a wooden spoon, as with a *maionese,* until the pesto is creamy and smooth.

*In Liguria, a special small-leaf basil is used.

MAKING PESTO WITH MEZZALUNA

12 walnuts, shelled

2 tablespoons pignoli

4 ounces pancetta

6 handfuls fresh basil leaves (about 3 cups)

1 heaping tablespoon chopped, cooked spinach

3 medium cloves garlic, peeled

4 ounces freshly grated Parmigiano

4 ounces freshly grated Sardo, Romano, or additional Parmigiano

Salt and freshly ground black pepper

1½ cups of olive oil, approximately

CHOP the walnuts, pignoli, and *pancetta* very fine with *mezzaluna,* then transfer to a bowl.

Chop the basil leaves, cooked spinach (squeezed until it is quite dry), and garlic very fine, then add to the bowl as well.

Add the grated cheeses and season with salt and pepper. Add the olive oil, little by little and stirring constantly, until you have a smooth sauce.

MAKING PESTO WITH BLENDER OR FOOD PROCESSOR

Use the same ingredients as for pesto made with the *mezzaluna.* Place ½ cup of the olive oil, plus all the other ingredients, in the blender or food processor and grind very fine. Add the remaining olive oil and blend for a few seconds, until very smooth.

Briciolata

*A*n excellent sauce for dried pasta, based on quality olive oil and good bread crumbs, *briciolata* derives from the world *briciole* for bread crumbs. Widely used all over Italy when homemade bread and bread crumbs were staples, it really depends on the high quality of its two principal ingredients. It uses no tomato or Parmigiano.

1 cup olive oil
*3 tablespoons unseasoned bread
   crumbs (see page 58),
   preferably homemade*

*Salt and freshly ground black
  pepper*

FIVE minutes before your pasta has finished cooking, begin to make the *briciolata.*

Heat the olive oil in a saucepan over low heat. When the oil is warm, add the bread crumbs and salt to taste. Sauté very gently until the bread crumbs are lightly golden, then remove the pan from the heat and sprinkle with pepper.

When the pasta is drained, pour the *briciolata* over it and mix thoroughly. Serve immediately. Absolutely do *not* add grated cheese.

NOTE: You can, if you wish, add 5 sprigs of Italian parsley, leaves only, chopped.

Antipasti

~

Sedano, finocchi, carciofi in pinzimonio

RAW CELERY, FENNEL, AND ARTICHOKE
IN PINZIMONIO

I talians are very fond of raw vegetables dipped in a sauce as an antipasto. The Tuscan version of this is called *in pinzimonio,* which means that the vegetables are eaten held between two fingers, grasping the vegetable as in *pinze,* or tweezers. This metaphor is necessary for the Italians because, as the inventors of forks and eating implements, they do not readily accept the idea of eating anything with their hands, and they must turn it into a story.

The "sauce" for *pinzimonio* in Tuscany is just high-quality olive oil with lots of salt and pepper. The saltiness of dishes such as *pinzimonio* is the opposite extreme from the saltlessness of their bread and some other dishes. The range in salting in Tuscan food is very wide; there is not a single degree of saltiness that applies to all dishes. It is the two extreme ends, saltlessness and extreme saltiness, that takes some getting used to, but I believe one eventually comes to see the advantages of this nonuniformity. (Perhaps the closest approach to this is in Chinese cooking, in which "salt" dishes are in a special category of their own.)

Fresh celery and fennel are the best vegetables to use for this dish. Leave the small, fresh leaves of the celery on, as they are the best part for catching the sauce and are delicious eaten in this way. Slice the fennel into long, thin sticks, removing the leaves, of course. In Florence itself, the favorite vegetable for *pinzimonio* is the small, tender raw artichoke. If you are ever there in the winter, do try it.

FOR EACH SERVING

¼ cup virgin olive oil
1 heaping teaspoon salt

½ teaspoon of freshly ground
black pepper

COMBINE all the ingredients.

To serve, place sliced vegetables on a serving dish. At each setting, place a small bowl with a portion of sauce as described above.

Each diner helps himself to vegetables, dips them, and eats.

Foglie di salvia ripiene

SAGE "SANDWICHES"

SERVES 6

*T*hese miniature deep-fried "sandwiches" of sage leaves between mozzarella squares make a very good appetizer to serve with *aperitivi,* before sitting down at the table. They are also useful for buffets.

1 cup unbleached all-purpose
  flour
Salt
2 tablespoons olive oil
1 extra-large egg, separated
3 tablespoons dry white wine
½ cup cold water,
  approximately (for a
  medium-thick batter)

8 ounces mozzarella
30 small leaves sage, fresh or
  preserved in salt (page 19)
1 quart vegetable oil (see page
  22)

SIFT the flour, then combine in a bowl with a pinch of salt, the olive oil, egg yolk, white wine, and cold water. Mix well with a wooden spoon, then let stand in a cool place (not the refrigerator), covered, for 2 hours.

Pat the mozzarella dry with a paper towel. Cut first into slices ½ inch thick, then into 1-inch squares. (If the cheese is still not very dry, absorb the excess liquid by patting the squares with more paper towels.) Using 2 sage leaves for each "sandwich," make miniature three-layer "sandwiches" by placing sage leaves between squares of mozzarella.

Heat the vegetable oil in a large frying pan. While it is heating, beat the egg white with a wire whisk in a copper bowl and fold into the batter.

When the oil is hot, dip the mozzarella "sandwiches" in the batter and deep-fry until golden all over. Remove from the fat, drain on paper towels, and immediately sprinkle with salt. Serve hot.

Insalata di riso

RICE SALAD

SERVES 8

*T*his cold rice appetizer, very often served at buffets, is especially good in the summer, when it is also used as a first course. With good Arborio rice, a little crispness from the celery and tomato, and a piquant touch from capers, anchovies, tuna, and olives, it is a welcome opener to a meal.

Coarse salt
1 pound raw rice, preferably
*   Italian Arborio*
Juice of 3 lemons
Salt to taste
Maionese (see page 64)
5 whole anchovies in salt or 10
*   anchovy fillets in oil,*
*   drained*
1 8-ounce can tuna fish in olive
*   oil, drained*

4 ounces capers in wine vinegar
1 celery heart
¾ pound large Greek olives
Freshly ground black pepper to
*   taste*
3 extra-large eggs
3 ripe, but not overripe, fresh
*   tomatoes*

BRING a large pot of cold water to a boil, add coarse salt, then the rice, stir with a ladle, and cook until the rice is al dente (about 14 minutes). When rice is ready, drain it in a colander, then place in a bowl and add the lemon juice and salt to taste. Mix thoroughly and let cool, covered, until needed.

Prepare the *maionese;* refrigerate until needed. If whole anchovies preserved in salt are used, clean and bone them under cold running water. Cut the anchovies into small pieces and place them in a large bowl.

Drain the capers and add them to the large bowl containing the anchovies. Cut the celery heart into ½-inch pieces, then add to the bowl, along with the tuna and two-thirds of the olives. Add the *maionese* to the bowl with the other ingredients and mix very well.

Add the cooled rice to the bowl. Season with salt and pepper to taste, then mix thoroughly. Place the bowl, covered with a lid or aluminum foil, in the refrigerator until needed.

Place a saucepan containing 4 or 5 cups of cold, salted water and the eggs over medium heat. When the water reaches the boiling point, cook the eggs until hard (about 9 minutes). Meanwhile, slice the tomatoes into ½-inch slices. When the eggs are ready, shell them and cut them in quarters.

Remove the bowl containing the rice mixture from the refrigerator and transfer the contents to a large serving dish. Arrange two rings of garnish around the rice, the first of tomato slices, the second of egg quarters. Finally, garnish with the remaining olives and serve, quite cold.

Polenta fritta

FRIED POLENTA APPETIZER

*L*eftover polenta (page 476) without sauce can be utilized as a delicious salty, crisp appetizer by deep-frying, then salting thin slices of it. It is particularly appropriate for the winter months.

TAKE polenta (a day old and still cold from refrigeration) and slice it into strips ½ inch thick and 2 inches long.

Heat a large quantity of olive oil, or a mixture of vegetable oil and lard in a frying pan. When the oil is hot (about 375 degrees), add some polenta strips and deep-fry, turning them, until they are golden on all sides.

Prepare a serving dish by placing some paper towels on the bottom. As the polenta slices are cooked, transfer them to the dish. When all the slices are on the serving dish, sprinkle them with salt and remove the paper towels.

Serve immediately, very hot.

Riso forte o pasticcio di riso amaro

PEPPERY RICE PASTICCIO

SERVES 8

*T*his is a very special dish, in which the rice is mixed with three kinds of cheese: pecorino Romano, a sheep's cheese; Parmigiano; and pecorino Toscano, the Tuscan sheep's cheese. Since the third is not always available outside of Italy, it is necessary to find a cheese that has a similar soft, unaged sheep's cheese flavor. *Ricotta salata,* a lightly salted dry ricotta, works very well. This ricotta is exported from southern Italy and is available at many cheese stores. If you can't find it, substitute more Parmigiano, though it is likely that cheese shops that carry really good Parmigiano could also obtain *ricotta salata.*

The fresh black pepper is really the main flavoring of this rice *pasticcio,* and should be tasted not only for its "hot" quality but also for its flavor.

10 cups cold water
1 tablespoon coarse-grained salt
10 ounces raw rice, preferably Italian Arborio
4 ounces freshly grated Parmigiano
2 ounces pecorino Toscano, ricotta salata, or additional Parmigiano
2 ounces freshly grated Romano

4 teaspoons freshly ground black pepper
6 tablespoons unseasoned bread crumbs, preferably homemade (see page 58)
Freshly grated nutmeg to taste
¼ teaspoon ground cinnamon
6 extra-large eggs
2 cups milk

PUT the water in a flameproof casserole, and bring to the boiling point. Add salt, then the rice, stir with a wooden spoon, and cook until the rice is soft (about 13 to 15 minutes).

Meanwhile, put the cheeses in a large bowl; preheat the oven to 375 degrees.

When the rice is done, drain it in a colander and cool under cold running water. Add it to the bowl with the cheeses. Mix well with a wooden spoon, then add the pepper, 2 tablespoons of the bread crumbs, the nutmeg, and cinnamon. Add the eggs, one at a time, mixing thoroughly, then the cold milk.

Butter a loaf pan and coat with the remaining bread crumbs. Place the rice mixture in the pan and bake in the preheated oven for 40 or 45 minutes.

Remove from oven, allow to cool for 15 minutes, then unmold onto a serving dish. Serve immediately or cold, as an appetizer.

Mozzarella in carrozza

MOZZARELLA "IN A CARRIAGE"

SERVES 6

*M*ozzarella "in a carriage"—that is, wrapped in bread slices, dipped in egg, and deep-fried—is sprinkled with salt and served hot, as an appetizer. It is especially good served with an *aperitivo* of cold white wine.

8 ounces mozzarella	*Salt*
12 slices white bread	*2 cups vegetable oil (see page*
4 extra-large eggs	*22)*

CUT the mozzarella into 6 slices, then cut each slice in half. Cut each slice of bread in half and place a piece of mozzarella between 2 bread slices.

Beat the eggs in a bowl with a pinch of salt.

Heat the oil in a frying pan. While it is getting hot, prepare a serving dish by lining the bottom with paper towels.

When the oil is hot, about 375 degrees, dip each "sandwich" into beaten egg and deep-fry until golden on one side. Turn over to fry other side; the mozzarella will melt. Place the deep-fried "sandwiches" on the serving dish to drain.

In Italy mozzarella is unsalted, but abroad it is sometimes salted. If the cheese is unsalted, when the "sandwiches" are on the serving dish, sprinkle them with salt. Serve hot.

Tortino di melanzane alla fiorentina

EGGPLANT BAKED IN BATTER, FLORENTINE STYLE

SERVES 6 TO 8

*J*n this Florentine version, the eggplant, first fried, are then baked in a batter of tomato sauce and separated eggs, the whipped egg whites causing it to rise in the manner of a soufflé. The bread crumbs and Parmigiano are in the batter itself, not sprinkled on top. The version from Ferrara included in my *Classic Techniques of Italian Cooking* is closer to the *Tortino di carciofi* of this book, see page 512, in that the eggplant is simply mixed with eggs, unseparated. It is the marjoram flavoring of that dish which gives it its special position. And even in Ferrara, so close to Parma, they do not add Parmigiano to obscure the dominant fragrance of its main herb. Compare the two versions; they are both wonderful.

4 medium eggplants, about 2 pounds

FOR THE TOMATO SAUCE
1 pound fresh tomatoes or 1 pound canned tomatoes, preferably imported Italian, drained
1 medium clove garlic, peeled
2 tablespoons olive oil
5 leaves basil, fresh or preserved in salt (see page 18)

PLUS
5 tablespoons unseasoned bread crumbs, preferably homemade
3 extra-large eggs, whole
3 extra-large eggs, separated

2 tablespoons coarse-grained salt

Salt and freshly ground black pepper
1 quart vegetable oil (see page 22)
¼ cup olive oil
1 cup unbleached all-purpose flour

4 tablespoons freshly grated Parmigiano
Salt and freshly ground black pepper to taste

CUT off the tops of the eggplants, peel and cut them horizontally into slices less than ½ inch thick. Put the slices in a large bowl and sprinkle them with the coarse salt. Place a dish as a weight over the slices to help squeeze out the dark bitter liquid and let stand for about ½ hour.

Meanwhile prepare the tomato sauce. If fresh, first cut the tomatoes into 1-inch squares. Put tomatoes in a small saucepan with the garlic, oil and basil, place the pan over medium heat and let cook for 20 minutes, mixing every so often with a wooden spoon. Pass the contents of the pan through a food mill, using the disc with the smallest holes, into a second small saucepan. Reheat the strained tomato sauce, add salt and pepper and let simmer for 5 minutes, then transfer the sauce into a large crockery or glass bowl and let cool for about ½ hour. When the eggplants are ready, carefully wash them in cold water to remove the salt and pat them dry with paper towels. Prepare a serving dish by lining it with paper towels. Heat the vegetable oil along with the olive oil in a frying pan. When the oil is very hot, about 375 degrees, lightly flour the eggplant slices and fry them, a few at a time, until they are lightly golden on both sides (about 3 minutes). Remove the fried slices from the pan and put them on the prepared serving dish to drain. When all the slices are on the dish, cover them with more paper towels to absorb all the excess fat.

Lightly oil a 13½ × 8¾ × 1¾-inch baking dish, and coat with 3 tablespoons of the bread crumbs. Preheat the oven to 375 degrees. Add the whole eggs and the egg yolks to the tomato sauce along with the Parmigiano, the remaining bread crumbs and salt and pepper to taste, and mix very well with a wooden spoon. Using a copper bowl and wire whisk, beat the egg whites until stiff and gently fold them into the tomato sauce mixture. Line the bottom of the baking dish with half of the eggplant slices, then pour over half of the batter then repeat procedure to make another layer each of eggplant and batter. Bake for 35 to 40 minutes.

Remove and serve immediately.

Pasticcetti con acciuga

ANCHOVY PASTRIES

SERVES 6

*L*ittle deep-fried anchovy pastries. Crisp and salty, they make a perfect accompaniment to a cold *aperitivo* wine. They should be cooked at the last moment, as they must be served hot.

*2 anchovies in salt or 4 anchovy
   fillets in oil, drained*
*1¾ cups unbleached all-purpose
   flour*
*4 tablespoons (2 ounces) sweet
   butter*

1 extra-large egg
Salt
*½ cup cold milk, approximately
   (for a smooth dough)*
*1 quart vegetable oil (see page
   22)*

IF using anchovies in salt, bone them under cold running water to remove excess salt. If using anchovy fillets in oil, dry them very carefully. Cut each anchovy into 8 pieces and set aside.

Place the flour in a mound on a pasta board. Make a well in the center.

Melt the butter and allow to cool for 10 minutes, then put in the well, along with the egg and a pinch of salt, and mix together thoroughly, not yet incorporating any flour. Add the milk and mix until all the ingredients are well incorporated into the flour.

Knead the dough for 20 minutes, until very smooth, then divide into halves. Spread out one half with your hands and arrange the anchovy pieces over the surface.

Spread out the other half of the dough until it is the same size as the first half, then place the second half evenly over the first. Press it down lightly, then roll with a rolling pin until the dough is ⅓ inch thick. Using cookie cutters of different shapes, cut out the dough.

Heat the oil in a large frying pan. When it is hot, about 375 degrees, deep-fry *pasticcetti* on both sides until golden.

Remove them from the pan, drain on paper towels, and sprinkle with salt. Serve very hot.

Crostini al ginepro

CANAPÉS OF LIVER PASTE AND JUNIPER BERRIES

SERVES 6

*C*rostini are the Italian canapés. However, hearty country bread is used, the slices, though thin, are not delicate, and the crusts are left on the bread. *Crostini* of liver paste cooked with juniper berries evoke the autumn hunting season.

10 chicken livers, cleaned

2 medium cloves garlic, peeled but left whole

4 large sage leaves, fresh or preserved in salt

¼ cup olive oil

1 tablespoon (½ ounce) sweet butter

Salt and freshly ground black pepper to taste

7 juniper berries

2 cups chicken or meat broth, preferably homemade

2 whole anchovies in salt or 4 anchovy fillets in oil, drained

1 tablespoon capers in wine vinegar, drained

24 small, thin slices day-old Tuscan bread (see page 39)

CHOP the chicken livers coarsely, then place them in a saucepan with the garlic cloves, sage, olive oil, and butter. Sauté very lightly for 10 minutes, then add a pinch of salt, pepper, and the juniper berries. Add 1 cup of the broth and let cook for 20 minutes over medium heat.

Remove the pan from the stove. Drain and save the liquid. Place the solid contents of the pan on a board and chop fine, then return to the pan, along with the reserved liquid. Add the remaining cup of broth and cook again, very gently, until almost all the broth has evaporated.

If using anchovies in salt, fillet them under cold running water to remove excess salt. Chop the anchovies fine, along with the capers, then incorporate with a fork into the chicken livers. Taste for salt and pepper and remove the pan from the stove.

Spread some of this paste on each slice of bread, either toasted or plain, place them in a serving dish, and serve. *Crostini* on untoasted bread are eaten cold. In Tuscany the bread is either toasted or used plain. However, bread slices fried in olive oil also work very well.

Melanzane marinate

MARINATED EGGPLANT

SERVES 6 TO 8

*E*ggplant slices, fried, marinated in olive oil, wine vinegar, basil, garlic, salt, and pepper, and then served cold. The dish may be served in the evening if prepared in the morning, but it is better if it marinates for at least a day. Best for an antipasto course at the table or for a buffet.

2 large or 4 medium eggplants
Coarse salt
1 cup fresh basil leaves
2 large cloves garlic, peeled
Vegetable oil for deep frying
    (see page 22)

Salt and freshly ground black
    pepper
½ cup very good quality red
    wine vinegar

SLICE the eggplants vertically into ½-inch slices; do not peel. Place the slices on a large plate, sprinkle liberally with coarse salt, and let stand for 1 hour with a weight on top. (The eggplant will shed some dark liquid.)

Tear the basil leaves and place in small bowl. Chop the garlic fine and add to the basil. Mix very well with a wooden spoon.

Rinse and dry the eggplant slices with paper towels, and deep-fry them, in a large quantity of vegetable oil, until golden all over. After all the slices are fried, do not drain off the oil on absorbent paper as usual; you will layer the undrained slices in a serving dish.

Put down a layer of eggplant; cover with basil and garlic, then sprinkle with salt and pepper. Put down another layer of eggplant; cover with more basil and garlic, then salt and pepper. Repeat until all the eggplant slices are in the serving dish.

Pour in the wine vinegar, let cool, and then place in refrigerator, covered with aluminum foil.

After 1 hour, gently turn the eggplant slices over. Return to the refrigerator, still covered, for at least 3 hours more. (This dish is even better when made a day in advance.)

The marinated eggplant can be preserved through the entire winter by covering it with olive oil in a jar with a lid and keeping it in the refrigerator.

Crostini con burro di acciughe

CROSTINI WITH ANCHOVY BUTTER

MAKES ABOUT 14

*A*nchovy butter spreads on rustic slices of Tuscan bread—one of the simplest of appetizers, widely used with before-dinner drinks and at the beginning of a buffet.

8 tablespoons (4 ounces) sweet butter

8 whole anchovies in salt or 16 anchovy fillets in oil, drained

2 ounces capers in wine vinegar, drained

14 small, thin slices day-old Tuscan bread (see page 39)

PLACE the butter in a bowl and mash it gently with a wooden spoon for 15 minutes, until it has a soft, creamy texture.

If using anchovies in salt, bone and clean them under cold running water. Place the anchovy fillets in a second bowl and mash them into a paste, then incorporate the paste into the butter. Continue to mix until the butter and anchovies are completely combined and homogenous. Cover the bowl with aluminum foil and refrigerate for 1 hour.

Spread the anchovy butter on the *crostini* and place on a serving dish. Serve each *crostino* with one or two capers in the center.

Peperoni ripieni

STUFFED PEPPERS

SERVES 4

*T*hese baked peppers are stuffed with a rather elaborate filling in which the meat is flavored with a variety of elements, including *odori* (aromatic vegetables), the chopped pepper tops, wine, prosciutto, Parmigiano, and broth. For this recipe you may use green, yellow, orange, or red peppers. (Do not confuse the sweet red ones with fresh pimientos). I personally prefer the yellow or orange ones for flavor, but the green ones are also excellent and have the advantage of being easy to find.

This Tuscan version does not cover the stuffed peppers with tomato sauce. The stuffing itself provides enough flavor. The baked peppers may be eaten cold as an appetizer, warm as a main dish, or as part of a buffet. When served as the main course, *peperoni ripieni* may be accompanied by *spaghetti alla fiaccheraia* (page 178) and *fagioli al forno* (page 520) with *ricotta fritta* (page 599) for a dessert.

4 large green, yellow, orange, or red peppers

1 small red onion, cleaned

1 large clove garlic, peeled

5 sprigs Italian parsley, leaves only

½ medium carrot, scraped

3 tablespoons olive oil

½ pound ground meat

Salt and freshly ground black pepper to taste

½ cup dry red wine

2 canned tomatoes, seeded, preferably imported Italian, drained

1 slice prosciutto, pancetta, or boiled ham (about 2 ounces)

1 extra-large egg yolk

2 tablespoons freshly grated Parmigiano

½ cup unseasoned bread crumbs, preferably homemade (see page 58)

½ cup meat or chicken broth, preferably homemade

SOAK the peppers in cold water for 10 minutes, then drain. Cut the tops off the peppers and remove the seeds from inside. Set the pepper bottoms aside then discard the stems and finely chop the top parts of the peppers, along with the onion, garlic, parsley, and carrot.

Place a saucepan containing 2 tablespoons of the olive oil over medium heat. When the oil is hot, add the chopped ingredients and sauté for 5 minutes, or until lightly golden. Add the ground meat, season with salt and pepper, and sauté for 10 more minutes. Add the wine and simmer until it is evaporated (about 6 to 8 minutes), then put in the tomatoes and cook until the sauce is thick (about 15 minutes), stirring continuously with a wooden spoon. Remove the saucepan from the stove and allow to cool (about 20 to 25 minutes).

Preheat the oven to 375 degrees.

When the contents of the pan are cool, coarsely chop the prosciutto (or *pancetta* or boiled ham) and add to the pan. Mix very well with a wooden spoon, then add the egg yolk and Parmigiano, mixing thoroughly.

Fill the reserved peppers with the contents of the pan. Sprinkle the tops with the bread crumbs, then put the peppers in a 13½ × 8¾-inch baking dish and pour in the broth and remaining 1 tablespoon olive oil. Place the baking dish in the preheated oven for 40 minutes, until the peppers are soft.

Remove the baking dish from oven, allow to cool for 10 minutes, then transfer the peppers to a serving dish with a spatula. Serve hot or cold.

Uova ripiene

STUFFED EGGS

SERVES 8 AS AN APPETIZER

*R*emoving the yolks of hard-cooked eggs, mashing them with flavorings, and refilling the whites with the mixture is a technique that again goes back at least as far as the fourteenth century. This is a version of somewhat more recent origin that is often used in present-day Italy. It is useful both as an appetizer and for buffets.

4 extra-large eggs
2 whole anchovies in salt or 4 anchovy fillets in oil, drained
1 ½ ounces capers in wine vinegar, drained
1 can (10 ounces) tuna in olive oil, drained
5 sprigs Italian parsley, leaves only

Salt and freshly ground black pepper to taste
1 tablespoon olive oil
Maionese (made with 1 egg yolk, 1 cup oil, and 1 teaspoon lemon juice; for procedure see page 64)
4 green olives stuffed with peppers or pimiento

HARD-COOK the eggs for 10 minutes. Let cool, then remove the shells and cut in half lengthwise. Remove the yolks, taking care not to break the whites. Place the whites on a plate and the yolks on a chopping board.

If using anchovies in salt, clean and fillet them under cold running water, then place, along with the capers, tuna, and parsley, on the chopping board with the yolks. Chop everything fine, then put in a bowl, taste for salt and pepper, and add the olive oil. Mix until thoroughly combined.

Fill each white half with enough of the yolk mixture to reconstruct the shape of a whole egg. Place the stuffed egg halves on a serving dish and cover with the *maionese*. Cut the green olives in half crossways, and place around the plate. Serve cold.

Panzanella

BREAD SALAD

SERVES 6

*O*ne of the most characteristic of all Florentine dishes, the earliest recipe for this was written down among the poems in the notebooks of the great painter Bronzino, pupil of Michelangelo himself, in the sixteenth century. Without doubt a summer dish, because it depends upon fresh summer vegetables.

Most important for making a good *panzanella* is to have a good, dark Tuscan bread, some days old, so that when it is soaked and the water squeezed out, it flakes into a texture that is very light and dry, almost a powder. (What must be avoided is sogginess, a danger lurking in light bread, or bread that is too fresh.)

This is probably one of the most difficult dishes to imagine if you have never experienced it, but follow the instructions carefully, take the trouble to make Tuscan dark bread, use good virgin olive oil, and you will have a real addition to your repertoire of refreshing dishes for summer eating.

(If the ingredients are not available, especially the Tuscan bread, do not attempt to make substitutions. All attention in the dish is focused on just these ingredients, and it cannot succeed without them.)

1 large red onion, cleaned
10 large fresh basil leaves
2 large ripe tomatoes
1 pound Tuscan dark bread (see
page 43), several days old

Salt and freshly ground black
pepper to taste
½ cup virgin olive oil
1 tablespoon red wine vinegar,
approximately

RINSE the onion, basil leaves, and tomatoes as well.

Soak the bread in very cold water with the whole tomatoes, onion, and basil for 15 to 20 minutes, then squeeze the bread to remove all liquid and place in a plastic container.

Cut the onion in quarters and finely slice each quarter. Place the onion pieces over the soaked bread. Tear each basil leaf into two or three pieces and arrange them over the onions, then dice the tomatoes

(continued)

113

PANZANELLA *(continued)*

into ½-inch squares and place these on top of the basil. Cover the plastic container and place in the refrigerator for at least 2 hours.

Remove the container from refrigerator and transfer the contents to a bowl. Season with salt, pepper, oil, and vinegar and mix thoroughly. Serve immediately.

Porrata

LEEK PIE

SERVES 12

*S*trangely enough, the word "puree" seems to derive from the Italian word for leeks, *porri*. A soup made from *porri* was called a *"porrea."* At the annual festival held at San Lorenzo (of the famous Michelangelo sacristy), from the fourteenth century on they served a *passato,* or puree, of leeks, and it appears that anything pureed gradually came to be called a *"purea,"* which became "puree" in French and English.

Porrata is a large leek pie with a crust made of yeast dough. The leeks are sautéed in olive oil and butter and flavored with *pancetta*. This is even better cold than warm, and may be prepared in advance. A perfect antipasto to serve at a buffet or with before-dinner drinks, it is also suitable for a fancy occasion, and can serve a function similar to a quiche.

5 bunches leeks (about 20 leeks)
3 tablespoons olive oil
1 tablespoon (½ ounce) sweet butter
Salt and freshly ground black pepper to taste
2 ounces (4 cakes) compressed fresh yeast or 4 packages active dry yeast

3 cups unbleached all-purpose flour
1 cup lukewarm or hot water, depending on the yeast
6 extra-large eggs
6 ounces **pancetta** *or 6 ounces* **prosciutto**

RINSE the leeks well, discard the green part, then slice them into rings ½ inch thick. Place the pieces in a large bowl of cold water for 30 minutes. Rinse several times to remove all grains of sand.

Heat the olive oil and butter in a large heavy casserole. When the butter is melted, add the leeks and sprinkle with salt and pepper. Cover the casserole and cook very slowly until the leeks are soft (30 to 40 minutes), stirring frequently with a wooden spoon. Remove the casserole from the heat and let the leeks stand until cold (about 1 hour). Meanwhile, make the crust.

Dissolve the yeast in the lukewarm or hot water.

Place the flour in a mound on a pasta board. Make a well in the flour, then pour in the dissolved yeast and add 2 eggs and salt. Mix with a wooden spoon, incorporating the flour from the inside rim of the well, little by little. When the dough is firm, start kneading. Knead until all but 2 tablespoons of flour is incorporated (about 20 minutes).

Sprinkle the dough with the remaining flour and cover it with a cotton dishtowel. Let stand in a warm place, away from drafts, until doubled in size (about 1½ hours).

Chop the *pancetta* coarsely and set aside in a dish until needed; place the remaining 4 eggs in the casserole with the leeks and mix well with a wooden spoon.

Oil a 10-inch springform pan; preheat the oven to 400 degrees.

When the dough has risen, gently roll it, using a rolling pin, into a large sheet less than ½ inch thick. Fit the sheet of dough into the springform pan, letting the excess dough hang out over the edges.

Sprinkle the chopped *pancetta* over the dough, then, using a strainer-skimmer, fill the springform pan with the leeks. With a knife, cut off the dough around the edges of the pan. Turn the edges inward, over the leeks, to make a border. Sprinkle with abundant freshly ground pepper (the dish should be peppery), then place the springform in the preheated oven for 45 to 50 minutes.

Remove the *porrata* from the oven and allow it to cool for 15 minutes before opening the springform. Remove from the springform and transfer to a serving dish. To serve, cut it like a pie. (The *porrata* may also be eaten cold.)

FRITTATE

*T*here is no translation of frittata that conveys what it is. They are not omelets,* which are really closer to egg *crespelle,* nor are they thin, pancakelike forms that are stuffed and rolled up. Rather, the pieces of vegetable or meat are sautéed or fried and incorporated into the eggs in the form of a low cake.

Frittate are used cold for appetizers and warm for main dishes of a light dinner. Like omelets, they are made with a large variety of different vegetables or meats cut into pieces and mixed into the egg.

Among the great favorites are frittate of leeks *(porri),* of fried green tomato slices, and with basil. The technique of cooking them once the eggs have been added is described in detail in each individual recipe.

Frittata di porri

FRITTATA OF LEEKS

SERVES 4

5 large leeks	**6 extra-large eggs**
¼ cup olive oil	
Salt and freshly ground black	
pepper to taste	

RINSE the leeks well, discard the green part, then cut them into rings ½ inch thick. Place the pieces in a bowl of cold water and let them soak for 30 minutes, then drain and rinse carefully under cold running water.

Heat 3 tablespoons of the olive oil in a flameproof casserole. When it is warm, add the leeks, season with salt and pepper, and sauté for about 30 minutes, until soft. Transfer the leeks to a bowl and allow them to cool for 1 hour.

*Omelets, called *uova di pesce,* existed in Renaissance Florence.

In a large bowl, lightly beat eggs with a pinch of salt. Add the cooled leeks and mix thoroughly.

Place a large omelet pan over medium heat with the remaining tablespoon of olive oil. When the oil is hot, add the leek-egg mixture. When eggs are well set and the frittata is well detached from the bottom of the pan, put a plate, face down, over the pan. Holding the plate firmly, reverse the pan and turn the frittata out.

Return the pan to the flame. Carefully slide the frittata onto the pan to cook the other side. After 2 minutes, reverse the frittata onto a serving dish. It may be served either hot or cold.

Frittata al basilico

FRITTATA WITH BASIL

SERVES 6

½ cup fresh basil leaves
7 extra-large eggs
Salt and freshly ground black
  pepper

3 tablespoons freshly grated
  Tuscan pecorino or
  Parmigiano
1½ teaspoons olive oil

RINSE the basil leaves and dry them with a paper towel. Tear each leaf into two or three pieces and place them in a dish.

In a large bowl, lightly beat the eggs with a pinch of salt and pepper.

Add the pecorino to the bowl and mix thoroughly, then add the basil leaves and stir gently.

Heat the olive oil in an 11-inch omelet pan. When the oil is hot, pour in the contents of the bowl. When the eggs are well set and the frittata is well detached from the bottom of the pan, place a plate, face down, over the pan. Holding the plate firmly, reverse the pan and turn the frittata out.

Return the pan to the flame. Carefully slide the frittata into the pan to cook the other side. After 1 minute, reverse the frittata onto a serving dish. It may be served either hot or cold.

Frittata di pomodori verdi

FRITTATA OF GREEN TOMATOES

SERVES 6

4 large fresh green tomatoes
1 cup plus 1 tablespoon olive oil
1 cup all-purpose flour,
  approximately

6 extra-large eggs
Salt and freshly ground black
  pepper

RINSE the tomatoes very well and cut them into ½-inch slices.

Heat the 1 cup oil in a frying pan. (Do not use more than 1 cup of oil, as the tomato slices should not be completely covered.) While the oil is heating, flour the tomato slices.

When the oil begins to sizzle, place only as many tomato slices in pan as will make a single layer. Sauté until golden on both sides, then transfer to a paper towel to drain; sprinkle with salt and pepper. Fry the remaining tomato slices the same way.

Beat the eggs very lightly with a pinch of salt and set aside.

Heat the 1 tablespoon of olive oil in an 11-inch omelet pan. When it is hot, add the tomato slices to the pan. (The slices are reduced in size from having been sautéed, so they should all fit in one layer.) Pour the eggs over the tomato slices. When the eggs are well set and the frittata is well detached from the bottom of the pan, place a plate, face down, over the pan. Holding the plate firmly, reverse the pan and turn the frittata out.

Return the pan to the flame. Carefully slide the frittata into the pan to cook the other side. After 1 minute, reverse the frittata onto a serving dish. It may be served either hot or cold.

Fettunta

*I*n the regions of Italy that have olive oil, it is a great treat for snack or appetizer to have large slices of country bread toasted, rubbed with garlic, and covered with green oil, especially in the season of the year when the olives are newly pressed. The oil, still warm from the olive press, is poured over the bread, creating a flavor never to be forgotten. The Tuscan word for this is *fetta unta,* or "oily slice." In Rome and southern Italy, it is called *bruschetta.* To compare the Roman and Tuscan ways of preparing it gives an insight into the way the Tuscans have of lightening their cooking. In Rome the bread is fried in the oil, while in Tuscany the bread is toasted, over charcoal or wood, if possible. Then the oil is heated, but not cooked, and poured over.

Fettunta can be successfully prepared in your kitchen with Tuscan bread (see page 39) and good olive oil. The bread may be toasted in the oven. If you are preparing something on the charcoal broiler, it is even better to toast the bread that way. Unlike the more usual garlic bread prepared to eat with meals, *fettunta* is a dish in its own right and should be eaten as an appetizer or as a snack.

4 large slices Tuscan bread
2 medium cloves garlic, peeled and cut in half

½ cup olive oil
Salt and freshly ground black pepper

PLACE the bread slices on a cookie sheet and place them in an oven preheated to 375 degrees. Toast the bread for about 8 minutes on each side, then rub both sides of the bread with the cut garlic.

Warm the oil in a small saucepan over very low heat for 5 minutes, then immediately pour onto the bread arranged on a serving dish. Sprinkle with salt and pepper and serve immediately.

Fagioli, tonno e cipolle

TUSCAN BEANS, TUNA, AND FRESH ONIONS

SERVES 4

A very basic, rustic appetizer. Easier to make if you have some cooked beans left over, and always very satisfying. Quite popular in Italy.

2 cups dried cannellini beans	*3 tablespoons olive oil*
Coarse-grained salt	*Freshly ground black pepper*
2 medium red onions, cleaned	*Salt to taste*
1 can (6 ounces) tuna, in olive oil, drained	

SOAK the beans overnight in a bowl of cold water (about 8 cups).

The next day, drain the beans and place in a stockpot with about 10 cups cold water and coarse salt. Simmer very slowly for about 45 minutes or more, depending on the dryness of the beans, until soft, then remove the stockpot from the heat and allow the beans to cool in the liquid for 1 hour. Drain the beans in a colander and transfer to a bowl. Cover and refrigerate for about 1 hour.

Meanwhile, soak one of the onions in cold water for 30 minutes, then chop coarsely and place in a small bowl.

Drain the tuna and add to the small bowl containing the onion.

Break the tuna up with a fork and mix it with the onion. Add the olive oil and let stand in the refrigerator until needed.

When the beans have been refrigerated for 1 hour, remove both bowls from the refrigerator and add contents of the small one to the beans. Mix very well with a wooden spoon and transfer to a serving dish. Sprinkle generously with freshly ground black pepper, then taste for salt and place the second red onion, left whole, in the center of the serving dish.

NOTE: This dish may be prepared several hours in advance; if so, keep the serving dish in the refrigerator, covered.

Carote all' agro

MARINATED RAW SHREDDED CARROTS

SEE PAGE 504.

Pomodori e tonno

TOMATO HALVES WITH TUNA, CAPERS,
AND MAYONNAISE

SEE PAGE 507.

Soups

*T*he popularity of the pastas often unjustly overshadows the great range of Italian soups. In many parts of Italy, pasta is eaten perhaps less than many non-Italians suppose, not at the evening meal and not every day at lunch. Soups are most often eaten instead, soups ranging from light broth and consommé, both with a little pasta, through broth- and stock-based soups of many kinds—onion, leek, vegetable, and so forth.

There are stock-based purees of vegetables and, of course, the substantial hearty *minestre,* minestroni, and finally bean and pasta soups, the latter with almost no liquid at all. I include examples of the entire range of these.

Let me begin, however, with a discussion of broth and consommé, stock and *gelatina;* then I present four lighter soups, in which the broth or stock base still determines the basic thickness: the very special *ginestrata;* two onion soups, one old and one modern; and a leek soup covered with grated cheese.

BROTH AND CONSOMMÉ

*I*n Italy, when one wants to make a really quality broth, one only uses beef. When one wants to economize, bones and scraps may be substituted, but we should not think that this is to be preferred. If the meat is of top quality, and if one begins with cold water and coarse salt and allows the stockpot only to simmer slowly, little or no impurity will come to the top of the pot. While Florentines are as well known as the Genoese for economy, this is one thing they feel is too important to compromise on.

The above rule applies to a soup broth or basic broth for consommé. For stock used in the preparation of other dishes, a less refined result is satisfactory, and bones and scraps may be substituted. On the other hand, chicken is never used for soup broth or consommé, though of course chicken stock is called for in making some dishes, and may often be substituted for beef stock.

The meat that is used in making broth must cook for 3 hours. If a cut that also requires so long a cooking time is used, such as brisket or short ribs, then the meat can also be eaten. If a meat is used that ordinarily requires a somewhat shorter cooking time, then it will be cooked out and useless. Often in Italy, it is necessary to discard the meat used for making broth.

The meat used for making broth into consommé is of necessity discarded.

See recipes for such dishes as *lesso rifatto con porri* (page 335), *polpettone con tonno* (page 392), or simply, boiled beef (page 329) for utilization of beef left over from making broth.

Many Italians prefer to clarify broths and aspics with whole eggs rather than whites alone. That is the older tradition there, and I personally still prefer it, but I have used egg whites in the instructions here.

Meat broth

MAKES ABOUT 2½ QUARTS

1¼ pounds beef
15 cups of cold water (3¾
quarts)
1 tablespoon coarse-grained salt
1 medium carrot, scraped
1 small red onion, cleaned

1 medium celery rib
5 sprigs Italian parsley, leaves
only
1 small ripe tomato or 2 ripe
cherry tomatoes

PLACE a stockpot containing the meat, cold water, and coarse salt over low heat. When the water reaches the boiling point, add the carrot, onion, celery, Italian parsley, and tomato, all whole, and simmer very slowly for 3 hours, half covered. While simmering, spoon off any foam or impurities that come to the surface of the broth.

Remove the meat from stockpot. Strain the broth through a colander into a large crockery or glass bowl.

Allow the broth to cool completely (about 1 hour), then place the bowl, covered, in the refrigerator for at least 1 hour. Then remove all fat from the surface.

Clarified broth

MAKES ABOUT 2 QUARTS

LIGHTLY beat 2 egg whites in a small bowl with 2 tablespoons of broth.

Place the beaten whites in the bowl with cold broth and stir thoroughly with a whisk.

Transfer the contents of the bowl to a stockpot, turn the heat on to medium, and stir continuously until the broth reaches the boiling point, then let simmer, very slowly and without stirring, for about 10 minutes.

Meanwhile, wet a piece of cheesecloth with cold water and place it in the refrigerator for about 10 minutes.

Place the cheesecloth over a large bowl and pour the hot broth through it; the broth should be absolutely transparent.

COLORING BROTH

It is possible to give different shades to broth, from very light brown to dark brown. This is done with 2 tablespoons of dry Marsala or from 1 to 2 teaspoons of caramelized sugar (melt the sugar in a spoon over a flame). The Marsala or sugar must be added to the broth when it reaches the boiling point while clarifying. Marsala flavors the broth a bit, while the caramelized sugar has almost no taste.

Consommé

SERVES 6

9 cups clarified broth (see
    above), made without the
    tomato
½ pound beef, without any fat
1 small carrot, scraped

1 very small red onion, cleaned
1 small celery rib
5 sprigs Italian parsley, leaves
    only
1 extra-large egg white

AFTER the broth is clarified, put it back into a clean stockpot.

Chop the beef coarsely and place it in a small bowl. Add the egg white to the bowl and mix it thoroughly into the meat, stirring for 5 or 6 minutes. Add the contents of the bowl to the stockpot and stir it into the broth.

Add carrot, onion, celery, and parsley, all whole, then place the stockpot over low heat and simmer for 1 hour, covered.

Wet a piece of cheesecloth with cold water and place it in the refrigerator for 10 minutes. Place the cheesecloth over a large bowl and pass the broth through it. The consommé may be eaten warm or cold.

NOTE: Consommé is served in a cup rather than a bowl, probably because it is concentrated and a smaller portion of it is served than of broth or soup.

Gelatina

ABOUT 3 CUPS

*G*elatina is the Italian form of what is called aspic in English, French, and German. The kind of meat used to make it depends on the dish it accompanies. To make a *gelatina* to accompany a capon, a second capon will be the base of the *gelatina*. The same would be true of chicken, fish, pork, or beef. The recipe below is based on beef and may accompany boiled beef, but also chicken or capon.

10 cups cold water
2 pounds beef for boiling
1 medium calf's foot
1 pig's foot (optional)
1 chicken neck or one small piece of chicken
1 carrot, scraped
1 celery rib

1 small red onion, cleaned
1½ teaspoons coarse-grained salt
¼ pound lean boneless veal
3 extra-large egg whites
1 to 2 teaspoons granulated sugar

PLACE the water, beef, calf's foot, optional pig's foot, chicken neck, carrot, celery, onion, and salt in a large stockpot. Set over medium heat and let simmer very slowly, half covered, for about 4½ hours. By that time, the water should have reduced to less than half.

Remove the pot from the heat. Strain the broth through a piece of cheesecloth into a large bowl and let stand until cool (about 1 hour). When cool, cover the bowl and place it in the refrigerator until completely cold (at least 4 hours).

Remove the bowl from refrigerator; all the fat will have risen to the top. Carefully remove it with a small spatula, wiping up the last bits with a paper towel.

CLARIFYING GELATINA

Using a wire whisk, beat egg whites with 2 tablespoons of the broth. Coarsely chop the veal, then add along with the beaten egg whites to the bowl with the cold broth. Mix thoroughly, then transfer the contents of the bowl to an absolutely clean stockpot. Place it over very low heat and stir continuously with the whisk until the broth reaches the boiling point. (In this way the beaten egg whites will become completely absorbed in the broth.)

At the moment the broth reaches boiling point, half-cover the pot with the lid and lower the heat to minimum. Let simmer for 10 to 12 minutes. In this time eggs rise to the top with all the impurities absorbed and the broth should at a critical moment become completely transparent.

COLORING GELATINA

You can give *gelatina* the shade you like, depending on the quantity of caramelized sugar you add.

Put sugar in a metal spoon and place spoon directly on flame until sugar liquifies and turns brown.

Pour it in simmering broth drop by drop and stop when it reaches the shade you wish.

STRAINING AND CLARIFYING GELATINA

Wet a piece of cheesecloth with cold water and place it in refrigerator for 10 minutes.

Place cheesecloth on colander and rest colander on large bowl.

Gently pour broth into colander with cheesecloth. Broth passing through should be absolutely clear and transparent.

Wet the mold you have chosen with cold water.

Transfer broth to mold and let stand until cool.

Place mold in refrigerator until firm.

UNMOLDING GELATINA

Hold serving dish upside down tightly over mold and reverse them together.

Wet a towel with hot water and squeeze it.

Place the hot towel over the reversed mold. Repeat procedure with the hot towel until *gelatina* detaches. Lift off mold.

You can serve *gelatina* in the shape of the mold or cut it into 1-inch squares.

Stock

*S*tock to be used in making other dishes is a by-product of boiled meat and fish dishes (see pages 328 and 284). Simply save the broth that results from boiling the meats, strain it, let it cool, defat it, and use it as stock. This is of course different from the French stock made by boiling bones, etc. for hours. Italians do not generally do this. Stock in these recipes refers to the Italian one, the broth left from making *bollito*.

Topini di patate con petto di pollo in brodo

TOPINI OF POTATO AND CHICKEN BREAST IN BROTH

SERVES 8

A marvelous variant of *topini* of potatoes (see page 276) is one made with chopped chicken breast added to the potatoes. The recipe is slightly more complicated, requiring egg yolks and Parmigiano to be added as well, but the procedure is the same. They are eaten in broth, rather than with sauce.

1¼ pounds boiling potatoes, but not new potatoes
1 whole chicken breast
2 extra-large egg yolks
½ cup freshly grated Parmigiano
5 sprigs Italian parsley, leaves only

2½ cups unbleached all-purpose flour
Salt, freshly ground black pepper, and freshly grated nutmeg to taste
6 cups chicken or meat broth, preferably homemade
Coarse-grained salt

STEAM (do not boil) potatoes until cooked but firm. Set aside until needed.

Heat 3 cups of cold water in a saucepan. When it reaches the boiling point, add the salt, then chicken breast, and let cook until soft (about 20 minutes).

Meanwhile, place the egg yolks in a small bowl. Add ¼ cup of the grated Parmigiano and mix very well with a wooden spoon. Chop the parsley fine and add to the bowl with the egg yolks and Parmigiano.

When the chicken breast is done, transfer it from saucepan to chopping board and remove both skin and bone. Chop the meat fine and add it to the bowl with the other ingredients.

Spread the flour on a pasta board. Peel the potatoes and pass them through a potato ricer onto the flour. Sprinkle the potatoes with salt, a little pepper, and a pinch of nutmeg, then add the contents of the small bowl to potatoes. Start incorporating flour, little by little, into the potato mixture until the dough is homogenous and firm. Knead gently for 5 or 6 minutes.

Cut the dough into several pieces and roll each piece into a long thin roll about ½ inch in diameter. Cut each roll into 1-inch pieces.

Use the dull inside of a convex hand cheese grater. Hold a 1-inch piece at the top of the grater with the middle fingers of one hand. Lightly draw the piece around in a motion that makes the cursive letter "c." The resultant shape should be the quasi-shell the Florentines think resembles "little mice," and which they prefer to the more usual *gnocchi*.

Heat the broth in a stockpot; heat a large quantity of cold water in a second stockpot.

When the water is boiling, add salt, then raise the heat and quickly drop all the *topini,* one by one, into the stockpot. Lightly stir the water with a wooden spoon, to keep the *topini* from sticking. After a few seconds, the *topini* will come to the surface of the water; let them cook for 1 minute more. With a strainer-skimmer, remove the *topini* from the stockpot to individual soup bowls. Quickly pour some hot broth over the *topini* in each bowl, sprinkle with some of the remaining Parmigiano, and serve immediately.

Taglierini in brodo

PASTA IN BROTH

SERVES 6

*F*inely cut fresh pasta in broth. A light and versatile first dish, suitable for all occasions.

2 cups unbleached all-purpose flour
2 extra-large eggs
Pinch of salt
2 teaspoons olive or vegetable oil

4½ cups meat broth (see page 126), approximately, preferably homemade
Coarse-grained salt
6 tablespoons freshly grated Parmigiano

MAKE the *taglierini,* using the flour, eggs, salt, and oil. For procedure, see pages 157–162, and to cut into *taglierini,* see page 162. Let the *taglierini* stand on a pasta board, covered with a cotton dishtowel, until needed.

Heat a large quantity of cold water in a stockpot. Meanwhile, in a second stockpot, heat the broth.

When the water in the first stockpot reaches the boiling point, add coarse salt, then the *taglierini,* stir with a wooden spoon, and let them cook for 15 seconds, then strain quickly and transfer to the second stockpot, with the heated broth.

Serve immediately, sprinkling each serving with a tablespoon of freshly grated Parmigiano.

Palline ripiene in brodo

LITTLE MUSHROOM-FILLED PUFFS IN BROTH

SERVES 6

*L*ittle balls of cream-puff pastry, filled with dried wild mushrooms, in a fine broth. Appropriate to the most formal and elegant occasions.

FOR THE PALLINE (PASTA SOFFIATA)

¾ cup cold water
Pinch of salt
6 tablespoons (3 ounces) sweet butter
¾ cup unbleached all-purpose flour
2 extra-large eggs

Pinch of freshly grated nutmeg
Salsa di funghi (see page 79)
5 cups meat broth (see page 126), approximately, preferably homemade
6 tablespoons freshly grated Parmigiano

MAKE the *pasta soffiata* with the ingredients listed above. For procedure see page 572, adding the pinch of nutmeg when the eggs are incorporated.

Butter a cookie sheet; preheat the oven to 375 degrees.

Place the *pasta soffiata* in a syringe or pastry bag and form small balls (about ½ inch in diameter) with it on the cookie sheet, then bake in the preheated oven for about 20 minutes. Do not open the oven for 15 minutes after you put the cookie sheet in.

Remove the cookie sheet from oven and let *palline* rest until cool (about 30 minutes).

Prepare *salsa di funghi,* but make sure the mushrooms are chopped very fine. Let the sauce rest until cool (about 30 minutes), then place in a syringe and fill the *palline.* Place 5 or 6 *palline* in each individual soup bowl.

Heat the broth. When it is warm, pour one ladleful of broth (about ¾ cup) in each soup bowl with the *palline,* then sprinkle with Parmigiano and serve immediately.

Acquacotta

TUSCAN SOUP

SERVES 8 TO 10

*A*cquacotta, meaning "cooked water," is obviously a name for a soup made with water, rather than broth, as a base. There is the typically understated Tuscan humor in the name as well. It is a real *zuppa* because it has a slice of bread at the bottom of the bowl. *Acquacotta* is completely vegetarian, being based on dried *porcini* mushrooms combined with the classic *odori*. The tomatoes which are now a common ingredient were probably a later addition, in the nineteenth century, and most likely the pinch of red pepper was added together with the tomatoes. Belonging to the earlier stage are the eggs, mixed in at the last moment, as in the famous Roman *Stracciatella* with grated Parmigiano.

As so often happens nowadays, some make *acquacotta* with broth rather than water, contradicting its very essence.

The main technical feature of making this soup is that the vegetables, after being sautéed in olive oil, are combined with cold rather than hot water and so they stop sautéing abruptly and have to begin cooking all over again. The recipe is also an instance of the use of hot pepper and grated cheese together. This breaking of the norm can perhaps be explained by understanding that the pepper was added with the tomatoes at a later stage.

1 ounce dried **porcini** *mushrooms*
2 medium carrots, scraped
2 large celery stalks
1 medium red onion, cleaned
1 small clove garlic, peeled
½ cup olive oil
1½ pounds ripe fresh tomatoes or 1½ pounds canned tomatoes, preferably imported Italian, drained
1 tablespoon tomato paste, preferably imported Italian
Salt and freshly ground black pepper
Pinch hot red pepper flakes
2 quarts cold water
2 extra-large eggs
8 tablespoons freshly grated Parmigiano

PLUS

*2 cups croutons (piccoli crostini fritti, see page 51), small bread
pieces fried in olive oil, or 8 slices Tuscan bread, toasted*

SOAK the mushrooms in a bowl of lukewarm water for ½ hour. Drain*
and be sure that no sand remains attached to the stems. Finely chop
carrots, celery, onion, garlic, and the soaked mushrooms all together on
board. Heat the oil in a heavy casserole over medium heat. When the
oil is warm, add the chopped ingredients and sauté for 10 minutes,
stirring with a wooden spoon as needed. Meanwhile pass the tomatoes
through a food mill, using the disc with the smallest holes, into a small
bowl. Add the strained tomatoes along with the tomato paste, then salt,
pepper, and red pepper flakes. Let simmer for 15 minutes, mixing every
so often. Add the cold water, mix very well, and when the broth returns
to a boil, let simmer for 55 minutes. Place the two eggs in a crockery
or china soup tureen and mix them very well with the Parmigiano.
When the soup is ready, ladle it into the tureen, and using a wooden
spoon, mix each addition very well with the egg-cheese combination, in
order to avoid curdling.

When the broth is very smooth and the eggs completely amalgamated, add the croutons and serve immediately. If using bread slices
instead, place a slice in each soup bowl and ladle the broth over it. Serve
immediately.

Ginestrata

RENAISSANCE CINNAMON BROTH

SERVES 6

*G*inestrata starts with a rich "eating" broth (not a stock). Making it
requires more technique than the usual soup. The cold, defatted
broth is mixed with the egg yolks and other ingredients and strained
through cheesecloth. Then it is placed over low heat and stirred without

(continued)

*Reserve mushroom water for other uses. See page 25.

stopping. It must be taken from the heat just before it reaches the boiling point.

The texture should be a homogenous, creamy one, a suspension, in which the egg particles should not be separately visible. Be sure to use very fresh eggs. When the *ginestrata* does not succeed, it curdles in part, and the egg particles are separately visible. When it succeeds, it is a dream, an unforgettable flavor in which individual ingredients lose their identity in a perfect whole.

Ginestrata is a classic Renaissance broth, and appears in sixteenth-century cookbooks. The name refers to the yellow color of broom flowers, *ginestre*. Dishes the color of *ginestre* formed one of the color groups so dear to Renaissance Florentines. It is unusual for a dish of this color not to contain saffron, but the desired color is achieved in other ways, with egg yolks and Marsala.

At the time there were many sweet fortified wines that were used, but since the eighteenth century, Marsala has gradually replaced most of them.

5 extra-large egg yolks	*6 tablespoons (3 ounces) sweet*
2 teaspoons ground cinnamon	*butter*
¾ cup dry Marsala	*3 teaspoons granulated sugar*
1 quart cold chicken or meat	*Freshly grated nutmeg*
broth (not stock),	
completely defatted,	
preferably homemade	

PLACE the egg yolks in a large bowl and add the cinnamon and Marsala. Mix very well with a wooden spoon, then add the cold broth and mix thoroughly. Pass the ingredients of the bowl through a piece of cheesecloth into a large flameproof casserole and add the salt and butter.

Warm 6 terra-cotta soup bowls in the oven.

Place the casserole over low heat and stir continuously until the moment before the broth reaches the boiling point; do not allow it to boil. Remove immediately from the heat and ladle into the individual heated soup bowls. Sprinkle each bowl with ½ teaspoon sugar and a "smell" (less than a pinch) of fresly grated nutmeg. Serve immediately.

Carabaccia

RENAISSANCE ONION SOUP

SERVES 8

*C*arabaccia has the Renaissance flavorings of ground almonds and a little sugar and cinnamon, but the lemon juice and olive oil make the taste a little sweet and sour. The soup does not require the careful technique of *ginestrata,* and the base can be an ordinary broth, left over from a *bollito.* It also dates from a sixteenth-century cookbook.

Coarse-grained salt
8 large red onions, cleaned
¼ cup olive oil
3 quarts chicken or meat broth,
    defatted, preferably
    homemade

Juice of 3 lemons
8 ounces almonds, blanched
Salt and freshly ground black
    pepper
5 teaspoons ground cinnamon
4 teaspoons granulated sugar

BRING a large quantity of cold water to a boil in a stockpot. Add coarse salt to taste. Leave the onions whole. Cook them in boiling water for 5 minutes, then drain, dry, and chop them coarsely.

Heat the olive oil in a large saucepan. When it is hot, add the chopped onions and sauté them very gently for 5 to 8 minutes. Heat the broth in a stockpot, then pour it into the saucepan with the onions. Simmer until the onions are soft (about 1 hour).

Warm the lemon juice in a small saucepan, then add the blanched almonds and simmer very slowly for 4 or 5 minutes.

Remove the onions from the broth by straining it into a bowl. Pass the onions through food mill, using the disc with the smallest holes, into a large bowl, then return, along with the broth, to the saucepan. Taste for salt and pepper, add 1 teaspoon of the cinnamon, and place the pan back on the heat. When the broth reaches the boiling point, add the almonds in the lemon juice and simmer for 2 or 3 minutes more. Meanwhile, heat 8 terra-cotta soup bowls in the oven.

Remove the saucepan from the heat and ladle the *carabaccia* into the individual heated bowls. Sprinkle ½ teaspoon each sugar and cinnamon on each portion and serve very hot.

Cipollata

MODERN TUSCAN ONION SOUP

SERVES 4

*L*ighter than French onion soup because the onions are parboiled rather than sautéed in butter. *Pancetta,* olive oil, and Parmigiano provide the Italian flavor, while the specifically Tuscan touch is the slices of good bread placed at the bottom of the bowl. Though post-Renaissance, the recipe is still an old one.

4 large white onions, cleaned
Coarse-grained salt
2 ounces pancetta *or prosciutto*
¼ cup olive oil
5 cups hot chicken or meat
*   broth, preferably homemade*

4 slices Tuscan bread (see
*   page 39)*
Salt and freshly ground black
*   pepper*
¼ cup freshly grated
*   Parmigiano, approximately*

LEAVE the onions whole. Cook them in a large quantity of boiling, salted water for 10 minutes, then drain them, place under cold running water to cool, and chop coarsely. Transfer to a bowl.

Chop the *pancetta* coarsely and sauté very lightly in the olive oil in a flameproof casserole, preferably terra-cotta. Add the chopped onions and sauté until they are golden, then add the hot broth. Cover the casserole and simmer for 35 minutes.

Toast the bread slices on both sides. Place one in each of 4 heated terra-cotta soup bowls.

Taste the soup for salt and pepper, then pour into the bowls. Sprinkle with Parmigiano and freshly ground black pepper, then cover the bowls with lids and allow to rest for 5 minutes before serving.

Zuppa di porri

LEEK SOUP

SERVES 4

*T*he leeks are sautéed in butter, and then simmered in broth. The soup is poured over toasted Tuscan bread in a terra-cotta bowl, the grated Groviera is sprinkled generously over and allowed to melt from just the heat of the hot soup. Not a thick soup, but a rich one.

There are two variants: in one, ½ cup of rice is cooked in the simmering broth and the bread is omitted; in the second, a separately poached chicken breast is cut into long, thin strips and used instead of either bread or rice.

5 medium leeks
4 tablespoons (2 ounces) sweet
  butter
2 tablespoons unbleached all-
  purpose flour
4 cups hot meat or chicken
  broth, preferably homemade

Salt and freshly ground black
  pepper
4 slices Tuscan bread (see
  page 39)
½ cup freshly grated Groviera

RINSE the leeks well, discard the green parts, then cut into ½-inch slices. Soak in cold water for 30 minutes, then rinse the pieces very well in cold water.

Heat the butter in a large flameproof casserole, preferably terra-cotta. When the butter is completely melted, add the leeks and sauté until translucent (15 to 20 minutes). Sprinkle the flour over the leeks and mix it in well with a wooden spoon, then pour in the hot broth and stir thoroughly for 1 minute. Taste for salt and pepper and simmer, covered, for 25 minutes.

Toast the bread slices on each side and place one in each heated terra-cotta soup bowl. Sprinkle 1 tablespoon of grated cheese over each bread slice, then pour over the soup, and sprinkle with the remaining cheese and freshly ground black pepper. Cover the individual bowls with their lids. Let rest for 10 minutes, then serve.

PASSATI

*T*his category of Italian soups deserves to be better known. Pureed vegetables are added to a good broth, then Parmigiano is sprinkled over and sometimes good homemade croutons float on top. Though they are sometimes also known as creme, comparable to our "cream of," no cream is used. It is the creaminess of the soup itself that suggests that name. *Passato* means "passed through."

The favorite types are those made from mixed vegetables, from spinach, and from Tuscan beans; the recipes for all three follow. The first two are useful for a light repast in the evening.

Passato di verdura

PUREED VEGETABLE SOUP

SERVES 4

*P*ureed mixed vegetables in a meat- or chicken-stock base, with some homemade croutons and good Parmigiano floating on top, is a very satisfying beginning to a light meal.

Of the vegetables specified, if Savoy cabbage, Swiss chard, or stringbeans are out of season, increase the quantities of all the other vegetables to compensate; there should be about 1¼ pounds of vegetables in all.

The vegetables are simmered first without any water or broth; they create their own liquid. Then they are passed through a food mill and added to the broth.

2 leaves Savoy cabbage
1 small potato
1 small red onion
1 carrot
5 sprigs Italian parsley, leaves only
2 celery ribs

5 large leaves Swiss chard
3 ounces fresh spinach
1 ripe fresh tomato or ½ cup canned tomatoes, preferably imported Italian, drained
1 handful stringbeans

5 tablespoons olive oil

Salt to taste

5 cups warm chicken or meat
   broth, preferably
   homemade, defatted (see
   page 126)

Pinch of freshly ground black
   pepper

¹/₄ cup freshly grated
   Parmigiano

4 heaping tablespoons deep-
   fried crostini (see page 51)
   or 4 tablespoons of rice,
   preferably Italian Arborio
   (optional)

RINSE, trim, and clean, then cut or slice all the vegetables (except the canned tomatoes, if used) into medium-sized pieces, then place in a bowl of cold water and let soak for 30 minutes. Then, without drying them, transfer all the vegetables (including the fresh or canned tomatoes) from bowl to stockpot.

Add the olive oil and salt to the stockpot and place over medium heat. Cover and let simmer very slowly, without lifting the lid and without adding any water or broth, for about 25 minutes. Remove the stockpot from the heat and pass all the vegetables through a food mill, using the disc with the smallest holes, into a large bowl.

Heat the broth in a saucepan.

Place the pureed vegetables back in the stockpot and add the warm broth. Place over medium heat and let simmer slowly, uncovered, for about 25 minutes, stirring every so often. Taste for salt and add black pepper.

After 25 minutes, the *passato di verdura* is ready to be served. If you prefer to eat it with *crostini,* prepare them while the soup is simmering. Then place them in individual soup bowls, and when the *passato* is ready, pour it over the *crostini,* sprinkle with Parmigiano, and serve immediately.

If you prefer to eat *passato di verdura* with rice, cook the rice in salted water in a small saucepan for about 15 minutes and add to the stockpot when *passato* is ready, after it has cooked for 25 minutes. Serve in individual soup bowls, sprinkled with grated Parmigiano.

Passato di fagioli

TUSCAN PUREED BEAN SOUP

SERVES 4

1½ cups dried cannellini beans
2 ounces **pancetta** *or prosciutto*
1 medium clove garlic, whole
    and unpeeled
Salt
¼ cup olive oil
1 large slice Tuscan bread,
    white (see page 39) or dark
    (see page 43)

1 tablespoon rosemary leaves,
    fresh or preserved in salt or
    dried and blanched
4 ounces good-quality imported
    dried pasta (small shells)
Freshly ground black pepper to
    taste

SOAK the beans overnight in a bowl of cold water. The next day, drain and rinse the beans and put them in a stockpot with 7 cups of cold water.* Add the *pancetta,* unpeeled garlic, and 1 tablespoon of salt. Place the pot over the heat and simmer until the beans are very soft (1 to 1½ hours).

Drain beans, saving the cooking water, and pass them through a food mill, using the disc with the smallest holes, into a bowl. Put back into stockpot, along with the water. Return the pot to the heat and simmer until the texture of the soup resembles a smooth light cream.

Heat the olive oil in a frying pan. Cut the bread slice in quarters and fry lightly. Remove the bread from the oil and save it for later use, then add the rosemary leaves to the pan. Let them sauté for 3 or 4 minutes, then pour the oil containing the rosemary into the bean soup. Taste for salt and pepper; there should be a lot of both.

Cook the dried pasta in the soup until al dente (10 to 15 minutes), then remove the soup from the heat and let rest for 10 to 15 minutes.

Place one piece of the fried bread in each of 4 soup bowls and pour the *passato* over. Serve hot.

NOTE: This soup is equally good served cold the following day, especially in summer. If you are making the soup to be served cold, add

*See Beans, page 29.

the bread pieces to the stockpot at the time you are putting in the dried pasta.

Passato di spinaci

CREAMED SPINACH SOUP

SERVES 4

he spinach is cooked in water with some *odori* (aromatic vege-tables) and then strained. This is to remove the bitterness from the spinach before it is added to the stock.

1 ½ pounds fresh spinach
Coarse-grained salt
½ carrot, scraped
1 small red onion, cleaned
½ celery rib

3 cups chicken or meat broth,
preferably homemade (see
page 126)
¼ cup freshly grated
Parmigiano

REMOVE the large stems from the spinach, then wash and let soak in cold water for 30 minutes.

Put 4 cups of cold water in a flameproof casserole over high heat. When the water reaches the boiling point, add coarse salt to taste, then the drained spinach, carrot, onion, and celery, and boil for 10 minutes. Meanwhile, heat the broth in a large saucepan. Drain the spinach, carrot, onion, and celery and add them to the saucepan with broth. Simmer for about 20 minutes, covered, then remove the saucepan from the heat and pass the contents through a food mill using the disc with the smallest holes, into a second saucepan.

Place the second saucepan, with the *passato,* on the flame. Taste for salt and pepper and simmer very slowly for 10 minutes more. Remove the saucepan from stove and serve the soup immediately. Sprinkle each serving with a tablespoon of grated Parmigiano.

NOTE: Homemade croutons (see *crostini,* page 51) may be added to the soup when served.

MINESTRONI AND MINESTRE

$\mathcal{E}$very part of Italy has its own particular minestrone, with vegetables, beans, and pasta or rice. In Tuscany, slices of Tuscan bread are usually substituted for pasta.

Following are the recipes for a number of different types: *minestrone di riso,* eaten hot or cooled; *minestrone alla contadina,* the usual Tuscan "country" minestrone; and the *ribollita* that is made from it the next day.

There are two special *minestre* from the mountainous Garfagnana region: *incavolata,* featuring kale and cannellini, lightly thickened with a little yellow corn meal, and the *minestra "povera" di patate.*

Finally, we have the *pasta e fagioli* (pasta and beans) category. Again, every part of Italy has its own version. Included here are two Tuscan versions, one with cannellini beans and the other with chick-peas, or *ceci.*

Minestrone di riso

TUSCAN MINESTRONE WITH RICE

SERVES 8

$\mathcal{O}$ne of the few Tuscan soups not using bread, obviously because rice is used. Unlike most minestroni, it begins with chicken and meat broth. Even the rice is cooked separately in stock before it is added to the minestrone.

Minestrone di riso may be eaten hot, but it is more often eaten cooled *(semifreddo),* not chilled or refrigerated, in the summer. It is one of the staples of the trattoria menu in the summertime.

To get the authentic flavor, be careful to use wrinkled Savoy cabbage rather than the more common type and to get a piece of the rind of the prosciutto from your Italian market. Otherwise, it can be made with no great difficulty and with sure result.

1 ½ cups dried cannellini beans
Coarse-grained salt
8 ounces fresh spinach, large
    stems removed
1 small bunch Swiss chard,
    cleaned
½ small head Savoy cabbage,
    cleaned
10 sprigs Italian parsley, leaves
    only
2 medium cloves garlic, peeled
2 ounces prosciutto, in one piece
1 small piece prosciutto rind
3 tablespoons olive oil
2 celery ribs
1 carrot, scraped

1 medium red onion, cleaned
1 medium potato, peeled
1 handful stringbeans, cleaned
1 small zucchini, cleaned
1 tablespoon tomato paste,
    preferably imported Italian
2 quarts chicken or meat broth,
    approximately, preferably
    homemade
Salt and freshly ground black
    pepper to taste
¾ cup raw rice, preferably
    Italian Arborio
½ cup freshly grated
    Parmigiano

SOAK the cannellini beans in a bowl of cold water overnight. The next day, drain the beans and partially cook them in salted water for 10 to 15 minutes.

Rinse the spinach, Swiss chard, and cabbage, then cut into strips. Cook in another saucepan for 15 minutes, with salt and only the water left on the leaves after washing. Drain the cooked vegetables, lightly squeeze them, and set aside.

Coarsely chop the parsley, garlic, prosciutto, and prosciutto rind. Place in a stockpot with the olive oil and sauté very gently for 15 minutes, until golden. Meanwhile, cut celery, carrot, onion, potato, stringbeans, and zucchini into ½-inch pieces. Add to the stockpot and sauté for 5 minutes more.

Transfer the partially cooked beans, and their water, to the stockpot, then add the spinach, Swiss chard, and cabbage. Add the tomato paste and enough broth (about 8 cups) to cover the vegetables by about 4 inches. Simmer very slowly until all the ingredients are cooked (about 40 minutes).

While the vegetables are cooking, partially cook the rice (for 10

(continued)

minutes) in the remaining broth with some water added. Drain the rice, add it to the stockpot, and cook until the rice is completely cooked (8 to 10 minutes more). Taste for salt and pepper and serve immediately, hot (sprinkling about a tablespoon of Parmigiano over each serving), or serve cool the next day.

Minestrone alla contadina

TUSCAN MINESTRONE, COUNTRY STYLE

SERVES 6 TO 8

*T*he standard Tuscan "country" minestrone, including among its vegetables Savoy cabbage, kale, and a few cannellini beans, served over slices of Tuscan bread with Parmigiano floating on top. It is flavored with the full battery of *odori* (aromatic vegetables) and with olive oil. If you have homemade croutons, you may substitute them for the bread slices.

Minestrone alla contadina is also served the following day as *ribollita* (see page 148).

8 ounces dried cannellini beans
1 slice prosciutto (about 3 ounces) or pancetta
1 large red onion, cleaned
1 celery rib
2 large cloves garlic, peeled
1 carrot, scraped
10 sprigs Italian parsley, leaves only
½ cup olive oil
½ small head Savoy cabbage, cleaned
1½ bunches kale
1 medium potato, cleaned

1 cup canned tomatoes, preferably imported Italian, drained and seeded
1 small bunch Swiss chard, cleaned
12 large, thick slices Tuscan bread (see page 39), several days old, or 1 cup homemade crostini *(see page 51)*
Salt and freshly ground black pepper
6 to 8 tablespoons freshly grated Parmigiano

SOAK the dried beans overnight in a bowl of cold water. The next day, drain the beans and cook them in a large flameproof casserole with 2 quarts of salted water and the prosciutto or *pancetta*. As the beans absorb water, keep adding enough hot water to maintain 2 quarts of liquid *(broda)* at the end of the cooking time. When the beans are tender (about 1 hour),* remove from the flame and let stand until needed.

Coarsely chop the onion, celery, garlic, carrot, and parsley and sauté them in a stockpot, with the olive oil, for 12 to 15 minutes. Meanwhile, finely slice the Savoy cabbage; remove the stems from the kale and cut into small pieces; peel the potato and cut it into small squares.

When the *odori* are golden, add the cabbage, kale, and potato to the stockpot, along with the tomatoes. Cover and simmer for 15 minutes, then add the Swiss chard, stems removed and cut up.

Remove the prosciutto from the bean casserole. Pass two-thirds of the beans through a food mill, using the disc with the smallest holes, into the stockpot. Simmer together for about ½ hour more, until Savoy cabbage and kale are almost cooked.

Drain the remaining beans, reserving the broth, and return them to the original casserole. Add the bean broth to the stockpot, little by little, whenever more liquid is needed, until all is used.

When the cabbage and kale are ready, add the remaining beans, whole. Taste for salt and pepper, then let cook for 5 minutes more.

If using bread, make a layer of bread slices on the bottom of a tureen and pour over two full ladles of soup. Make other layers of bread, each time pouring the soup over, until all the bread is used. Pour the remaining soup on top, cover the tureen, and let stand for 20 minutes before serving, with a tablespoon of grated Parmigiano sprinkled over each portion.

If using croutons instead of bread slices, place 2 tablespoons of croutons in each individual soup bowl. Allow the soup to stand for 20 minutes after cooking, then pour over the croutons. Sprinkle with Parmigiano and serve.

*See Beans, p. 29.

Ribollita

"REBOILED" TUSCAN MINESTRONE

SERVES 6

*M*inestrone alla contadina is usually made in a large quantity so there will be enough left over to make *ribollita* the next day. *Ribollita* means, literally, "reboiled."

Most Florentines prefer the *ribollita* to the minestrone itself, so it is a very popular, standard winter dish. One of the standard items on all *trattorie* menus in Florence, it resembles *pappa,* the "bread soup" (see *pappa al pomodoro,* page 273), more than a *minestra.* Try it.

Overnight, the minestrone will thicken even further. Heat it, and allow it to boil for about 1 minute. With a wooden spoon, mix well, breaking up the bread slices until the texture is almost homogenous. Ladle into individual bowls, preferably of terra-cotta with handles, and pour 2 teaspoons of good olive oil over each serving.

Incavolata

KALE AND BEAN SOUP

SERVES 6 TO 8

A minestra of kale and beans, flavored with sage and *pancetta.* At a certain point, a little yellow corn meal *(farina gialla)* is added, creating a unique texture, only slightly thick. *Incavolata* is a specialty of the mountain area north of Lucca, called Garfagnana. That part of Tuscany has its own, very special *cucina.*

Special care must be taken when the corn meal is added; this must be done very slowly, while stirring, so it does not lump together.

1 pound dried cannellini beans

4 leaves sage, fresh or preserved
   in salt

4 ounces pancetta or
   prosciutto, in one piece

1 clove garlic, peeled but left
   whole

Coarse-grained salt

1 pound kale

1 tablespoon tomato paste,
   preferably imported Italian

1/2 cup coarse Italian yellow
   corn meal

Salt and freshly ground black
   pepper to taste

SOAK the beans overnight in a large bowl of cold water. The next day, drain the beans and put in a stockpot, preferably terra-cotta, along with 12 cups cold water, the sage, the whole clove of garlic, and pancetta, cut into pieces. Season with coarse salt, cover, and simmer very slowly until the beans are tender (about 1 hour, depending on the freshness of the beans).*

Meanwhile, remove the stems completely from the kale and cut up the leaves coarsely. Soak in a large bowl of cold water for 1 hour.

Drain the cooked beans in a colander, letting the bean water pour off into another large bowl. Pour the bean water back into the stockpot. Pass half of the beans through a food mill, using the disc with the smallest holes, back into the stockpot; leave the remaining beans in the colander.

Return the stockpot to the heat and add the kale and tomato paste. Simmer until the kale is very soft (about 1 hour), then pour in the yellow corn meal, little by little, stirring continuously with a wooden spoon. Simmer very slowly for 30 minutes.

Just 5 minutes before removing the pot from the heat, add remaining whole beans from the colander and mix thoroughly. Taste for salt and pepper, then remove from the flame and serve immediately.

*See Beans, p. 29.

Minestra "povera" di patate

SIMPLE POTATO SOUP

SERVES 4

A potato soup, also from the Garfagnana. In Tuscany, the word *"povera,"* meaning "poor," is sometimes used, in a form of reverse snobbism, to mean "genuine" or "good" when referring to food. The implication is that nothing sophisticated and unnatural is used. Most times *taglierini* are added (see note below), but there is also an alternative version that adds thin strips of chicken breast. This second version would be less starchy and probably more to foreign tastes. It is, however, a completely authentic alternative.

1½ pounds of boiling potatoes,
* but not new potatoes*
12 cups cold water
1 celery rib
1 large red onion, cleaned
1 large clove garlic, peeled
1 carrot, scraped
10 sprigs Italian parsley, leaves
* only*

2 ounces of **pancetta** *or*
* prosciutto, in one piece*
¼ cup olive oil
2 small fresh tomatoes or 2
* canned tomatoes, preferably*
* imported Italian, drained*
* and seeded*
Salt

FOR POACHING THE CHICKEN BREAST
1 carrot, scraped
1 very small red onion, cleaned
½ celery rib
3 or 4 sprigs Italian parsley,
* leaves only*
Coarse-grained salt

1 whole chicken breast, boned
¼ cup freshly grated
* Parmigiano*
Freshly ground black pepper to
** taste**

PEEL and rinse the potatoes, then place them in a stockpot, preferably terra-cotta, with the cold water. Coarsely chop the celery, onion, garlic, carrot, parsley, and *pancetta.* Add to the stockpot, along with the olive oil, tomatoes (skinned and seeded, if fresh), and salt. Place the stockpot on the heat and simmer, covered, for 2 hours.

150

While the soup is simmering, place the poaching *odori* (carrot, onion, celery, and parsley) in a saucepan with water to cover and coarse salt. When the water boils, poach the chicken breast for 16 to 18 minutes. Transfer to a board, remove the skin, and cut the meat into long thin strips.

When the soup is ready, place a few strips of chicken breast on bottom of each individual terra-cotta soup bowl. Pour the soup over, and sprinkle each serving with 1 tablespoon of Parmigiano. Grind some fresh black pepper into each bowl, then cover each bowl with its lid and let stand for 5 minutes before serving.

NOTE: This soup is most frequently served with fresh *taglierini* in place of the strips of chicken breast. (Rice may also be substituted.) We prefer the version with chicken breast because it is lighter. If you wish to use *taglierini* instead of chicken breast, make them according to the recipe on page 157, using 1 egg, 1 cup unbleached all-purpose flour, a pinch of salt, and 1 teaspoon olive oil.

Pasta e fagioli

PASTA AND BEAN SOUP

SERVES 6

*T*he famous "hearty" pasta and beans.

Flavored with prosciutto rind *(cotenna)*, garlic, and pepper, it is served with Parmigiano. A high-quality imported dried pasta should be used, one that is also fairly substantial in shape, such as the medium-sized *chiocciole* (snails or shells), which are known by some other names as well.

2 cups dried cannellini beans
1 small slice prosciutto rind
1 small potato
1 medium red onion, cleaned
2 large cloves garlic, peeled
¼ cup olive oil
10 cups water
1 cup canned tomatoes,
 preferably imported Italian,
 drained

Salt and freshly ground black
 pepper
8 ounces good-quality imported
 dried pasta (medium shells
 or large elbow macaroni)
6 heaping teaspoons freshly
 grated Parmigiano

SOAK the beans overnight in cold water.

The next day, cook the prosciutto rind in boiling water for 2 minutes, then rinse well under cold running water and cut into small pieces; peel the potato and cut into small squares.

Chop the onion and garlic coarsely and place them in a stockpot, preferably terra-cotta, along with the olive oil. Sauté very gently until light golden, then add the drained beans, the potato pieces, cold water, tomatoes, and pieces of prosciutto rind. Cover and simmer very slowly for about 45 minutes or until beans are cooked but not overcooked. Taste for salt and pepper, then add the pasta to the pot and cook until al dente, 9 to 12 minutes, depending on brand. Allow to cool for 10 minutes, then serve, sprinkling Parmigiano and freshly ground black pepper over each individual serving.

Pasta e ceci

PASTA AND CHICK-PEAS

SERVES 6

*C*hick-peas, *ceci,* are widely used in Tuscany and all over Italy. There is a well-known *torta* or "pie" of *ceci,* and we have seen that they were used in Renaissance cooking, antedating cannellini. Olive oil, rosemary, garlic, and pepper complement their fine flavor. Use the smaller type of pasta, such as *avemarie.* Grated cheese is not used with this dish; instead, some good uncooked olive oil is spooned over each bowl when the *pasta e ceci* is served.

8 ounces dried chick-peas
8 cups cold water
6 tablespoons olive oil
1 medium clove garlic, peeled
    but left whole
½ cup canned tomatoes,
    preferably imported Italian,
    drained and seeded

1 teaspoon rosemary leaves,
    fresh or preserved in salt or
    dried and blanched
Salt and freshly ground black
    pepper to taste
6 ounces good-quality imported
    dried short pasta (such as
    avemarie)

SOAK the chick-peas overnight in a large bowl of cold water.

The next day, put 8 cups of cold water in a flameproof casserole, preferably terra-cotta, along with 6 tablespoons of the olive oil, the whole clove of garlic, the tomatoes, and rosemary leaves. Set it on the heat, and when the water is warm, add the chick-peas. Season with salt, cover, and simmer very slowly until the chick-peas are soft (about 1½ hours).

Remove half the chick-peas from the casserole and pass through a food mill, using the disc with the smallest holes, back into the casserole. Taste for salt and pepper, then add the dried pasta and cook until al dente, 9 to 12 minutes, depending on brand.

Remove the casserole from the heat and serve; the soup should be quite thick and smooth. Put 1 teaspoon of the remaining olive oil, uncooked, on each serving; do *not* add any grated Parmigiano.

Zuppa lombarda

BEAN SOUP FOR THE LOMBARDS

SERVES 4

*S*oup *for* the Lombards, not Lombard soup. When the Milanese Lombards, fighting for the German emperor, succeeded in their siege of Florence in 1525, they were famished when they broke into the city. The besieged Florentines had very little food left, but they put together this dish with some beans, days-old bread, olive oil, and some broth. If you think it doesn't sound appetizing, try it and you'll know why it is still eaten very often, without the benefit of a siege. It is a useful dish to make with leftover *fagioli* (see page 516). But as often as not, the beans are made on purpose just to be able to make this dish.

It was in this siege that the Germans set fire to the Renaissance façade of the famous Cathedral of Florence. For some centuries it stayed without a façade, until a reconstruction was made in the nineteenth century.

6 large thick slices Tuscan
*   bread (see page 39), at least*
*   3 days old*
2 cups beans and all the liquid
*   from the flask from* **fagioli**
*   al fiasco *(see page 516)*

4 cups meat broth,
*   approximately, preferably*
*   homemade (see page 126)*
4 teaspoons olive oil
Abundant coarsely ground
*   black pepper*

CUT the bread into thirds and place in a tureen.

Heat the beans, with their liquid, in a saucepan; in another saucepan, heat the broth. When hot, pour the beans and liquid over the bread. Add enough broth so the liquid covers the beans and bread by ½ inch. (The amount of broth will vary depending on the amount of bean broth already present.) Cover tureen and let stand for about 20 minutes.

Mix the beans and bread together with a ladle, then ladle out into terra-cotta soup bowls. Sprinkle 1 teaspoon of olive oil and abundant coarsely ground black pepper over each serving.

Pasta

*T*he widespread myth that Marco Polo introduced pasta from China into Italy is not true. There still exists the manuscript of a will, drawn up in Genoa two years before the return of Marco Polo, which leaves the heirs a chestful of dried pasta.

In any case, most historians of gastronomy trace the origins of pasta to ancient Roman times. Sicily's woods had been cut down in order to make it the granary of the Roman Empire, a one-crop area for wheat. The Romans of Sicily made the excess wheat into pasta, which was preserved by drying it in the sun.

Though stuffed pasta dishes appear in Renaissance cookbooks, the standardization of the large-scale use of any pasta for the first course did not occur until rather recently, well into the nineteenth century in northern Italy, perhaps a little earlier in the south. The order of courses fixed in the sixteenth century in Florence continued, as we have mentioned before, into the nineteenth century in Italy and France, the first course after antipasti consisting of a variety of boiled dishes. By the beginning of the nineteenth century this had narrowed down to a *minestra* course. With the passage of the nineteenth century, pasta gradually moved north and began to alternate with *minestra* as the first course. Friends of mine in the Veneto tell me that pasta was not eaten often as recently as the generation of their grandparents.

Unstuffed pasta did not come into its own until Corrado, the great cook of the Neopolitan Bourbon court, made it respectable in court circles in the second half of the eighteenth century. As a matter of fact, the three-pronged fork was invented to make it possible to eat spaghetti in a polite way, not with the hands, as was done on the street by the common folk. The triumphant progress northward began in the early nineteenth century, when a machine was invented to produce dried pasta in quantity. (The adoption of dried pasta as the chief first course for many families was a product of the Industrial Revolution.)

Stuffed fresh pasta has been used at least since the fourteenth century, when Florentine cookbooks discuss *tortelli*. It was probably taken to Bologna from Florence. Fresh pasta is not always made with eggs, as exemplified by the pasta that is made in modern Genoa.

We begin with a discussion of fresh pasta—how to make it, how to cut it for various dishes—and then we present recipes for dishes made with it.

Following is a discussion of some popular types of dried pasta, some advice about buying it, and some recipes using it.

Finally, we have a section on stuffed fresh pasta—how to make the various kinds, along with a variety of stuffings and recipes for dishes made with it.

FRESH PASTA

*T*his is the basic "yellow" egg pasta. It is cut into *taglierini, tagliatelle* (fettuccine), *pappardelle, farfalle,* homemade spaghetti, and *penne* to be eaten with sauce. It is cut into *taglierini* (again) and *quadrucci* to be eaten with broth. And finally, it is used to make the stuffed pasta: *tortelli* (ravioli), tortellini, and *cappelletti* (smaller tortellini for broth) and cannelloni. The squares made for cannelloni are also used to make the layered lasagne.

1 cup unbleached all-purpose flour
1 extra-large egg

1 teaspoon olive or vegetable oil
Pinch of salt

The proportion of ingredients to each other is given, rather than a fixed amount per serving, because the amounts vary depending on which dish the pasta is being made for. Definite amounts are given in ingredients for each recipe.

Flour Unbleached all-purpose flour refers to the type of unbleached

For book-length treatment and many additional recipes of fresh and dried pasta, see *Bugialli on Pasta.*

white flour used for making pasta in Italy, and called by different names in different countries. This is more commonly employed than semolina, which is reserved for some special regional fresh pastas and of course is used exclusively for dried pasta. Indeed, much of the wheat used in Italy is imported, some of it probably American. The difference in method of grinding becomes significant only for dark flour used in making bread (see page 38). Unbleached flour is preferable, but bleached is also usable. All-purpose flour is generally partially sifted and states this on the package. Use it as it comes, without additional sifting.

Eggs If you use large instead of extra-large eggs, you will need an extra egg for every 5 or 6. If the eggs are still smaller, add an extra one for every 3 or 4. Flour absorbs less egg in damp weather, so you may have to add a little more egg under such conditions.

Oil If you do not use olive oil, be sure that the vegetable oil you do use is one such as sunflower or corn oil, without a strong taste.

TUSCAN fresh pasta varies from that of the Bologna region. Oil and salt are used in Tuscany, and the pasta is generally rolled finer. A little oil makes the pasta more flexible so it can be rolled a little finer, and is lighter when cooked. This pasta when stuffed can be sealed without being dampened, or if left to dry a little, may be sealed by being dampened very slightly with a finger dipped in water.

I repeat that the amount of pasta necessary for each serving varies, especially according to whether it is used with sauce or with broth, or again whether it is to be filled. The proportion of the ingredients remains the same. See each individual recipe for specific amounts.

Making fresh pasta is an area in which I take a slightly heretical position. I believe that pasta made with a hand pasta machine is at least as good as that rolled out with a wooden rolling pin. Perhaps this is because I have the Tuscan preference for pasta that is fine and soft. (The Bolognese *sfoglia* of 1 millimeter is too thick for my taste.) Taking the pasta machine's roller to the last notch, it can be made even finer. The little oil in the Tuscan pasta makes that fineness possible, without holes.

Hand-rolled pasta is necessary, however, for dishes that require a large single sheet, wider than is possible with the machine, such as the *rotolo di pasta ripieno* on page 229, where the hand rolling process is described. Even by hand, however, I still prefer it finer than the thickness that is usual in Bologna or in the south of Italy.*

Pasta board A pasta board 18 × 26 inches provides a good wooden surface to work on.

Rolling pin Use either the long, thin Italian rolling pin or the rotary rolling pin, which is shorter and rotates. The rotary action actually makes it easier to use.

Pasta machine When you invest in a pasta machine, buy one made in Italy and be careful of the trademark. They are not equally good, and some of the brands that are most often exported are inferior. Use of the different parts of the machine is explained below.

Making Fresh Pasta

Place the flour in a mound on a pasta board. Make a well in the center and put in the egg, olive oil, and salt (see the illustration on page 160). With a fork, first mix together the yolk, white, oil, and salt, then begin to incorporate the flour from the inner rim of the well, always incorporating fresh flour from the lower part, pushing it under the dough to keep the dough detached.

When almost half of the flour has been absorbed, start kneading, always using the palms of your hands in a folding motion, not the fingers. Continue absorbing the flour until almost all of it has been incorporated. The small fraction of flour that remains unabsorbed should be passed through a sifter to remove bits of dough and kept to coat dough during the succeeding steps. Now you are ready to use the pasta machine.

The machine has two main parts, one for rolling, the other for cutting. The first part of the machine consists of two rollers, the distance between which can be adjusted by a little wheel on the side. On the opposite side fits a detachable handle, to turn the rollers. The second part, for cutting, is sometimes detachable. It consists of two rows of teeth, one to cut into narrow strips *(taglierini)*, the other wide (the width of *tagliatelle*).

*For the many regional variants in fresh pasta making, see *Bugialli on Pasta*.

Attach the machine to your table by tightening the clamp at the bottom. (See illustration opposite for the position of the body in relation to the pasta machine.) Set the wheel for the rollers at the widest setting.

If the dough has been made with more than one egg, cut it into the same number of pieces as eggs or several eggs, if you can handle it. Repeat the following steps with each piece of dough.

Turning the handle, pass the dough through the rollers. Fold the dough into thirds and press down (see illustration opposite). Sprinkle with flour and repeat the rolling and folding eight to ten times, until the dough is very smooth. (These steps take the place of hand kneading.)

Move the wheel to the next notch, which places the rollers a little closer together. Pass the dough through rollers once; do not fold. Move the wheel to each successive notch, each time passing the dough through the rollers once. After passing each time, sprinkle the dough with a little flour. Each successive notch produces a thinner layer of pasta. Stop when the layer reaches the thickness desired; I always go to the last notch.

Caution Beginning with the step in which you first pass the pasta through the rollers without folding, do not hold it with your fingers, but let it hang over your whole left hand.

Making fresh pasta: Break the eggs into the well in the flour.

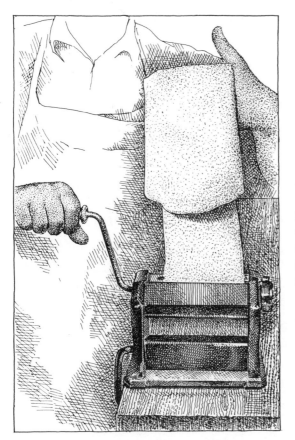

Pasta hanging over the whole left hand. Notice the position of the body in relation to the pasta machine.

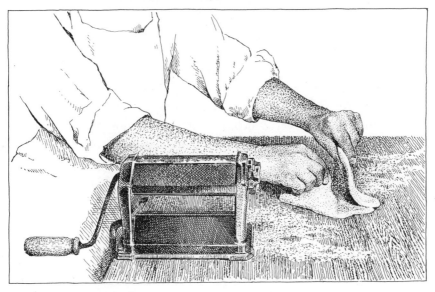

Fold the dough into thirds.

When the long sheet of pasta has finished passing through the rollers, take the end gently in your fingers and carefully pull the layer out to its full length, free of folds. Sprinkle a cotton dishtowel with flour and lay the sheet of pasta upon it until a thin film forms, before cutting. If the kitchen is hot or drafty, cover the pasta with another dishtowel.

Cutting Fresh Pasta (types made by machine)

Tagliatelle For *tagliatelle,* simply pass the sheet of pasta through the wide teeth of the cutting section (see illustration opposite).

Taglierini For *taglierini,* pass the sheets of pasta through the narrow teeth of the cutting section.

Spaghetti For homemade spaghetti, when you are passing the pasta through the rollers to thin it, stop when you arrive at two notches from the last and leave the sheets of pasta this thick. When the pasta has dried a bit, cut it by passing it through the narrow teeth. The shape of the cut pasta will be almost round. (Generally, the dried pasta form of spaghetti is used; the freshly made ones are an infrequent treat.)

Cutting Fresh Pasta (types made by hand)

Pappardelle See the recipe for *pappardelle sulla lepre* (page 174) and illustration opposite.

Farfalle (or fiocchi) With a pastry wheel, cut your sheet of pasta in half lengthwise, and every 2 inches widthwise, making rectangles.

Take each rectangle in the center, lengthwise, between two fingers, and press the two sides toward each other, making the pasta piece take the shape of a bow (see the illustration on page 164). This shape of fresh pasta may be substituted for *tagliatelle* in any of the recipes given and used with any kind of tomato sauce.

Penne Using the same rectangles as for *farfalle* (see above), roll the pasta around the end of a wooden spoon (see the illustration on page 164). Press down the outside edge of the pasta to seal the side; the form should be a tube. Pull the spoon end off and let dry.

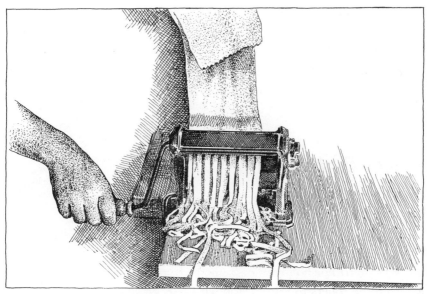

How to cut fresh *tagliatelle*.

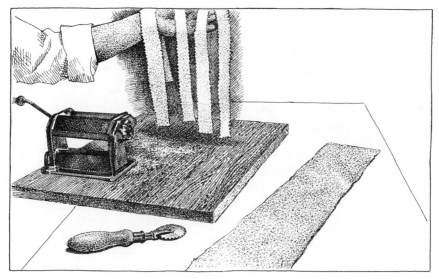

How to cut fresh *pappardelle* by hand.

Shaping the *farfalle,* or *fiocchi.*

Roll a pasta square around the handle of a wooden spoon to make *penne.*

Do not substitute these for dry *penne,* but rather for other fresh pasta.

Cannelloni See the recipe for *cannelloni con carne* (page 209).

Lasagne See the recipe for *lasagne* (page 221).

Tortellini See the recipe for *tortellini* (page 194).

Mezzelune See the recipe for "half-moon" *tortelli* (page 194).

Tortelli See the recipe for *tortelli* (page 192).

Pasta verde

GREEN PASTA

SERVES 3

5 to 6 ounces fresh spinach, weighed before stems are removed

Coarse-grained salt

2 extra-large eggs

3½ cups unbleached all-purpose flour

2 teaspoons olive or vegetable oil

Pinch of salt

REMOVE the stems completely from the spinach, leaving only the leaves.

Place a large saucepan containing a large quantity of cold water on the heat. Meanwhile rinse the spinach leaves thoroughly.

When the water has reached the boiling point, add salt, then the spinach leaves and cook for 10 to 12 minutes. Drain the spinach, cool under cold running water, and squeeze very dry. Chop the spinach extremely fine and measure 1 heaping tablespoon of it. (If there is a little left over, discard it.) At this point, using the remaining ingredients, follow the directions on pages 159–162, noting that this recipe uses 1¾ cups of flour for each egg instead of 1 cup, and placing the chopped spinach in the well along with the other ingredients. Follow the remaining directions exactly, but the drying time will be a little bit longer.

Green pasta may be used for *tagliatelle* and *taglierini.* To cut pasta into those shapes, see pages 162–163.

To cut green pasta for lasagne or cannelloni, see *cannelloni con carne* (page 209).

Pasta rossa

RED PASTA

SERVES 3

*1 medium red beet with stems
and leaves*
Coarse-grained salt
*3½ cups unbleached all-purpose
flour*

2 extra-large eggs
*2 teaspoons olive or vegetable
oil*
Pinch of salt

CAREFULLY rinse the beet.

Place a saucepan containing a large quantity of cold water on the heat. When the water reaches the boiling point, add coarse salt to taste, then the beet and cook for 1 to 1½ hours, until soft. Peel off the beet's outer layer under cold running water, discard stems and leaves then chop the beet extremely fine. Measure 1 heaping tablespoon of finely chopped beet. (If there is a little left over, discard it.)

At this point, using the remaining ingredients, follow the directions on pages 159–162, noting that this recipe uses 1¾ cups of flour to each egg instead of 1 cup. Place the chopped beet in the well along with the other ingredients. Follow the remaining directions exactly as for green pasta.

Red pasta may be used for *taglierini, tagliatelle,* or even cannelloni. To cut pasta into these shapes, see pages 162–163 and 209.

Taglierini al pomodoro fresco

TAGLIERINI WITH FRESH TOMATO SAUCE

SERVES 4

*T*he thinly cut, delicate *taglierini* go best with the lightest sauce, one made from ripe, fresh tomatoes, cooked very lightly and then adorned only with fresh basil leaves to bring out the quality of the tomatoes.

With good imported Italian canned plum tomatoes, and basil pre-served in salt, a very creditable version can also be made in the winter. The fresh *taglierini* need be cooked for only 15 seconds. Green *taglierini* (see page 165) are also used to good advantage in this dish.

FOR THE PASTA

2 cups unbleached all-purpose flour

2 extra-large eggs

2 teaspoons olive or vegetable oil

Pinch of salt

Sugo di pomodoro fresco (see page 81)

4 tablespoons (2 ounces) sweet butter or ¼ cup olive oil

Coarse-grained salt

¼ cup freshly grated Parmigiano

Freshly ground black pepper

3 or 4 leaves fresh basil (see note below)

MAKE the *taglierini,* using the quantities listed above, according to direc-tions on pages 159–162. To cut into *taglierini,* see page 162. Let the *taglierini* stand on a pasta board, covered with a cotton dishtowel, until needed.

Make the sauce as directed. Let it stand in the casserole, covered, until needed.

Put a large quantity of cold water in a stockpot and set on the heat.

Prepare a serving dish with butter or olive oil. Cut the butter into pats and spread them or the olive oil over the bottom of the dish. Then spread on about 6 tablespoons of tomato sauce. Heat the remaining sauce in its casserole.

When the water reaches the boiling point, add coarse salt to taste, then the *taglierini,* stir with a wooden spoon, and allow them to boil for 15 seconds *only.* Immediately drain the *taglierini* in a colander and arrange them on the serving dish, on the tomato sauce.

Pour the remaining tomato sauce over the *taglierini* and sprinkle with Parmigiano and black pepper. Tear the basil leaves into 3 or 4 pieces and sprinkle them over sauce. Serve immediately.

NOTE: If fresh basil is not available, omit basil at the end. Do not substitute basil under salt or dried basil leaves.

Tagliatelle al sugo di carne

FRESH TAGLIATELLE WITH MEAT SAUCE

SERVES 6

*T*agliatelle, somewhat wider than *taglierini* but no thicker, go best with a richer sauce, a meat sauce. Indeed, this is the cut of fresh pasta that is generally used with meat sauce. (On San Lorenzo day, sometimes the wider *pappardelle* are used with meat sauce if the hare sauce is not available.)

This is one of the most widely used pasta dishes in Italy and abroad. Cooking time for fresh *tagliatelle* is about 30 seconds. Green *tagliatelle* (see page 165) may also be used.

Sugo di carne *(see page 86)*

FOR THE PASTA

3 cups unbleached all-purpose
    flour
3 extra-large eggs

Coarse-grained salt

1 tablespoon olive or vegetable
    oil
Pinch of salt

6 tablespoons freshly grated
    Parmigiano

MAKE the sauce. Let it stand in the casserole, covered, until needed.

Make fresh *tagliatelle,* using the quantities listed above, according to the directions on page 159. To cut into *tagliatelle,* see page 162. Let the *tagliatelle* stand on a pasta board, covered with a cotton dishtowel, until needed.

Put a large quantity of cold water in a stockpot and set on the heat. Meanwhile, prepare a serving dish by spreading 4 or 5 tablespoons of sauce over the bottom; heat the remaining sauce in its casserole.

When the water reaches the boiling point, add coarse salt to taste, then the *tagliatelle,* stir with a wooden spoon, and let them cook for only about 30 seconds. Immediately drain the *tagliatelle* in colander and arrange in the serving dish.

Pour the remaining sauce over the *tagliatelle.* Toss very well, sprinkle with the Parmigiano, and serve immediately.

Tagliatelle alla panna

SERVES 6

*T*he simple, classic butter-and-cream sauce used for fresh pasta is called by several different names, *alla panna* or cream sauce in Bologna and Florence, *doppio burro* being the correct term for it in Rome. The sauce is probably of northern rather than Roman origin, and calling it "Alfredo" is giving too much credit to a restaurateur in Rome who clearly did not invent it. The fresh pasta, called in standard Italian *tagliatelle,* are known in Roman dialect as fettuccine.

In Italy, there are two kinds of heavy cream, that used for whipping and an almost solid cream used for cooking. For this dish you would use whipping cream, which fortunately corresponds to the heavy cream, or whipping cream, we find elsewhere.

FOR THE PASTA

3 cups unbleached all-purpose flour

3 extra-large eggs

12 tablespoons (6 ounces) sweet butter

2 cups heavy cream

1 tablespoon olive or vegetable oil

Pinch of salt

4 ounces freshly grated Parmigiano

Freshly ground white pepper

Freshly grated nutmeg

MAKE fresh *tagliatelle,* using the quantities listed above, as directed on page 159. To cut into *tagliatelle,* see page 162. Let the *tagliatelle* stand on a pasta board, covered with a cotton dishtowel, until needed. Place a stockpot containing a large quantity of cold water on the heat. After about 10 minutes, when the water is giving off steam but is not yet boiling, place a frying pan containing the butter over the stockpot to melt the butter. Keep the butter warm, but do not allow it to boil.

When the water is boiling vigorously, add coarse salt to taste, then the fresh pasta. The pasta will rise to the surface almost immediately. Quickly drain it in a colander. *(continued)*

TAGLIATELLE ALLA PANNA *(continued)*

Place the frying pan containing the butter over very low heat and add the cooked pasta. Toss gently with two forks.

Add the heavy cream, unheated, and the Parmigiano, and keep tossing gently until the sauce is homogenously creamy (about 1 minute). Sprinkle with white pepper and nutmeg and serve.

Sformato di tagliatelle verdi

GREEN PASTA "SOUFFLÉ"

SERVES 4

*T*his is a soufflélike dish made with green *tagliatelle*. The green pasta is cooked a little less than usual, for about 20 seconds. Then it is mixed with *balsamella,* Parmigiano, and egg yolk. Stiffly beaten egg whites are folded in, and the soufflé dish is placed in the oven. After it is baked, it is unmolded in the manner of Italian *sformati.*

An elaborate treatment, suitable for a stylish dinner.

FOR THE GREEN PASTA

1 extra-large egg

1¾ cups unbleached all-purpose flour

1 teaspoon olive or vegetable oil

4 ounces fresh spinach, weighed with part of the stems removed (enough to make 1 scant tablespoon chopped, boiled spinach)

Pinch of salt

1 tablespoon vegetable oil

FOR THE BALSAMELLA

6 tablespoons (3 ounces) sweet butter

½ cup unbleached all-purpose flour

2 cups milk

Pinch of salt

Coarse-grained salt

FOR THE SOUFFLÉ

3 extra-large eggs, separated,
plus 1 extra-large egg white
2 tablespoons freshly grated
Parmigiano
4 ounces boiled ham

Salt, freshly ground white
pepper, and freshly grated
nutmeg to taste
Sweet butter and unbleached
all-purpose flour

USING the ingredients in the proportions listed above, make the green pasta according to the directions on page 165.

Cut the green pasta into *tagliatelle* (see page 162). Set aside, covered with a cotton dishtowel, until needed.

Using the ingredients in the proportions listed above, make the *balsamella* according to the directions on page 62. Cover the saucepan and let the *balsamella* cool for 20 minutes.

Place a stockpot containing a large quantity of cold water on the heat. While the water is heating, put about 10 cups of cold water and the tablespoon of oil into a large bowl.

When the water reaches the boiling point, add coarse salt to taste, then the *tagliatelle* and cook for about 20 seconds. Drain them, then put into the bowl of cold water for about 1 minute.

Wet a cotton dishtowel with cold water and spread it out on a pasta board. Lifting the *tagliatelle* very gently, place them on the damp towel.

Preheat the oven to 400 degrees.

Beat the egg yolks in a large bowl with a wooden spoon. Add the cooled *balsamella* and grated Parmigiano. Mix very well, then add the ham, coarsely chopped, and seasonings and mix very gently. Let rest for 15 minutes. Meanwhile, beat the egg whites until stiff.

Add the *tagliatelle* to the bowl containing the ham mixture, then fold in the egg whites. Toss very gently, taking care not to break up the *tagliatelle*. Pour carefully into a soufflé dish well greased with butter and coated with flour, and bake in the preheated oven for 40 minutes, until puffed and golden. Serve immediately.

Tagliatelle con cibreo

FRESH TAGLIATELLE WITH CIBREO SAUCE

SERVES 6

*T*agliatelle also go well with the special *cibreo* sauce, the sauce with the almost gamelike flavor, made from chicken livers and crests and little unlaid eggs if they are available. Like *sugo di carne,* this sauce requires the slightly wider pasta. It can also be made with green *tagliatelle* (see page 165).

Cibreo *(see page 88)*

FOR THE PASTA

3 cups unbleached all-purpose
    flour
3 extra-large eggs

1 tablespoon olive or vegetable
    oil
Pinch of salt

Coarse-grained salt

MAKE the sauce. (If you cannot get the crests and unlaid eggs, use 1 whole pound of chicken livers.) Let the sauce stand covered, until needed.

Make fresh *tagliatelle* using the flour, eggs, oil, and pinch of salt, according to the directions on page 159. To cut into *tagliatelle,* see page 162. Let the *tagliatelle* stand on a pasta board, covered with a cotton dishtowel.

Put a large quantity of cold water in a stockpot, and set on the heat. While the water is heating, prepare a serving dish by spreading 4 or 5 tablespoons of sauce over the bottom; heat the remaining sauce in its casserole.

When the water reaches the boiling point, add coarse salt to taste, then the *tagliatelle,* stir with a wooden spoon, and let them cook for only about 30 seconds. Immediately drain the *tagliatelle* in a colander and arrange in the serving dish.

Pour the remaining sauce over the *tagliatelle.* Toss very well, and serve immediately.

Tagliatelle al sugo di fegatini

FRESH TAGLIATELLE WITH CHICKEN LIVER SAUCE

SERVES 6

his sauce differs from the straight chicken liver version of *cibreo* in that it is made with a thickened broth base and less wine. The texture of this sauce again calls for the *tagliatelle* cut; it can also be made with green *tagliatelle* (see page 165).

Salsa di fegatini *(see page 90)*

FOR THE PASTA

3 cups unbleached all-purpose flour

3 extra-large eggs

1 tablespoon olive or vegetable oil

Pinch of salt

Coarse-grained salt

MAKE the sauce. Let it stand in its pan, covered, until needed.

Make fresh *tagliatelle,* using the quantities listed above, according to the directions on page 159. To cut into *tagliatelle,* see page 162. Let the *tagliatelle* stand on a pasta board, covered with a cotton dishtowel.

Put a large quantity of cold water in a stockpot and set on the heat. While the water is heating, prepare a serving dish by spreading 4 or 5 tablespoons of sauce over the bottom; heat the remaining sauce in its pan.

When the water reaches the boiling point, add coarse salt to taste, then the *tagliatelle,* stir with a wooden spoon, and let them cook for only about 30 seconds. Immediately drain the *tagliatelle* in a colander and arrange in the serving dish.

Pour the remaining sauce over the *tagliatelle.* Toss very well and serve immediately.

Pappardelle sulla lepre

PAPPARDELLE WITH HARE SAUCE

SERVES 6

*O*ne of the great Tuscan dishes, a still wider pasta with a sauce made from wild hare. This famous dish is of course characteristic of the hunting season in Italy. Hare may be found in many markets and in those specializing in game. If you hunt yourself, so much the better. Be careful when buying hare that it be a hare with dark meat, not a wild rabbit. (If the animal is very large, with light meat, it is not what you are looking for to make this dish.)

The sauce of hare is not given separately, as it is used only for this dish, wedded (without the possibility of divorce) with the *pappardelle. Pappardelle* are always made with "yellow" pasta.

FOR THE PASTA

4 cups unbleached all-purpose flour

4 extra-large eggs

4 teaspoons olive or vegetable oil

Pinch of salt

Coarse-grained salt

FOR THE SAUCE

1 hare (about 3 pounds), liver reserved

½ cup red wine vinegar

1 medium red onion, cleaned

1 carrot, scraped

1 celery rib

10 sprigs Italian parsley, leaves only

4 ounces pancetta *or* prosciutto, *in one piece*

¼ cup olive oil

4 tablespoons (2 ounces) sweet butter

Salt and freshly ground black pepper to taste

½ cup dry red wine

2½ cups chicken or meat broth, approximately, preferably homemade (see page 126)

2 tablespoons tomato paste, preferably imported Italian

Pinch of freshly grated nutmeg

6 tablespoons freshly grated Parmigiano, optional

MAKE the pasta, using the ingredients in the quantities listed, according to the directions on page 159. When the sheet of pasta is ready, cut it with a jagged pastry cutter into strips ¾ inch wide and about 12 inches long. Place the *pappardelle* on a floured board, cover with a cotton dishtowel, and let stand until needed.

Cut the hare into large pieces. Rinse the pieces and place them in a large bowl with 3 cups cold water and the vinegar. Let soak for 1 hour; this will remove the strong "gamey" flavor.

Finely chop the *odori* (onion, carrot, celery, and parsley); coarsely chop the *pancetta*.

Heat the olive oil and butter in a large casserole. When the butter is melted, add the chopped ingredients and sauté until golden (about 20 minutes), stirring continuously with a wooden spoon.

Rinse the hare pieces under cold running water and add them to the casserole. Sprinkle with salt and pepper, then sauté, turning, until the pieces are golden on all sides (about 20 minutes). Add the wine and let evaporate very slowly (from 15 to 20 minutes). Meanwhile heat the broth in a saucepan.

When the wine has evaporated, add the tomato paste and 1 cup of the hot broth. Let cook very slowly, adding hot broth as needed, for about 1 hour. Coarsely chop the reserved hare liver and add it to the casserole. Sauté for about 10 minutes more, then remove the hare from the casserole. (The hare meat is not needed in this sauce and may be eaten separately at another meal.)

Taste for salt and pepper and add a pinch of nutmeg. Reduce the sauce very slowly, for about 10 minutes, until it is quite thick, then remove the casserole from the heat and let the sauce rest until needed.

Put a large quantity of cold water in a stockpot and heat until it reaches boiling point. Meanwhile, spread 4 or 5 tablespoons of the sauce over the bottom of a large serving dish; heat the remaining sauce in its casserole.

When the water reaches the boiling point, add coarse salt to taste, then the *pappardelle*. If the pasta is very fresh, it will rise to the surface almost immediately. Let the pasta cook only 30 seconds from that point; quickly remove it from the water. (If the pasta has been made several

(continued)

hours in advance, and is somewhat dried, cooking time will be from 1 to 1½ minutes after the pasta rises to the surface.)

Drain the *pappardelle* in a colander, then transfer to the serving dish. Pour the remaining sauce on top, mix, if using, with the Parmigiano, and serve immediately.

Trenette al pesto

TRENETTE WITH BASIL SAUCE

SERVES 4

*T*he pasta most classically associated with pesto is called *trenette.* Since the spread of dried pasta in the last century and a half, packaged dried *trenette* are gradually replacing the fresh pasta even in Genoa itself. Indeed, fresh *trenette* have become sufficiently rare so that some current cookbooks confuse them with *tagliatelle* or fettuccine. *Trenette* have a different shape from *tagliatelle,* having curled edges, but the significant difference is that *trenette* are made without eggs.

Most genuinely Genoese pasta, such as *trofie* and the specifically Ligurian ravioli,* is eggless. Genoese cookbooks of the nineteenth and twentieth centuries began to include the egg pastas from other places, and that has added to the confusion that exists in cookbooks published in Italy and elsewhere.

The following is the way some Genoese friends of mine of the older generation make fresh *trenette.* The pasta without egg is more elastic when cooked.

FOR THE PASTA

2½ cups unbleached all-purpose flour

1 cup cold water

2 teaspoons olive or vegetable oil

Coarse-grained salt

Pinch of salt

Pesto (see page 92)

1 large potato

*See Bugialli on Pasta for recipes.

PREPARE the pasta, using the quantities listed above, according to the directions on page 159. The technique of making this kind of pasta, without eggs, is just the same as for that with eggs. Place the cold water, olive oil, and salt in the well of the flour. Then continue with the same procedure and technique.

When the sheet of pasta is ready, cut it on one side with a jagged pastry cutter, on the other side with a knife, into strips ½ inch wide and about 12 inches long. The strips should be jagged on one side, straight on the other. Place the *trenette* on a floured board and cover with a cotton dishtowel. Let stand until needed.

Prepare the pesto. (Since quantities and ingredients depend on whether you wish to make it with mortar and pestle, *mezzaluna,* or blender, see the recipes for all three, pages 94–95.)

When the pesto is done, place a large stockpot of cold water on the heat. While the water is heating, peel the potato, then cut it into paper-thin slices; put them into stockpot. Place a large serving dish and the bowl of *pesto* sauce close by.

When the water reaches the boiling point, be sure potatoes are cooked, then add coarse salt to taste. Put in the *trenette,* stir with a wooden spoon, and let them boil for 30 seconds. Meanwhile, take 2 tablespoons of boiling water from the stockpot and put them into a bowl with the pesto sauce. Mix thoroughly.

Quickly drain the *trenette* and place in the serving dish. Put the pesto on top, toss gently, and serve immediately.

NOTE: If dried *trenette* (widely available both in Italy and abroad) are used, the only difference will be in the cooking time of the pasta. Dried *trenette* require 9 to 12 minutes to cook.

DRIED PASTA

*T*here are scores of varieties of dried pasta. Italians feel that a particular shape and thickness lends itself best to certain sauces or treatments. And, conversely, each sauce has a particular dried pasta, or perhaps two, especially suited to it.

Dried pasta made in Italy is still in a class by itself. It is lighter and more finely made than versions made outside of Italy, and fortunately it is widely exported.

Of the multitude of dried pasta dishes, I am going to suggest a limited number that I feel have culinary distinction, though they are often simple enough. Spaghetti (from *spaghi,* meaning "little strings") remains the prototype and the most popular kind of dried pasta. I include treatments that are best for this type of pasta and more recipes for *chiocciole* (snails or shells), for *penne* (short tubular pasta), and for rigatoni. Most of these are Tuscan treatments, but several come from other parts of Italy. My principal criterion has been that they retain a relative lightness consistent with the approach in the rest of the book. There are also recipes for pasta with tomato and meat sauces given in the sauce chapter.

Al dente cooking time for dried pasta is given as 12 minutes. With some brands, it may be as little as 8 minutes. Check package instructions.

Spaghetti alla fiaccheraia

SPAGHETTI, COACHMEN'S STYLE

SERVES 4

A very spicy red-peppery dish that is Tuscan, but also close to similar dishes in other parts of Italy—a dish that should give lie to the idea that red-peppery dishes exist only in the south of Italy. The name means "in the style of coachmen," who are supposed to be the prototypical tough, rough-hewn city types in Italy. A rare example of combining hot pepper and cheese in a dish.

2 ounces **pancetta** or
    prosciutto, in one piece
5 tablespoons olive oil
1 small red onion, cleaned
2 cups canned tomatoes,
    preferably imported Italian,
    drained and seeded
1 tablespoon tomato paste,
    preferably imported Italian

Salt and freshly ground black
    pepper to taste
½ teaspoon hot red pepper
    flakes
Coarse-grained salt
1 pound spaghetti, preferably
    imported Italian
¼ cup freshly grated
    Parmigiano or Romano

CUT the *pancetta* into tiny pieces.

Heat the olive oil in a saucepan. When it is hot, add the *pancetta* and sauté until golden (about 15 minutes). Meanwhile, chop the onion coarsely.

Remove the *pancetta* from the saucepan with a slotted spoon and set it aside. Add the onion to the oil in the saucepan and sauté gently until soft and translucent (about 15 minutes). Add the tomatoes and tomato paste, then taste for salt and pepper and add the hot pepper flakes. Reduce the sauce very slowly for about 20 minutes.

While the sauce is reducing, place a stockpot containing a large quantity of cold water on the heat. When the water boils, add salt to taste, then the spaghetti, and cook until al dente (9 to 12 minutes, depending on the brand).

When the sauce is reduced and the spaghetti almost cooked, place the *pancetta* back in the sauce and simmer it for 1 minute more. Remove the pan from the flame.

Drain the spaghetti in a colander and place it in a serving bowl. Pour the sauce on top and sprinkle with the Parmigiano. Toss very well and serve hot.

NOTE: No extra cheese should be added at the table.

Spaghetti alla carbonara

SPAGHETTI WITH EGG-PANCETTA SAUCE

SERVES 4

*T*his Roman dish is sometimes called "spaghetti with bacon and eggs" on tourist menus. *Pancetta,* of course, is not bacon, because it is not smoked; do not substitute bacon. To make it well and with as much lightness as possible, cook the *pancetta* slowly to remove the fat. This recipe contains just enough *pancetta* fat and eggs to have all the sauce well incorporated. There is nothing worse in *carbonara* than to have excess fat and unincorporated egg sitting on the bottom. This version should give a spicy, but not greasy *carbonara,* one that is as light as the dish can be.

4 ounces **pancetta**
2 large cloves garlic, peeled
3 tablespoons olive oil
*¹/₂ teaspoon hot red pepper
    flakes, optional*
Salt
2 extra-large eggs

*¹/₃ cup freshly grated pecorino
    Romana or Parmigiano*
Coarse-grained salt
*1 pound spaghetti, preferably
    imported Italian*
Freshly ground black pepper

PUT a large quantity of cold water in a stockpot. Set on the heat.

While the water is heating, cut *pancetta* into small pieces and chop the garlic very fine. Put the *pancetta* and garlic in a saucepan with the olive oil, hot pepper flakes, if used, and salt. (Salt should be added depending on the saltiness of the *pancetta.*) Place the saucepan on very low heat for 12 to 15 minutes. The *pancetta* should brown very, very slowly, so that all the fat is rendered out.

In the meantime, beat the eggs and combine with the grated cheese.

When the water reaches the boiling point, add coarse salt to taste, then the pasta and cook until it is al dente (9 to 12 minutes, depending on brand). Drain the spaghetti well, then place it in a serving bowl. Quickly spoon the hot contents of saucepan over it. Toss; then, just as quickly, add the eggs and cheese. Grind black pepper plentifully over the dish, as it should be very peppery, then toss very well and serve hot.

Pasta alla puttanesca

PASTA WITH A SAUCE OF UNCOOKED
TOMATOES AND HERBS

SERVES 4

*T*he most perfect of all summer pasta dishes, for freshness and for lightness. Everything in the sauce—tomatoes, basil, and olive oil—is uncooked. The fresh, summery ingredients must be made very cold (even left for a few minutes in the freezer), and then quickly tossed with the steaming pasta, just out of the boiling water. The contact of the very hot with the very cold releases an unforgettable flavor; this dish could be a real discovery for many people. Use a substantial pasta, shaped to catch some of the sauce. (I won't translate the name, nor even speculate as to why those ladies should prefer their pasta this way.)

1 ½ pounds very ripe tomatoes or 1 ½ pounds canned tomatoes, preferably imported Italian, drained
4 medium cloves garlic, peeled
25 large leaves fresh basil
½ cup olive oil
Salt

Generous amount of freshly ground black pepper
Coarse-grained salt
1 pound dried pasta, such as chiocciole *(shells or snails) or* penne, *preferably imported Italian*

IF fresh tomatoes are used, rinse them, then cut them into small pieces and put in a bowl. Chop the garlic coarsely and add to bowl, then tear the basil leaves into thirds and add to the bowl, along with the oil, salt, and pepper. Mix all the ingredients together, then cover the bowl and place it in the refrigerator for at least 2 hours before serving time.

About 30 minutes before serving time, heat a large amount of cold water in a stockpot. When the water boils, add coarse salt to taste, then the pasta and cook it until al dente (9 to 12 minutes, depending on brand). Drain quickly and place it in a serving bowl.

While the pasta is still hot, pour the refrigerated sauce over it. (The reaction of very hot and very cold releases the flavor of this dish.) Toss well and serve at once; do *not* add grated cheese.

Chiocciole ai gamberi

SHELLS WITH SHRIMP SAUCE

SERVES 4 TO 6

A light sauce, especially useful in hot weather, is that made with uncooked vegetables and boiled shrimp, then cooled and used to dress the hot pasta. This combination of freshly cooked hot pasta and cold sauce is much more popular in Italy than completely cold pasta salads. Italians do not like cold pasta very much and above all would never eat stuffed pasta, such as tortellini, cold. Here the shell-shaped dried pasta combines well with the cold, flavorful sauce. Cold sauces for pasta often are a little piquant or strongly flavorful and quite often incorporate fish.

1 1/2 pounds medium shrimp, unshelled

1 lemon

Coarse-grained salt

1 medium red onion, cleaned

1 very small clove garlic, peeled

3/4 pound ripe, but not overripe, fresh tomatoes

10 sprigs Italian parsley, leaves only, coarsely chopped

2 medium inner stalks celery, without leaves

1/2 cup olive oil

Salt and freshly ground black pepper

1 pound chiocciole (shells or snails), preferably imported Italian

TO COOK THE PASTA

Coarse-grained salt

TO SERVE

15 large leaves fresh basil

SOAK the shrimp in a bowl of cold water with the lemon cut in half and a little of the coarse salt for 30 minutes.

Place a medium-sized pot of cold water over medium heat and when the water reaches a boil, add coarse salt to taste, then drain the shrimp, rinse them under cold running water, and add to the pot of boiling water to cook for 2 minutes. Drain the shrimp, then shell and devein them, and place in a crockery or glass bowl.

Coarsely chop the onion and finely chop the garlic and soak in a bowl of cold water for 30 minutes. Clean the tomatoes, then cut them, without removing seeds and skin, into ½-inch cubes and place them on top of the shrimp along with the parsley. Cut the celery into pieces about 1 × ½ inch and add it to bowl. Drain the onion and garlic and add to bowl. Pour the oil over and season with salt and pepper. Do not mix, but cover the bowl and refrigerate for at least 1 hour before using.

When ready to serve, place a large pot of cold water over medium heat and when the water reaches a boil, add coarse salt to taste, then the pasta, and cook for 9 to 12 minutes, depending on the brand. Drain the pasta, transfer to a large serving platter, mix the sauce very well and pour it over. Mix very well, arrange the basil leaves all over, and serve with more freshly ground black pepper. (Do not add grated cheese.)

Spaghetti all'acciugata

SPAGHETTI WITH ANCHOVY SAUCE

SERVES 4

*S*paghetti is the best pasta for anchovy sauce and this dish is perhaps the most useful of all for last-minute cooking if you need a quick first dish.

Coarse-grained salt	*1 pound spaghetti, preferably*
Acciugata *(see page 73)*	*imported Italian*
	Freshly ground black pepper

PUT a large quantity of cold water in a stockpot and set on the heat. While the water is heating, prepare the *acciugata*. Let stand until needed.

When the water reaches the boiling point, add coarse salt to taste, then the spaghetti, stir thoroughly with a wooden spoon, and let it cook until al dente (9 to 12 minutes, depending on brand). Immediately drain the spaghetti in a colander and place it in a serving dish.

Pour the *acciugata* over and toss thoroughly. Sprinkle with freshly ground pepper and serve immediately; do not add any grated cheese.

Denti di cavallo o rigatoni alla salsicce

RIGATONI WITH SAUSAGE-FLAVORED SAUCE

SERVES 4 TO 6

*H*ere is a pasta treatment related to *"alla carbonara,"* unique to Tuscany. Instead of *pancetta,* sausage is used, in small but whole pieces, not broken up. In place of the Roman pecorino, that of Tuscany is preferred and the best substitute is Parmigiano. A type of pasta called *denti di cavallo,* "horses' teeth," is employed for the dish in its place of origin, but rigatoni are quite similar and much more widely available.

4 Italian sweet sausages, without fennel seeds, or 12 ounces ground pork mixed with 1 teaspoon of salt and ½ teaspoon freshly ground black pepper
4 tablespoons olive oil
3 extra-large eggs

6 tablespoons freshly grated Tuscan pecorino or Parmigiano
2 medium cloves garlic, peeled
Salt and freshly ground black pepper to taste
1 pound denti di cavallo or rigatoni, preferably imported Italian

TO COOK THE PASTA
Coarse-grained salt

TO SERVE
10 sprigs Italian parsley, leaves only, coarsely chopped

REMOVE the casing from the sausages and cut them into 1-inch pieces. Place a large skillet with the oil over low heat and when the oil is warm, add the sausages and garlic and sauté until completely cooked, for about 10 minutes. Discard the garlic. Meanwhile bring a large pot of cold water to a boil, and when the water reaches a boil, add coarse salt to taste, then the pasta and cook until al dente for 9 to 12 minutes, depending on the brand. Meanwhile mix the eggs with the cheese in a small crockery or glass bowl. Raise the heat on the sausages and season with salt and pepper. Keep stirring to be sure the sausages do not stick to skillet. When the pasta is ready, drain it and transfer to skillet over high heat, sprinkle with more pepper, and sauté for a few seconds, mixing very well with two forks. Remove skillet from the heat, pour the mixed eggs over the pasta, sprinkle with parsley, mix again thoroughly, and serve directly from the pan.

Spaghetti al sugo di "cipolle"

SPAGHETTI WITH CHICKEN GIZZARD SAUCE

SERVES 4

A really unusual and delicious dish. The long-cooked sauce of chopped chicken gizzards has a rich flavor reminiscent of game. Spaghetti is the pasta that goes best with it.

Sugo di "cipolle" *(see page 85)*	*1 pound spaghetti, preferably imported Italian*
Coarse-grained salt	*¼ cup freshly grated Parmigiano*

MAKE the sauce. Let it stand in the casserole, covered, until needed.

Put a large quantity of cold water in a stockpot, then set on the heat. While the water is heating, prepare a large serving dish by spreading 4 or 5 tablespoons of the sauce over the bottom; heat the remaining sauce in its casserole.

When the water reaches the boiling point, add coarse salt to taste, then the spaghetti, stir with a wooden spoon, and cook on a medium flame until al dente (9 to 12 minutes, depending on brand). When the pasta is cooked, drain it in a colander and place it in the serving dish.

Pour the remaining hot sauce over the spaghetti and toss very well. Sprinkle with Parmigiano and serve immediately.

Spaghetti al sugo "metà e metà"

SPAGHETTI WITH "HALF AND HALF" SAUCE

SERVES 4 TO 6

*M*eat sauces which combine several different types of meat occur throughout Italy. Perhaps the extreme of this is the wonderful sauce containing four different meats which is popular in Abruzzi; it can be found in *Bugialli on Pasta,* page 144. This sauce mixing two meats is about as far as they go in Tuscany, where the emphasis is usually on simplicity and a minimum of ingredients. However, the two meats, flavored with *odori,* sage, wine, and spices, merge into a straightforward flavor still expressive of the Tuscan palette. A delicious alternative to the classic *Sugo di carne.*

1 medium red onion, cleaned

1 celery stalk

1 carrot, scraped

10 sprigs Italian parsley, leaves only

1 large clove garlic, peeled

4 large leaves sage, fresh or preserved in salt

½ cup olive oil

½ cup dry white wine

8 ounces ground beef

8 ounces ground pork

Salt and freshly ground black pepper

Large pinch of hot red pepper flakes

6 tablespoons tomato paste, preferably imported Italian

2 cups beef broth, preferably homemade

1 pound spaghetti, preferably imported Italian

TO COOK THE PASTA

Coarse-grained salt

FINELY chop onion, celery, carrot, parsley, garlic, and sage all together on a board. Heat the oil in a medium-sized casserole, preferably of terra-cotta, over medium heat and when the oil is warm, add the chopped ingredients and sauté for 10 minutes, stirring every so often with a wooden spoon. Add the wine, raise the heat, and cook for 2 minutes more. Add the meats, lower the heat, season with salt, pepper, and hot pepper flakes, and cook for 15 minutes. Dissolve the tomato paste in the broth and add to casserole. Simmer, covered, for 1 hour, stirring every so often with a wooden spoon.

Bring a large pot of cold water to a boil, add coarse salt to taste, then the pasta and cook it for 9 to 12 minutes, depending on the brand. Taste the sauce and transfer to a large skillet over medium heat. Drain the pasta, transfer to the skillet and sauté over high heat for 30 seconds. Serve hot directly from the skillet without adding cheese.

Spaghetti con briciolata

SPAGHETTI WITH BREAD CRUMB SAUCE

SERVES 4

*S*paghetti with *briciolata,* the sauce made with homemade bread crumbs, was one of the most popular first courses throughout Italy when everyone still made his own bread crumbs. It is worth going to that trouble if only to be able to retain this dish in your repertoire. (Commercial bread crumbs just aren't good enough to carry the entire burden of the dish.)

10 sprigs Italian parsley, leaves only
Coarse-grained salt

1 pound spaghetti, preferably imported Italian
Briciolata (see page 96)
Freshly ground black pepper

HEAT a large quantity of cold water in a stockpot. Meanwhile, chop the parsley coarsely and let stand until needed.

When the water reaches the boiling point, add coarse salt to taste, then the spaghetti, stir with a wooden spoon, and let cook until al dente (9 to 12 minutes depending on brand).

Meanwhile, prepare the *briciolata.*

When the spaghetti is ready, quickly drain it in a colander and place it in a serving dish. Pour on the hot sauce, then sprinkle with the chopped parsley and freshly ground black pepper. Toss thoroughly and serve immediately; do not add grated cheese.

Penne ai peperoni

PENNE WITH A SWEET BELL PEPPER SAUCE

SERVES 4 TO 6

*T*hough it is southern Italy that has so many marvelous pasta and vegetable combinations, Tuscany does have some characteristic ones. The small town of Empoli in the Arno valley, where the composer and pianist Busoni was born, is especially known for its fine peppers. In this dish, the peppers are peeled, cut into strips, and sautéed with *odori*. The herb of choice is parsley and the preferred pasta shape is the tubular penne, probably for visual as well as taste reasons, the shapes combining well. If you wish to sprinkle it with cheese, try to get Tuscan pecorino for the optimum taste combination, otherwise Parmigiano is the best substitute.

4 large yellow sweet bell peppers
1 large red onion, cleaned
1 stalk celery
2 medium carrots, scraped
4 ounces **pancetta** *or prosciutto, in one piece*
½ cup olive oil

Salt and freshly ground black pepper
15 sprigs Italian parsley, leaves only
1 pound penne or penne rigate, preferably imported Italian

TO COOK THE PASTA
Coarse-grained salt

OPTIONAL
4 to 6 tablespoons of freshly grated Tuscan pecorino or Parmigiano

REMOVE the skin from the peppers (see page 544) or see another method in my *Foods of Italy* (see page 26). Cut the peppers into strips less than ½ inch wide. Finely chop onion, celery, and carrots all together on a board. Cut *pancetta* into tiny pieces. Heat the oil in a medium-sized casserole over medium heat and when the oil is warm, add the chopped ingredients along with the *pancetta* and sauté for 10 minutes, stirring with a wooden spoon every so often. Add the peppers, season with salt and pepper, and cook for 15 minutes more, stirring with a wooden spoon every so often and adding some lukewarm water (up to ½ cup) as more liquid is needed.

Meanwhile, coarsely chop the parsley and bring a large pot of cold water to a boil. When the water reaches a boil and the sauce is ready, add the parsley to casserole and coarse salt to taste to the pot for the pasta. Put pasta in the water and cook for 9 to 12 minutes, depending on the brand. Drain the pasta, transfer to a large warm serving dish, pour the sauce all over, mix very well, and serve immediately with the cheese.

Chiocciole con salsa di tonno

SHELLS WITH TUNA SAUCE

SERVES 4

*A*nother treatment useful for those evenings when you would like a first dish, but have almost no time to make it. The flavorsome *salsa di tonno* (tuna sauce) requires a heavier pasta that will, again, "catch" some of the sauce. *Chiocciole* are perfect.

Salsa di tonno *(see page 88)*
Coarse-grained salt

1 pound **chiocciole** *(shells or snails), preferably imported Italian*

MAKE the sauce. While the sauce is cooking, put a large quantity of cold water in a stockpot and set on the heat.

When sauce is almost ready and the water in stockpot has reached the boiling point, add coarse salt to taste, then the *chiocciole*. Stir with a wooden spoon, and allow them to cook until al dente (9 to 12 minutes, depending on brand). Drain the pasta in a colander and place in a serving bowl.

Pour over the sauce; toss thoroughly, and serve very hot; do not add any grated cheese.

Pasta con pommarola
o Pasta con sugo scappato

PASTA WITH SUMMER OR WINTER TOMATO SAUCE

Coarse-grained salt
1 pound any kind of dried
*   pasta, preferably imported*
*   Italian*

2 cups Pommarola *(see page*
*   83) or* Sugo scappato *(see*
*   page 84)*

BRING a large quantity of cold water to a boil, add coarse salt to taste, then the pasta and cook from 9 to 12 minutes, depending on brand. Drain and dress with *Pommarola* or *Sugo scappato.*

Pasta con sugo di carne

PASTA WITH MEAT SAUCE

GIVEN on page 168 with fresh *tagliatelle,* this may also be used with any dried pasta. Use 2 cups of sauce to 1 pound of dried pasta.

Coarse-grained salt
1 pound any kind of dried
*   pasta, preferably imported*
*   Italian*

2 cups Sugo di carne

BRING a large quantity of cold water to a boil, add coarse salt to taste, then the pasta, and cook from 9 to 12 minutes, depending on brand. Drain and dress with *Sugo di carne.*

Pasta con sugo di pomodoro

PASTA WITH FRESH TOMATO SAUCE

Coarse-grained salt
1 pound any kind of dried
 pasta, preferably imported
 Italian

2 cups **Sugo di pomodoro**
(see page 166)

BRING a large quantity of cold water to a boil, add coarse salt to taste, then the pasta, and cook from 9 to 12 minutes, depending on brand. Drain and dress with *Sugo di pomodoro.*

STUFFED FRESH PASTA

Tortelli, the earliest known stuffed pasta, appear along with lasagne in the earliest Florentine cookbooks and were always made with egg pasta. The Bolognese would probably be shocked to know, as they certainly do not know any longer, that their beloved egg pasta and tortellini came to Bologna from Florence. The earliest Bolognese cookbook is a copy of an earlier Florentine one that contains these types of pasta.

Tortelli are similar to what are known in other places as "ravioli." They may be cut in a circular shape with a special *tortelli* or ravioli cutter, or even a cookie cutter. They may also be made in a rectangular form, cut with a pastry wheel. It is typical that the edges of the circles or rectangles be jagged. (It is difficult to understand why many books state that this type of stuffed pasta is of more recent Genoese origin. If you wish to be amused, read *Larousse Gastronomique*'s account of the source of "ravioli," in which the origin is left ambiguously hovering between Genoese and French.)

Tortellini means, of course, "little *tortelli*." In Florence the term refers to something close to "half-moon" *tortelli,* but curved around a finger and joined at the end. They are made with circles of pasta about 1½ inches in diameter. The smaller versions are called *cappelletti* in Florence, and are eaten in broth.* The names tortellini, *cappelletti,* and even *tortelloni* differ slightly in meaning depending on the region in which they are used, but they all derive from the ancient Florentine stuffed pasta called *tortelli.*

First, we present the directions for making *tortelli,* and "half-moon" *tortelli,* and tortellini. Then recipes for *tortelli* with a fresh mint sauce; for half-moon *tortelli* stuffed with spinach and ricotta and covered with butter and cheese; for *tortelli* with a gorgonzola stuffing and a light tomato sauce. There is a special recipe that features a rabbit sauce from the mountainous Mugello and, finally, one for the sweet *tortelli* of squash from Modena. Two recipes for tortellini conclude the section, demonstrating the versatility of one filling for two very different sauces.

Half-moon *tortelli,* filled with a tortellini chicken-breast stuffing, are also used in the dish *cannelloni alla sorpresa* on page 216, and tortellini are also used in the dish *timballo di tortellini* on page 241.

Making Tortelli

Follow the recipe for fresh pasta on pages 157–162, through the drying of the pasta sheet before cutting. Then lay out the long sheet of pasta, and starting an inch from the top and side edges, begin a lengthwise row of dots of filling, each one 2 inches from its neighbor. Each dot should be made with 1 teaspoon of filling. Continue the row until it reaches close to halfway down the length of the pasta sheet. If sheet is narrow, make only 1 such row. If it is wide enough, make a second row, 1 inch in from the other side.

With a wet finger, draw 3 vertical lines (2 if only 1 row of dots), half the length of the pasta, one down each side and one through the center; then draw lines across, between the dots of filling. In this way, when cut, the edges of each *tortello* will be moist enough to seal well.

Carefully pick up bottom end of pasta sheet and fold it over the top

---

* For differences in making tortellini and *cappelletti,* see *Giuliano Bugialli's Classic Techniques of Italian Cooking.*

half (see illustration below). Quickly press down around the dots of filling. Using a 2-inch round scalloped pastry cutter, cut out circles, pressing well to be sure all edges are detached. As you lift out each *tortello,* press the edges all around between two fingers, to make sure they are completely sealed.

Let rest until needed on a floured wooden surface or floured cotton

Making *tortelli:* Fold the pasta sheet over the filling.

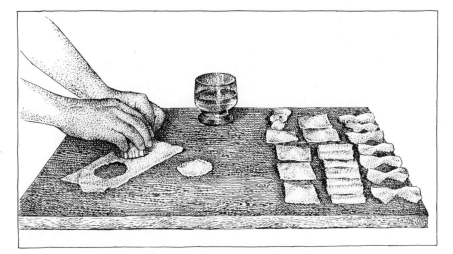

Making *tortelli:* Cut out the *tortelli.*

dishtowel. If the *tortelli* are to stand more than 30 minutes before cooking, cover them with a cotton towel so they do not dry out.

NOTE: *Tortelli* may also be made square. Cut into squares using a pastry wheel instead of a round cutter.

Making "Half-Moon" Tortelli

Follow the recipe for fresh pasta on pages 157–162, through the drying of the pasta sheet before cutting. Then lay out the long sheet of pasta on a wooden surface. With a pastry wheel or knife, cut the sheet in half lengthwise.

Starting 1½ inches from top, begin a lengthwise row of dots of filling, in the center of each half-sheet. Each dot should be made with 1 teaspoon of filling. Continue the row down entire length of the half-sheet.

With a wet finger, moisten entire length of one edge of each half-sheet. Then make lines of moisture across, between the dots of filling. In this way, when cut, each half-moon will be moist enough to seal well.

Carefully pick up one of the sides with both hands and fold the half-sheet lengthwise in half. Quickly press down around the dots of filling. Repeat with the other half-sheet.

Cut out half-moons, that is semicircles, by placing only half of a round 2-inch jagged pastry cutter over the area containing the filling. As you lift out each half-moon, press the edges on the semicircular side between two fingers, to be sure they are completely sealed.

Let rest until needed on a floured wooden surface or floured cotton dishtowel. If the half-moon *tortelli* are to stand more than 30 minutes before cooking, cover them with a cotton towel so they do not become too dry.

Making Tortellini

To make tortellini, make fresh pasta according to the directions on pages 157–162, but do not wait for the pasta to dry. As each piece of dough is rolled out, begin to make tortellini with it immediately.

Cut the sheet of pasta into circles with a 1½-inch round cookie cutter. Place a scant ½ teaspoon of filling in the center of each circle. Moisten the edges, then double over one side of the pasta circle, but not all the way to the other side; leave a little border arc of the pasta undoubled. Seal the moistened edges (see illustration below).

Wrap the half-moon around your index finger, the top of the finger reaching only to the top of the filled section (see bottom illustration below). With your thumbs, connect the two edges of the half-moon. The overlap of pasta above your index finger should be curled outward.

Making tortellini: Double the pasta over and seal it.

Curve the tortellini around the finger.

Tortelli alla menta

TORTELLI WITH FRESH MINT

SERVES 8

*H*ow can one adequately describe the summery freshness of this dish, in which the fresh mint plays the role usually assigned to fresh basil in bringing out the full flavor of fresh tomato? The mint leaves are chopped and placed in the stuffing itself, while basil leaves are placed in the fresh sauce.

FOR THE SAUCE

2 1/2 pounds ripe tomatoes or 2 1/2 pounds canned tomatoes, preferably imported Italian, drained
Salt and freshly ground black pepper to taste

8 tablespoons (4 ounces) sweet butter
10 to 12 large basil leaves, fresh

FOR THE FILLING

15 ounces of ricotta, drained
4 extra-large egg yolks
1 cup freshly grated Parmigiano
1 1/2 tablespoons finely chopped fresh mint leaves

1 1/2 tablespoons coarsely chopped fresh mint leaves
Salt, freshly ground black pepper, and freshly grated nutmeg to taste

FOR THE PASTA

4 cups unbleached all-purpose flour
4 extra-large eggs

4 teaspoons olive or vegetable oil
Pinch of salt

PLUS

Coarse-grained salt

1/2 cup freshly grated Parmigiano

PREPARE the sauce first. Cut the tomatoes into pieces, if fresh, and put them in a saucepan with salt. Place the pan over medium heat and simmer for 20 to 30 minutes, then pass the tomatoes through a food mill, using the disc with the smallest holes, into a bowl. Return the tomato sauce to saucepan and place it over low heat. Simmer for 5 more minutes, then taste for salt and pepper. Meanwhile, cut the butter into pats and place them on a serving dish. Set both sauce and serving dish aside while you prepare the filling.

Place the ricotta in a bowl and add the egg yolks, Parmigiano, and the finely and coarsely chopped mint. Mix very well with a wooden spoon, then season with salt, pepper, and nutmeg, and set aside.

Make the pasta, using the ingredients in the proportions listed above, according to the directions on page 159. Form the *tortelli* as directed on page 192, using the filling you have just prepared.

Bring a large quantity of cold water to a boil in a stockpot. Meanwhile, heat the sauce, then pour half of it over the butter in the serving dish. Tear 6 or 7 of the basil leaves in quarters and add them.

When the water is boiling, add coarse salt to taste, then the *tortelli* quickly but gently, being careful not to break them. If the *tortelli* have been made as much as an hour or two before, they will cook and rise to surface of water in 1 minute. If they are already dried, cooking time will be longer (about 3 to 4 minutes). Remove the *tortelli* with a strainer-skimmer and place them on the serving dish. Pour the rest of the sauce over them. Tear the remaining basil leaves and add them, sprinkle with the Parmigiano, and serve.

Tortelli della vigilia

"HALF-MOON" TORTELLI STUFFED WITH
SPINACH AND RICOTTA

SERVES 8

*P*erhaps the best-known stuffing for *tortelli,* that of ricotta, spinach, Parmigiano, eggs, and flavorings. Originally the stuffing for the eve of a holiday when meat was not eaten, it has surpassed the meat stuffings in popularity. Serve the *tortelli* with a light butter and cheese sauce.

FOR THE FILLING
3 pounds fresh spinach
Coarse-grained salt
15 ounces ricotta
2 extra-large eggs plus 2 extra-large egg yolks

1 cup freshly grated Parmigiano
Salt, freshly ground black pepper, and freshly grated nutmeg to taste

FOR THE PASTA
4 extra-large eggs
4 cups unbleached all-purpose flour

4 teaspoons olive or vegetable oil
Pinch of salt

FOR THE SAUCE
12 tablespoons (6 ounces) sweet butter
1 1/2 cups freshly grated Parmigiano

Freshly ground black pepper and freshly grated nutmeg

TO COOK THE PASTA
Coarse-grained salt

RINSE the spinach very well and cut off the larger stems, then cook in a large quantity of boiling, salted water for about 5 minutes. Drain the spinach, cool it under cold running water, and squeeze dry.

Chop the spinach very fine, then place it in a bowl, along with ricotta, eggs, egg yolks, Parmigiano, salt, pepper, and nutmeg. Blend with a wooden spoon until the mixture is thoroughly combined, then cover and let stand in the refrigerator until needed.

Make the pasta, using the ingredients in the proportions listed above, according to the directions on page 159, then form the "half-moon" *tortelli* as described on page 194, using the filling you have just made.

Begin preparing the sauce by melting 8 tablespoons (4 ounces) of the butter in a saucepan; let it stand, covered, until needed.

Bring a large quantity of cold water to a boil in a stockpot. Meanwhile, prepare a serving dish by pouring in half the melted butter. When the water is boiling, add coarse salt to taste, then the *tortelli* quickly but gently, being careful not to break them. If the *tortelli* have been made as much as an hour or two before, they will cook and rise to surface of water in 1 minute. If they are already dried, cooking time will be longer (about 3 to 4 minutes). Remove the *tortelli* with a strainer-skimmer and place them on the prepared serving dish.

Pour the rest of the melted butter over the *tortelli,* arrange the remaining 4 tablespoons of butter, in pats, on top, then sprinkle with the Parmigiano, freshly ground black pepper, freshly grated nutmeg, and serve.

Tortelli al gorgonzola

TORTELLI WITH GORGONZOLA STUFFING

SERVES 8

*G*orgonzola dolce, the sweet gorgonzola cheese, is mixed with ricotta, Parmigiano, egg yolks, and nutmeg to produce a rich and unusual stuffing for *tortelli*. It is covered with a very light tomato sauce and some melted, but not cooked, butter. Useful for those occasions when you crave something "rich."

FOR THE SAUCE
2 pounds fresh tomatoes, or 2 pounds canned tomatoes, preferably imported Italian, drained
Salt and freshly ground black pepper to taste

8 tablespoons (4 ounces) sweet butter
8 tablespoons freshly grated Parmigiano

FOR THE STUFFING
8 ounces ricotta
8 ounces gorgonzola, preferably dolce
4 extra-large egg yolks

6 tablespoons freshly grated Parmigiano
Salt, freshly ground black pepper, and freshly grated nutmeg to taste

FOR THE PASTA
4 extra-large eggs
4 cups unbleached all-purpose flour

4 teaspoons olive or vegetable oil
Pinch of salt

TO COOK THE PASTA
Coarse-grained salt

MAKE the sauce first.

If using fresh tomatoes, cut them into pieces, then place the fresh or canned tomatoes in a flameproof casserole and simmer very slowly for 25 to 30 minutes. Season with salt and pepper, then pass through a food mill, using the disc with the smallest holes, back into the casserole. Simmer for 5 minutes longer. Remove the casserole from the stove and add 4 tablespoons of the butter, then cover and let rest until needed.

Make the filling by combining the ricotta and the gorgonzola in a bowl. Mix with a wooden spoon until thoroughly combined, then add the egg yolks and Parmigiano. Season with salt, pepper, and nutmeg and mix thoroughly with the wooden spoon.

Make the pasta, using the ingredients in the proportions listed above, according to the directions on page 159. Form into *tortelli* as directed on page 192, using the filling you have just made.

Bring a large quantity of cold water to a boil in a large stockpot. Meanwhile, reheat the sauce, then pour half of it into a serving dish.

When the water is boiling, add coarse salt to taste, then the *tortelli* quickly but gently, being careful not to break them. If the *tortelli* have been made as much as an hour or two before, they will cook and rise to surface of water in 1 minute. If they are already dried, cooking time will be longer (about 3 to 4 minutes). Remove the *tortelli* with a strainer-skimmer and place them on the prepared serving dish.

Pour the remaining sauce over, dot with remaining butter, sprinkle with the Parmigiano, and serve.

Tortelli di zucca alla modenese

SQUASH TORTELLI, MODENA STYLE

SERVES 8

*F*estive, sweet *tortelli*, eaten as a first dish. Made with fresh baked butternut squash, the bitter almond taste of *amaretti*, egg, bread crumbs, and Parmigiano, its mixture of sweet and "salt" reveals it as a survivor of the Renaissance. It is really a good idea for an Italian Thanksgiving dinner, because the fresh squash is appropriate and available. Do not make it if fresh squash cannot be found; they are basically the same as the Italian *zucche* used for the dish.

FOR THE STUFFING

1 butternut squash (for a yield of 1 cup of pulp after baking and straining)
1 ounce of amaretti (imported Italian almond cookies)
¼ cup bread crumbs, preferably homemade (see page 58)

1 extra-large egg
5 heaping tablespoons freshly grated Parmigiano
Salt to taste
Pinch of freshly grated nutmeg
Coarse-grained salt

FOR THE PASTA

4 extra-large eggs
4 cups unbleached all-purpose flour

4 teaspoons olive or vegetable oil
Pinch of salt

FOR THE SAUCE

6 tablespoons butter

5 or 6 heaping tablespoons freshly grated Parmigiano

TO COOK THE PASTA

Coarse-grained salt

FOR the stuffing, bake the squash on a cookie sheet in an oven preheated to 400 degrees for about 1 hour, then remove from the oven and lower the heat to 375 degrees. With fork and knife, peel the squash, divide in quarters, and remove the seeds and filaments. Place the pulp in a bowl and mash it with a fork, then strain it into another bowl.

Crush the *amaretti* very fine and pass them through a sifter. Toast the bread in the 375-degree oven on a cookie sheet, until golden (about 15 minutes).

Place the *amaretti* and toasted bread crumbs in the bowl containing the squash; mix very well with a wooden spoon, then add the egg, Parmigiano, salt, and nutmeg. Mix very well, without stopping, for about 10 minutes, then place the bowl in the refrigerator until the pasta is ready.

Make fresh *tortelli,* using the ingredients in the quantities listed, according to the directions on page 159. Form the *tortelli* as directed on page 192, using the filling you have just made.

Melt the butter for the sauce in a saucepan. Set aside until needed. Bring a large quantity of cold water to a boil in a stockpot. Meanwhile, prepare a serving dish by coating the bottom with 2 tablespoons of the melted butter. When water reaches the boiling point, add coarse salt to taste, then the *tortelli* quickly but gently, being careful not to break them. If the *tortelli* have been made as much as an hour or two before, they will cook and rise to the surface of the water in 1 minute. If they are already dried, cooking time will be longer (about 3 or 4 minutes). Remove the *tortelli* from the boiling water with a strainer-skimmer and arrange them in a layer in the prepared serving dish. Sprinkle with 2 more tablespoons of the butter and half the Parmigiano, then make a second layer of *tortelli* and cover with the remaining melted butter and Parmigiano. Serve hot.

Tortellini alla panna

TORTELLINI IN BUTTER AND CREAM SAUCE

SERVES 6

*T*ortellini tossed in the same butter and cream sauce as in *taglia-telle alla panna*. The sauce must be made in the pan with the cooked tortellini; it does not exist in its own right.

The dish is very popular in Bologna. It requires homemade tortellini, very tender, and should not be made with the prepackaged kind.

FOR THE STUFFING

2 ounces prosciutto, in 1 slice
2 ounces mortadella of Bologna,
*   in 1 large slice, or*
*   additional prosciutto*
¼ pound chicken breast, in 1
*   piece*
¼ pound pork, in 1 piece
1 whole bay leaf
1 teaspoon sweet butter

1 tablespoon olive oil
Salt, freshly ground black
*   pepper, and freshly grated*
*   nutmeg*
2 extra-large eggs
1 cup freshly grated
*   Parmigiano*

FOR THE PASTA

3 extra-large eggs
3 cups unbleached all-purpose
*   flour*

1 tablespoon olive oil or
*   vegetable oil*
Pinch of salt
Coarse-grained salt

FOR THE SAUCE

12 tablespoons (6 ounces) sweet
*   butter*
2 cups heavy cream
4 ounces freshly grated
*   Parmigiano cheese*

Freshly ground white pepper to
*   taste*
Freshly grated nutmeg to taste

TO COOK THE PASTA

Coarse-grained salt

To make the stuffing, cut the prosciutto and mortadella into small squares.

Heat the butter and oil in a saucepan and add the meat squares, along with the chicken breast, pork, bay leaf, salt, pepper, and nutmeg. Sauté very lightly for 10 minutes, remove the mixture from the pan, discarding the bay leaf, and chop very fine. Mix in the eggs and Parmigiano, then stir well until entire mixture is thoroughly combined.

Make the pasta, using the ingredients in the quantities listed, according to the directions on page 159. Form the tortellini as directed on page 194, using the stuffing you have just made.

To cook the tortellini, put a large quantity of cold water in a stockpot and set on the heat. When the water reaches the boiling point, add coarse salt, then the tortellini, a few at a time, until all are in the pot. Freshly made tortellini will be cooked in 2 or 3 minutes, those made several hours before require a few minutes more. (Test them, as cooking time can also vary with the weather.) When they are cooked, quickly remove the tortellini with a strainer-skimmer.

Place a large frying pan containing the 12 tablespoons of butter over very low heat and add the tortellini. Toss gently with a large metal spoon. Add the heavy cream, unheated, and the grated Parmigiano. Keep mixing gently until the sauce is homogenously creamy (about 2 minutes). Sprinkle with white pepper and nutmeg and serve immediately.

Tortelli al coniglio

TORTELLI IN RABBIT SAUCE

SERVES 8

A rather elaborate country dish, from the mountainous Mugello, the area where Giotto and Fra Angelico were born.

The sauce is made by cooking out the essence of the rabbit with *odori* (aromatic vegetables), red wine, *pancetta,* butter, and olive oil, broth, and a little tomato. The liver is chopped and added; the rabbit is discarded or saved for a family snack. The *tortelli* are lightly stuffed with a filling flavored with a little of the sauce and butter. But the lion's share of the sauce is put over the *tortelli* after they are cooked.

This is a dish very little known even in Florence itself, and once when I made it for a public occasion there, it became the subject of an article in one of the Florentine newspapers. (My co-citizens are not used to coming in contact with a new dish that they actually like.)

FOR THE SAUCE

1 small rabbit (about 3 pounds), liver reserved

4 ounces **pancetta** *or prosciutto, in one piece*

4 tablespoons (2 ounces) sweet butter

3 tablespoons olive oil

1 medium red onion, cleaned

1 large or 2 small carrots, scraped

1 medium celery rib

5 sprigs Italian parsley, leaves only

1 large clove garlic, peeled

1 cup dry red wine

Salt and freshly ground black pepper to taste

3 ounces tomato paste, preferably imported Italian

2 cups meat broth, preferably homemade (see page 126)

FOR THE FILLING

2 large potatoes for boiling, but not new potatoes

Coarse-grained salt

8 tablespoons (4 ounces) sweet butter

1/2 cup of the sauce (see above)

2 extra-large egg yolks

1/4 cup freshly grated Parmigiano

Salt, freshly ground black pepper, and freshly grated nutmeg to taste

FOR THE PASTA

4 extra-large eggs
4 cups unbleached all-purpose
flour

4 teaspoons olive or vegetable
oil
Pinch of salt

TO COOK THE PASTA
Coarse-grained salt

PLUS

4 tablespoons (2 ounces) sweet
butter

5 tablespoons freshly grated
Parmigiano

PREPARE the sauce first.

Be sure the cavity of rabbit is well cleaned. Rinse the rabbit very well and place it in a metal casserole. Cover the casserole and place over medium heat for 10 minutes; do not add anything, as the rabbit will shed liquid. Remove the casserole from the heat and throw away the liquid the rabbit has shed (it would give the dish too gamey a taste), then rinse rabbit in cold water again and set it aside.

Cut the *pancetta* into tiny pieces, then place it in a flameproof casserole with the butter and olive oil and sauté very gently for 10 to 12 minutes. Add the rabbit and sauté until golden all over (about 15 minutes).

Meanwhile, finely chop the onion, carrots, celery, parsley, and garlic. Add these chopped *odori* to the casserole and sauté very slowly until golden. Add the red wine and let it evaporate (about 15 minutes), then season with salt and pepper. Add the tomato paste and 1 cup of the meat broth, cover, and let simmer very slowly for 15 to 20 minutes until the broth is reduced and the tomato paste is completely incorporated. Taste for salt and pepper, add 1 more cup of broth, and simmer again until almost all the broth is evaporated (about 20 minutes).

Remove rabbit and set aside for another purpose (it is no longer needed for this dish), then chop the rabbit liver very fine and add it to the casserole. Cook for 5 minutes more, continually stirring with a wooden spoon, then remove the casserole from the heat, cover, and let rest until needed.

Make the filling. Boil the potatoes, in their skins, in salted water

(continued)

207

(about 25 to 35 minutes, depending on the potatoes), then peel and pass them through a potato ricer into a small flameproof casserole. Add the butter and ½ cup of the rabbit sauce to riced potatoes and place the casserole over medium heat for about 15 minutes, stirring constantly with a wooden spoon. Remove the casserole from the heat and transfer the contents to bowl to cool for about 20 minutes.

When cool, add the egg yolks, grated Parmigiano, salt, pepper, and nutmeg and mix very well with a wooden spoon.

Make the pasta using the ingredients in the proportions listed above, according to the directions on page 159. Form into *tortelli* as directed on page 192, using the filling you have just made.

Bring a large quantity of cold water to a boil in a stockpot. Meanwhile, reheat the sauce and pour half of it into a serving dish with 4 tablespoons of butter.

When the water is boiling, add coarse salt to taste, then the *tortelli* quickly but gently, being careful not to break them. If the *tortelli* have been made as much as an hour or two before, they will cook and rise to surface of water in 1 minute. If they are already dried, cooking time will be longer (about 3 to 4 minutes). Remove the *tortelli* with a strainer-skimmer and place them on the prepared serving dish.

Pour over the remaining sauce, sprinkle with Parmigiano, and serve.

Tortellini al sugo di carne

TORTELLINI IN MEAT SAUCE

SERVES 6

*T*hese little stuffed pasta are very versatile; they also go very well with the *sugo di carne* used with *tagliatelle*. Throughout Italy this is the sauce which is most often used with them.

Make the *sugo di carne* as described on page 86. After the *sugo* has cooked for 1 hour and has another hour to cook, make the tortellini, preparing the pasta, filling it, and then cooking the tortellini, all as described in the recipe for *tortellini alla panna,* using the same stuffing but omitting the sauce.

When the tortellini are cooked, quickly remove them from the boiling water with a strainer-skimmer.

Arrange the tortellini in a serving platter and pour the *sugo di carne* over them. Serve hot, sprinkling each serving with a tablespoon of grated Parmigiano.

NOTE: The *sugo di carne* may be prepared as much as a day in advance.

LARGE STUFFED PASTA DISHES

Cannelloni con carne

CANNELLONI WITH MEAT

MAKES 8 TO 10

$\mathcal{C}$ annelloni are stuffed, rolled-up squares of pasta. They may be made from yellow or green pasta and stuffed with a variety of fillings. Sometimes they are also made with *crespelle* instead of pasta squares; this is not in imitation of French crêpes, but rather a survival of Italian *crespelle* from earlier centuries. The recipes given here are for the more usual type made with pasta.

After the long strips of pasta have been cut into squares, the squares are precooked for some seconds. A few tablespoons of the stuffing are placed at one end, and the square is rolled up in the form of a tube.

People abroad serve cannelloni as a main dish, but this is never done in Italy. Cannelloni are always a first dish, even if they are stuffed with meat, and are eaten in a quantity appropriate to that course. Two cannelloni is an adequate portion, and for light eaters one often suffices.

This basic recipe, for meat cannelloni, contains the procedure for how to prepare them in detail. Following are cannelloni for the eve of a holiday, containing spinach and ricotta, cannelloni filled with ricotta and cheese, green cannelloni stuffed with ricotta and cheese, and the very

(continued)

CANNELLONI CON CARNE *(continued)*

special *cannelloni alla sorpresa,* the apotheosis of cannelloni, which are filled with *tortelli alla panna.*

Cannelloni are always baked, covered with "strips" of *balsamella* so the top does not become dry.

FOR THE STUFFING

1 ounce dried **porcini** *mushrooms*
1 small carrot, scraped
1 medium red onion, cleaned
1/2 celery rib
10 sprigs Italian parsley, leaves only
1 medium clove garlic, peeled
5 tablespoons olive oil
1/2 pound pork
1/2 pound ground beef
1/2 chicken breast, from a 3 1/2-pound chicken

1/2 cup dry red wine
1 tablespoon tomato paste, preferably imported Italian
2 cups hot meat or chicken broth, preferably homemade (see page 126)
1/4 pound prosciutto, in one piece
Salt and freshly ground black pepper to taste
1/2 cup freshly grated Parmigiano
Freshly grated nutmeg to taste

FOR THE PASTA

2 cups unbleached all-purpose flour
2 extra-large eggs

2 teaspoons olive or vegetable oil
Pinch of salt

PLUS

Coarse-grained salt

2 tablespoons olive or vegetable oil

FOR THE BALSAMELLA

3 tablespoons (1 1/2 ounces) sweet butter
1/4 cups unbleached all-purpose flour

2 cups milk
Salt and freshly grated nutmeg to taste

MAKE the stuffing first.

Soak the mushrooms in lukewarm water for 30 minutes.

Meanwhile, chop the carrot, onion, celery, parsley, and garlic very fine. Place a saucepan, preferably terra-cotta, with the olive oil over medium heat. When the oil is warm add the chopped ingredients and sauté until the onion is translucent.

Add the pork, beef, and chicken breast and sauté for 15 to 20 minutes more, then add the wine and cook until evaporated (about 15 minutes). Add the tomato paste and 1 cup of the hot broth and reduce for 15 minutes.

Transfer the pork and chicken breast to a board and chop them very fine. Drain the mushrooms and clean them very well, removing all the sand attached to the stems. (If the soaking water is saved for another dish, strain it through several layers of paper towels to remove sand. The water may be frozen in ice cube trays.) Place the meats back in the pan, adding the second cup of broth, the mushrooms, salt, and pepper. Reduce for about 15 minutes, until the sauce is quite thick, then chop the prosciutto very fine, add it to the sauce, and cook for 1 more minute.

Remove the pan from flame. Add the grated Parmigiano and nutmeg and mix very well, then let the sauce cool before stuffing the pasta.

Make fresh pasta, using the ingredients in the quantities listed, according to the directions on page 159. Then, with a jagged-edged wheel (pastry wheel), cut the pasta sheets to make squares (see the illustration on page 212).

Bring a large amount of cold water to a boil. Meanwhile, fill a large bowl with cold water and 2 tablespoons of olive oil; dampen 4 cotton dishtowels with cold water.

When the water is boiling, add coarse salt, then one by one, put squares of pasta into the pot for several seconds, until they rise to the top of the water. Transfer each to the bowl of cold water with a slotted spoon to cool, then place on the dampened towels, stack if necessary, and allow to rest for 20 minutes (see the illustrations on pages 212 and 213).

Meanwhile, make the *balsamella,* using the ingredients in the quantities listed, following the directions on page 62. Transfer the sauce to a

(continued)

Cannelloni con carne: Cut the pasta into squares.

Transfer the half-cooked pasta square to the bowl of cold water.

Place the pasta squares on the dampened cotton dishtowel.

Roll up the cannelloni. Notice that the finished cannelloni are placed in the baking dish with the jagged edges on top.

CANNELLONI CON CARNE *(continued)*

crockery or glass bowl and cover with a piece of buttered wax paper.

When you are ready to put the cannelloni together, preheat the oven to 375 degrees, then transfer a pasta square to a board. Spread 3 heaping tablespoons of the stuffing along one of the jagged edges, then roll, starting at the edge containing the stuffing and ending with the other jagged edge on top (see the illustration on page 213). Repeat until all the cannelloni are rolled.

Place the cannelloni in 1 or 2 well-buttered 13½ × 8¾-inch baking dishes. A maximum of 8 will fit in one dish of this size, so be guided by the number of cannelloni you have.

Pour a "strip" of *balsamella* along the length of each of the cannelloni and another strip between each two, then bake in the preheated oven for 20 minutes. Allow to cool for 10 minutes before serving, then serve with a large spatula.

Cannelloni verdi di ricotta

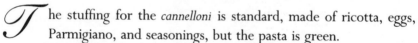

GREEN CANNELLONI WITH RICOTTA FILLING

MAKES 10 TO 12

*T*he stuffing for the *cannelloni* is standard, made of ricotta, eggs, Parmigiano, and seasonings, but the pasta is green.

FOR THE STUFFING

20 sprigs Italian parsley, leaves
   only
8 ounces ricotta, well drained
1 cup freshly grated
   Parmigiano

2 extra-large eggs plus 2 extra-
   large egg yolks
Salt, freshly ground black
   pepper, and freshly grated
   nutmeg to taste

FOR THE BALSAMELLA

3 tablespoons (1½ ounces)
   sweet butter
¼ cup unbleached all-purpose
   flour

2 cups milk
Salt to taste

FOR THE PASTA

3¹/₂ cups unbleached all-purpose
    flour
2 extra-large eggs
5 to 6 ounces fresh spinach,
    weighed before stems are
    removed

2 teaspoons olive or vegetable
    oil
Pinch of salt

PLUS

Coarse-grained salt

2 tablespoons olive or vegetable
    oil

MAKE the stuffing first.

Remove the stems from the parsley and chop the leaves coarsely. Place in a large bowl with the ricotta, Parmigiano, eggs, and egg yolks. Mix well with a wooden spoon, then season with salt, pepper, and nutmeg and mix thoroughly. Cover the bowl and place it in the refrigerator until needed.

From this point on, proceed as directed in the recipe for *cannelloni con carne* on page 209, but making the green pasta according to the directions on page 165.

Cannelloni alla sorpresa

GREEN CANNELLONI STUFFED WITH
TORTELLI ALLA PANNA

MAKES 16

*T*he apotheosis of cannelloni, a very fancy treatment in which green pasta is used for the outside roll, while inside, under a lining consisting of a thin slice of *prosciutto cotto,* is a stuffing of "half-moon" *tortelli,* made of yellow pasta and stuffed in turn with chicken breast, prosciutto, and seasonings, then tossed in *alla panna* sauce, some of which is spooned inside the cannelloni along with the *tortelli.* A noteworthy dish, worth the trouble of making the two kinds of pasta and the *tortelli.* It makes a strong impression at an important dinner.

PASTA FOR THE GREEN CANNELLONI

5 to 6 ounces fresh spinach, weighed before stems are removed

3½ cups unbleached all-purpose flour

2 extra-large eggs

2 teaspoons olive or vegetable oil

Pinch of salt

PLUS

Coarse-grained salt

2 tablespoons olive or vegetable oil

FOR THE TORTELLI FILLING

3 tablespoons olive oil

2 tablespoons (1 ounce) sweet butter

1 whole chicken breast, from a 3½-pound chicken

1 bay leaf

Salt and freshly ground black pepper to taste

¼ cup freshly grated Parmigiano

2 extra-large eggs yolks

Freshly grated nutmeg to taste

PASTA FOR THE "HALF-MOON" TORTELLI

3 cups unbleached all-purpose flour

3 extra-large eggs

1 tablespoon olive or vegetable oil

Pinch of salt

TO COOK THE "HALF-MOON" TORTELLI
Coarse-grained salt

FOR THE ALLA PANNA SAUCE

**8 tablespoon (4 ounces) sweet
  butter**
1 cup heavy cream
**5 tablespoons freshly grated
  Parmigiano**

**Salt, freshly ground white
  pepper, and freshly grated
  nutmeg to taste**

FOR THE BALSAMELLA

**3 tablespoons (1½ ounces)
  sweet butter**
**¼ cup unbleached all-purpose
  flour**

2 cups milk
Pinch of salt

PLUS

16 thin slices boiled ham

MAKE the green pasta, using the ingredients in the quantities listed,
according to the directions on page 165. Prepare the pasta for cannelloni, cutting it and precooking it, as directed on page 209. Let stand on
the damp cotton dishtowel until needed. Begin the "half-moon" *tortelli*,
making the filling first.

Heat the oil and butter in a saucepan. When the butter is melted,
add the whole chicken breast, along with the bay leaf. Season with salt
and freshly ground black pepper and sauté lightly for about 20 minutes,
turning several times.

Remove the saucepan from the heat, discarding the bay leaf but
saving the sautéing fat, and transfer chicken breast to a chopping board.
Remove the bones and chop the meat fine.

Place the chopped meat in a small bowl, along with the Parmigiano,
egg yolks, and reserved sautéing fat. Taste for salt and pepper, add a
pinch of freshly grated nutmeg, and mix thoroughly with a wooden
spoon. Cover the bowl and let stand until needed.

Make the pasta for the "half-moon" *tortelli*, as directed on pages
159–162, using the ingredients in the quantities listed, then form the

(continued)

CANNELLONI ALLA SORPRESA *(continued)*

tortelli as directed on page 192, using the filling you have just made.

When you have finished making the *tortelli,* put a large quantity of cold water in a stockpot and set it on the heat. While the water is heating, melt 8 tablespoons of butter in a large frying pan to prepare for making *tortelli alla panna.*

When the water in the stockpot reaches the boiling point, add coarse salt to taste, then all the *tortelli,* one by one, into the pot. Stir with a wooden spoon and let cook about 35 seconds, in the meantime turning the heat to low under the pan containing the melted butter. When the *tortelli* are ready, quickly transfer them with a strainer-skimmer from pot to the warm butter in the frying pan. Pour the heavy cream over the *tortelli,* and then sprinkle them with the Parmigiano, a little white pepper, and nutmeg to taste.

With a slotted spoon, very gently mix the heavy cream, Parmigiano, and *tortelli* together. Allow the *tortelli* to simmer for 30 seconds, gently stirring without stopping, then remove the pan from the heat and let the *tortelli* cool for ½ hour.

Meanwhile make the *balsamella,* using the ingredients in the quantities listed, according to the directions on page 62, then transfer to a crockery or glass bowl and press over it a piece of buttered wax paper and let cool for 1 hour.

Preheat the oven to 375 degrees.

To assemble the dish, place a whole slice of boiled ham on each square of green pasta. Arrange 4 or 5 *tortelli,* with a little of the sauce, along one jagged edge of each pasta square and roll up. Place the rolled cannelloni in two well-buttered (13½ X 8¾-inch) baking dishes, then pour *balsamella* all over. Place the baking dishes in the preheated oven for 20 minutes. Allow to cool for 10 minutes, then serve with a wide spatula.

NOTE: You can prepare this dish as much as 1 day in advance. Put the dish together up to and including pouring on the *balsamella.* Wrap the baking dishes in plastic wrap and place in refrigerator until needed.

Forty-five minutes before serving, remove the wrap and place in an oven preheated to 375 degrees for 30 minutes. Allow to stand for about 10 minutes and serve.

Cannelloni con ricotta

CANNELLONI STUFFED WITH RICOTTA

MAKES 8 TO 10

*H*ere the ricotta-eggs-Parmigiano stuffing is flavored with Italian parsley.

FOR THE FILLING

20 sprigs Italian parsley, leaves
only
15 ounces ricotta
1 cup freshly grated
Parmigiano cheese

2 extra-large eggs plus 2 extra-
large egg yolks
Salt, freshly ground black
pepper, and freshly grated
nutmeg to taste

FOR THE BALSAMELLA

3 tablespoons (1½ ounces)
sweet butter
¼ cup unbleached all-purpose
flour

2 cups of milk
Salt

FOR THE PASTA

2 cups unbleached all-purpose
flour
2 extra-large eggs

2 teaspoons olive or vegetable
oil
Pinch of salt

MAKE the filling first.

Chop the parsley very fine. Place in a bowl with the ricotta, Parmigiano, eggs, egg yolks, salt, pepper, and nutmeg. Mix together with a wooden spoon until all the ingredients are well combined. Cover the bowl and let stand in the refrigerator until needed.

From this point on, proceed exactly as directed in the recipe for *cannelloni con carne* on page 209; the procedures for making the pasta and *balsamella* and assembling the dish are exactly the same.

Cannelloni della vigilia

CANNELLONI STUFFED WITH SPINACH AND RICOTTA

MAKES 8 TO 10

FOR THE FILLING

3 pounds fresh spinach

Coarse-grained salt

15 ounces ricotta, well drained

2 extra-large eggs plus 2 extra-large egg yolks

1 cup freshly grated Parmigiano cheese

Salt, freshly ground black pepper, and freshly grated nutmeg to taste

FOR THE BALSAMELLA

3 tablespoons (1½ ounces) sweet butter

¼ cup unbleached all-purpose flour

2 cups milk

Salt to taste

FOR THE PASTA

2 extra-large eggs

2 cups unbleached all-purpose flour

2 teaspoons olive or vegetable oil

Pinch of salt

PLUS

Coarse-grained salt

2 tablespoons olive or vegetable oil

MAKE the filling first.

Rinse the spinach very well and cut off the larger stems. Put a large quantity of cold water in a stockpot and set it on the heat. When the water boils, add coarse salt, to taste, then the spinach and cook for about 5 minutes. Drain the spinach, cool it under cold running water, and squeeze dry.

Chop the spinach very fine, then place it in a bowl with the ricotta, eggs, egg yolks, Parmigiano, salt, pepper, and nutmeg. Mix together with a wooden spoon until well combined, then cover and let stand in the refrigerator until needed.

From this point on, proceed exactly as directed in the recipe for *cannelloni con carne* on page 209. The procedures for making the pasta and *balsamella* and assembling the dish are identical.

Lasagne al forno

BAKED LASAGNE, NORTHERN ITALIAN STYLE

SERVES 8 TO 10

*L*asagne are layers of pasta, made from the same squares of pasta as cannelloni, with layers of sauce or stuffing placed between the layers of pasta. The dish is then baked in the oven.

The northern Italian lasagne are made with light fresh pasta, yellow, green, or both. The classical dish is an alternation of three sauce/stuffings: meat sauce, *balsamella,* and grated mozzarella and Parmigiano. Quite different from lasagne made with dried lasagne noodles and heavier sauces, it is usually a revelation of lightness to non-Italians.

This recipe includes the three sauces and suggests alternating yellow and green pasta. Alternating the two colors adds further distinction to the presentation, and of course to the taste. The meat sauce uses the same ingredients as the filling for *cannelloni con carne* on page 210, but in different proportions.

FOR THE MEAT SAUCE

1 ounce dried **porcini** *mushrooms*

1 large carrot, scraped

1 large red onion, cleaned

1 celery rib

10 sprigs Italian parsley, leaves only

1 medium clove garlic, peeled

5 tablespoons olive oil

¼ pound ground pork

½ pound ground beef

½ chicken breast, from a 3½-pound chicken

½ cup dry red wine

1 tablespoon tomato paste

2 cups hot meat or chicken broth, preferably homemade

¼ pound prosciutto or boiled ham, in one piece

Salt, freshly ground black pepper, and freshly grated nutmeg to taste

(continued)

LASAGNA AL FORNO *(continued)*

FOR THE BALSAMELLA

**6 tablespoons (3 ounces) sweet
butter**
**1/2 cup unbleached all-purpose
flour**

4 cups milk
**Salt and freshly grated nutmeg
to taste**

FOR THE CHEESE STUFFING

8 ounces mozzarella

**1 1/2 cups freshly grated
Parmigiano**

FOR THE YELLOW PASTA

2 extra-large eggs
**2 cups unbleached all-purpose
flour**

**2 teaspoons olive or vegetable
oil**
Pinch of salt

FOR THE GREEN PASTA

**5 to 6 ounces fresh spinach,
weighed before stems are
removed**
Coarse-grained salt
2 extra-large eggs

**3 1/2 cups unbleached all-purpose
flour**
**2 teaspoons olive or vegetable
oil**
Pinch of salt

PLUS

Coarse-grained salt

**2 tablespoons olive or vegetable
oil**

MAKE the meat sauce, using the ingredients in the quantities listed, according to the directions given in *cannelloni con carne* on page 209, omitting the Parmigiano. Otherwise, follow the procedure exactly. When the meat sauce is cooked, cover the saucepan and be sure you allow it to cool for 1 to 1 1/2 hours before using.

Make the *balsamella,* using the ingredients in the quantities listed, according to the directions on page 62. When finished, transfer to a crockery or glass bowl and press a piece of buttered wax paper over the surface and let cool for 1 hour.

Make the cheese stuffing by coarsely grating the mozzarella into a bowl. Add the grated Parmigiano and mix together with a wooden spoon, then cover and place in the refrigerator until needed.

Make fresh pasta, using the ingredients in the quantities listed, according to the directions on page 159, then cut and precook it as for cannelloni (see page 209). Make the green pasta according to the directions on page 165. (If you prefer, use green pasta only, which would make the dish *lasagne alla ferrarese.*) An especially beautiful dish is made by alternating layers of yellow pasta with green pasta.

Preheat the oven to 375 degrees.

To put the dish together, heavily butter a 13½ × 8¾-inch baking dish. Spread 1 tablespoon of the meat sauce over bottom of dish; then fit in enough squares of precooked pasta to cover the bottom of the baking dish and to allow about 1 inch to hang out over the edges all around the dish; sprinkle with some of the cheese stuffing (see illustrations below and at the top of page 224).

Add another layer of pasta, this time covering only the inside of the dish. Cover with *balsamella* (see illustration at the bottom of page 224). Keep alternating the three fillings (cheese, *balsamella,* and meat sauce), covering each layer of filling with a layer of pasta (see illustrations on page 225). The last layer should be either cheese or *balsamella,* covered with 3 squares of pasta. *(continued)*

Lasagne al forno: After putting some sauce in a prepared baking dish, cover the bottom of the dish with squares of pasta.

Over the first layer of cheese "stuffing," add another layer of pasta. Notice the bottom layer of pasta overlapping the sides.

Cover the second layer of pasta with a layer of *balsamella*.

Cover a third layer of pasta with a layer of meat sauce.

Folding the pasta ends from the bottom layer over the top layer of pasta.

LASAGNA AL FORNO (continued)

Take the pasta ends hanging over the edges of the baking dish and fold them in, over the top layer of pasta; then place the dish in the preheated oven for about 25 minutes, until the top layer is lightly golden and crisp. Remove the dish from the oven and allow to cool for 15 minutes before serving.

When ready to serve, cut the lasagne, in the baking dish, in half lengthwise, then cut each half into 4 or 5 servings. Transfer the servings to individual plates with a spatula.

NOTE: This dish may be prepared a day in advance. If so, after the dish is assembled but not baked, wrap in plastic wrap and place in the refrigerator. When needed, unwrap and place in a preheated 375 degree oven for 35 to 40 minutes.

Lasagne all'anitra all'aretina

LASAGNE WITH DUCK, IN THE STYLE OF AREZZO

SERVES 8 TO 10

*L*asagne with duck as made in the Tuscan town of Arezzo, home of the frescoes by the great Piero della Francesca and an old Etruscan town with its own tradition of cooking. Only an authentic version of Peking duck matches the haughtiness with which the duck meat itself is treated after it is used to make the dish. Here the essence is extracted from the duck by cooking it for a long time in the sauce. And it is only the sauce, and a little of the duck fat and its liver, which are then used for the dish. As far as the Aretini are concerned, the duck itself may be tossed out. (But if you have some close family or friends, who won't tell on you, you can keep it for a snack, because as you can imagine it is still quite good.)

The pasta squares prepared for the lasagne should be all yellow pasta. The duck sauce is alternated with each layer of pasta until you reach the last one. Then a substantial layer of *balsamella* is placed over the last layer of pasta, and is then itself covered with a thin coating of homemade bread crumbs. This is a rare dish, in all senses, and one you will remember.

FOR THE SAUCE

*1 fat domestic duck (about 5
    pounds), liver reserved*
*Salt and freshly ground black
    pepper to taste*
*1 tablespoon (¹/₂ ounce) sweet
    butter*
¹/₄ cup olive oil
1 large red onion, cleaned
2 large carrots, scraped
*1 large or 2 small cloves garlic,
    peeled*
*10 sprigs Italian parsley, leaves
    only*
4 medium celery ribs

*¹/₄ pound boiled ham, in one
    piece*
*2 ounces prosciutto or
    pancetta, in one piece*
*Salt, freshly ground black
    pepper, and freshly grated
    nutmeg*
*4 large, ripe, fresh tomatoes
    (about 1 pound), or 1
    pound canned tomatoes,
    preferably imported Italian,
    drained*
*1 to 2 cups meat or chicken
    broth, preferably homemade
    (see page 126)*

FOR THE PASTA

*4 cups unbleached all-purpose
    flour*
4 extra-large eggs

*4 teaspoons olive or vegetable
    oil*
Pinch of salt

PLUS

Coarse-grained salt

*2 tablespoons olive or vegetable
    oil*

FOR THE BALSAMELLA

*6 tablespoons (3 ounces) sweet
    butter*

*¹/₄ cup unbleached all-purpose
    flour*
2 cups milk

FOR THE FILLING AND TOPPING

*8 ounces freshly grated
    Parmigiano*

*¹/₃ cup unflavored bread
    crumbs, preferably
    homemade, from Tuscan
    bread (see pages 39
    and 58)*

(continued)

LASAGNA ALL'ANITRA ALL'ARETINA *(continued)*

MAKE the sauce first.

Clean the duck very well, setting the liver aside, then sprinkle inside and out with salt and pepper. Put the tablespoon of butter inside the duck, then place it in a large oval casserole, along with the olive oil. Put the casserole over medium heat and sauté the duck until it is lightly golden on all sides (about 30 to 35 minutes). Meanwhile, chop the onion, carrots, garlic, parsley, celery, boiled ham, and prosciutto together, all very fine.

When duck is browned, add the chopped ingredients to the casserole and sauté gently for 25 to 30 minutes more, turning the duck over two or three times. Add salt, pepper, and nutmeg to taste and mix thoroughly.

Pass the fresh or canned tomatoes through a food mill, using the disc with the smallest holes, into bowl and add them to the casserole. Simmer slowly, covered, for 1 hour, adding broth if the sauce becomes too thick, then remove the duck from the sauce. (The cooked duck may be eaten separately, but it is no longer necessary for this dish.) Chop the reserved duck liver very fine and add it to the sauce. Taste for salt and pepper and let simmer for 5 or 6 minutes more.

Transfer the sauce to a bowl and allow it to cool for at least 1 hour. Remove half of the grease from the top.

Make fresh pasta, using the ingredients in the proportions listed, according to the directions on page 159, then cut and precook it as for cannelloni (see page 209).

Make the *balsamella,* using the ingredients in the quantities listed, according to the directions on page 62, then transfer to a crockery or glass bowl, press a piece of buttered wax paper over the surface and let cool for 1 hour.

Preheat the oven to 400 degrees.

Butter a 13½ × 8¾-inch glass baking dish generously, since in this type of lasagne no sauce is placed on the bottom, then fit in enough precooked pasta squares to cover the bottom and allow about ½ inch to hang out over the edges all the way around. Cover the layer of pasta generously with the duck sauce, then sprinkle abundant grated Parmigiano over the sauce.

Make another layer of pasta (with no overlap) and repeat the procedure with sauce and Parmigiano. Keep making layers (this amount of pasta should make about 6 or 7), putting sauce and Parmigiano over each layer except the last. Cover the last layer with the *balsamella* and cover the *balsamella* with the bread crumbs. Fold the pasta edges over the ends of the bread crumb layer.

Bake in the preheated oven for 20 to 25 minutes, then allow to cool for 15 minutes before serving.

NOTE: This dish may be prepared a day in advance. If so, after the dish is assembled but not baked, wrap it in plastic wrap and place in the refrigerator. When needed, unwrap and place in a preheated 400-degree oven for 35 to 40 minutes.

Rotolo di pasta ripieno

STUFFED PASTA ROLL

SERVES 8

FOR THE FILLING

3 pounds fresh spinach
Coarse-grained salt
15 ounces ricotta, well drained
2 extra-large eggs plus 2 extra-
     large egg yolks

1 1/2 cups freshly grated
     Parmigiano
Salt, freshly ground black
     pepper, and freshly grated
     nutmeg to taste

FOR THE BALSAMELLA

4 tablespoons (2 ounces) sweet
     butter

4 teaspoons unbleached all-
     purpose flour
1 1/2 cups milk

FOR THE PASTA

2 cups unbleached all-purpose
     flour
2 extra-large eggs

2 teaspoons olive or vegetable
     oil
Pinch of salt

PLUS

2 tablespoons olive or vegetable
     oil

Coarse-grained salt

(continued)

ROTOLO DI PASTA RIPIENO *(continued)*

REMOVE the large stems from the spinach and rinse very carefully. Put a large quantity of cold water in a stockpot and set on the heat. When the water reaches boiling point, add coarse salt to taste, then put in the spinach. Cook for about 5 minutes, then drain in a colander, cool under cold running water and squeeze dry.

Chop the spinach fine, then put it in a large bowl, along with the ricotta, eggs, and egg yolks. Mix very well with a wooden spoon, then, when well combined, add 1 cup of the Parmigiano and salt, pepper, and nutmeg. Stir until homogenous, then cover and refrigerate until needed.

Prepare the *balsamella,* using the ingredients in the quantities listed, according to the directions on page 62.

Make fresh pasta, using the ingredients in the proportions listed, according to the directions on page 159, then knead it and roll it out by hand as directed below.

After the flour has been absorbed, knead the dough for about 10 minutes more. (This parallels the early steps of passing it through the machine.)

After making sure that your pasta board and rolling pin are absolutely dry and smooth, dust the board with the clean remaining flour. (Illustrations show ball-bearing type of rolling pin.*)

NOTE: The pasta for the *rotolo* should be a bit thicker than that rolled by machine. That paper-thin pasta is less than 1/16 of an inch. But the large single *rotolo* sheet must be a bit thicker in order to handle it as a single whole sheet that must be precooked and then stuffed and placed in the oven, all in one piece.

Gently roll out the ball of dough to a uniform thickness of 1/16 of an inch, in the following stages:

Holding the rolling pin firmly in both hands, quickly roll back and forth over the ball of dough until it is flat. At this point it will be longer than it is wide. Turn the dough 45 degrees and roll it until the width is about equal to the length.

Sprinkle with flour and turn the pasta over. Repeat the rolling as described above. Sprinkle with flour and turn over again.

(continued)

---

*For use of long Italian rolling pin, see *Bugialli on Pasta.*

Wrap the sheet of pasta around a rolling pin.

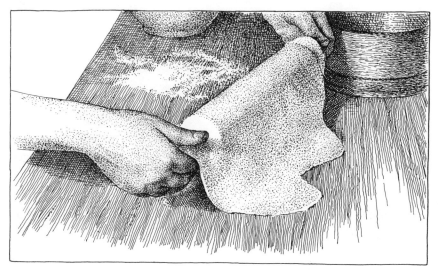

Unroll the sheet of pasta on the other side of the rolling pin.

For *Rotolo di pasta ripieno,* put the sheet of pasta in boiling water.

Transfer the insert containing the sheet of pasta to a bowl of cold water.

ROTOLO DI PASTA RIPIENO *(continued)*

Repeat the procedure about 4 times on both sides. At that point, the sheet should be almost as thin as needed. (After the second rolling out, it becomes more difficult to lift the sheet for turning. To make it easier, lightly wrap the sheet of pasta around the rolling pin. Then, hold the end of the sheet and reverse the direction of the rolling pin. The sheet of pasta should unroll on the reverse side; see illustration opposite).

In the final stage, pay careful attention to rolling the edges to the same thickness as the rest of the sheet. (With the ball-bearing rolling pin it is not necessary to use any special procedure for the edges, such as rolling them around the pin.) Before stopping, be sure the sheet of pasta is of uniform thickness all over.

Let the sheet of pasta dry on the board for 2 minutes. Meanwhile, put a large quantity of cold water in a large stockpot with insert. Set on the heat.

Prepare a very large bowl (or substitute a second stockpot) with about 20 cups of cold water and the 2 tablespoons of oil.

When the water in the pot reaches the boiling point, add coarse-grained salt to taste, then carefully place the entire sheet of pasta in insert of the pot, holding the ends with both hands and being sure not to fold it (see illustration opposite). Let the sheet of pasta cook for 50 seconds, then remove the insert with the sheet of pasta inside and quickly place it in the bowl of cold water and oil and let cool for 2 minutes (see illustration opposite).

Wet 2 large cotton dishtowels with cold water and spread out on a board. Remove the sheet of pasta from the cold water and spread it out flat on the towel. Spread out the second towel over the sheet of pasta and let rest for 5 minutes, then, with a jagged pastry wheel, trim edge of one side in a straight line. Cut the opposite side similarly to make a sheet uniformly 13 inches wide. (The other two sides need not be cut, and can be as long as the pasta board.)

Transfer the filling from the bowl onto the sheet of pasta. Using a long spatula, spread out the filling to cover the sheet, leaving a ½-inch edge of pasta all around (see illustration at the top of page 234). Sprinkle the remaining ½ cup of grated Parmigiano over.

Preheat the oven to 375 degrees. *(continued)*

The filling spread over the pasta sheet.

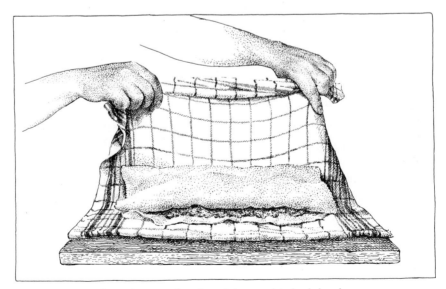

Roll up the *rotolo* by picking up the edge of the towel in both hands.

ROTOLO DI PASTA RIPIENO *(continued)*

To roll up *rotolo,* take one of the untrimmed sides in both hands and fold it over about 1 inch of the filling. Then pick up the edge of the towel in both hands. As you keep lifting the edge of the towel a little higher, the pasta sheet will continue to roll over until it is rolled up like a jelly roll (see illustration opposite); the other untrimmed end should now be on top.

Place the *rotolo* in a well-buttered 13½ × 8¾-inch glass baking dish. Cover the top with the *balsamella.* Place in the preheated oven for about 25 minutes, until the top part is lightly golden. Remove from oven and allow to cool 10 to 15 minutes before serving.

To serve, slice through, like a jelly roll, so that all of the layering shows through.

NOTE: This dish may be prepared, up to and including the rolling and covering with *balsamella,* in advance. If you don't wish to cook the *rotolo* immediately, wrap the dish in plastic wrap and place it in the refrigerator. When you wish to serve it, unwrap it and bake it at 375 degrees for 35 to 40 minutes.

TIMBALLO DISHES

PASTRY DRUMS

$\mathcal{T}$he *timballo,* or pastry drum, is used for elegant presentation of various dishes, consisting of chicken, meat, pasta, or dessert. The French, who also use it, call it *timbale.* The type of pastry used depends on whether it holds a "salty" or "sweet" dish (two opposing categories that are used in Italian cooking, "salty" meaning anything not sweet). Both types of pastry may be eaten, but an elaborate pretense is made that they are for presentation only. Sooner or later, however, someone wants to taste the pastry and everyone joins in.

There are simpler dishes that are called by this name that have crisp bread crumb crusts, but they are not real *timballi,* being rather more like *pasticci.* For a sweet *timballo,* see page 582.

Timballo di piccioni

SERVES 6

*T*his "salty" *timballo* dish includes the recipe for the nonsweet timballo pastry and directions for making the drum.

FOR THE PASTRY DRUM

12 tablespoons (6 ounces) sweet butter

5 cups unbleached all-purpose flour

2 extra-large egg yolks

1 cup cold water

4 tablespoons olive oil

Pinch of salt

1 extra-large egg (for the glaze)

2 pounds of any dried beans, the cheaper the better

FOR THE BALSAMELLA

3 tablespoons (1½ ounces) sweet butter

¼ cup unbleached all-purpose flour

1½ cups of milk

Salt to taste

FOR THE SQUAB-MACARONI FILLING

2 squab

2 small celery ribs

1 small red onion, cleaned

2 small carrots, scraped

3 tablespoons olive oil

½ cup dry red wine

1 cup chicken or meat broth, preferably homemade

Salt, freshly ground black pepper, and freshly grated nutmeg to taste

¾ pound dried elbow macaroni, preferably imported Italian

4 ounces boiled ham, in one piece

FOR THE TOPPING

6 tablespoons (3 ounces) sweet butter, cut into pats

2 tablespoons freshly grated Parmigiano

Freshly grated nutmeg to taste

MAKE the pastry drum first.

Melt the butter in a small bowl, using a double boiler or *bagnomaria*. Let the butter cool for ½ hour.

Make a mound of the flour on a pasta board and make a well in the flour. Pour the melted butter, the egg yolks, water, oil, and salt into the well. Use a fork to mix all the ingredients in the well together; then start incorporating the flour from the inside rim of the well until only ½ cup of the flour remains unincorporated. Use your hands to gather the dough together; then knead it for 2 minutes and form the dough into a ball. Put the ball of dough in plastic wrap and let it rest in a cool place for 2 hours.

Preheat the oven to 375 degrees.

Finish the pastry drum. Unwrap the dough and knead it for 1 minute on a pasta board. Sprinkle the board with the remaining flour; then cut the dough into 3 equal pieces. Using a rolling pin, roll out 1 piece to a thickness of a little less than ¼ inch. Make the "lid" of the *timballo* by placing the removable bottom of a 10-inch springform pan on the sheet of dough and cutting around it with a scalloped pastry wheel (see illustration at the top of page 238).

Butter a baking sheet and place the *timballo* lid on it. Use a fork to make punctures all over the lid so the dough does not rise while it is baking. Cut out a circle or square of dough of about 2 inches and place it in the center of the *timballo* lid to make a little handle.

Prepare the glaze. Beat the egg in a small bowl and use a pastry brush to spread it over the top of the lid.

Bake the lid for 35 minutes, or until the pastry is golden.

While the lid is baking, roll out a second piece of the dough to the same thickness as the first. Cut out a circular bottom for the *timballo* by placing the removable bottom of the springform pan on the pastry and cutting out a circle ½ inch larger than the bottom of the springform pan.

Put the springform pan together and butter it. Fit the bottom layer of the *timballo* into the pan; the ½-inch overlap of pastry should be curled up along the sides of the pan (see illustration at the bottom of page 238).

Take the third piece of dough and roll it out into a strip long

(continued)

Making a *timballo:* Cut out the pastry lid.

Fit the bottom of the pastry drum into the springform pan.

Fit the long strips of dough against the sides of the springform pan, overlapping with the bottom.

Fit a sheet of aluminum foil inside the drum and fill it with beans so the pastry will stay flat while baking.

TIMBALLO DI PICCIONI *(continued)*

enough to circle the inside of the springform pan. This strip will form the sides of the *timballo*. Use the rolling pin to stretch the strip of dough to a width of 3½ inches. Fit the strip of dough inside the springform pan, along the sides, fitting it inside the overlapping pastry from the *timballo* bottom (see illustration at the top of page 239).

Use the palm of your hand to press down the pastry hanging over the top edge of the pan. Then use a knife to cut around the top to remove the extra pastry.

Fit a piece of aluminum foil shiny-side down loosely inside the *timballo;* then put in weights or dried beans to keep the pastry from rising as it bakes (see illustration at the bottom of page 239). Place the springform pan in the oven and bake for 1 hour.

By the time the pastry form is ready for the oven, the lid should have finished baking. Remove it from the oven and put it on a rack to cool.

Make the *balsamella,* using the ingredients in the quantities listed, according to the directions on page 62. Cover the saucepan and let rest until needed.

To make the filling with the squab and macaroni, rinse the squab well, discarding the livers, and set aside.

Coarsely chop the celery, onion, and carrot, then heat the olive oil in a large flameproof casserole. When the oil is warm, add the chopped ingredients and sauté for 15 minutes, stirring with a wooden spoon, until golden. Add the squab and sauté very slowly for 15 to 20 minutes, turning them over two or three times. Add the wine, season with salt and pepper, and let the wine evaporate very slowly (about 10 minutes).

Heat the broth in a saucepan. When the wine has evaporated, add the broth and simmer for about 25 minutes more.

Remove the casserole from the heat. Transfer the squab to a board, remove all the meat from the bones, and coarsely chop it. Coarsely chop the boiled ham as well, and set both meats aside.

Put a large quantity of cold water in a stockpot and set on the heat. When the water reaches the boiling point, add coarse salt to taste, then the macaroni and let cook for 11 to 12 minutes. Meanwhile, put the casserole with the sauce back over low heat.

Drain the macaroni in a colander, then transfer it to the casserole. Mix thoroughly with a wooden spoon. Add the squab meat, chopped ham, and *balsamella*. Stir while the sauce simmers.

Meanwhile, preheat the oven to 400 degrees.

Remove the casserole from the flame. Fill the *timballo,* still in the springform, with the contents of the casserole, top with the pats of butter, and sprinkle with Parmigiano and freshly grated nutmeg. Cover the *timballo* with its own lid and place in the preheated oven for 15 minutes, then remove from the oven and allow to cool for 5 minutes before opening the springform.

Transfer the *timballo* to a serving dish with its lid in place for presentation. Serve immediately, lifting the lid, using serving spoons to dish out each portion.

Timballo di tortellini

TORTELLINI IN A PASTRY DRUM

SERVES 6

*I*n this dish, *tortellini alla panna* (see page 204) are served in a pastry drum, made and baked as described on page 237.

MAKE the *timballo* first, then, when it is out of the oven and cooling, make the tortellini. The *timballo* may even be made as much as a day in advance and kept, but while the tortellini can be made up several hours in advance (to be cooked a few minutes longer if they dry out a bit), they must be cooked and combined with the *alla panna* sauce only immediately before they are poured into the pastry drum and served.

Rice
First Courses

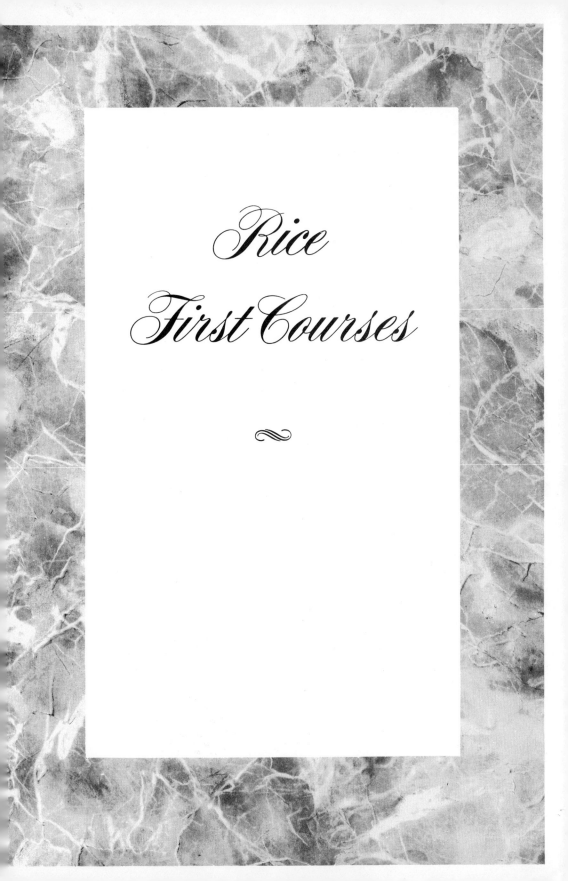

RISOTTI

*R*isotto is an entire category of first courses, based on a particular way of cooking rice, a way that as far as I know is unique to northern Italy. This area, and the Po valley in particular, produces a wide-grained rice that has a pearly white spot on it. It is especially suitable for *risotti,* because when cooked in that manner it remains al dente, firm and chewy. In making risotto it is worth the trouble to find the Po Valley rice, the Arborio type, generally found in Italian markets abroad as well as in "gourmet" shops, where you should ask for Italian Arborio rice.

The rice is not precooked in water at all, and no water as such is used in making the dish, so that nothing of the flavor of the rice is lost. The raw rice is sautéed first in hot butter or olive oil and seasonings until it is very hot. Then hot broth is added, little by little, while stirring, and the hot rice quickly absorbs the broth. More broth is added only after that previously put in has been absorbed. It is important to stir without stopping so that the rice does not stick or burn. Only enough hot broth is used to get the rice to that point of al dente firmness and chewiness. Then the risotto is done.

There are many kinds of *risotti.* We include eleven, the first being the simplest and most common treatment, *in bianco*—with the rice sautéed in butter and olive oil and a little onion, with Parmigiano added —the last being the marvelous *risotto di mare,* made with the broth of the *cacciucco* fish soup on page 308. The section ends with a rustic *timballo* of risotto, hearty enough for a second course.

Risotto in bianco

RISOTTO

SERVES 3

1 small white onion, cleaned
2 tablespoons olive oil
5 tablespoons (2½ ounces)
*   sweet butter*
1 cup raw rice, preferably
*   Italian Arborio*

2 cups meat or chicken broth,
*   preferably homemade (see*
*   page 126)*
Salt and freshly ground white
*   pepper to taste*
¼ cup freshly grated
*   Parmigiano*

CHOP the onion fine.

Put the olive oil and 4 tablespoons of the butter in a large casserole. Set over medium heat, and when the butter is melted, add the chopped onion and sauté until lightly golden (3 to 5 minutes). Meanwhile, heat the broth to boiling in a saucepan.

Place the rice in the casserole with the onion and sauté for 3 minutes, stirring constantly with a wooden spoon. Pour in ½ cup of the boiling broth and keep stirring very gently until the rice has incorporated all the broth (3 or 4 minutes). Season with salt and pepper. Then continue to add hot broth, little by little, stirring continuously until all the broth is absorbed and the rice is cooked (about 18 minutes in all). The rice should be al dente, not overcooked, and no liquid should be left unabsorbed.

Remove the casserole from the heat and add the remaining tablespoon of butter and all the Parmigiano. Mix thoroughly with a wooden spoon, then transfer the risotto into a tureen and serve.

Risotto in bianco con agliata

RISOTTO WITH GARLIC SAUCE

SERVES 3

*T*his risotto is prepared using the same ingredients and procedure as for *risotto in bianco* (see page 245). However, omit the Parmigiano and pour some *agliata* sauce, the ancient white garlic sauce (see page 91), over each portion at serving time.

Risotto con carciofi

RISOTTO WITH ARTICHOKES

SERVES 3

*T*he artichoke pieces are soaked in lemon, then sautéed together with garlic, prosciutto, and *pancetta*. After the risotto has been made, the artichoke and its seasoning are mixed in and Parmigiano is added.

1 large artichoke
1 lemon
1 large clove garlic, peeled
5 sprigs Italian parsley, leaves only
2 ounces prosciutto, in one piece
1 ounce pancetta *or prosciutto, in one piece*
1 small red onion, cleaned
3 tablespoons olive oil

Salt and freshly ground black pepper to taste
4 tablespoons (2 ounces) sweet butter
1 cup raw rice, preferably Italian Arborio
2 cups meat or chicken broth, preferably homemade
¼ cup freshly grated Parmigiano

PLACE the whole artichoke in a bowl of cold water with a lemon cut in half, for 30 minutes. Meanwhile, coarsely chop the garlic, parsley, prosciutto, and *pancetta* on a board; chop the onion separately and set it aside.

After the artichoke has soaked, remove the outer leaves and inside "choke" (see page 510). Cut the remainder in small pieces, using both body and stem, and place, along with the chopped ingredients, in a saucepan with the olive oil. Sauté very gently for 10 to 12 minutes, then taste for salt and pepper and simmer for 10 minutes more, until the artichoke pieces are soft, adding cold water if necessary. Remove the saucepan from the stove, cover, and let stand until needed.

Heat 2 tablespoons of the butter in a flameproof casserole. When the butter is completely melted, add the chopped onion and sauté slowly, stirring with a wooden spoon, until the onion is golden (about 10 minutes). Meanwhile, in another saucepan, heat the broth to boiling.

When the onion is golden and translucent add the rice and stir for 3 minutes. Pour in 1 cup of boiling broth, and keep stirring. Continue mixing and adding hot broth as needed until the rice is completely cooked (about 18 minutes in all). All the broth should be completely absorbed.

Remove the saucepan from the stove, add the artichoke pieces and remaining butter, and mix very well. Transfer the risotto to a serving dish, sprinkle with the Parmigiano, and serve immediately.

Risotto con funghi

RISOTTO WITH DRIED MUSHROOMS

SERVES 6

*W*hen this risotto is prepared, red wine is added before the broth. The imported dried *porcini* mushrooms are prepared by soaking them, then are added after the first cup of broth. Like all dishes depending on the flavor of the dried *porcini,* this is a memorable one.

2 ounces dried **porcini** *mushrooms*
1 medium red onion, cleaned
1 large clove garlic, peeled
10 sprigs Italian parsley, leaves only
6 tablespoons (3 ounces) sweet butter
1 tablespoon olive oil
⅓ cup dry red wine

4 cups chicken or meat broth, preferably homemade (see page 126)
2 cups raw rice, preferably Italian Arborio
Salt and freshly ground black pepper
¼ cup freshly grated Parmigiano

SOAK the dried mushrooms in a small bowl of lukewarm water for 20 minutes. Meanwhile, chop the onion, garlic, and parsley fine. Drain the mushrooms and rinse them, removing the sand attached to the stems. (Mushroom water is not used in this recipe. See Mushrooms, page 24.)

Put 4 tablespoons of the butter and the oil in a flameproof casserole and set over medium heat. When the butter is melted, add the chopped ingredients and sauté very gently until golden (about 12 to 14 minutes), then add the wine and let it evaporate slowly (3 or 4 minutes). Meanwhile, heat the broth to boiling in a saucepan.

Place the rice in the casserole and sauté for 3 minutes, stirring constantly with a wooden spoon. Add 1 cup of boiling broth and keep stirring. Season with salt and pepper.

When the first cup of broth is completely incorporated (about 2 or 3 minutes), add the mushrooms and, still stirring constantly, add hot broth as needed until the rice is completely cooked (about 18 minutes in all). All the broth should be completely absorbed.

Remove the casserole from the heat. Add the remaining butter and Parmigiano and mix thoroughly, then transfer the risotto to a tureen and serve immediately.

Risotto con salsicce

RISOTTO WITH SAUSAGES

SERVES 3

2 Italian sweet sausages without fennel seeds or 6 ounces ground pork
1 medium red onion, cleaned
6 tablespoons (3 ounces) sweet butter
2 tablespoons olive oil

1 cup raw rice, preferably Italian Arborio
2 cups meat or chicken broth, preferably homemade
1/4 cup freshly grated Parmigiano
Salt and freshly ground black pepper to taste

REMOVE the skin from the sausage and cut it into small pieces; coarsely chop the onion.

Heat 4 tablespoons butter and olive oil in a flameproof casserole, then add the sausage pieces and chopped onion and sauté very gently until golden, stirring every so often. Meanwhile, heat the broth to boiling in a saucepan.

When the contents of the casserole are golden, add the rice and stir constantly for 3 minutes. Add 1 cup of boiling broth, still stirring constantly. Keep stirring for about 18 minutes in all, adding broth as needed; by then the rice should be al dente and all the broth absorbed. Taste for salt and pepper.

Remove the casserole from the heat, add the remaining butter and grated Parmigiano, and mix thoroughly. Serve immediately.

Risotto agli spinaci

RISOTTO WITH SPINACH

SERVES 6 TO 8

*Y*ou would expect that one of the Florentine versions of risotto would be with spinach. And those few Tuscan dishes which use cream really emphasize that ingredient; you don't find a casual tablespoon of cream added to many other ingredients in this *cucina.* Here, heavy cream is added as the final liquid after the chicken broth and is highlighted by the use of butter and Parmigiano. One may eat this delicious creamy spinach risotto as is, or give it a fresh summery touch by adding diced fresh tomatoes and fresh mint. The summer version is even more special. Try it both ways.

1 pound fresh spinach, leaves only

Coarse-grained salt

1 tablespoon olive oil

4 tablespoon (2 ounces) sweet butter

Salt and freshly ground black pepper to taste

Pinch of freshly grated nutmeg

2 cups raw rice, preferably Italian Arborio

2½ cups chicken broth, preferably homemade

¾ cup heavy cream

½ cup freshly grated Parmigiano

PLUS (OPTIONAL)

1 pound fresh ripe tomatoes

2 tablespoons olive oil

Salt and freshly ground black pepper

10 leaves fresh mint

SOAK the spinach in a bowl of cold water for a half hour. Meanwhile bring a large stockpot of cold water to a boil, add coarse salt to taste, then the spinach, and boil for 10 minutes. Drain the spinach and cool it under cold running water, but do not squeeze it. Pass the spinach through a food mill, using the disc with the smallest holes, into a small crockery or glass bowl.

Heat the oil and 1 tablespoon of the butter in a skillet over medium heat, and when the butter is melted, add the pureed spinach and sauté for 2 minutes, mixing with a wooden spoon. Season with salt, pepper, and nutmeg. Transfer the sautéed spinach to a crockery bowl and let stand until needed.

Melt the remaining butter in a heavy casserole over medium heat and when the butter is completely melted, add the rice and sauté for 4 minutes, stirring constantly with a wooden spoon. Then add spinach. Meanwhile heat the broth to a boil in a separate pan. Start adding the hot broth, ¼ cup at a time, stirring constantly. Do not add more broth until that previously added has been completely absorbed. When all the broth has been incorporated, start adding the cold heavy cream, a little at a time, stirring constantly. Taste for salt and pepper. When all the liquid has been incorporated (18 minutes in all), the rice should be cooked but still al dente. Remove the casserole from the heat, add Parmigiano, stir very well, transfer to a warmed serving dish, and serve immediately.

If the risotto is served with tomatoes, coarsely chop them on a board, transfer to a crockery bowl, adding oil, salt, and pepper to taste, and let rest, covered, in the refrigerator for a half hour before using. When the risotto is ready to be served, arrange the marinated tomatoes on top and sprinkle the mint leaves all over.

Risotto alla toscana

RISOTTO WITH MEAT SAUCE

SERVES 6

A meat sauce is prepared with chopped beef, coarsely chopped chicken livers, red wine, a little tomato, and *odori* (aromatic vegetables). After the rice is sautéed, a little sauce is stirred in before the broth is added. After the risotto is cooked, the rest of the sauce is served with it, to be added to the individual servings.

FOR THE SAUCE

½ small red onion, cleaned
1 small celery rib
1 small clove garlic, peeled
1 carrot, scraped
10 sprigs Italian parsley, leaves only
2 tablespoons (1 ounce) sweet butter
¼ cup olive oil

½ pound ground beef
Salt and freshly ground black pepper to taste
½ cup dry red wine
1 cup canned tomatoes, preferably imported Italian, drained
2 or 3 chicken livers

FOR THE RISOTTO

½ small red onion, cleaned
4 tablespoons (2 ounces) sweet butter
2 tablespoons olive oil
2 cups raw rice, preferably Italian Arborio

4 cups chicken or meat broth, preferably homemade
½ cup freshly grated Parmigiano

MAKE the sauce first. Finely chop the onion, celery, garlic, carrot, and parsley all together. Heat the butter and oil in a saucepan, and when the butter is melted put in the chopped *odori* and sauté until lightly golden (about 15 minutes), stirring constantly with a wooden spoon. Add the ground meat and sauté for 10 minutes more, then season with salt and pepper.

Add the wine and let evaporate slowly (about 10 minutes), then pass the tomatoes through a food mill, using the disc with the smallest holes, into the saucepan and simmer for 25 minutes more.

Coarsely chop the chicken livers and place in the saucepan. Cook for 5 minutes, then remove the saucepan from the heat and let rest while you start the risotto.

Chop the onion coarsely.

Put the butter and oil in a flameproof casserole and set over medium heat.

When the butter is melted, add the chopped onion and sauté very gently until golden (about 10 minutes). Meanwhile, heat the broth to boiling in a saucepan.

Add the rice to the casserole and sauté for 3 minutes, stirring constantly, then add ½ cup of sauce to the casserole and stir for 2 minutes more. Add 1 cup of boiling broth, stirring with a wooden spoon. Keep stirring and adding broth as needed; in about 18 minutes all the broth should be absorbed and the rice properly cooked al dente.

Remove the casserole from the stove and transfer the risotto to a serving dish. Place the remaining sauce all around the rice in a ring, then sprinkle with the Parmigiano and serve immediately.

Risotto con gamberetti in bianco

RISOTTO WITH SHRIMP

SERVES 3

*T*he shrimps are sautéed in a saucepan with the olive oil and white wine. Then the risotto is prepared and 5 minutes before it is finished cooking, the shrimp are added to the rice. Fish broth may be used instead of meat or chicken broth in this dish, but it is not essential.

1 large clove garlic, peeled
10 sprigs Italian parsley, leaves
*   only*
1/2 pound small shrimp,
*   unshelled*
Coarse-grained salt
5 tablespoons olive oil
Salt and freshly ground black
*   pepper to taste*
1/2 cup dry white wine

1/2 small white onion, cleaned
3 tablespoons (1 1/2 ounces)
*   sweet butter*
1 cup raw rice, preferably
*   Italian Arborio*
1 1/2 cups of fish, meat, or
*   chicken broth,*
*   approximately, preferably*
*   homemade*

CHOP the garlic fine, and chop the parsley coarsely; shell the shrimp and place them in a bowl of cold water with a little coarse salt added.

Heat 3 tablespoons of the olive oil in a saucepan, and when it is warm, add the garlic and parsley and sauté very lightly for about 4 minutes. Add the shrimp, season with salt and pepper, and stir thoroughly with a wooden spoon. Sauté for 2 minutes longer.

Pour the wine into the saucepan and let it evaporate over high heat for 1 minute, then remove the saucepan from the heat and transfer the shrimp to a small bowl, leaving the liquid in the saucepan. Cover the bowl. Add enough broth to the saucepan to have 2 cups of liquid. Set aside while you start the risotto.

Chop the onion fine.

Heat 2 tablespoons of the butter and the remaining 2 tablespoons of olive oil in a flameproof casserole. When the butter is melted, add the chopped onion and sauté very gently until golden (about 10 minutes). Meanwhile, heat the liquid in the saucepan.

When onion is golden, add the rice and stir constantly for about 3 minutes with a wooden spoon. Add ½ cup of boiling broth to the casserole and keep stirring very gently until the rice has incorporated all the broth (3 or 4 minutes). Taste for salt and pepper, then continue to add broth, little by little, stirring continuously, until all the broth is absorbed and the rice is al dente (about 18 minutes in all).

Just 2 minutes before the rice is completely cooked, add the shrimp to the casserole. Remove the casserole from the flame, add the remaining butter, and mix thoroughly. Transfer the risotto to a serving dish and serve immediately.

Risotto alla marinara

RISOTTO WITH FISH BROTH

SERVES 3

*F*ish broth is essential to this dish. The procedure is basically the same as for *in bianco* (see page 245), but after the onions are sautéed, a little tomato paste is mixed in before the raw rice is added. This is a good first course for a fish dinner.

2 cups broth left over from poaching a fish (see page 284)
1 small red onion, cleaned
2 tablespoons olive oil
2 tablespoons (1 ounce) sweet butter

2 tablespoons tomato paste, preferably imported Italian
1 cup raw rice, preferably Italian Arborio
Salt and freshly ground black pepper to taste

STRAIN the poaching broth; chop the onion fine.

Heat the oil and 1 tablespoon of the butter in a flameproof casserole. When the butter is melted, add the chopped onion and sauté gently until lightly golden. Meanwhile, heat the broth to boiling in a saucepan.

Add the tomato paste to the casserole and stir thoroughly until it is completely incorporated. Add the rice and sauté for 3 minutes, stirring constantly with wooden spoon, then pour in ½ cup of the boiling broth and keep stirring very gently until the rice has absorbed all the broth (about 3 minutes). Taste for salt and pepper, then continue to add hot broth, little by little, stirring continuously until all the broth is absorbed and the rice is al dente (about 18 minutes in all).

Remove the casserole from the flame, add the remaining butter, and mix thoroughly. Transfer the risotto to a serving dish and serve immediately.

Risotto di mare

RISOTTO WITH CACCIUCCO BROTH

SERVES 3

*I*t is difficult to decide which is more delicious, the *cacciucco* itself or the risotto made with its broth. It is good to save some little morsels of fish and shellfish from the *cacciucco* along with the broth, to mix in at the last moment in order to make an even more interesting texture.

1 small red onion, cleaned
2 tablespoons olive oil
2 tablespoons (1 ounce) sweet
  butter
2 cups broth left over from
  cacciucco *(see page 308)*

1 cup raw rice, preferably
  Italian Arborio
Salt and freshly ground black
  pepper to taste

CHOP the onion fine. Heat the olive oil and 1 tablespoon of the butter in a flameproof casserole. When the butter is melted, add the chopped onion and sauté gently until lightly golden. Meanwhile, heat the broth to boiling in a saucepan.

Add the rice to the casserole with the onion and sauté for 3 minutes, stirring continuously with a wooden spoon. Pour in ½ cup of the boiling broth and keep stirring very gently until the rice has incorporated all the broth (3 or 4 minutes). Taste for salt and pepper (generally no salt or pepper are necessary because the broth left over from *cacciucco* is very spicy), then continue to add hot broth, little by little, stirring continuously until all the broth is absorbed and the rice is al dente (about 18 minutes in all).

Remove the casserole from heat, add the remaining butter, and mix thoroughly with a wooden spoon. Transfer the risotto to a serving dish. Place any pieces of fish left over from *cacciucco* over the risotto and serve immediately.

Risotto ai fagioli con l'occhio

RISOTTO WITH BLACK-EYED PEAS FROM TUSCANY

SERVES 6 TO 8

*T*he rice and beans combination is rare in Italian cooking, pasta with beans holding such a beloved place in the repertory. Barley and beans are savored in Friuli. It is black-eyed peas which are singled out for combination with risotto and it is in bean-eating Tuscany where one finds it. Black-eyed peas were taken from Africa to the Americas, where they became an intrinsic part of the southern U.S. diet. An Eastern Hemisphere bean, in Europe, it was the Tuscans who most enthusiastically adopted them as an alternative to cannellini and especially for this dish. Thyme is the dominant herb flavoring.

TO COOK THE BLACK-EYED PEAS

1 cup dried black-eyed peas
Coarse-grained salt
2 tablespoons olive oil
1 large clove garlic, peeled but left whole

1 medium fresh tomato, skinned and seeded or 2 canned tomatoes, preferably imported Italian, seeded
1 teaspoon dried thyme
Salt and freshly ground black pepper

FOR THE RISOTTO

2 large cloves garlic, peeled
1 teaspoon dried thyme
5 tablespoons olive oil
2 cups raw rice, preferably Italian Arborio

4 cups chicken or beef broth, preferably homemade
Salt and freshly ground black pepper

PLUS

6 to 8 teaspoons olive oil

OPTIONAL

6 to 8 tablespoons freshly grated Parmigiano

SOAK the black-eyed peas in a bowl of cold water overnight. Next morning bring a large pot with 2 quarts of cold water to a boil over medium heat, then add coarse salt to taste. Drain the black-eyed peas, rinse them under cold running water, and add them to pot along with the olive oil, garlic, tomato, and thyme. Cover and let simmer until the beans are cooked but still firm (from 45 minutes to 1 hour, depending on the dryness). When ready, taste for salt and pepper. Then drain the black-eyed peas, discarding the garlic, and put them in a crockery or glass bowl to let stand, covered, until needed.

Prepare the risotto. Finely chop garlic and thyme together on board. Place a heavy casserole, preferably of terra-cotta, over low heat with the oil and when oil is warm, add the chopped ingredients and sauté for 1 minute. Add the rice and sauté for 4 minutes, continuously stirring with a wooden spoon. Meanwhile bring the broth to a boil over medium heat. When the rice is ready, start adding the broth, ½ cup at a time, continuously stirring with a wooden spoon and not adding additional broth until the previous half cup has been completely absorbed by the rice. When 3 cups of the broth have been incorporated, taste for salt and pepper and add the cooked black-eyed peas. Finish the risotto by adding the remaining cup of broth little by little, stirring constantly until all the broth is absorbed and the rice is al dente (about 18 minutes in all). Transfer it to a warmed serving dish. Pour 1 teaspoon of oil and tablespoon of optional cheese over each serving.

Timballo di riso (Bomba con salsicce)

RICE TIMBALLO STUFFED WITH SAUSAGES

SERVES 6

*M*olded to the shape of a drum, this rustic dish from the Apennine Mountains is called a *timballo,* though the outside of the drum is not of pastry. It is, rather, shaped in the mold from half-cooked rice. The stuffing is of sausage pieces, dried wild mushrooms, and seasoning. The whole is then covered with homemade bread crumbs, and when baked acquires a crisp outer crust. A gastronomic treat that is also useful as a hearty second dish, it is served hot.

FOR THE CRUST

3 cups raw rice, preferably Italian Arborio

Coarse-grained salt

3 extra-large eggs

3 tablespoons freshly grated Parmigiano

Salt and freshly ground black pepper to taste

Pinch of freshly grated nutmeg

½ cup bread crumbs, preferably homemade (see page 58)

FOR THE FILLING

2 ounces dried **porcini** *mushrooms*

1 medium red onion, cleaned

2 tablespoons olive oil

1 teaspoon butter

6 Italian sweet sausages, without fennel seeds or 18 ounces ground pork

1½ pounds ripe fresh tomatoes or 1½ pounds canned tomatoes, preferably imported Italian, drained

1 cup meat or chicken broth, preferably homemade

Salt and freshly ground black pepper to taste

PREPARE the crust first.

Put the rice in a saucepan with a large quantity of cold water and a pinch of coarse salt. Set the saucepan over high heat and stir the rice with a wooden spoon until the water reaches the boiling point. When the rice is half cooked (about 8 minutes), remove the saucepan from the heat and drain the rice. Run cold water over it to cool it completely, then drain again and put it in a bowl. Add the eggs, Parmigiano, salt, pepper, and nutmeg and stir well until completely combined. Set aside while you prepare the filling.

Soak the dried mushrooms in lukewarm water for 30 minutes. Meanwhile, chop the onion coarsely. Heat the olive oil and the butter in a saucepan. When they are hot, add the chopped onion and sauté gently for 10 to 12 minutes.

Remove the skin from the sausages and cut them into 5 or 6 pieces each. When the onion is golden, add the sausage pieces and sauté for 10 to 15 minutes. If using fresh tomatoes, cut them into pieces, then pass the fresh or canned tomatoes through a food mill, using the disc with the smallest holes, into a bowl. Add them to the pan and simmer very slowly for 15 minutes more. Add the broth, taste for salt and pepper, and let cook slowly, until the broth has completely evaporated and the mixture is thick and homogenous (about 30 minutes).

Meanwhile, drain the mushrooms, saving the soaking liquid. Clean the mushrooms, removing all the sand attached to the stems and clean the soaking water by passing it through different layers of paper towels into a small bowl. Add the soaked mushrooms and 3 or 4 tablespoons of the soaking water. Let cook until the water has evaporated, then remove the saucepan from the heat and transfer the filling mixture to another bowl to cool (about 30 minutes).

When cool, transfer 2 or 3 tablespoons of liquid from the filling mixture to the bowl with the rice.

When you are ready to assemble the *timballo,* preheat the oven to 400 degrees; butter well the bottom and sides of a 10-inch diameter glass casserole and line it with some of the bread crumbs.

Stir the rice very well once more and cover the bottom and sides of the prepared mold with three-quarters of it. Pour the filling mixture sauce into the center, then make a layer on top with the rest of the rice. Sprinkle the remaining bread crumbs over, then place the casserole in the preheated oven and bake for 25 to 30 minutes.

Remove from the oven and let cool for 15 minutes, then unmold on a serving dish. The rice should form a uniform outer crust, in one piece, to resemble a *timballo.* Serve hot, slicing it like a cake.

Miscellaneous First Courses

~

Batuffoli alla livornese

POLENTA WITH MEAT SAUCE, LIVORNO STYLE

SERVES 10 TO 12

*I*n this version, the prepared polenta is alternated in layers with a rich beef sauce and baked. The whole piece of meat is sautéed before being chopped and is combined with *pancetta, odori,* wine, wild mushrooms, and tomato paste or concentrate, not tomatoes. Concentrate, that much maligned ingredient, has its own flavor and is legitimately used in some recipes. It should not, of course, be used as a substitute for tomatoes and the quality of the ingredient should be high, imported Italian or homemade (See *Bugialli on Pasta,* page 349).

Polenta, in general, is served for very rustic dinners. Alternating layers of polenta and sauce—as in this polenta dish which can be cut into neat pieces—it is served for a less rustic repast.

FOR THE SAUCE

½ ounce dried **porcini** *mushrooms*

2 cups lukewarm water

4 ounces **pancetta** *or prosciutto, in one piece*

4 tablespoons olive oil

1 medium red onion, cleaned

1 stalk celery

1 medium carrot, scraped

1 small clove garlic, peeled

1 pound beef, in one piece

1 cup dry white wine

4 tablespoons tomato paste, preferably imported Italian

1 cup lukewarm chicken or beef broth, preferably homemade (see page 126)

Salt and freshly ground black pepper to taste

Pinch of freshly grated nutmeg

FOR THE POLENTA

3 quarts chicken or beef broth, preferably homemade (see page 126)

1 pound coarse Italian yellow corn meal

TO SERVE

1 cup freshly grated Parmigiano

2 tablespoons (1 ounce) sweet butter, cut into small pieces

PREPARE the sauce first. Soak the mushrooms in a bowl with the 2 cups of water for a half hour. Cut the *pancetta* into tiny pieces, then place a medium-sized heavy casserole with the oil over medium heat and when the oil is warm, add the *pancetta* and sauté for 5 minutes, until the pieces are very crisp. Meanwhile finely chop onion, celery, carrot, and garlic on board, add them to casserole and sauté for 10 minutes more, stirring every so often with a wooden spoon. Drain mushrooms, saving the soaking water, and clean the mushrooms very well, being sure that no sand remains attached to the stems. Strain the mushroom water, passing it through several layers of paper towels, into a small bowl. Put the whole piece of meat in the casserole and sauté for 10 minutes, turning several times, until lightly golden on all sides. Add wine and let it evaporate for 5 minutes, then dissolve the tomato paste in the lukewarm broth, add it to casserole, season with salt, pepper, and nutmeg and let simmer for 20 minutes. Transfer the meat to a board, finely chop it together with the mushrooms, add to casserole with 1 cup of the mushroom water and simmer for 25 minutes more.

Meanwhile heat the broth for the polenta in a large pot over medium heat and when broth comes to a boil, start pouring in the corn meal in a very slow stream, stirring continuously with a flat wooden spoon. Be sure to pour slowly and steadily and to keep stirring, or the polenta will easily become very lumpy. Stir slowly, without stopping, for 50 minutes from the moment the last of the corn meal was added to the pot.

Lightly butter a large ovenproof casserole and preheat oven to 375 degrees. Ladle one fourth of the polenta into the prepared casserole, then spoon on one fourth of the sauce and of the Parmigiano. Make 3 more layers of polenta, sauce, and Parmigiano. The top layer will be of sauce and cheese. Arrange the butter pieces over the top and bake for 20 minutes. Remove from oven, let rest for a few minutes, and serve.

Gnocchi di farina gialla

CORN MEAL GNOCCHI

SERVES 6 TO 8

*T*he corn meal is prepared as though you were going to make polenta. It is then put in individual terra-cotta bowls in layers, alternating with layers of *sugo di carne* (meat sauce), with Parmigiano sprinkled on each layer of sauce. The polenta is not cut into discs nor into layers, but is ladled into the bowls while still hot. The dish is allowed to rest after all the layers are made, to permit the ingredients to amalgamate into a single delicious whole.

Sugo di carne *(see page 86)*

FOR THE GNOCCHI

¾ pound coarse Italian yellow corn meal

8 cups cold water

2 teaspoons salt

1 cup freshly grated Parmigiano

MAKE the sauce, then set aside, covered, until needed. Prepare the *gnocchi,* with the quantities listed above, according to the directions on page 476, up to and including the cooking and stirring for 35 minutes. (More water is added to the corn meal in this recipe than in that for polenta as the cooked *farina gialla* should be less thick for *gnocchi* than for polenta.) Keep it over low heat while you prepare 6 or 8 small terra-cotta bowls with handles.

Put a tablespoon of meat sauce in each individual bowl, then make a layer of *gnocchi,* using about ¼ cup, or half a ladleful, in each bowl. Sprinkle with some more sauce and some of the grated Parmigiano.

Make another layer of *gnocchi* and again add sauce and Parmigiano. Continue this alternation of layers until you have used everything up. The top layer should be meat sauce and Parmigiano. Cover each terra-cotta bowl with its lid, if it has one, or aluminum foil and let rest for about 15 minutes, then serve. (If you used aluminum foil to cover the bowls, remove before serving.)

Pomodori ripieni

STUFFED TOMATOES

SERVES 6

*T*he tomatoes are stuffed and baked with a very light touch. The stuffing is basically tomato itself, with chopped garlic and basil, and just a little rice. The tomatoes are covered with their own "lids" and baked in a dish containing tomato-flavored liquid, olive oil, and more basil. Served warm or cold, they make a good opener or addition to a buffet, and they have a refreshing taste in which everything contributes to bring out the flavor of the tomato itself.

6 large, ripe tomatoes and 1 small, very ripe tomato
10 large leaves fresh basil
1 large clove garlic, peeled
6 heaping tablespoons raw rice, preferably Italian Arborio

5 tablespoons olive oil
1 cup cold water
2 tablespoons tomato paste, preferably imported Italian
Salt and freshly ground black pepper to taste

SOAK all the tomatoes in cold water for 10 minutes, then drain and slice off the tops of the 6 large tomatoes. Put the tops aside to be used later. Using a melon-ball cutter, empty the seeds and juice of the tomatoes into a large bowl without breaking up the inside pulp. Strain the juice into another bowl and save seeds in a strainer. Put the tomatoes into a 13½ × 8¾-inch glass baking dish.

Pass the small tomato through a food mill using the disc with the smallest holes, into the bowl containing the juice of other tomatoes. Chop the garlic and 6 of the basil leaves fine and add them to the bowl, then put in the rice and season with salt and pepper.

Fill each tomato two-thirds full with the stuffing mixture. Sprinkle ½ teaspoon of the olive oil on top of the stuffing in each tomato, then cover each with its top.

Preheat the oven to 375 degrees.

Pass the 1 cup of water through the seeds left in strainer into a bowl. Then mix in the tomato paste, remaining 2 tablespoons olive oil,

(continued)

Pomodori ripieni *(continued)*

salt, pepper, and the remaining 4 basil leaves. Pour into the baking dish with the tomatoes. If the liquid does not reach one-third the height of the tomatoes, add enough water to do so.

Bake in the preheated oven for about 40 minutes, then remove the dish from the oven and transfer the tomatoes very carefully to a serving dish. Allow to cool 10 to 15 minutes before serving; you may also serve the tomatoes cold.

Ravioli nudi

NAKED RAVIOLI OR RAVIOLI ALLA FIORENTINA

SERVES 8

*R*avioli nudi, one of the prides of the city on the Arno, are never called "spinach *gnocchi*" there—for that is another dish made in other places. The recipe is a simple, classic one, with enough egg yolks and cheese to bind together the chopped spinach and ricotta mixture. If properly done, it should not be necessary to add flour to hold the mixture together; this makes the "ravioli" too tough. Though the standards for making this dish are very high in its native city, or perhaps because of it, you will never find the dish on the menu of a restaurant. Perhaps because of the confusion with the above-mentioned *gnocchi*, one sees some very strange recipes for this dish in cookbooks.

The *nudi* part of the name refers to the fact that the filling is not covered with pasta.

3 pounds fresh spinach
Coarse-grained salt
15 ounces ricotta, well drained
5 extra-large egg yolks
3 cups freshly grated
  Parmigiano
Salt and freshly ground black
  pepper to taste

½ teaspoon freshly grated
  nutmeg
2 cups unbleached all-purpose
  flour
8 tablespoons (4 ounces) sweet
  butter

RINSE the spinach very well and cut off the large stems. Place a stockpot containing a large quantity of cold water on the heat. When the water boils, add coarse salt to taste, then the spinach and cook for about 10 minutes, then drain and cool under cold running water. Squeeze dry.

Chop the spinach very fine, then place in a bowl, along with the ricotta, egg yolks, 2 cups of the Parmigiano, salt, pepper, and nutmeg. Mix together with a wooden spoon until thoroughly combined. Refill the stockpot with a large quantity of cold water and set on the heat.

While the water is heating, place a sheet of wax paper on the table and spread the flour over. Take 1 tablespoon of the mixture from the bowl and roll it on the floured foil surface into a little ball. Be sure the ball is uniformly compact, with no empty spaces inside; the outside should be uniformly floured.

When the water is boiling, add coarse salt to taste, then drop this first ball in, to test it. It should retain its shape and rise to the top, cooked, after a minute or two. (If it falls apart, you have allowed too much liquid to remain in the spinach. To save the dish, you can add 2 tablespoons of flour to the mixture. However, this is a compromise and should not be done regularly; even that little flour will make the taste inauthentic.) After testing, as described above, continue to make ravioli, rolling them in flour, until all the contents of the bowl have been used up.

Melt the butter and pour into a serving dish; place the serving dish close to the stockpot.

Drop the ravioli into the boiling water, 5 or 6 at a time, and as they rise to the surface, remove them with a strainer-skimmer, transferring them directly onto the serving dish. They should be placed in one layer, not one on top of another.

When all the ravioli are on the serving dish, sprinkle with the remaining Parmigiano and serve immediately.

Gnocchi di pesce

FISH GNOCCHI

SERVES 6

A recipe of Jarro, the famous Florentine gastronome of the turn of the century. This was the period when Florence had emerged from its life as the charming capital of the Grand Duchy of Tuscany to become briefly the capital, and then the artistic and intellectual center, of the kingdom of Italy. The cafés of the Piazza Vittorio Emanuele* were ablaze with the great literary artistic groups of their day. The international social set, including many of the reigning monarchs, spent the winter season in Rome and summered in their villas in the hills outside of Florence, Henry James's American social set joining in. Bernard Berenson in his villa entertained everyone from Bertrand Russell to the King of Sweden and, in his last days, Harry Truman. This was the period when Jarro was one of the arbiters of Florentine gastronomy.

The chopped raw fish, all light in flavor, are held together with egg yolks and cheese and flavored with other ingredients. They are baked, much in the manner of *gnocchi di semolino*. A delicious and unusual first dish to begin a fish dinner.

FOR THE FISH MIXTURE

2 pounds of raw fish, a combination of 2 or more light-flavored fleshy fish (pike, striped bass, mullet, red snapper, whiting)

2 extra-large eggs, separated, plus 2 extra-large egg yolks

1 cup milk

½ cup unbleached all-purpose flour

6 tablespoons (3 ounces) sweet butter

Salt and freshly ground black pepper to taste

4 tablespoons freshly grated Parmigiano

Freshly grated nutmeg to taste

*Now Piazza della Repubblica.

270

PLUS

1 tablespoon olive oil   *3 tablespoons freshly grated*
2 tablespoons (1 ounce) sweet   *Parmigiano*
    butter

REMOVE bones, skin, and heads from all the fish, so that only filleted meat remains (about 1½ pounds). Chop the fish very fine, until homogenous and soft. Put into a large bowl.

Use a copper bowl and wire whisk to beat the egg whites until stiff. Add the egg yolks to the fish, and when they are thoroughly incorporated, fold in the beaten egg whites.

Put the fish mixture into a saucepan over low heat and begin stirring gently with a wooden spoon. When the fish mixture begins to bubble, add the milk and then the flour, little by little. When the flour is all incorporated and the mixture is smooth, add the 6 tablespoons of butter, salt, and pepper. Keep stirring for 10 to 12 minutes more, to allow the flour to cook.

Remove from the heat and add the 4 tablespoons of the Parmigiano and the nutmeg. Season with additional salt and pepper.

Preheat the oven to 375 degrees.

Use the 1 tablespoon of oil to oil a marble or formica surface. Place the contents of the pan upon the oiled surface. With a wet spatula, spread out uniformly to a thickness of ½ inch. Let rest until cool, then cut into round shapes with a 2-inch cookie cutter.

With the 2 tablespoons butter, butter a 13½ × 8¾-inch glass baking dish. Place the discs in it, in a single layer, then place in the preheated oven for about 15 minutes.

Remove from the oven, sprinkle with the 3 tablespoons Parmigiano, and serve hot.

Ravioli nudi di pesce

NAKED FISH RAVIOLI

SERVES 6

*T*he chopped fish is held together like *ravioli nudi* (see below), with egg yolks and cheese, but also with a little flour. They are poached like their namesake. Another good fish first course.

FOR THE FISH MIXTURE (see page 270)

1 extra-large egg yolk
6 tablespoons freshly grated
 Parmigiano
2 heaping tablespoons
 unbleached all-purpose
 flour, plus ½ cup for
 coating

2 tablespoons (1 ounce) sweet
 butter
Coarse-grained salt

PREPARE and cook the fish mixture, up to and including the addition of the Parmigiano, salt, and pepper.

Place the contents of the saucepan in a bowl and let rest until cool. Then add the egg yolk, 2 tablespoons of the above Parmigiano, and 2 tablespoons of the above flour. Mix very well until all these ingredients are incorporated, then make little balls 1 inch in diameter and coat them very gently with additional flour.

Meanwhile, put a stockpot containing abundant cold water on the heat; melt the butter in another saucepan and pour over the bottom of a serving dish.

When the water boils, add coarse salt to taste, then drop in the little fish balls, one at a time. In about 30 seconds they will rise to the surface of the water; let them cook for 1 minute more and then, with a slotted spoon, remove them from the water and place in the buttered serving dish. Sprinkle the remaining 4 tablespoons Parmigiano over them and serve hot.

Pappa al pomodoro

BREAD SOUP

SERVES 4 TO 6

*P*erhaps another descendant of the ancient Roman *puls,* but made with bread instead of corn meal. Though similar dishes exist in other parts of Italy, it is the Florentine version that is the most famous and that is considered one of the most characteristic dishes of that town, for simple home dinners or in *trattorie.* As with *panzanella* (see page 113), it is most important that the bread not be soggy. It should be sufficiently old, several days at least, rather hard, and if possible dark rather than light. The quantities of liquid given are just enough to produce the right texture. The broth, tomatoes, olive oil, basil, and garlic provide the marvelous flavor.

Another dish that makes it even more worthwhile to take the trouble to make the Tuscan bread.

3 large cloves garlic, peeled
½ cup olive oil
Pinch of hot red pepper flakes
1 pound very ripe fresh
  tomatoes or 1 pound canned
  tomatoes, preferably
  imported Italian, drained
  and seeded
1 pound Tuscan bread, white
  (see page 39) or dark (see
  page 43), several days old

3 cups hot chicken or meat
  broth, preferably homemade
  (see page 126)
Salt and freshly ground black
  pepper
5 leaves basil, fresh or preserved
  in salt (see page 18)

CHOP the garlic coarsely, then place in a stockpot, preferably terra-cotta, along with ¼ cup of the olive oil and the pepper flakes. Sauté very gently for 10 to 12 minutes.

If fresh tomatoes are used, blanch them in salted boiling water, then cut them into 3 or 4 pieces, remove the seeds, then add to the pot. Simmer for 15 minutes.

(continued)

Cut the bread into small pieces and add to the pot, along with the broth, salt, black pepper, and whole basil leaves. Stir very well and simmer for 15 minutes longer, then remove from the heat, cover, and let rest for 1 to 2 hours.

When ready to serve, stir very well to break up all the bread pieces and place in individual soup bowls. At the table, sprinkle 1 teaspoon of the remaining olive oil on each serving, and grind some fresh black pepper into each bowl.

NOTE: Though considered a soup, the consistency of *pappa* is not liquid at all. It may be eaten lukewarm or cold, or reheated and hot the following day. Do not add any grated cheese.

Gnocchi di semolino

SEMOLINA GNOCCHI

SERVES 4

*G*nocchi of semolina or *alla romana*. First the milk is boiled and some butter and flavorings added. The semolina flour must be added slowly and carefully in a steady stream so that lumps do not form, and it must be stirred without stopping while cooking for the same reason.

When the semolina is cooked and cooled, the egg yolks and Parmigiano are added. The mixture is spread out, cut into discs and arranged in one or more layers for baking. (Occasionally, with the same proportions, the cooled mixture becomes too soft and does not hold its shape. If this happens, reduce the amount of butter a little the next time.)

5 cups milk
8 tablespoons (4 ounces) sweet
  butter
Salt, freshly ground black
  pepper, and freshly grated
  nutmeg to taste

1 1/4 cups very fine semolina
  flour
4 extra-large egg yolks
1 3/4 cups freshly grated
  Parmigiano

RESERVE 2 tablespoons of milk; pour the rest into a flameproof casserole. Heat the milk. The moment before it boils, add 4 tablespoons of the butter and a pinch each of salt, pepper, and nutmeg. Then add the semolina, pouring in a continuous slow stream, at the same time mixing steadily with a wooden spoon. As soon as all the semolina is in the casserole, quickly raise the heat so the contents will reach the boiling point almost immediately. (The longer it takes to reach the boiling point, the more possibility there is for lumps to form.) Lower the heat and allow the mixture to boil slowly for 15 to 20 minutes, stirring continuously, until smooth and homogenous. Remove from the heat and let cool for 10 minutes.

Dilute the egg yolks with the 2 tablespoons cold milk, mixing with a wooden spoon. Add this to the semolina mixture, then add half the Parmigiano. Continue to stir, being careful to keep the mixture from sticking to the bottom and sides of the pan.

Oil a marble or formica surface. Pour the semolina mixture over this surface, and spread it out with a metal spatula wet with warm water to make a sheet about ½ inch thick. Let the sheet rest for 1½ hours.

Meanwhile, melt the remaining butter in a saucepan; preheat the over to 400 degrees.

Cut the semolina mixture into discs with a 2-inch round cookie cutter. Make a layer of semolina discs in a buttered 13½ × 8¾-inch glass baking dish. Cover this layer with some of the melted butter and some of the remaining grated Parmigiano. Make additional layers of semolina discs, covering each layer with butter and Parmigiano until you get to the final semolina layer. Leave this layer without butter or cheese. (A top layer of cheese would brown and become bitter in taste.)

Place the baking dish in the preheated oven. When the top is golden (25 to 30 minutes), remove from the oven. Sprinkle with Parmigiano and serve hot.

Topini di patate

POTATO GNOCCHI

SERVES 6

*T*opini di patate are the Florentine counterpart of gnocchi, but are made into the shape of "little mice." The potatoes must be steamed, not boiled, both to retain all their flavor and to absorb as little moisture as possible. They are passed through a ricer and mixed with flour to make a dough. The knack of pulling the dough pieces across a curved grater to acquire the proper shape is acquired with just a little practice in making the right hand movement.

Topini are versatile, and may be served with a variety of sauces— fresh tomato, butter and cheese, pesto.

1 pound potatoes for boiling, but not new potatoes	*Salt and freshly grated nutmeg*
1¾ cup unbleached all-purpose flour	*4 tablespoons (2 ounces) sweet butter*
	Coarse-grained salt

STEAM (do not boil) the potatoes until cooked but firm, then peel.

Spread the flour on a pasta board. Pass the potatoes through a potato ricer onto the flour. Sprinkle with a pinch of salt and nutmeg, then start incorporating the flour, little by little, into the potatoes until the dough is homogeneous and all but ½ cup of the flour is incorporated. Knead gently for 5 or 6 minutes.

Cut the dough into several pieces and roll each piece into a long thin roll about ½ inch in diameter. Cut each roll into 1-inch pieces.

Use the dull inside of a convex hand cheese grater. Hold a 1-inch piece of dough at the top of the grater with the middle fingers of one hand. Lightly draw the piece around in a motion that makes the cursive letter "c" (see illustration). The resultant shape should be the quasi-shells which the Florentines think resemble "little mice," and which they prefer to more usual *gnocchi*. Use the remaining flour to flour the grater and continue to shape the *topini* until all the dough is used.

Place a stockpot containing a large quantity of cold water on the heat. While the water is heating, melt the butter in a small saucepan and pour it into a serving dish. Place the serving dish next to the stockpot.

When the water is boiling, add coarse salt to taste, then raise the heat and quickly drop all the *topini*, one by one, into the stockpot.

Lightly stir the water with a wooden spoon, to keep the *topini* from sticking. After a few seconds, the *topini* will come to the surface of the water; let them cook for 1 minute more. With a strainer-skimmer, remove the *topini* to the serving dish. Serve hot, with the sauce of your choice.

Shape the *topini* against the dull side of a convex cheese grater.

Torta pasqualina

EASTER TORTA

SERVES 12

*O*ne of the specialties of the fine Genoese cooking. The *torta pasqualina* reveals in its very name that it is primarily a dish for the Easter holiday. The pastry is the Genoese pastry without eggs or yeast, and with a minimum of oil; it is almost a severe flour and water dough. It must be rolled very, very thin, and about ten layers of it are used, five on the bottom and five on top. The manifold thin layers separated by air are a little related to strudel, but this pastry is even more difficult to handle because it has very little shortening in it; the layers do not quite become paper thin.

One of the great specialties of northern Italian cooking, at one time no Easter feast would have been conceivable without its *torta pasqualina.* If you are fond of artichokes, mushrooms, and fine pastry, this makes a spectacular antipasto for an elegant dinner. It is served cold.

Though in Italy, a large one is often eaten over a period of several days, in the course of which the pastry loses its crispness, I believe non-Italians would prefer to eat it fresh, while the pastry is still crisp. It may be followed by a lamb dish and fruit dessert.

FOR THE DOUGH

5 cups unbleached all-purpose flour
1½ to 2 cups very cold water

1 tablespoon olive oil
Pinch of salt

FOR THE ARTICHOKE STUFFING

2 ounces dried porcini mushrooms
5 medium artichokes
Juice of 2 lemons
2 medium red onions, cleaned
2 large cloves garlic, peeled
10 sprigs Italian parsley, approximately, leaves only

¼ cup olive oil
2 tablespoons (1 ounce) sweet butter
Salt and freshly ground black pepper to taste
½ cup meat or chicken broth, approximately, preferably homemade

FOR THE RICOTTA STUFFING

15 ounces ricotta, well drained

3 extra-large eggs

¼ cup freshly grated
Parmigiano

1 tablespoon unbleached all-
purpose flour

Salt, freshly ground black
pepper, and freshly grated
nutmeg to taste

½ cup olive oil, approximately

7 or 8 teaspoons butter

4 extra-large eggs

MAKE the dough first.

Arrange the flour in a mound on a pasta board and make a well in the center. Put the cold water, olive oil, and salt in the well. Little by little, mix the flour from the inside rim of the well into the liquid; absorb as much flour as possible. When a solid dough is formed, start kneading, always using a folding motion. Knead the dough for about 25 minutes.

Dampen a cotton dishtowel with cold water. Place the dough in the damp towel and let rest for 2 hours in a cool place or in the bottom shelf of your refrigerator while you make the stuffings.

For the artichoke stuffing, soak the mushrooms in a small bowl of lukewarm water for 30 minutes.

Meanwhile, clean the artichokes (see page 510) and cut them into ½-inch pieces. Put the artichoke pieces into a bowl of cold water with the lemon juice and let stand until needed.

Coarsely chop the onions, garlic, and parsley all together.

Heat the olive oil and butter in a large flameproof casserole, terracotta if possible, and when the butter is melted, add the chopped ingredients and sauté very gently for about 15 minutes, until lightly golden. Add the artichoke pieces, mix thoroughly, and sauté for 15 minutes more.

Drain the mushrooms and clean them, removing all the sand attached to the stems. (Discard or freeze [see note, page 25] the soaking water.) Then add the mushrooms to the casserole. Season with salt and pepper and let cook very slowly until artichokes are cooked and soft (about 25 minutes), adding broth as needed (about ½ cup).

Remove the casserole from the heat and transfer its contents to a

(continued)

large bowl. Let cool completely (about 1 hour) while you make the ricotta stuffing.

Drain the ricotta in cheesecloth to remove excess liquid, then place in a large bowl and add the eggs, Parmigiano, and flour. Mix all the ingredients together with a wooden spoon, then add salt, freshly ground pepper, and nutmeg to taste and mix thoroughly. Cover the bowl and place it in the refrigerator until needed.

When you are ready to assemble the dish, preheat the oven to 375 degrees. Cut the dough into 10 equal pieces. With a rolling pin, roll each piece of dough into a circular sheet, as thin as you can get it (not less than 14 inches in diameter).

Oil a 10-inch springform pan and line it with a first layer of dough, letting an overlap of pastry hang over the sides. Oil the top side of the pastry sheet in the pan and place a second sheet on top of it; oil the second sheet. Repeat this procedure until there are 5 sheets of pastry in all.

On top of the fifth layer, arrange the cold artichoke stuffing, then put 3 or 4 pats of butter on top. Make a layer of the ricotta stuffing on top of the layer of artichokes. In this ricotta layer, make 4 small depressions, each the width of an egg; in each one break a raw egg. Place a pat of butter on top of each egg and sprinkle with salt and pepper.

Over the ricotta layer, place a sixth sheet of pastry, still letting the sides overlap. Oil the sixth sheet of pastry and add the remaining sheets, oiling each except for the last one. (With these top 5 sheets it is important to leave some air between the layers.) Gently press all the layers together at the edge of the springform and cut off all the overlapping parts with a knife.

Place the springform pan in the preheated oven and bake for about 40 minutes, then remove from the oven and let cool for about 4 or 5 hours. Do not cover the pan; otherwise, the crust will become soggy.

When cool, open the springform pan, place the *torta pasqualina* on a serving dish, and serve, slicing it like a cake.

Fish

*T*he Arno river is one of the central facts of Tuscany. Florence, Pisa, and a host of smaller towns are situated on it. At one time the river was not only navigable by large vessels but the river and its tributaries were teeming with fish. Sturgeon was not a rarity. In 1558 two gigantic sturgeon fished from the Arno fed the entire company at one of the gigantic Medici royal weddings. The old cookbooks have recipes for carp, salmon, turbot, as well as sturgeon. The tributaries such as the Bisenzio, a few miles from Florence, were famous throughout Europe for the quality of their fresh pike, tench, and so on. These recipes which have remained on after the fish themselves have gone from the local waters are useful in areas where many of these species are still to be found. In recent times the specialties of the Arno are tiny fish and baby eels which the Arno folk love to deep-fry.

Standing also at the foot of the Apennine mountains, Florence nowadays depends on the mountain streams for marvelous and abundant fresh trout, which are prepared in a wide variety of ways. Eels and lampreys, snails, and frogs have also given rise to a large repertoire of dishes.

The long seacoast of Tuscany gives access to the varieties of fish on Italy's western Mediterranean coast. (It is often said that the Adriatic has the best fish but the Mediterranean side the best ways of cooking it.) Since its lagoon silted up several centuries ago and Pisa is now inland, the most famous sea dishes are those of Livorno (Leghorn), Viareggio, and Massa. The fish soup of Livorno is a direct descendant of the ancient Greek ones, and shares the highly spiced quality of Livornese cooking.

Among the varieties of Mediterranean fish used in Tuscan cooking that are available also in the Atlantic are the following: *spigola,* sea bass, and its relative, striped bass; *triglia,* the larger ones like red mullet; *cernia,* spotted grouper; *pesce spada,* swordfish; *tonno,* fresh tuna; *cefalo* or *muggine,* striped or gray mullet; *nasello* or *merluzzo,* hake or its less tasty relative whiting. Fresh sardines are increasingly available in the United

States. Though only dried salted cod, *baccalà,* is available in Italy, fresh cod is available in other countries and makes a more subtle and not inauthentic version of some, though not all, of the Italian cod dishes. Salted herring is used more in Italy than most suspect. Bluefish, though related to *ombrina,* is too strong in taste to substitute for it, as delicious porgy is really too strong to approximate its relative, *dentice,* though one sees these substitutions suggested often enough. Though the Atlantic sole is related to the flounder family of flatfish *(Pleuronectidae)* rather than that of the Mediterranean and Dover sole *(Solidae),* if the dish is not a subtle and very exposed one, small, thin Atlantic sole can sometimes be substituted with success.

Squid and ink-squid or cuttlefish are also much used. The smaller shrimp are generally preferred to the larger ones for most dishes, except for grilling on the spit. Mediterranean clams are much smaller than Atlantic ones and are eaten steamed in the shell with flavorings or used with pasta. Mussels are used in fish soups and cooked *alla marinara.* Oyster and turtle recipes exist in old cookbooks, though these species are rarely used in Italy now. (Turtles may always have been imported for eating, even in the sixteenth century.) Lobsters are characteristic of the islands off Tuscany, Giglio, and Elba, and of Sardinia. Crabs are most plentiful in the Adriatic.

The sampling of fish dishes which follows is just an introduction to this large area of Tuscan cooking.

BUYING AND HANDLING FISH

*T*here are some basic things you should know about buying and handling fish, most important of all is how to recognize whether a fish is fresh:

1. The smell of ocean fish must be extremely light; there should be no smell at all for freshwater fish.
2. The eyes must be very bright and not sunken.

3. The skin must be smooth and still pulled tight.

4. The gills must be rose or red in color.

5. The body of the fish must be firm and not soft.

When using slices cut from a very large fish (such as cod, haddock, etc.), note that the fish is generally tougher than a small whole fish and should be soaked in cold milk for an hour, then dried with paper towels, before using.

Finally, always handle fish with wet hands. To remove any smell from your hands it will be enough to moisten them with some lemon juice or better with toothpaste, and then wash them as you ordinarily do.

Pesce bollito

POACHED FISH

One of the most common ways of cooking fish is by poaching. Many kinds of fish can be prepared this way, and the fish-poaching broth we give below can be generally used (see page 285 for an exception). Observe the directions below in order to obtain the best taste result with each kind of fish.

First of all, the best pot for poaching fish is a long, heavy tin-lined copper fish poacher, which in Italy is called a *"pesciaiola."* If you don't have a fish poacher, copper or tin, make a cheesecloth sling on which the fish may rest immersed in the broth in a large saucepan.

Before poaching, ocean fish must be washed in salted cold water, while fresh-water fish must be rinsed in cold water containing some lemon juice (*acqua acidulata,* as it is called in Italy). The fish can then be poached in the following broth (the amount of water is for 2 pounds of fish).

Poached fish should be preceded by a light soup or pasta, accompanied by boiled vegetables, and followed by almost any dessert.

1 carrot, scraped
1 medium red onion, cleaned
1 celery rib
1 small clove garlic, peeled
5 or 6 sprigs Italian parsley,
*   leaves only*
1 large bay leaf

½ teaspoon dried thyme
½ cup dry white wine
1 tablespoon coarse-grained salt
2 quarts water
2 pounds fish, ocean or
*   freshwater*

PLACE all the ingredients except the fish in your fish poacher, then cover and place over medium heat. Let the broth simmer very slowly for about 30 minutes, then strain through a wire strainer into a large bowl. Return the broth to the poacher.

Then follow either of these procedures; the first is for ocean fish.

Allow the broth to become cold. Place the ocean fish in the cold broth, then cover the poacher and heat until the broth reaches the boiling point. Simmer very slowly until cooked. (Time depends on individual fish and its size; see the list below for times for various fish.) Remove the poacher from the heat and let stand without opening the pot for 5 or 6 minutes.

For freshwater fish, place the fish in very hot broth (not yet boiling), then cover the poacher and simmer very slowly until the fish is cooked. Remove the poacher from the heat and let stand without opening for about 10 minutes.

NOTE: The broth left over after poaching fish may be used for *risotto di mare* (see page 257).

COOKING TIMES

Sea bass, 2 pounds, or striped bass, 2-pound piece, 20–25 minutes.
Swordfish, 2-pound piece, 20–30 minutes.
Fresh cod or haddock, 2-pound piece, 20–30 minutes.
Hake or whiting, 2 pounds, 15–20 minutes.
Sole filet, medium-sized, about 12 minutes.
Dried, salted cod, soaked overnight, boiled 20–30 minutes.
Trout (see page 287).

A SUGGESTED DINNER

WINE

BERTAGNI SOAVE

Gnocchi di pesce

(SEE PAGE 270)

Trota bollita con maionese

(SEE BELOW)

Spinaci saltati

(SEE PAGE 546)

Torta di ricotta

(SEE PAGE 580)

Trota bollita con maionese

BOILED TROUT WITH MAYONNAISE

SERVES 4

*F*reshwater trout, poached in a good broth and served with homemade *maionese,* is one of the great treats, though it is among the simplest of things to prepare. Trout is widely available, and this dish may be served in either the most informal or highly formal circumstances.

Trout is a very delicate fish, and for this reason the broth in which it is cooked differs from ordinary fish poaching broth in that the garlic and onion are omitted.

Maionese *(see page 64)*
1 lemon, cut in wedges
5 sprigs Italian parsley, leaves
* only*

Broth for poaching fish *(see*
* page 284), but omitting the*
* garlic and onion*
4 brook trout (about 2 pounds)

MAKE the *maionese,* then set aside until needed.

Prepare the broth for poaching fish, then poach the trout in it for about 15 minutes.

When the trout are done, let them stand, covered, for about 10 minutes, then lift them out of the fish poacher and carefully cut off the heads and tails. Open each trout lengthwise and gently lift out the central bone, leaving each filleted half-fish in one piece. Place the trout fillets on a serving dish and surround with the lemon wedges and parsley sprigs. Serve, accompanied by the *maionese* in a sauceboat.

NOTE: This dish can be served either warm or cold.

A SUGGESTED DINNER

WINE

CORTESE DI GAVI LA BOLLINA

Risotto con gamberetti in bianco
(SEE PAGE 254)

Trota al piatto
(SEE BELOW)

Pomodori al forno
(SEE PAGE 550)

Meringhe alla panna
(SEE PAGE 598)

Trota al piatto

TROUT COOKED ON A PLATE

SERVES 4

A special way to cook filleted trout. The fillets are put on oven-proof plates with a little wine, lemon juice, and olive oil, then the plate is placed over a steaming stockpot. While simple to prepare, the presentation of this fish generally provides a touch of drama, and the result is delicious.

4 brook trout (about 2 pounds)
5 sprigs Italian parsley, leaves
    only
Juice of ½ lemon

¼ cup dry white wine
2 teaspoons olive oil
Salt and freshly ground white
    pepper

WET your hands, then cut off the heads and tails of the trout with a knife. Open stomachs to clean out the viscera. With a boning knife, extend each stomach opening down to the tail end, to open the fish completely, then insert the point of the knife alongside the backbone, at the head end. Move the knife downward to the tail end. Repeat the procedure on the other side of the bone, then lift the bone out.

Coarsely chop the parsley and set it aside.

Put the lemon juice in a small bowl, along with the wine, olive oil, and salt and white pepper to taste. Stir very well with a wooden spoon.

Oil 4 ovenproof plates and on them place the trout fillets, with their skins on. Pour the liquid in the bowl over the trout and sprinkle the chopped parsley on top, then wrap the plates completely in aluminum foil.

Put a large quantity of water in 4 saucepans and set them on the heat. When the water reaches the boiling point, lower the heat to a simmer and place the plates on top of the saucepans. Let the fish steam for 16 to 18 minutes.

Remove the plates from the saucepans, carefully remove the foil, and serve immediately.

Pesce arrosto

ROASTED FISH

SERVES 4

A roasted fish retains its full flavor if it is left whole, with the head and tail still on, since cutting these off would create openings through which a large part of the flavor vanishes. (If the head and tail bother you, cut them off only before serving.)

The touch of garlic here blends ideally with the fish, at least as well as with meat. Be careful not to overcook. Test with a fork; the bones may still be slightly pinkish when the fish is ready to be removed from the oven.

1 large whole fish such as red snapper, spotted grouper, or gray mullet (about 4 pounds)	*Salt and freshly ground black pepper to taste*
3 large cloves garlic, peeled	*5 tablespoons olive oil*
1 tablespoon rosemary leaves, fresh or preserved in salt or dried and blanched	*Juice of 1 lemon*
	Lemon wedges

CLEAN the fish very well, removing the scales but not the head, and cutting off only the lower half of the tail. Make 2 or 3 short slits in the skin of the fish.

Cut the garlic cloves into quarters, then put some inside each slit and inside the fish's cavity, along with the rosemary, salt, and pepper.

Preheat the oven to 375 degrees.

Place 4 tablespoons of the olive oil in a roasting pan. Place the fish on the oil, sprinkle on the remaining olive oil and a little salt, and place in the preheated oven for about 30 minutes. (It is very difficult to give the exact time for roasting fish, because not only do different kinds of fish take different lengths of time to cook, but even among fish of the same kind there are big differences, according to the size of the fish, how big the bones are, the freshness of the fish, in which period of the year the fish has been caught and where.) The best judge for doneness of fish is a fork. When the fork goes down very easily and the meat makes no resistance, the fish is ready.

Remove the fish from the oven, sprinkle with the juice of a lemon, and serve in the same roasting pan, garnished with lemon wedges.

A SUGGESTED DINNER

WINE
ANTINORI EST! EST!! EST!!!

Risotto alla marinara
(SEE PAGE 256)

Pesce arrosto
(SEE ABOVE)

Cardi dorati
(SEE PAGE 528)

Budino di ricotta
(SEE PAGE 627)

A SUGGESTED DINNER

WINE

FELLUGA PINOT BIANCO

Risotto con agliata

(SEE PAGE 246)

Pesce al cartoccio

(SEE BELOW)

Fagiolini in fricassea

(SEE PAGE 522)

Frittura mista di frutta

(SEE PAGE 634)

Pesce al cartoccio

FISH COOKED IN A PAPER BAG

SERVES 4

*A*nother way of roasting fish, this time wrapped up to hold in the flavor and to keep the fish moist. Years back, the fish used to be cooked in an oiled brown paper bag, but parchment paper produces just as good a result and has taken the place of the oiled paper. Garlic, rosemary, and lemon are the flavorings. This method is very widely used in Italy.

1 sea bass or red snapper (about
3½ pounds)
Salt and freshly ground black
pepper to taste
1 tablespoon rosemary leaves,
fresh or preserved in salt or
dried and blanched

2 large cloves garlic, peeled
Lemon wedges

MAKE sure that the cavity of the fish is very well cleaned, then rinse the fish in salted water and wipe it off with paper towels.

Preheat the oven to 375 degrees.

Place a large sheet of parchment paper skin-side up on a board and sprinkle it with a little salt, pepper, and some of the rosemary leaves. Place the fish on the parchment paper.

Cut the cloves of garlic into small pieces. Into the cavity of the fish put half of the remaining rosemary leaves, half of the garlic pieces, salt, and pepper. Sprinkle the outside of the fish with the remaining rosemary leaves, garlic, and more salt and pepper.

Wrap fish completely in the parchment paper and place it in a baking pan, then place in the preheated oven for 17 minutes. Gently turn the fish over and bake for 17 minutes more, then remove the pan from oven and let the fish cool for 5 minutes.

Unwrap the fish onto a serving dish and serve hot, with lemon wedges.

SQUID

*F*or most dishes, the smaller the squid the better and the more tender. For *calamari ripieni* (see page 302) the squid should be larger, since they are to be stuffed, but not extremely large.

To clean the squid, pull the tentacles away from the casing, or stomach, until the entire head is outside. Detach the head from the stomach by pulling. Cut off the head below the eyes and discard, leaving the tentacles attached to the lower part (see illustration opposite).

Turn the lower part upside down. The tentacles will now hang over the sides, and the inside of the lower head will be pulled open to reveal a black spot, which is the mouth. Pull it out (see illustration opposite).

Remove the membranes remaining inside the stomach by squeezing the stomach from the bottom. Discard the membranes, then pull out the transparent "bone" from inside the stomach (see illustration on page 296) and rinse out the inside of the stomach very carefully.

Under cold running water, pull the thin layer of dark outer skin from the stomach and tentacles so the white under layer is exposed (see illustration on page 296). (Leaving on the outer skin is the most common mistake of those inexperienced with squid; no amount of cooking can remove its toughness.)

The "fins" attached along the sides of the bottom half of the stomach are of the same quality as the stomach. Cut them off, being careful not to open the stomach, and save them.

At this point the squid is ready to be used for a variety of dishes. Unless you are going to stuff the whole stomach, cut it into rings (see illustration on page 297). If the tentacles are larger than an inch or so, cut them into 1-inch sections.

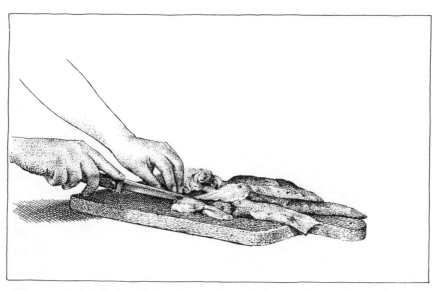

Cleaning squid: Cut the head below the eyes, leaving the tentacles attached to the lower part of the head.

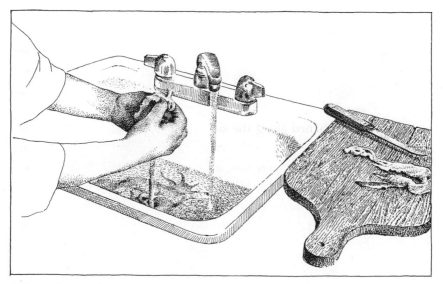

Pull out the mouth.

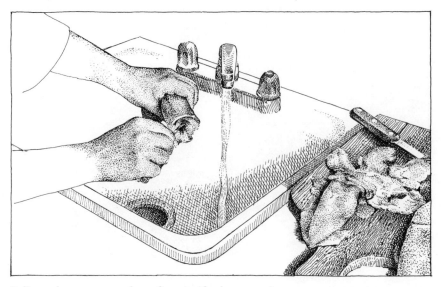

Pull out the transparent bone from inside the stomach.

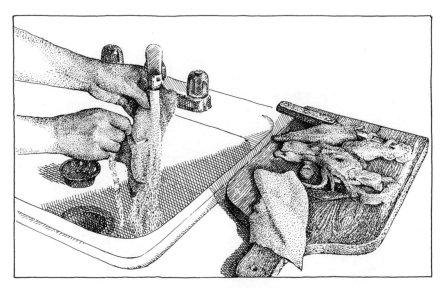

Pull the thin layer of dark outer skin off the stomach under cold running water.

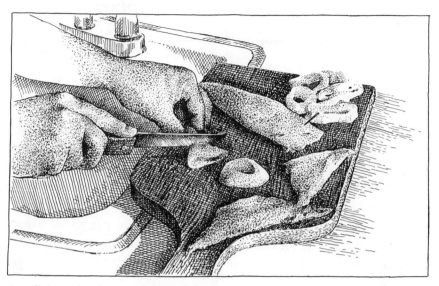

A stuffed squid and cutting squid into rings.

Fritto di calamari e gamberi

DEEP-FRIED SQUID AND SHRIMP

SERVES 4

$\mathcal{T}$he lightness and crispness of fried shrimp and squid in Tuscany is widely admired. It is important not to use a thick batter. The Tuscan method is to shake the shellfish in a colander with some flour, so that only what clings to the fish remains. Then, after being lightly dipped in egg, it is cooked in very hot, light oil and placed in paper towels to absorb any excess grease. As in any kind of deep-frying, if the oil is light and hot enough, very little fat is absorbed by the fish, as you will see when you place them on towels and see how little excess grease comes off. Most of the fish in Tuscany is fried according to this method or the *alla pescatora* method described on pages 338–339.

1 pound squid	*Salt to taste*
½ pound medium shrimp,	*3 extra-large eggs*
unshelled	*1 quart vegetable oil*
Coarse-grained salt	*Lemon wedges*
2 cups unbleached all-purpose	
flour	

CLEAN the squid well according to the directions on page 294, then cut the stomachs into rings and the tentacles into 2 or 3 pieces; shell and devein the shrimp. Soak the squid and shrimp in a bowl of cold water, with a pinch of salt, for 10 to 15 minutes, then drain, rinse under cold running water and dry with paper towels to absorb excess water.

Put the fish in a large colander, sprinkle over the flour, then shake the colander to remove the excess. The pieces should be fully, but lightly, covered with flour.

Beat the eggs in a second bowl with a pinch of salt and set aside while you heat the vegetable oil in a deep-fat fryer. While it is getting hot (about 375 degrees), line a serving dish with paper towels.

When the oil is hot, dip each piece of floured squid or shrimp into the beaten eggs and fry until golden all over. Transfer onto the serving dish lined with paper towel, so grease is absorbed.

When all the fish is cooked, remove the paper towels from the bottom of the serving dish, sprinkle with salt, and serve hot with lemon wedges.

A SUGGESTED DINNER

WINE
MASTROBERARDINO GRECO DI TUFO

Pomodori ripieni
(SEE PAGE 267)

Fritto di calamari e gamberi
(SEE ABOVE)

Zucchini fritti
(SEE PAGE 552)

Biscotti di Prato
(SEE PAGE 596)

Calamari in zimino

SQUID WITH SPINACH

SERVES 4

*W*hen Americans overcome their resistance to squid, they are generally very happy with their discovery; it is, after all, one of the very best gifts of the sea. For most dishes, the smaller squid are best because they are more tender. Squid rings and pieces, cooked together with spinach in white wine and slightly spiced with red pepper flakes, is one of the classic Florentine recipes. All Italian fish markets abroad carry fresh squid.

2 pounds of squid
Coarse-grained salt
3 pounds fresh spinach, cleaned
    and large stems removed
1 small red onion, cleaned
1 carrot, scraped
5 tablespoons olive oil
Salt and freshly ground black
    pepper to taste

Large pinch of hot red pepper
    flakes
½ cup dry white wine
1 tablespoon tomato paste,
    preferably imported Italian
10 sprigs Italian parsley, leaves
    only
Juice of 1 lemon

CLEAN the squid according to the directions on page 294, then cut the stomachs into rings and the tentacles into small pieces. Let the squid pieces soak in a bowl of salted water until needed.

Put a large quantity of cold water into a stockpot and bring it to a boil. When the water reaches a boil, add coarse salt to taste, then the spinach and cook for 15 minutes. Drain the spinach and cool under cold running water, then squeeze and chop it coarsely. Set aside.

Coarsely chop the onion and carrot. Heat the oil in a medium-sized casserole over medium heat and when the oil is warm, add the chopped aromatic vegetables and sauté for 5 minutes. Season with salt, pepper, and hot pepper. Drain the squid, rinse in cold water, and add to the casserole. Sauté for 15 minutes.

Add the white wine, let the wine evaporate, then add the spinach and tomato paste and cook very slowly for 20 minutes more.

Chop the parsley coarsely, then add it to the casserole and cook for 1 minute more. Taste for salt and pepper. By this time the squid should be tender, if not add some lukewarm water and cook until tender. Remove from the flame, add the lemon juice, and serve hot.

NOTE: Swiss chard *(bietola)* may be used instead of or in combination with the spinach.

A SUGGESTED DINNER

WINE

GAVI LA GIUSTINIANA

Gnocchi di semolino

(SEE PAGE 274)

Calamari in zimino

(SEE ABOVE)

Pomodori in insalata

(SEE PAGE 502)

Fresh fruit

Calamari ripieni

STUFFED SQUID

SERVES 4

*S*tuffed squid requires larger squid, as the so-called stomach sections must be large enough to stuff. When cooked, these look like attractive white sausages, and they are stuffed with the squids' tentacles, chopped, mixed with *mollica* (the inside part of bread), white wine, and seasoning. We strongly urge you to try this, especially if you share the frequent resistance to squid.

8 large squid
Coarse-grained salt
2 large cloves garlic, peeled
15 sprigs Italian parsley, leaves
 only

2 slices white bread
½ cup olive oil
Salt and freshly ground black
 pepper
1½ cups dry white wine

CLEAN the squid very well, without cutting the stomachs, according to the directions on page 294, then remove the tentacles from the bottom part of the heads and soak them, along with the stomachs, in cold salted water for 10 to 15 minutes. Be sure that nothing remains in the bottom of the stomachs. Drain the squid and rinse in cold water.

Chop the tentacles fine, together with the garlic and parsley; remove the crusts from the bread slices.

Heat ¼ cup of the oil in a saucepan, and when it is warm, add the chopped ingredients and the bread slices. Sauté over medium heat, mixing very well until the bread is completely incorporated with the other ingredients (about 12 to 15 minutes). Season with salt and pepper, then remove the saucepan from the heat and allow to cool for 20 minutes.

Preheat the oven to 375 degrees.

Stuff the squid stomachs with the contents of the saucepan, but not too full or they will split. Fasten the open end of each with a toothpick, then place in a 13½ × 8¾-inch glass baking dish.

Combine the wine and remaining ¼ cup of olive oil and pour over the calamari. Sprinkle with salt and pepper, then place in the preheated oven and cook for 25 to 35 minutes or until tender; the squid should be tender when pricked with a fork.

Remove the dish from the oven, transfer the squid to a serving dish, remove the toothpicks, and serve hot.

A SUGGESTED DINNER

WINE

Carpené Malvolti Prosecco Di Conegliano

Frittata di porri
(SEE PAGE 116)

Calamari ripieni
(SEE ABOVE)

Finocchi in sugo finto
(SEE PAGE 537)

Pesche ripiene
(SEE PAGE 629)

Baccalà alla fiorentina

DRIED SALTED COD, FLORENTINE STYLE

SERVES 4

accalà is dried salted cod. It can be found in most Italian markets, as well as in other ethnic markets such as Greek, Spanish, and Chinese. (In Italy, dried cod is also found unsalted and called *stoccafisso*.)

The dried fish must be soaked before cooking. In Italy, the classic way to do this is to leave it in a bowl under slowly running water overnight, for 9 or 10 hours. Many trying to sleep, however, would consider this "the Italian torture treatment," so most will prefer the below-mentioned compromise; it is, however, important to change the water quite often.

Every part of Italy has its own way of cooking *baccalà*. In Florence, in common with some other parts of italy, it is done with olive oil, garlic, and tomatoes. But it is crisped in the oil before the tomatoes are added, in moderation, and because it is not cooked too long, it does not become heavy.

Atlantic countries have fresh cod, which they do not in Italy. However, the dried salted cod has its own special flavor.

1 pound dried salted cod fillet
½ cup unbleached all-purpose
   flour
3 large cloves garlic, peeled
Scant ½ cup olive oil
1 pound ripe fresh tomatoes or
   1 pound canned tomatoes,
   preferably imported Italian,
   drained

Salt and freshly ground black
   pepper to taste
10 sprigs Italian parsley, leaves
   only

CUT the dried cod into large pieces (about 4 × 3 inches) and let soak in cold water for 24 hours, changing the water quite often. Dry on paper towels.

Spread the flour on the counter and flour the pieces well; coarsely chop the garlic. Heat the olive oil in a large frying pan. When it is hot, add the *baccalà* to the pan, along with the garlic, and fry lightly on both sides until golden (about 12 minutes). Pass the fresh or canned tomatoes through a food mill, using the disc with the smallest holes, into the pan and let simmer for 15 minutes over low heat. Taste before adding salt (the saltiness of the fish is variable) and add fresh pepper to taste. Simmer for 4 to 5 minutes more.

Transfer the *baccalà* pieces from pan to serving dish, coarsely chop the parsley and sprinkle it over. Pour over the hot sauce from the pan and serve.

A SUGGESTED DINNER

WINE
ANTINORI CASTELLO DELLA SALA
ORVIETO CLASSICO *(SECCO)*

Risotto alla toscana
(SEE PAGE 252)

Baccalà alla fiorentina
(SEE ABOVE)

Boiled potatoes
Fresh fruit

Sogliola alla livornese

SOLE, LIVORNO STYLE

SERVES 4

*M*editerranean sole is a species we do not find everywhere. It is very delicate and thinner than ocean sole, which is related to the flounder family. For this reason, I don't recommend it for light sautéing or frying. But if you can find small whole sole, this spicy treatment of *sogliola alla livornese* will not suffer with the ocean species. Leave the sole whole; do not have them filleted, just cleaned.

A very Mediterranean treatment of a small whole fish, in the style of the seaport of Livorno (Leghorn). It is even more often made with *triglie* (small red mullet, *rouget* in French), difficult to find outside the Mediterranean.

4 small whole sole
Coarse-grained salt
10 sprigs Italian parsley, leaves
*   only*
2 large cloves garlic, peeled
1 small celery rib
6 tablespoons olive oil

1 pound ripe fresh tomatoes or
*   1 pound canned tomatoes,*
*   preferably imported Italian,*
*   drained*
Salt and freshly ground black
*   pepper to taste*
Large pinch of hot red pepper
*   flakes*

BE sure that sole are cleaned well, then rinse them in salted water; finely chop the parsley, garlic, and celery all together.

Heat 3 tablespoons of the olive oil in a frying pan over medium heat. When the oil is hot, add the chopped ingredients to the pan and sauté them very gently for 10 minutes. Pass the tomatoes through a food mill, using the disc with the smallest holes, into the frying pan. Taste for salt and pepper and let cook for 10 minutes more, then remove all the solid ingredients from the pan with a strainer-skimmer and set aside.

Add the remaining 3 tablespoons of olive oil to the pan, and when it is hot, place all 4 whole sole in the pan. Sprinkle salt, freshly ground black pepper, and red pepper over the fish and sauté for 1 minute.

Sprinkle the sole with the solid ingredients previously set aside, then cover the pan and very gently cook for about 16 minutes, turning the fish once after about 8 minutes.

Serve very hot.

A SUGGESTED DINNER

WINE
TRAMINER COLLIO

Risotto con carciofi
(SEE PAGE 246)

Sogliola alla livornese
(SEE ABOVE)

Boiled potatoes
Fragole al vino rosso
(SEE PAGE 631)

A SUGGESTED DINNER

WINE

BROLIO BIANCO TOSCANO

Sformato di carciofi

(SEE PAGE 554)

Cacciucco

(SEE BELOW)

Bruciate ubriache

(SEE PAGE 613)

Cacciucco

TUSCAN FISH SOUP, LIVORNO STYLE

SERVES 6

*O*ne of the favorite dishes of the ancient Greeks was a rich fish soup, and all of the cities the Greeks settled along the Mediterranean—such as Marseilles and Naples—retain this great old tradition. Each Italian seacoast town has its *zuppa di pesce,* and the one characteristic of the Tuscan seacoast is *cacciucco.* It uses a variety of fish* and shellfish, which are served over toasted Tuscan bread slices covered with some of the rich broth as sauce. However, the bulk of the broth is retained for making another dish the next day, *risotto di mare* (see page 257). A great treat that yields two unforgettable meals, *cacciucco* is a main course, and should be preceded by something quite light.

The Mediterranean fish used in Italy such as *palombo,* small *triglie,* or

*Some fish traditional for *cacciucco,* such as *triglie* and *scorfano,* are also classic for the *bouillabaisse* of Marseilles.

FISH

cicale (a type of shellfish that has no meat but is added for flavor), are not found everywhere. For *palombo,* a full-fleshed fish may be substituted, such as cod, haddock, or striped bass. Smelts may be substituted for *triglie,* and crabs, preferably soft-shelled, for the sweet flavor of the *cicale.* Seafood used in Italy and found almost everywhere are *calamari* (squid), shrimp (added raw, in their shells), clams, and mussels. The *cacciucco* can be made perfectly well with a variety of combinations. To be avoided are fatty fish and any with a flavor so strong as to overwhelm the others.

6 pounds assorted fish and
    shellfish (see above), plus 2
    or 3 additional large fish
    heads
Coarse-grained salt
1 large red onion, cleaned
20 sprigs Italian parsley, leaves
    only
6 large cloves garlic, peeled
7 tablespoons olive oil
2 cups canned tomatoes,
    preferably imported Italian,
    drained

2 tablespoons tomato paste,
    preferably imported Italian
Salt and freshly ground black
    pepper to taste
1 teaspoon hot red pepper flakes
1/4 cup red wine vinegar
8 cups meat broth, preferably
    homemade
6 large slices Tuscan bread,
    preferably dark
    (see page 43)

CLEAN all the fish, detaching heads and tails, and cut into pieces about 1½ inch square (cutting full-fleshed fish across the width to leave the bones in, rather than filleting); reserve heads. Clean squid well (see page 294) and cut the stomachs into rings and the tentacles into small pieces. Leave shrimp in their shells.

Place all the seafood in a large bowl containing 2 quarts of cold water and 1 tablespoon of coarse salt, and let stand until needed.

Coarsely chop the onion, 10 sprigs of the parsley, and 2 cloves of the garlic, then place them in a large stockpot, along with the olive oil, and sauté for 5 minutes.

Add the tomatoes and tomato paste to the stockpot, season with
(continued)

309

CACCIUCCO (*continued*)

salt, pepper, and red pepper, and simmer for 15 minutes longer. Add the wine vinegar and all the reserved fish heads and bones and cook for 15 minutes more.

In a saucepan, heat the broth to the boiling point, then add to the stockpot and simmer, with the lid on, for 2 hours.

Strain the contents of the pot, forcing the solids through the strainer, into another bowl, then transfer the contents of the bowl back to the stockpot, and return the latter to the heat. Taste for salt and pepper, remembering that it should be spicy.

Pour the soaked fish pieces into a colander, letting the water run off, then rinse them under cold running water and add them to the stockpot in the following stages:

First put in squid, which take about 30 minutes; then, 20 minutes later add the full-fleshed fish. A few minutes after that, add shrimp, crabs, and smelts, which all take 4 to 5 minutes.

Meanwhile, chop the remaining 10 sprigs of parsley and set aside; cut the remaining garlic cloves into halves; preheat the oven to 375 degrees.

Toast the bread slices in the preheated oven for about 10 minutes on each side, then remove from the oven and immediately rub them on both sides with the cut garlic. Place 1 slice of bread in each individual soup plate.

When all the fish is cooked, remove the stockpot from the flame and let rest for 10 minutes, then, with a large ladle, select a sampling of each fish for each serving. Pour about ½ cup of broth over the fish and bread in each plate. Sprinkle with a little chopped parsley, and serve hot.

NOTE: There will be abundant broth remaining, which is sometimes eaten separately the next day but is most often used to make *risotto di mare.*

A SUGGESTED DINNER

WINE

CERETTO ARNEIS

Tagliatelle alla panna
(SEE PAGE 169)

Pastello di pesce
(SEE BELOW)

Spinaci alla fiorentina
(SEE PAGE 547)

Timballo di pere
(SEE PAGE 582)

Pastello di pesce

BONED   WHOLE   FISH,   BAKED   IN   A   CRUST

SERVES 6

*A*n elaborate, impressive dish, it is appropriate for a special occasion. The recipe comes from a Florentine cookbook of the 1300s. Much Florentine food of that period is extremely complicated and uses many different spices; the classic Florentine food, using a few excellent ingredients in just the right proportions, was developed in the course of the centuries of the Renaissance. Dishes such as this *pastello* were indirectly responsible for the discovery of America, as these were the famous spices of the Indies that Columbus sought, after the Venetians and other shippers were cut off from the East by the Turks.

Fish should be used which has only one, central bone, and whose

(continued)

flesh is not too soft. In Italy *spigola* or *orata* is best. Away from the Mediterranean, use a fish such as bass or snapper.

2 cups unbleached all-purpose flour	**1 level teaspoon ground cumin**
2/3 cup cold water	**1/2 teaspoon freshly grated nutmeg**
3 tablespoons olive oil	**Pinch of ground saffron**
Salt	**1 level teaspoon ground cardamom**
1 large fish (about 4 or 5 pounds before boning), such as striped bass	**5 black peppercorns**
1/2 teaspoon freshly ground black pepper	**Pinch of ground cinnamon**
1/4 teaspoon cayenne pepper	**5 sprigs Italian parsley, leaves only**
1/2 teaspoon ground ginger	**2 ounces pancetta or prosciutto**
1/2 teaspoon ground cloves	**1/4 cup rose water**

MAKE the crust first. Place the flour in a mound on a pasta board and make a well in it. Pour in the water, 1 tablespoon of the olive oil, and a pinch of salt. Using a fork and mixing outward from the center, completely absorb the flour into the liquid. Keep mixing until very smooth (about 15 minutes), then knead for at least 15 minutes. Wrap the dough in a dampened cotton dishtowel and put it in a cool place for 2 hours, or on the bottom shelf of the refrigerator.

Meanwhile, prepare the fish. Rinse it very carefully, then, after wetting your hands with cold water, completely remove the scales from the outside.

Now bone the fish. Open the stomach completely, using a boning knife, then cut out the backbone in one piece, without cutting the back, and cut the connection to the head on one end and to the tail on the other. Cut off the bottom half of the tail; the upper part of the tail should be left so the bottom end of the fish remains completely closed (see the illustrations on pages 313 and 314).

Open the fish flat, with the inside facing up, and sprinkle 1 level

(continued)

Open the stomach of the fish completely before boning.

Remove the backbone in one piece.

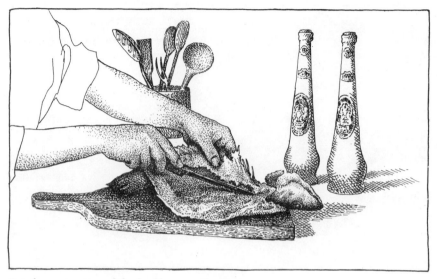

Cut the connection of the backbone to the head.

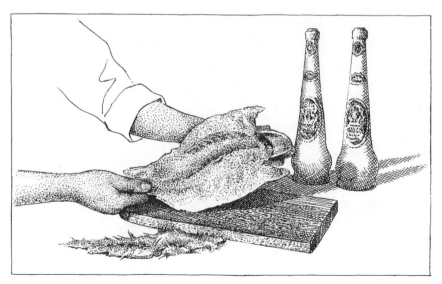

Open the fish out flat.

tablespoon salt and all the spices uniformly over the entire cavity. Arrange the parsley leaves down the length of the fish, in the center, then cut up the *pancetta* coarsely and arrange it uniformly all over the cavity. Close the fish.

Preheat the oven to 350 degrees.

With a rolling pin, roll out the dough into a large, paper-thin sheet. Place the fish on the sheet of dough and wrap it completely, but only once.

Lay out a large sheet of aluminum foil or parchment paper and puncture it all over with about 20 little holes. Place a grill on a jelly-roll pan and put the punctured foil or paper on the grill; oil the foil or paper with the remaining 2 tablespoons of oil.

Place the fish on the foil or paper. (In this way, if there is excess fat, it can drip off without softening the crispness of the bottom crust.) Make two little holes on the top side of the dough enclosing the fish, one near the head, the other near the tail (these will be necessary at a later stage to pour in the rose water), then place the pan in the pre-heated oven for 20 minutes.

Remove the pan from the oven and pour the rose water in through the two holes in the crust. Replace the pan in the oven and raise the oven temperature to 375 degrees for about 15 minutes more. (Be careful not to overcook the fish, but be sure the crust is a light golden brown.)

Remove the pan from the oven and let cool for 5 minutes, then transfer the fish to a serving dish. Starting from the tail end, cut the fish across into at least 6 pieces and serve.

A SUGGESTED DINNER

WINE
PIO CESARE CHARDONNAY

Ravioli nudi di pesce
(SEE PAGE 272)

Pesce ripieno in gelatina
(SEE BELOW)

Bietole saltate
(SEE PAGE 549)

Ciambella di frutta
(SEE PAGE 620)

Pesce ripieno in gelatina

STUFFED WHOLE FISH IN ASPIC

SERVES 6

*S*tuffed whole fish in aspic is a dish for an important dinner. The fish is boned before it is stuffed with a shrimp and mushroom filling. When served, it can be cut right through, each slice containing fish and stuffing and still encased in aspic.

We prefer beef aspic, as that made from fish, in our experience, produces too "fishy" a result for most people. The beef aspic blends quite well with the stuffed fish.

This dish may be served at the most formal of dinners and is also useful for a fancy buffet. Since it is cold, it goes particularly well in warm weather, but need not be restricted to that time.

316

GELATINA

20 cups cold water
4 pounds beef for boiling
1 large calf's foot
2 carrots, scraped
2 celery ribs

1 large red onion, cleaned
1 tablespoon coarse-grained salt
8 ounces lean boneless veal
5 extra-large egg whites
2 or 3 teaspoons sugar

STUFFING

5 sprigs Italian parsley, leaves
*   only*
2 large cloves garlic, peeled
1/2 pound medium shrimp,
*   unshelled*
Coarse-grained salt
1/2 pound fresh mushrooms, any
*   type*
3 tablespoons olive oil

Salt and freshly ground black
*   pepper to taste*
2 heaping tablespoons
*   unseasoned bread crumbs,*
*   preferably homemade*
1 large sea fish such as bass or
*   snapper (about 3 1/2 pounds)*
2 teaspoons rosemary leaves,
*   fresh or preserved in salt or*
*   dried and blanched*

MAKE the aspic with quantities listed above, according to the directions on page 128, but do not place it in the refrigerator to solidify.

Chop the parsley and garlic coarsely; shell the shrimp and rinse them with salted water; clean the mushrooms, removing the stem ends, rinse, then dry them with paper towels.

Heat the olive oil in a saucepan. When it is warm, add the parsley and garlic and sauté gently for 4 or 5 minutes, then add the shrimp, taste for salt and pepper, and cook for 2 to 3 minutes longer. Cut the mushrooms into quarters and add them to the saucepan. Mix thoroughly with a wooden spoon and let them cook for about 5 minutes. Add the bread crumbs, mix thoroughly, and cook for 5 minutes more.

Remove the saucepan from the heat. Transfer the contents of the pan to a crockery or glass bowl and let rest until completely cold (about 1 hour).

Preheat the oven to 375 degrees.

Clean and bone the fish, leaving on the head and tail, as described on page 312. Sprinkle the cavity of the fish with salt and pepper, then

(continued)

stuff it with the contents of the bowl, being careful not to overstuff the fish. Sew the fish together.

Lightly oil a sheet of aluminum foil (the shiny side) or parchment paper and place the whole fish on it. Sprinkle the outside part with salt, pepper, and rosemary leaves, then with 2 or 3 drops of olive oil. Place the foil or paper containing the fish in a baking dish and put it in the preheated oven for about 40 minutes.

Remove the dish from the oven and allow the fish to cool completely (about 1 hour), then place the fish in the refrigerator for 2 hours more.

Meanwhile prepare a mold, the same size as the fish, by lightly oiling it all over. Put ¾ cup of the aspic, cool but still liquid, in the mold and place in the refrigerator until the aspic is completely solid (about 3 hours).

When the aspic is solid, remove the fish from the refrigerator and carefully remove the thread. With a paper towel, gently remove the rosemary leaves from the top of the fish.

Lay the fish in the mold, on the solid aspic, and pour over the remaining, still-liquid aspic. Place the mold in the refrigerator until the second layer of aspic is solid (about 5 hours).

When the aspic is solid, remove the mold from the refrigerator and reverse it onto a serving dish. Loosen the aspic by placing hot towels on the outside of the mold (the aspic should unmold with ease) and serve.

A SUGGESTED DINNER

WINE
FELLUGA PINOT GRIGIO

Penne ai peperoni
(SEE PAGE 188)

Lattughe di gamberi
(SEE BELOW)

Rocchi di sedano
(SEE PAGE 458)

Fragole al vino rosso
(SEE PAGE 631)

Lattughe di gamberi

LETTUCE LEAVES STUFFED WITH SHRIMP

SERVES 6

*T*uscan shrimp dishes naturally come from towns on the coast such as Leghorn and Viareggio. The large shrimp, known as *mezzancolle,* tender, sweet and nutty, are a great favorite, quite simply grilled on the spit over a wood fire. The smaller shrimp are used in a variety of preparations, mostly in combination with other shellfish, but in a few by themselves. Shrimp prepared with pasta is a relative rarity.

From Leghorn we parboil the shrimp, then chop and employ it as a stuffing together with garlic, parsley, and eggs. Wrapped in delicate lettuce leaves, lighter than the more usual cabbage leaves so often stuffed, the delightful result is simmered in wine, olive oil, and some tomato and given the spicy Livornese touch with the hot pepper flakes.

(continued)

LATTUGHE DI GAMBERI *(continued)*

FOR THE STUFFING

**2 pounds medium shrimp,
    unshelled**
Coarse-grained salt .
1 lemon
**20 large sprigs Italian parsley,
    leaves only**

2 medium cloves garlic, peeled
2 extra-large eggs
**Salt and freshly ground black
    pepper**

PLUS

2 large heads Boston lettuce

Coarse-grained salt

FOR THE SAUCE

**30 large sprigs Italian parsley,
    leaves only**
4 large cloves garlic, peeled
½ cup olive oil
1 cup dry white wine
**Salt and freshly ground black
    pepper**

**½ teaspoon hot red pepper
    flakes**
**¾ pound canned tomatoes,
    preferably imported Italian,
    drained**

SOAK the shrimp in a bowl of cold water with 1 tablespoon of coarse-grained salt added, for 30 minutes.

Bring a medium-sized pot of cold water to a boil over medium heat and when the water reaches a boil, add coarse-grained salt to taste, then the lemon cut in half. Drain the shrimp, add them to pot and cook for 3 minutes. Drain the shrimp, cool under cold running water, then shell and devein them.

Finely chop parsley and garlic together on a board. Coarsely chop the shrimp and mix the garlic/parsley with them in a crockery or glass bowl. Add the eggs, and salt and pepper to taste. Mix very well, cover the bowl, and refrigerate until needed.

Clean and rinse the Boston lettuce and select 18 large whole leaves, with no breaks in them. Bring a large pot of cold water to a boil and fill a large bowl with cold water. When the water reaches a boil, add coarse-grained salt to taste, then the lettuce leaves and let cook for 1 minute. Carefully transfer the leaves from the boiling water to the bowl of cold water and let them remain until cold. Line a tray with paper towels and open out the leaves on the paper. Place 2 tablespoons of the stuffing in the center of each leaf, then wrap up the leaf around it. Let these little "packages" stand on the paper towels until needed, covered with a cotton towel dampened with cold water.

Prepare the sauce. Coarsely chop the parsley and finely chop the garlic on a board. Heat the oil in a large skillet over medium heat and when it is warm, add the chopped ingredients and sauté for 1 minute. Carefully transfer the lettuce "packages" to skillet with the lettuce ends on the bottom side. Sauté for 1 minute, then add the wine, season with salt, pepper, and red pepper flakes, cover, and let simmer for 5 minutes. Pass the tomatoes through a food mill, using the disc with smallest holes, into a crockery bowl. Add the tomatoes to the skillet and let cook, uncovered, for 5 minutes longer, spooning the sauce over the lettuce "packages" every so often. Remove from heat, let rest for a few minutes, then transfer the *lattughe* and the sauce to a large serving dish. Each serving consists of three "packages" and some sauce surrounding them.

Gamberi alla viareggina

SHRIMP AND CANNELLINI BEANS, VIAREGGIO STYLE

SERVES 8

*I*n Viareggio the shrimp are boiled simply with lemon and dressed with olive oil and salt. The beans, simmered with sage and garlic, are cooled. The onions, sautéed in butter, oil, and wine, either still warm or reheated are combined with the cooled shrimp and beans. Each portion is attractively served on a lettuce leaf, with parsley and basil. This is an especially refreshing warm weather dish, as appetizer or main course. The nearby Lucca area produces white onions, so they are used instead of the more common red ones.

FOR THE BEANS

1 cup dried cannellini beans
1 tablespoon olive oil
5 large leaves sage, fresh or preserved in salt

1 large clove garlic, peeled but left whole
Salt to taste

FOR THE ONIONS

1 1/2 pounds white onions, cleaned
4 tablespoons (2 ounces) sweet butter

2 tablespoons olive oil
4 cups dry white wine
Salt and freshly ground black pepper

FOR THE SHRIMP

Coarse-grained salt
2 pounds medium shrimp, unshelled

1 lemon

PLUS

15 sprigs Italian parsley, leaves only
4 tablespoons olive oil

Salt and freshly ground black pepper to taste
1 head Boston lettuce
8 large leaves fresh basil

A SUGGESTED DINNER

WINE

TERRUZZI & PUTHOD VERNACCIA DI SAN GIMIGNANO
RISERVA CARLO HAUNER MALVASIA LIPARI PASSITO

Pasta con pommarola
(SEE PAGE 190)

Gamberi alla viareggina
(SEE ABOVE)

Insalata composta
(SEE PAGE 501)

Biscotti di Prato
(SEE PAGE 596)

SOAK the beans in a bowl of cold water overnight. Next morning, drain the beans, rinse very well and put them in a medium-sized stock pot, adding 2 quarts of cold water, the oil, sage, and the whole clove of garlic. Place the pot over medium heat and when the water reaches a boil, add salt to taste and let simmer for 45 minutes to 1 hour or until the beans are cooked but still firm. Then drain beans and let them rest, covered, until needed.

Meanwhile thinly slice the onions in rings and soak them in a bowl of cold water for 30 minutes. Place a medium-sized casserole with the butter and oil over medium heat and when the butter is completely melted, drain onions, add them to casserole, cover, and let cook for 15 minutes. Start adding the wine, a half cup at a time, until the onions are very soft. Once the wine is all used up, add some lukewarm water. Taste for salt and pepper.

Bring a large pot of cold water to a boil, add coarse salt to taste,

(continued)

then add and cook the shrimp, along with the lemon cut into halves, for 3 to 4 minutes, depending on the size of the shrimp. Shell and devein shrimp, place them in a crockery bowl, add the oil, salt and pepper to taste, mix well, and refrigerate, covered, until needed.

To assemble the dish, first coarsely chop the parsley on a board. Mix the shrimp with beans and parsley in a large bowl. Prepare each individual dish with a large leaf of the lettuce and arrange the mixed cannellini and shrimp on the leaf. When ready to serve, reheat the onions, ladle some over each serving and top each with a basil leaf.

The

Boiled

Course

*W*e have seen in the discussion of a sixteenth-century Florentine dinner that the boiled course was a part of every large meal. Generally five different boiled and poached dishes were included in it. Here are some more examples of the Renaissance boiled course. A boiled course of March 18, 1546, included Malta eels with little green cabbages (probably Brussels sprouts), squid in a thick soup, ground pignoli soup, and filleted herrings with a walnut-garlic sauce. This more elaborate boiled course was for a feast day in August 1546: stuffed stomach of baby veal (like the modern *cima alla genovese*), boiled tripe, boiled kid Florentine style, boiled salted beef, boiled sausages and salamis with *ginestrata* soup (see recipe page 135) and *visciole* sour cherry sauce. We can see that this really approaches quite closely the modern *gran bollito misto* for feast days such as Christmas. The stuffed veal nowadays would be a main dish by itself. But boiled veal, kid, and beef could be contained in an elaborate *bollito.* The sausages and salamis have continued into the present as the boiled *cotechini* and *zamponi* still included in the modern *bollito.*

What happened to the boiled course as an everyday feature? Mainly, it evolved into the *minestra* or soup course. Also, boiled meats became occasional main dishes when the distinction "boiled course," then "fried course," or "roasted course" gave way to the modern *primo piatto* and *secondo piatto* in the nineteenth century.

Fortunately, some of the good boiled dishes survive—and many more that have become rare deserve to be revived. Following are the most basic boiled dishes of the modern-day repertory, as well as the combination *bollito misto,* used on feast days.

Boiled meats, fowl, and fish are always accompanied by boiled vegetables, never fried or roasted or prepared in any other way.

A SUGGESTED DINNER

WINE
MASTROBERARDINO FIANO DI AVELLINO

Spaghetti alla fiaccheraia
(SEE PAGE 178)

Boiled chicken or Boiled beef
(SEE BELOW)

with Salsa verde
(SEE PAGE 66)

Bietole all'agro
(SEE PAGE 548)

Fragole al vino rosso
(SEE PAGE 631)

Boiled fowl

*F*owl that are often eaten in boiled dishes are chicken, hen *(gallina)*, capon, and turkey. A hen is used exclusively for boiling because it is usually about two years old and must be cooked a long time. A boiled hen can be a marvelous dish, preferred by many to chicken for its richer taste. As we mentioned elsewhere, turkey was originally used to replace the very expensive and prestigious peacock in elaborate dishes, and is eaten boiled as well as roasted.

In the *gran bollito misto* (see page 332), there is always at least one fowl included and sometimes more than one. Boiled chicken is also used to make *pollo forte* (see page 380).

Great care must be taken in boiling a chicken not to overcook it. It is also pointless to boil a small, young chicken that can be better used for frying or broiling.

BOILING TIMES

Chicken: 45 minutes	Capon: 1½ hours
Hen: 4 to 5 hours	Turkey: 2 hours approximately

Enough cold water to well cover the fowl	**1 celery rib**
Coarse-grained salt	**5 sprigs Italian parsley, leaves only**
1 large carrot, scraped	**1 chicken, hen, capon, or turkey**
1 medium red onion, cleaned	

PUT a goodly amount of cold water in a stockpot over high heat. When the water reaches the boil, add coarse salt to taste, then add the carrot, onion, celery, and parsley and return to a boil.

When the water has reached the boiling point, add the fowl and let it boil very slowly, with the stockpot uncovered, until done according to the chart above, skimming off the foam from the surface. (The fowl must be well covered with water. Keep a saucepan of boiling water over low heat next to the stockpot to add if the stockpot water reduces to too low a level. For boiled hen it may be necessary to add water several times because of its long cooking time.)

NOTE: Boiled fowl are always served with one or more sauces on the side. See the recipes for sauces on pages 65–74.

Boiled beef

*T*he perfect meat for boiling is beef. Italian *manzo* is usually a little younger than U.S. beef, and different cuts of it are used boiled, depending on the relative festiveness and importance of the dinner. Abroad I generally use the breast cut called "brisket" and boil it for about 2½ hours. It is a meat that requires this long cooking time, and it is excellent for boiling, since it remains moist and retains its fine taste when boiled enough to become soft. Take care not to overcook it, however; if too soft, it becomes difficult to cut.

Boiled beef is almost always included in the *gran bollito misto* (see page 332).

For ingredients and procedure, see the recipe for boiled fowl opposite.

NOTE: Boiled beef is always served with one or more sauces on the side; see pages 65–74.

Boiled veal tongue

*T*his may be eaten as a separate dish or as part of the *bollito misto* (see page 332).

Veal tongue should be boiled for about 1½ hours; for ingredients and procedure, see recipe for boiled fowl. After boiling, the outer skin must be pulled off whole before the tongue is sliced and served.

NOTE: See pages 65–74 for sauces to accompany the tongue.

Boiled cotechino and zampone

*C*otechino and *zampone* are large pork sausages in the shape of salami. Though they are cured, they are almost always eaten boiled. Both can be eaten as a separate dish, usually accompanied by a puree of potatoes, or as part of the *gran bollito misto* (see page 332). *Cotechino* resembles an ordinary sausage, but *zampone* has a special shape as it is a stuffed pig's foot. The *zamponi* made in the town of Modena are celebrated in Italy, and when I am there for Christmas I make a trip to Modena to obtain one for Christmas dinner. *Cotechini* and *zamponi* are obtainable in many Italian specialty markets.

Cotechini and *zamponi* must be soaked for several hours and cooked for a long time, *cotechini* for 2 to 3 hours and *zamponi* for 4 to 5 hours. Usually cooked in a long fish poacher *(pesciaiola)*, they can be cooked together, but never in the same pot with other boiled meats because they give off a lot of grease. Unless they are served to a large group, generally these sausages are not completely consumed at one meal, so the water in which they are cooked is saved to be used for reheating them. They are always eaten hot.

1 cotechino *or* zampone   *Water to cover*
   sausage   *Coarse-grained salt*

PLACE the *cotechino* or *zampone* in a large bowl of cold water and soak for 2 or 3 hours. After soaking, make several punctures in the sausage with a large needle, then wrap completely in a cotton dishtowel and tie both ends with thread.

Place the sausage in a large pot of cold water and bring to a boil over medium heat. Meanwhile, put enough water to cover the sausage in a large fish poacher, add coarse salt, and set on the heat till it boils.

When the water containing the sausage reaches the boiling point, remove the pot from the heat, transfer the sausage to a board, and unwrap the towel. Place the *cotechino* in the boiling water in the fish poacher, add coarse salt to taste, then lower the heat and simmer until cooked. Cooking time varies even among *cotechini* or *zamponi* of the same brand, because cooking time is related to the freshness of the sausage and how coarsely chopped the meat inside is. The time for *zamponi* varies from 2 to 3 hours; for *cotechini,* 1 to 2.

Transfer the *cotechino* or *zampone* to a cutting board and cut into slices about ½ inch thick. (Cut only those slices you will need, as the rest will retain its flavor better if left in a large piece, resting in its own broth.) Arrange the discs of meat in a ring on a serving dish, and inside place a puree of potatoes or another accompanying vegetable.

Aside from puree of potatoes, these dishes may also be accompanied by *fagioli al fiasco* (see page 516), *fagioli all'uccelletto* (see page 519) or *rape saltate in padella* (see page 545).

Gran bollito misto

"GRAND" MIXED, BOILED DINNER

*T*he tradition of the elaborate boiled course, with many dishes, is principally represented today by the *gran bollito misto*. It is a tradition to serve it on Italian Christmas. It can, of course, be served on other festive occasions, and in some *ristoranti* it is available on ordinary days.

The components may vary slightly, but generally there is boiled beef, one or two kinds of boiled fowl, *cotechino* and *zampone,* veal tongue, *guancia* (the cheek part of the calf's head), calf's foot, and even occasionally ox's tail. These last two might be too gelatinous for some tastes, but if you should decide to use one or both, they must be cooked apart from the other meats—*zampa,* or foot, for 2½ to 3 hours and tail for about 2 hours. Cooking time for *guancia* is 2 to 2½ hours.

Hen, beef, turkey, capon, tongue, and chicken may all be cooked together and added in the order mentioned. Following the directions on page 328, start with the hen; after 2½ hours, add the beef, after ½ hour more add the turkey; after another ½ hour, capon and tongue; after 45 minutes more, the chicken. When the chicken is added, try the hen with a fork. If it is soft, remove it and put it back in when everything is finished. If it is not yet soft enough, leave it in to cook for the additional time.

Zampone should be placed to cook in the fish poacher at the same time as the hen in the other pot. Add *cotechino* 2 hours later. (See page 330 for directions on how to cook the sausages.)

In a third pot, boil *zampa,* starting about when you add the *cotechino.* Half an hour later, add *guancia;* another half hour later, add tail.

At the last moment before serving, combine all the boiled meats in a very large pot, preferably of copper, with some hot broth. To serve each individually, remove each meat one by one to a cutting board; cut off a slice and place the large piece back in the broth. Each person should get a slice of each meat. This is the most elegant way of serving the dish, painstaking though it may be.

If you don't have a large enough pot for everything, slice the different meats and arrange the different types in rings or rows on one of more serving dishes. Place puree of potatoes or another vegetable in the center and serve with a variety of the sauces found in pages 65–74.

NOTE: For Christmas, the first dish is usually tortellini (see page 194) in broth, which precedes the *bollito* very well.

A SUGGESTED DINNER

WINE
NEGRI SASSELLA

Palline ripiene in brodo
(SEE PAGE 133)

Gran bollito misto
(SEE ABOVE)

with Salsa verde
(SEE PAGE 66)

Salsa verde del Chianti
(SEE PAGE 67)

and Maionese
(SEE PAGE 64)

Puree of potatoes
Ritortelli pieni alla fiorentina
(SEE PAGE 600)

A SUGGESTED DINNER

WINE
BORGOGNO BARBERA D'ALBA

Melanzane marinate
(SEE PAGE 108)

Lesso rifatto con porri
(SEE BELOW)

Castagnaccio
(SEE PAGE 615)

Lesso rifatto con porri

LEFTOVER BOILED BEEF WITH LEEKS

SERVES 4

*O*ne of the best ways to convert leftover boiled meat into an exciting new dish. The meat is cooked a second time, covered with a layer of leeks. By covering the casserole, only the liquid given off by the leeks is used, so the boiled meat loses none of its own flavor but rather gains that of the leeks.

10 large leeks, cleaned
¼ cup olive oil
1½ pounds of boiled beef,
    approximately

Salt and freshly ground black
    pepper to taste

RINSE the leeks well, discard the green part, then cut them into rings. Soak them for 30 minutes in a bowl of cold water, then drain and rinse under cold running water.

Pour the olive oil into a large casserole, preferably terra-cotta, then add half the leeks. Place the whole piece of cold boiled meat over the leeks and cover it with the remaining leeks. Sprinkle with salt and freshly ground pepper, cover, and place the casserole over medium heat. Simmer very gently, stirring every so often with a wooden spoon, for about 1½ hours. The leeks should give off enough liquid so it will not be necessary to add any. If extra liquid is necessary, add up to ½ cup of hot water. After 1½ hours, the leeks should be very soft. When you stir, be sure to leave the boiled meat between two layers of leeks.

Taste for salt and pepper and simmer for 3 or 4 minutes more without the lid, then remove the casserole from the stove and let rest for 5 minutes.

Remove the boiled meat from the casserole and slice it on board. Arrange slices of meat on a serving dish and make a ring of leeks around them. Sprinkle with a little pepper and serve.

For another dish utilizing leftover *bollito*, see *Crocchette al limone,* page 432.

The Fried Course

~

"$\mathcal{E}$ven a bedroom slipper tastes good if it is deep-fried."

This saying conveys how much the Florentines love deep-fried meats and vegetables, and over the centuries they have developed a wide variety of techniques for deep frying.*

Though in recent decades some have attempted to minimize the consumption of fried foods because of their heaviness, it should be noted that this heaviness comes about only when the frying is poorly done. Indeed, roasted meats, which are often cooked for a very long time, are usually heavier. If the deep frying is properly done, the oil is not absorbed into the food itself, but merely serves to make the outside crisp. The oil—which in most cases should be a mixture of vegetable oils—must become very hot, so it is not absorbed into the meat or vegetable but affects only the outside. Detailed instructions are given in each recipe.

There are five main methods of deep-frying used in Florence, and all of them result in a very light dish. Even batter-dipped meat and vegetables have only a thin, light coating. (The kind of batter frying in which the batter is half an inch thick with a minute amount of meat inside, all very soggy, is unknown in Florentine cooking.)

The following are the procedures for coating different kinds of meats and vegetables; remember that fried meats are always accompanied by vegetables that are fried, not boiled, baked, pureed, or prepared in any other way:

1. Lightly floured by shaking the pieces in a colander with some flour. For fish and seafood, this method is sometimes referred to as *fritto*

---

*Again, the French owe all techniques of frying to Caterina de' Medici's cooks, as frying was unknown in France before their arrival. Even *tempura* was introduced to Japan from the West, by the Portuguese, who probably got the technique from the Florentines.

alla pescatora because it is the method used by fishermen. A whole fish or fillet, not in pieces, is rolled in flour and the excess flour is shaken off.

2. Coating with bread crumbs only. (In different parts of Italy, coarse semolina flour is used instead of bread crumbs.)
3. Flouring as described in method 1 above and then dipping lightly in salted beaten egg.
4. Marinated in lightly beaten egg with salt and coated lightly with bread crumbs.
5. Dipped in batter.

Pollo fritto

SERVES 4

*B*oned chicken pieces, dipped into a batter made with white wine and olive oil and flavored with nutmeg, are luscious, light, and crisp when deep-fried. Easy to make for a family dinner, when accompanied by zucchini or zucchini flowers dipped in the same batter and fried, a dish delicious enough to serve to the most discerning guests. On a family evening, if you really have little time, you can use the chicken unboned, and it will still work well. The batter must, however, be prepared 2 hours in advance and allowed to stand in a cool place, or on the lower shelf of the refrigerator.

FOR THE PASTELLA (BATTER)

1¾ cups unbleached all-purpose
flour
½ teaspoon salt
4 tablespoons olive oil

2 extra-large eggs, separated
Pinch of freshly grated nutmeg
⅓ cup dry white wine
1 cup cold water

FOR THE CHICKEN

1 small chicken, about 3
pounds
2 quarts vegetable oil (see note)

Salt to taste
Lemon wedges

SIFT the flour into a large bowl. Make a well in the flour, then one at a time, add the salt, olive oil, egg yolks, nutmeg, wine, and water. After each ingredient is added, mix it well with some of the flour before adding the next. When all are added, stir until the batter is smooth.

Let stand in a cool place for 2 hours, or on the lower shelf of the refrigerator. Set the egg whites aside for incorporation later.

Meanwhile, cut the chicken into about 24 small pieces, then remove the bone from each piece of chicken. (This is not absolutely necessary, but the dish is better when the pieces are boned. Boning the individual small pieces requires no special technique and need not be time consuming.) Remove the skin, however, whether boned or not.

Heat the vegetable oil in a deep-fat fryer until hot (about 375 degrees). Just before the oil reaches the point where it is ready for frying, beat the reserved egg whites with a wire whisk in copper bowl until they are stiff. Fold the whites into the batter and mix very gently and very little.

Dip each piece of chicken completely in the batter and gently place it into the hot oil. Let cook for 7 or 8 minutes. (With the bone, it will take a few minutes longer.)

Line a large serving dish with paper towels. As each piece of chicken is cooked, remove with strainer-skimmer and place on the paper towels.

When all the pieces are on the dish, remove the towels. Sprinkle with salt. Serve hot, with lemon wedges.

NOTE: Use a combination of corn oil and sunflower oil.

A SUGGESTED DINNER

WINE

CAPEZZANA CARMIGNANO

Rotolo di pasta ripieno
(SEE PAGE 229)

Pollo fritto
(SEE ABOVE)

*Zucchini fritti
and Fiori di zucca fritti*
(SEE PAGE 552)

Crespelle di farina dolce
(SEE PAGE 617)

Cervello fritto

FRIED CALF'S BRAINS

SERVES 4

The calf's brains are soaked for an hour in cold water, the membranes are removed, and then are soaked for 15 minutes in lemon juice. They are cut into small pieces, lightly floured, dipped in egg and deep-fried. This is a good dish to introduce you to brains if they are not already part of your repertory. Mixed together with fried artichoke pieces (see page 515), they make a very special dish called *fritto misto alla fiorentina* (see page 351).

1 whole calf's brain
Coarse-grained salt
2 extra-large eggs
Salt

1 cup unbleached all-purpose
flour, approximately
1 quart vegetable oil (see page
22)
Lemon wedges

SOAK the brains in a bowl of cold water for an hour. Meanwhile, bring about 1 quart of cold water to a boil in a saucepan, then add coarse salt to taste.

Drain the brains, put them back in the bowl, then cover with the boiling water. Leave the brains in the hot water for 5 minutes, then put them under cold running water, holding them with one hand while you remove the membranes with the other.

Return the brains to the bowl. Add the lemon juice to 1 cup of cold water and pour it over the brains. Let soak for 15 minutes, then dry very well with paper towels and cut into pieces about 2 inches square.

Lightly beat eggs in a bowl using a fork and add a pinch of salt; lightly flour the pieces of brain.

Heat the oil in a deep-fat fryer. When it is hot (about 375 degrees), dip the pieces of brain, one at a time, in the egg and gently place into the hot oil, turning them over when golden on one side.

Cover the bottom of a serving dish with paper towels. When pieces are golden on both sides, transfer them with slotted spoon onto the serving dish; the paper towels will absorb excess grease. When all the pieces are in the serving dish, remove the paper towels.

Sprinkle with salt, and serve hot with lemon wedges.

A SUGGESTED DINNER

WINE
MASTROBERARDINO TAURASI

Lasagne all'anitra
(SEE PAGE 226)

Cervello fritto
(SEE ABOVE)

Sformato di verdura
(SEE PAGE 554)

Tortelli dolci
(SEE PAGE 590)

Polpette alla fiorentina

DEEP-FRIED CHICKEN OR MEAT CROQUETTES

SERVES 6

*T*hough these croquettes are sometimes made with leftover chicken breast or boiled beef, more often the chicken is poached or the meat boiled especially to make this dish, which shows that it is important enough to the Florentines for them to start from scratch. When the croquette filling is rolled in homemade bread crumbs and deep-fried in a light vegetable oil, the result is a marvelously light, crisp *polpetta*.

2 large potatoes for boiling, but not new potatoes
Coarse-grained salt
4 slices white bread, crusts removed
1 cup cold milk
¾ pound boiled chicken breast or beef (see pages 328 and 329)
10 sprigs Italian parsley, leaves only
1 medium clove garlic, peeled

2 extra-large eggs
¼ cup freshly grated Parmigiano
Salt and freshly ground black pepper
1 cup unseasoned bread crumbs, preferably homemade (see page 58), approximately
2 quarts vegetable oil (see page 22)
Lemon wedges

BOIL potatoes in a saucepan of salted water for 25 to 30 minutes, until soft, then peel them and pass through a potato ricer into a large bowl.

Put the bread in a small bowl with the cold milk and soak for 10 to 12 minutes. Meanwhile, finely chop the boiled chicken (or beef), parsley, and garlic all together.

Transfer the chopped ingredients to the bowl with potatoes, then add the eggs and Parmigiano and mix very well with a wooden spoon. Squeeze the milk out of the bread and add to the bowl, then taste for salt and pepper and mix thoroughly.

Spread the bread crumbs out on a board. Take a heaping tablespoon of the croquette mixture, form into a sausage shape, and roll in the bread crumbs. Repeat until all the mixture is used.

Prepare a serving dish by lining it with paper towels.

Heat the oil in a frying pan, and when it is hot (about 375 degrees), put in the *polpette* and fry until golden on both sides. As they are cooked, place them to drain on the prepared serving dish.

When all the *polpette* are on the dish, remove the paper towels, sprinkle with salt. Serve hot with lemon wedges.

A SUGGESTED DINNER

WINE

PIO CESARE DOLCETTO

Incavolata

(SEE PAGE 148)

Polpette alla fiorentina

(SEE ABOVE)

Broccoli strascicati

(SEE PAGE 526)

Pesche ripiene con mandorle

(SEE PAGE 630)

A SUGGESTED DINNER

WINE
BERTANI VALPOLICELLA

Tagliatelle al cibreo
(SEE PAGE 172)

Cotolette d'agnello
(SEE BELOW)

Carciofi fritti
(SEE PAGE 515)

Insalata verde
(SEE PAGE 500)

Pere al vino
(SEE PAGE 632)

Cotolette d'agnello

LAMB CHOP, FLORENTINE STYLE

SERVES 4

*L*amb is eaten in Italy only very young, in the spring. In order to make these deep-fried lamb chops, you have to convince your butcher to cut them very thin, usually requiring that he cut a single chop into two slices. Insist, because they must be very thin for this dish.

8 small rib lamb chops, cut very thin, about ½ inch
2 extra-large eggs
Salt

¾ cup very fine unflavored bread crumbs, preferably homemade (see page 58), approximately
½ cup olive oil
Lemon wedges

REMOVE all the fat from the chops.

Use a fork to lightly beat the eggs in large bowl with a pinch of salt. Place the lamb chops, one by one, in the bowl with the beaten eggs, making sure all are well coated with egg. Let them marinate for 1 hour.

Spread the bread crumbs over a board. Remove the chops one at a time from the bowl and bread them on both sides. With your fingers, gently press each chop all over to make sure the bread crumbs are adhering to the other side.

Prepare a serving dish by lining it with paper towels.

Heat the vegetable oil and olive oil in a frying pan. When they are hot (about 375 degrees), place the chops, one by one, in the pan and cook for 2 or 3 minutes on each side, then raise the heat to make the bread crumbs a darker brown (what Italians call "frying a brunette," rather than a "blonde," color).

With a strainer-skimmer, transfer the chops from the pan to the prepared serving dish. When all the chops are on the dish, remove the paper towels. Sprinkle with salt, and serve immediately with lemon wedges.

A SUGGESTED DINNER

WINE

Pio Cesare Barbaresco

Tortelli alla menta
(SEE PAGE 196)

Braciole fritte
(SEE BELOW)

Fiori di zucca fritti
(SEE PAGE 552)

or Insalata mista
(SEE PAGE 500)

Schiacciata unta di Berlingaccio
(SEE PAGE 606)

Braciole fritte

DEEP-FRIED VEAL OR BEEF CUTLETS

SERVES 4

This dish is the Florentine counterpart of *cotolette alla milanese*. Cookbooks from the turn of the century mention that a *milanese* has a bone when it is cut from the loin, and is boneless when it is cut from the upper leg. (These are called respectively *costola* and *noce*.) At that time the *milanese* was cooked in enough butter so that it was really deep-fried. Nowadays, most *milanese* are made with the bone and use less butter, so they are almost sautéed rather than deep-fried.

This recipe is for a dish that the Florentines sometimes call a *milanese,* but I believe that, though they were once the same, both it and the *milanese* have changed in the past century. I call it *braciola* because it is made from meat, either veal or young beef, without the bone, pounded thin and tender with the *batticarne* (meat pounder). In Milan the dish is often swimming in butter; some recommend that the butter in which it has been cooked be poured over the dish when served. This obviously would not appeal to the Florentines with their horror of fat and heaviness. So, in Florence, the deep-frying of the old days remains, but done with the lighter *olio di semi.* The butter flavor is replaced by lemon juice and a little salt, which are added when the dish is served. It is also the practice there to marinate the meat in the beaten egg, rather than just dipping it.

4 boneless veal cutlets (about ¾ pound) or thin slices of a tender beef, such as sirloin
2 extra-large eggs
Salt
¾ cup very fine unseasoned bread crumbs, preferably homemade (see page 58), approximately

2 cups vegetable oil (see page 22)
Lemon wedges

IF any fat has been left on the meat cutlets, remove it with a knife.

Wet two sheets of wax paper and place the cutlets between them. Pound the cutlets with a meat pounder until they are about ⅛ inch thick.

In a large bowl, use a fork to lightly beat the eggs with a pinch of salt. Place the cutlets, one by one, in the bowl with the beaten eggs, making sure all are well coated with egg. Let the cutlets marinate for 1 hour.

Spread the bread crumbs over a board. Remove one cutlet at a time from the bowl and bread it on both sides; with your fingers, gently press each cutlet all over to make sure the other side is absorbing bread crumbs. *(continued)*

BRACIOLE FRITTE *(continued)*

Prepare a serving dish by lining it with paper towels.

Heat the vegetable oil in a frying pan. When it is hot (about 375 degrees), place the cutlets, one by one, in the pan and cook them for about 1 minute on each side, until very lightly golden. (In Italy we say that the *braciole* must be "blonde" and that breaded lamb cutlets must be "brunette.")

Transfer the cutlets from the pan to the prepared serving dish with a strainer-skimmer. When all cutlets are on the dish, remove the paper towels. Sprinkle with a little salt, and serve immediately with lemon wedges.

NOTE: You can also eat the cutlets cold, or plain with anchovy sauce (see page 73). If cold, use butter to fry the cutlets. While butter is heavier than the vegetable oil, it will give a better taste to the cold dish.

A SUGGESTED DINNER

WINE

BERTANI BARDOLINO CLASSICO SUPERIORE

Risotto con funghi
(SEE PAGE 428)

Fritto misto alla fiorentina
(SEE BELOW)

Insalata verde
(SEE PAGE 500)

Pesche al vino
(SEE PAGE 632)

THE FRIED COURSE

Fritto misto alla fiorentina

MIXED FRY, FLORENTINE STYLE

*T*he fried-dish counterpart to the *bollito misto* is called *fritto misto*. It is again a holdover from the days when the boiled course and the fried course were the *primi e secondi.*

The most usual mixture, if only two dishes are included, is that of fried calf's brain (see page 342) and fried artichokes (see page 515), a combination that appears on most restaurant menus as *fritto alla fiorentina.* However, the *misto* can be a more elaborate combination. For a really grand *misto,* you may include, for meats, fried chicken (see page 340), croquettes (see page 344), and the brains; for vegetables, zucchini (see page 552), zucchini flowers (see page 552), cauliflower (see page 533), potatoes, or any combination thereof.

To serve *fritto misto,* arrange the serving dish into as many wedges (like slices of a pie) as there are different dishes. Separate each wedge from the next by a row of lemon wedges. As much as possible, alternate wedges of meats with those of vegetables.

Eggs

*E*ggs make a very light but very satisfying main course. The first egg dish we present, the classically simple *uova al pomodoro* (eggs poached in tomatoes), is useful for the simplest of occasions or when a very light main dish is in order. Following is *uova alla fiorentina* the way the Florentines make it, and last comes *asparagi alla fiorentina,* a succulent dish of tender, thin young asparagus, sautéed with butter and topped with eggs fried a very special way.

It goes without saying that any of the *frittate* on pages 116–118, when freshly made and warm, may also be served as main courses.

A SUGGESTED DINNER

WINE

BROLIO RISERVA DI BARONE

Risotto con salsicce

(SEE PAGE 249)

Uova al pomodoro

(SEE BELOW)

Patate saltate alla salvia

(SEE PAGE 540)

Fresh fruit

Uova al pomodoro

EGGS POACHED IN TOMATOES

SERVES 6

A dish that can be marvelous—if the ingredients are good. Poaching in tomatoes rather than water preserves the full flavor of the eggs. Especially good in the summer when tomatoes and basil are fresh, this dish also works well with preserved tomatoes and basil in the winter.

2 pounds very ripe fresh tomatoes, or 2 pounds canned tomatoes, preferably imported Italian, drained
1 small clove garlic, peeled
¼ cup olive oil

Salt and freshly ground black pepper
6 leaves basil, fresh or preserved in salt (see page 18)
12 extra-large eggs

IF fresh tomatoes are used, first cut them into pieces (canned tomatoes may be left whole); cut the garlic into small pieces.

Heat the oil in a large saucepan, preferably terra-cotta. When it is hot, sauté the garlic lightly until light golden. Add the tomatoes and cook over low heat for about 15 minutes. Check to be sure they are very soft and of a saucelike consistency, and if necessary cook a little longer; do not add any water or broth. Add salt and pepper to taste.

If the basil is fresh, tear the leaves in half or in thirds. If preserved, keep the leaves whole, as they must be removed before the dish is served. Add basil to the saucepan.

Very carefully, break the eggs into the tomato sauce. Sprinkle salt and pepper over the eggs and let them poach for about 8 minutes, in total. Four minutes uncovered and 4 minutes covered. (Remove the preserved basil at this point.)

Bring the eggs to the table, in the pan, and serve hot.

NOTE: This dish is best prepared with fresh—not supermarket—eggs.

A SUGGESTED DINNER

WINE
MASI AMARONE

Spaghetti con briciolata
(SEE PAGE 187)

Uova alla fiorentina
(SEE BELOW)

Frittelle di riso
(SEE PAGE 622)

Uova alla fiorentina

SERVES 4

*T*he dish that is widely disseminated under the name "eggs Florentine" consists of spinach sautéed in butter, egg placed over it, everything covered with *balsamella* and Parmigiano or *groviera* (Mornay sauce in France), and then baked.

Though even modern Florentine cookbooks use this recipe and call it "eggs Florentine," I believe that this is a completely French dish. The French tend to call anything with spinach and Mornay sauce "Florentine," and there probably is some basis in the history of food for doing so.

However, I have never come across the sautéing of spinach in butter in the Florence of either the past or present. And while Mornay sauce is quite probably of Florentine origin, and is used on spinach to make *spinaci alla fiorentina* (see page 547), it is not used on eggs. The baking also probably comes from *spinaci alla fiorentina*.

The following is a dish that is widely used in Florence and is possibly the authentic eggs Florentine.

1 pound fresh spinach, cleaned	*Salt and freshly ground black*
Coarse-grained salt	*pepper*
3 tablespoons olive oil	*4 extra-large eggs*
1 small clove garlic, peeled	*Freshly grated nutmeg to taste*

USING the spinach, coarse salt, olive oil, garlic, and salt and pepper make *spinaci saltati* as directed on page 546, preferably using a terra-cotta saucepan.

Make 4 small wells in the spinach and place a raw egg in each. Salt and pepper each egg, then cover the pan and cook over very low heat for about 12 to 15 minutes; the eggs will steam inside the pan.

Sprinkle very lightly with nutmeg, then bring to the table in the pan and serve.

NOTE: This dish is best prepared with fresh—not supermarket—eggs.

357

Asparagi alla fiorentina

ASPARAGUS, FLORENTINE STYLE

SERVES 4

*B*ecause they have a short one-month season in the spring, asparagus are much prized in Italy and are treated as a main dish. In
contrast to some tastes, it is the thin asparagus that are preferred, for
their delicacy and taste as well as tenderness. Nowadays we are lucky to
have asparagus for much more of the year, often from the greenhouse,
and our large, thick asparagus are often good and tender. But do try the
thin ones, for taste, and to know how they are in their own season.

After the asparagus are boiled or steamed, they are sautéed in butter
and sprinkled with Parmigiano. Then the master touch is applied: *uova
in padella* (fried eggs) are arranged over them. The Italian expression,
"Non è buono a cuocere nemmeno un uovo" (he is not even able to cook an
egg) gives an incorrect impression, because to cook an egg well is really
an art—and the eggs as prepared here are truly artistic. They can stand
on their own, without the asparagus, very well indeed, and make an
excellent main course in themselves.

4 extra-large eggs
3 pounds thin asparagus
Coarse-grained salt
12 tablespoons (6 ounces) sweet
*   butter*

Salt and freshly ground black
*   pepper*
½ cup freshly grated
*   Parmigiano*

REMOVE eggs from the refrigerator at least 1 hour before you intend to
use them; they must be at room temperature for this dish.

Rinse the asparagus well, then clean the white part of each one by
scraping it with a knife. Arrange all asparagus in a bunch, with tips even.
Tie the bunch together, toward the bottom, with thread. Then, with a
knife, even off the ends.

Place the bunch of asparagus, standing with tips up, in a tall stockpot or asparagus cooker. Add enough cold water to cover the white
parts, at the lower end of the asparagus, then cover with pot and place

A SUGGESTED DINNER

WINE
MARCHESI DI BAROLO GRIGNOLINO DEL PIEMONTE

Tagliatelle al sugo di carne
(SEE PAGE 168)

Asparagi alla fiorentina
(SEE ABOVE)

Lamponi alla panna
(SEE PAGE 634)

it on the heat. Bring the water to a boil, add coarse salt, reduce the heat, and simmer for 20 minutes or less, according to the size of the asparagus, without removing the lid.

Remove the pot from the heat and transfer the asparagus to a chopping board. Untie the bunch and cut off the hard white ends.

Heat the butter in a large frying pan. When it is melted, add the asparagus and sauté for 6 or 7 minutes, turning gently with a wooden spoon several times. Sprinkle the grated Parmigiano, salt, and freshly ground black pepper over the asparagus, then cook, still turning gently, for 1 minute more.

Leaving the sautéing butter in the pan, transfer the asparagus from the frying pan to a large serving dish and arrange in a ring, with all the tips facing the center of the dish. Keep the serving dish in a warm place, near the stove if possible.

Heat the butter left over from cooking the asparagus over low heat. Break one of the eggs, and carefully pour the white into the pan with the asparagus butter, saving the yolk in its half-shell. Repeat with the

(continued)

ASPARAGI ALLA FIORENTINA *(continued)*

remaining eggs, keeping each white separate from the others in the pan.

When all the egg whites are arranged in the frying pan, sprinkle with salt, then place a yolk on top of each white, taking care not to break the yolk. Sprinkle each yolk with pepper, then cover the frying pan and let simmer very slowly for about 4 minutes.

Remove the pan from the heat, arrange the eggs over the asparagus on the serving dish, and serve immediately, sprinkled with a little freshly ground black pepper.

Poultry and Game

A SUGGESTED DINNER

WINE

BROLIO CHIANTI CLASSICO RESERVA

Lasagne al forno

(SEE PAGE 221)

Pollastrino alla griglia

(SEE BELOW)

Insalata mista

(SEE PAGE 500)

Torta di mele

(SEE PAGE 610)

Pollastrino alla griglia

GRILLED SQUAB CHICKEN

SERVES 1

*H*ere, the celebrated, two-month-old Arno Valley chickens are flattened and cooked simply on the iron *gratella,* the range-top grill. A good butcher can obtain young squab fryers or even fresh Cornish hens for you, and they work very well for this dish. Each person is served a whole tender, tiny chicken.

The *gratella* is a wonderful way of cooking. It is ridged so that the fat drips down and the chicken doesn't cook in it. If the grill is well seasoned, you will need no shortening; just salt the grill.

*1 squab fryer chicken or fresh
Cornish hen (1 to 1½
pounds)*

*2 teaspoons coarse-grained salt
Freshly ground black pepper
Lemon wedges*

CUT the chicken (or Cornish hen) lengthwise through the breast and open it. With your hands, flatten it out.

Heat a well-seasoned iron *gratella* on a low flame for about 5 minutes, then sprinkle the grill with the 2 teaspoons of salt. When the grill is very hot and the salt turns brown, place the flattened chicken on it and top with a weight such as an iron skillet wrapped in aluminum foil (see illustration below). Cook for about 10 minutes, then turn the chicken over, using a metal spatula, put the weight back on, and cook for 10 minutes more. (If the chicken is really very young, at this point it should be completely cooked and of a dark, golden color. Try with a fork to see if it is really cooked; if not, cook it for several more minutes, until completely done.)

Transfer the grilled chicken to serving dish, sprinkle with a little freshly ground black pepper and serve with lemon wedges.

Place the weight—an iron skillet wrapped in foil—on the chicken.

Petti di pollo alla fiorentina

CHICKEN BREASTS, FLORENTINE STYLE

SERVES 6

*C*hicken breasts and the tender insides of artichokes, cut into pieces and sautéed together in white wine and sprinkled with lemon juice. This is a dish that gives lie to the idea that artichokes and wine do not go together. In this dish, only the tenderest part of the artichoke is used so it can be cooked in a very short time, conveying a little of the idea of the taste of the raw tender artichokes the Florentines love to eat *in pinzimonio* (see page 98).

This is a dish that can be prepared in a short time.

3 large artichokes
2 lemons
½ cup olive oil
Salt and freshly ground black
*   pepper to taste*
3 whole chicken breasts, from a
*   3½-pound chicken, skinned*

1 cup unbleached all-purpose
*   flour, approximately*
½ cup dry white wine

CLEAN the artichokes according to the directions on page 510 and cut them into small pieces. Put artichoke pieces in a large bowl of cold water with one of the lemons, cut into halves, and let stand for 30 minutes.

Remove artichokes and dry them with paper towels.

Heat ¼ cup of the olive oil in a large, heavy casserole. When the oil is hot, add the artichoke pieces and sauté, over medium heat, for about 25 minutes, stirring every few minutes with a wooden spoon and adding lukewarm water as needed until artichokes are cooked and soft. Season with salt and pepper, then, with a strainer-skimmer, remove the artichokes from the casserole and transfer them to a second casserole. Cover with a lid and let stand until needed.

Remove bone from chicken breasts and cut them into 1-inch-square pieces. Lightly flour the chicken pieces.

Heat the remaining ¼ cup of olive oil in the first casserole and put in the chicken pieces. Sauté very gently until soft (about 15 minutes), then season with salt. When the meat is ready, transfer from the first casserole to the second, containing the artichokes.

Pour the wine in the first casserole, use a wooden spoon to help deglaze the casserole, and let it reduce very slowly (about 15 minutes), then pour the sauce over the artichoke and chicken mixture; squeeze the juice of the remaining lemon over and mix thoroughly.

Transfer the contents of the casserole to a serving dish and serve immediately.

A SUGGESTED DINNER

WINE
CESARI TRENTINO PINOT GRIGIO

Sformato di tagliatelle verdi
(SEE PAGE 170)

Petti di pollo alla fiorentina
(SEE ABOVE)

Schiacciata con zibibbo
(SEE PAGE 604)

A SUGGESTED DINNER

WINE
CONTRATTO BAROLO

Carabaccia
(SEE PAGE 137)

Pollo alle olive
(SEE BELOW)

Insalata mista
(SEE PAGE 500)

or Insalata composta
(SEE PAGE 501)

Dolce di polenta
(SEE PAGE 611)

Pollo alle olive

CHICKEN WITH BLACK OLIVES

SERVES 4

*U*nboned chicken pieces cooked with olives and flavored with thyme and bay leaf. Though thyme grows wild in many gardens in Florence, it is not used as much nowadays as in olden times. There are, however, several traditional dishes that use it. Here its flavor blends well with the Mediterranean olive flavor.

1 chicken (3 to 4 pounds)
8 tablespoons (4 ounces) sweet butter
1 tablespoon olive oil
Salt and freshly ground black pepper
1½ cups chicken or meat broth, preferably homemade

2 tablespoons unbleached all-purpose flour
1 bay leaf
1 teaspoon dried thyme
½ pound black olives, in brine, drained (see note)
10 sprigs Italian parsley, leaves only, coarsely chopped

Cut the chicken into 16 pieces. Heat the butter and olive oil in a large flameproof casserole. When the butter is melted, raise the heat, then put in the chicken pieces and sauté gently, turning them, until they are golden all over (about 15 minutes). Season with salt and pepper.

Heat the broth to the boiling point in a saucepan.

Meanwhile, sprinkle the chicken with the flour and stir it thoroughly with a wooden spoon for 1 minute. Immediately pour in the hot broth, stirring thoroughly to prevent lumps from forming, then add the bay leaf and the thyme to the casserole and simmer slowly for 20 minutes, stirring every so often. Remove the bay leaf from the casserole and add the olives. Taste for salt and pepper and simmer for about 10 minutes more.

Remove the casserole from the heat and transfer its contents to a serving dish. Sprinkle over the parsley and serve hot.

NOTE: Olives preserved in brine can be very salty. If so, soak them in cold water for ½ hour, rinse, and drain.

Fricassea di pollo

FLORENTINE CHICKEN FRICASSEE

SERVES 4

Le Cuisinier of La Varenne, which appeared in France about 1650, is full of fricassees. However, the Florentine and Ferrarese cookbooks of more than a century earlier also contain them. In fact La Varenne's book, which many consider an important step in the history of the development of haute cuisine, really does not differ all that much from the Italian cookbooks of the previous century. The book was translated in Bologna about 1690, and because the French and the Bolognese share a predilection for rich, creamy food, it may have played a role in the development of Bolognese cooking.

1½ ounces dried **porcini** mushrooms	1 tablespoon (½ ounce) sweet butter
1 chicken (about 3 pounds)	2 tablespoons olive oil
1 red onion, cleaned	1½ tablespoons unbleached all-purpose flour
1 celery rib	
10 sprigs Italian parsley, leaves only	2½ cups chicken or meat broth, approximately, preferably homemade
1 carrot, scraped	
1 large clove garlic, peeled	3 extra-large egg yolks
½ teaspoon rosemary leaves, fresh or preserved in salt or dried and blanched	1 lemon
	Salt and freshly ground black pepper to taste

SOAK mushrooms in lukewarm water for 30 minutes; cut the chicken in 8 pieces; coarsely chop and place the *odori* (onion, celery, parsley, carrot, garlic, and rosemary) on a piece of cheesecloth, tie into a bag, and set aside.

Heat the butter and olive oil in a flameproof casserole. When the butter is melted and hot, add the chicken pieces and sauté lightly over medium heat for 10 to 12 minutes. When the chicken pieces are golden, transfer them from the casserole onto a serving dish.

Leaving the casserole on the heat, add the flour to the remaining oil and cook, stirring very well, until golden (about 3 to 4 minutes). Meanwhile, heat the broth to boiling in a saucepan, then pour 1½ cups of it into the casserole and mix very well, to prevent lumps from forming. Meanwhile, drain the mushrooms and clean them, removing all the sand attached to the stems. If the soaking water is saved for another dish, strain it through several layers of paper towels to remove sand. The water may be frozen in ice cube trays.

Put the chicken pieces back into the casserole and add the cheesecloth bag containing the *odori*. Cover and simmer very slowly for 20 minutes, then remove the cheesecloth bag and taste for salt and pepper. Add the mushrooms and more hot broth if needed, cover, and simmer for 10 to 12 minutes more, stirring every so often with a wooden spoon.

When the cooking time is almost up, beat the egg yolks in a bowl. Remove the casserole from the heat and quickly add the beaten eggs, stirring continuously with a wooden spoon. When the eggs are well amalgamated, squeeze in the juice from the lemon and mix thoroughly.

Transfer to a serving dish and serve hot.

A SUGGESTED DINNER

WINE
NEGRI INFERNO

Risotto con funghi
(SEE PAGE 248)

Fricassea di pollo
(SEE ABOVE)

Sformato di fagiolini
(SEE PAGE 554)

Torta di mele
(SEE PAGE 610)

Pollo alla cacciatora

CHICKEN, HUNTER STYLE

SERVES 4

*A*ll over Italy, "hunter style," *alla cacciatora,* is applied to dishes made with fowl, perhaps originally with game birds. It is supposed to connote the basic but excellent style of preparation used by the hunters themselves. Naturally, the name covers a multitude of dishes, usually made with chicken rather than a game bird.

This is a Tuscan way of making it, using very little tomato but depending more on red wine and olive oil and full of herbs such as sage, rosemary, and bay leaf. The chicken is *spezzatino,* that is, cut into small pieces, each around a piece of bone.

It is worthwhile to try this version, especially if you know the heavier tomato sauce ones. It is not difficult to prepare.

1 chicken (3 to 3½ pounds)	Salt and freshly ground black
1 tablespoon rosemary leaves,	pepper to taste
fresh or preserved in salt or	Pinch of hot red pepper flakes
dried and blanched	½ cup dry red wine
10 leaves sage, fresh or	1 bay leaf
preserved in salt (see	2 tablespoons tomato paste,
page 19)	preferably imported Italian
2 large cloves garlic, peeled	1½ cups hot water
½ cup olive oil	

CUT the chicken into 16 pieces; coarsely chop the rosemary, sage, and garlic.

Heat the olive oil in a large casserole, preferably terra-cotta, and when it is hot, add the chopped ingredients and sauté gently until lightly golden (10 to 12 minutes). Add the chicken pieces and sauté them over moderately high heat until golden all over (about 15 minutes), then add salt, pepper, and hot pepper flakes.

Lower the heat and pour in the wine. Let it evaporate very slowly (about 10 minutes), then add the bay leaf, tomato paste, and ½ cup of the hot water. Cover and let simmer very slowly for 20 minutes, adding more hot water if needed.

. At this point, the chicken should be cooked, and there should be a small quantity of thick sauce. Remove the bay leaf and transfer the chicken pieces and sauce to a serving dish. Serve hot.

NOTE: This dish is even better when reheated.

A SUGGESTED DINNER

WINE
NEGRI GRUMELLO

Risotto in bianco
(SEE PAGE 245)

Pollo alla cacciatora
(SEE ABOVE)

Insalata composta
(SEE PAGE 501)

Bombe
(SEE PAGE 573)

Pollo in porchetta

CHICKEN MADE IN THE MANNER OF SUCKLING PIG

SERVES 4

*T*he famous *porchetta,* or suckling pig, is cooked filled with a large quantity of herbs, spices, and *pancetta.* This treatment is also very good with both chicken and duck. After the bird is stuffed, it is closed up tightly by sewing, and put in the oven. Suckling pig is indeed evoked, and one can make this dish more often than the *porchetta,* which after all requires a very special occasion.

FOR THE STUFFING

4 ounces **pancetta** *or prosciutto, in one piece*
14 large leaves sage, fresh or preserved in salt (see page 19)
10 juniper berries
1 large bay leaf

1 tablespoon rosemary leaves, fresh or preserved in salt or dried and blanched
6 or 7 whole black peppercorns
Salt and freshly ground black pepper

FOR THE CHICKEN

1 broiler chicken (about 3¹/₂ pounds), left whole

¹/₄ cup olive oil

PREPARE the stuffing by coarsely cutting the *pancetta,* and coarsely chopping 10 of the sage leaves, the juniper berries, bay leaf, and rosemary leaves; then mix in the peppercorns, 2 level teaspoons of salt, and ¹/₂ teaspoon pepper.

Preheat the oven to 400 degrees.

Rinse the chicken inside and out; leave in all the chicken fat. Fill the cavity of the chicken with the stuffing mixture and sew up both ends, placing the 4 remaining sage leaves in the neck end before sewing it up, then tie the chicken up as you would a roast.

Abundantly salt and pepper the outside of the chicken and place in a roasting pan along with the olive oil. Cook in the preheated oven for about 1 hour, turning the chicken over 3 or 4 times. By that time the chicken should be cooked and golden.

Transfer the chicken to a serving dish and serve hot.

A SUGGESTED DINNER

WINE
CHIANTI CLASSICO MONSANTO

Cipollata
(SEE PAGE 138)

Pollo in porchetta
(SEE ABOVE)

Fagioli all'uccelletto
(SEE PAGE 519)

Fresh fruit

Pollo affinocchiato

FENNELED CHICKEN

SERVES 4

*C*hicken prepared with fennel seeds and almonds is the oldest known Italian chicken recipe, going back at least to the fourteenth century, and for some centuries it was the favorite way of preparing chicken. When you try it, you'll understand why. The taste is a little unusual at first, but then you realize that it is one of the combinations that was meant to be. That it has disappeared in recent times can probably be explained by the movement away from using almonds as one of the bases of Mediterranean cooking. A dish that is worth reviving, that can be eaten often, with an unusual flavor, this is not extremely difficult to prepare, but makes a fine impression at an important dinner.

1 chicken (about 3 to 3½ pounds)
4 ounces pancetta *or* prosciutto, *in one piece*
1 medium red onion, cleaned
¼ cup of olive oil
2 cups chicken or meat broth, preferably homemade

4 ounces almonds, blanched
2 tablespoons unbleached all-purpose flour
1 heaping tablespoon fennel seeds
Salt and freshly ground black pepper to taste

CUT the chicken into 8 pieces, then rinse very carefully and dry with paper towels. Cut the *pancetta* into tiny pieces and coarsely chop the onion.

Heat the olive oil in a flameproof casserole, then add the *pancetta* and onion and sauté over medium heat until golden. Add the chicken pieces and let them sauté until light golden on both sides (about 15 minutes).

While the chicken is sautéing, heat the broth in a saucepan. When the broth is hot, lower the heat and put in the blanched almonds. Let the broth and almonds remain over low heat until needed.

When the chicken pieces are ready, sprinkle them with the flour. Wait a few seconds, then pour in the hot broth and almonds. Taste for salt and pepper, then add the fennel seeds and let everything simmer together for 25 to 30 minutes, until completely cooked, stirring every few minutes.

Remove the casserole from the heat, transfer the chicken and sauce to a serving dish, and serve hot. This dish is even better the next day, reheated, or served cold for a family dinner.

NOTE: Sometimes chickens give off a great deal of fat. If there is more than a thin layer at the top, remove excess before transferring chicken and sauce to serving dish.

A SUGGESTED DINNER

WINE

SAN FELICE CHIANTI CLASSICO

Gnocchi di pesce

(SEE PAGE 270)

Pollo affinocchiato

(SEE ABOVE)

Sformato di finocchi

(SEE PAGE 554)

Crostata di frutta

(SEE PAGE 576)

A SUGGESTED DINNER

WINE

FONTANA FREDDA GATTINARA

Taglierini al pomodoro fresco
(SEE PAGE 166)

Pollo in pane
(SEE BELOW)

Lattaiolo
(SEE PAGE 567)

Pollo in pane

WHOLE CHICKEN BAKED IN BREAD

SERVES 4

The whole chicken baked inside a bread and the boned whole stuffed chicken (see page 382) are the most elaborate chicken dishes in the Tuscan repertory, and probably in all Italian cooking. They are both dishes with an elaborate presentation that is appropriate to the most festive and formal occasions.

This dish, the less complicated of the two, is presented as a very large, freshly baked Tuscan bread. Then it is sliced open and inside is a whole, unboned chicken, which is stuffed in turn with coarsely cut *odori* (aromatic vegetables), chicken livers, red wine, and prosciutto. The stuffing is not in the form of a forcemeat, but is in recognizable small pieces. The bread absorbs some of the juice of the chicken and stuffing on the inside, and is delicious when chunks of it are served with the meat and stuffing.

1 chicken (3½ to 4 pounds)
1 medium red onion, cleaned
1 large celery rib
1 large clove garlic, peeled
2 carrots, scraped
3 ounces prosciutto or
    pancetta, in one piece

5 tablespoons olive oil
Salt, freshly ground black
    pepper, and freshly grated
    nutmeg
½ cup red wine
¼ pound chicken livers, cleaned
Tuscan bread (see page 39)

PREPARE the stuffing and the chicken first.

Rinse the chicken, inside and out, then dry with paper towels; cut the onion, celery, garlic, carrots, and prosciutto (or pancetta) into large pieces.

Heat the olive oil in a large frying pan, then add the cut-up ingredients and sauté gently for about 10 minutes.

Place the whole chicken in the frying pan. Season with salt, pepper, and nutmeg and sauté, turning on all sides, until golden all over (about 15 minutes). Add the red wine and let evaporate very slowly (about 15 minutes), continuing to turn the chicken on all sides.

Meanwhile, cut the chicken livers into quarters. Add them to the pan and cook for 2 or 3 minutes more, then remove the frying pan from the heat and let stand until cool (about 1 hour).

Prepare the "sponge" and then the dough for Tuscan bread according to the directions on page 40, up to the point that kneading of dough is completed.

Flour a pasta board. Spread the dough out very gently, with a rolling pin or with your hands, to a thickness of about 1 inch. Sprinkle the surface of the dough with salt and pepper.

Stuff the chicken with the ingredients in pan and then place the chicken on the dough (see the illustration on page 378). Sprinkle the top of the chicken with any ingredients left over in the pan, then fold the dough completely around the chicken so that from the outside it appears to be an oval-shaped bread (see the illustration on page 378).

Lightly flour a large jelly-roll pan and carefully place the dough-covered chicken on it. Cover with a cotton towel and let stand in a warm place, away from drafts, until the dough has risen and almost doubled in size (about 1 hour). (continued)

Pollo in pane: Place the stuffed chicken on the dough.

Fold the dough up around the chicken.

POLLO IN PANE *(continued)*

Preheat the oven to 400 degrees.

Place the pan in the preheated oven and bake for 60 to 70 minutes, depending on the size of the chicken, then remove the pan from the oven and transfer the whole bread with chicken inside onto a large serving dish.

To serve, cut off the top part of the bread; the chicken will appear, sitting in the middle of the loaf of bread with some vegetables surrounding it. Each serving should have a piece of chicken, some vegetable filling, and a piece of the bread crust.

A SUGGESTED DINNER

WINE

SANTA SOFIA BIANCO DI CUSTOZA

Panzanella

(SEE PAGE 113)

Pollo forte

(SEE BELOW)

Insalata composta

(SEE PAGE 501)

Pesche al vino

(SEE PAGE 632)

Pollo forte

SPICY CHICKEN APPETIZER

SERVES 8

*B*oiled chicken pieces, flavorsome and not overcooked, in a delicious, piquant sauce made with olive oil, broth, wine vinegar, garlic, and red peppers preserved in wine vinegar. Served cold, it is an extremely useful and versatile dish. Used mainly as an antipasto to whet the appetite, it serves also as a refreshing main dish for the hot weather.

1 boiled chicken (about 4 pounds), with its broth (see page 328)

2 tablespoons capers in wine vinegar, drained

4 whole anchovies in salt or 8 anchovy fillets in oil, drained

2 large cloves garlic, peeled

½ cup olive oil

1½ tablespoons unbleached all-purpose flour

2 sweet red bell peppers in wine vinegar, whole or in pieces (available in specialty stores)

Salt and freshly ground black pepper to taste

3 tablespoons red wine vinegar

PREPARE the boiled chicken according to the directions. Remove from the broth and let cool. Strain the broth and let cool for 1 hour.

Meanwhile, remove the skin from the chicken and lift the meat off the bones. Cut the meat into strips and arrange on a serving dish. Sprinkle the capers over. Set aside.

When the broth is cool, defat it thoroughly. Set aside.

Prepare the sauce. Clean and fillet the anchovies under cold, running water if the anchovies in salt are used. Set the fillets aside until needed.

Heat 1½ cups of defatted broth to the boiling point in a saucepan. Meanwhile, chop the garlic coarsely.

Heat the oil in a flameproof casserole over medium heat. When it is warm, add the anchovies, mashing them with a wooden spoon into a paste. Add the flour and stir until the flour is golden. Continuing to stir, add the boiling broth, all at once, and stir for 2 or 3 minutes more. Add one of the peppers, unchopped, and the chopped garlic. Let simmer for

about 10 minutes, then remove from the heat and put in a blender or food processor. Blend until homogenous.

Return the blended mixture to the casserole. Taste for salt and pepper and place over low heat. Simmer for about 15 minutes more, then remove the casserole from the heat. Add the wine vinegar, mix well, and pour immediately over the chicken.

Cut the remaining pepper into thin strips and arrange them over the chicken.

Let cool for 30 minutes, then wrap the serving dish and place in the refrigerator for at least 4 hours before serving.

A SUGGESTED BUFFET

WINES
CORVO BIANCO
FONTANA CANDIDA-ORVIETO
MARCHESE ANTINORI NATURE *(BRUT)*

Insalata di riso
(SEE PAGE 100)

Pollo forte
(SEE ABOVE)

Porrata
(SEE PAGE 114)

Melenzane marinate
(SEE PAGE 108)

Pesche ripiene con mandorle
(SEE PAGE 630)

with Crema zabaione
(SEE PAGE 565)

A SUGGESTED DINNER

WINE
BERTANI AMARONE GIANFRANCO D'ATTIMIS PICOLIT

Ravioli nudi
(SEE PAGE 268)

Pollo disossato ripieno
(SEE BELOW)

Fagioli al fiasco
(SEE PAGE 516)

Torta di riso uso garfagnana
(SEE PAGE 624)

Pollo disossato ripieno

BONED WHOLE STUFFED CHICKEN

SERVES FROM 8 TO 12

*O*ne of the great old Tuscan dishes, this requires much preparation, the time and skill to bone the chicken while leaving it whole, the elaborate stuffing, the cooking, weighting, and cooling. It is appropriate for the most elegant occasions, though it is eaten cold. The elaborate forcemeat with which it is stuffed contains four kinds of meat, red wine, Parmigiano, and boiled ham, in addition to *odori* (aromatic vegetables) and herbs. It is a much more complex dish than a *galantina,* * with which it is occasionally confused.

It is well worth the trouble, however, for it is one of the most delicious dishes imaginable, and makes an extraordinary presentation. It

*For various types of galantines, see my *Classic Techniques of Italian Cooking* and *Foods of Italy* (Galantine-sausage).

also has the advantage that it must be prepared in advance, so it can be done at your leisure. Don't be afraid to try it. The instructions for boning the chicken, making the stuffing, etc., are given in complete detail. Just follow them carefully, and with a little practice you'll have a dish that will give you reason to be proud.

4 extra-large eggs
Coarse grained salt
2 celery ribs
10 sprigs Italian parsley, leaves only
2 large cloves garlic, peeled
1 carrot, scraped
5 tablespoons olive oil
1 bay leaf
1 pork chop (for a yield of ¼ pound meat)
½ pound ground beef
1 whole chicken breast, from 4-pound chicken, skinned
¾ cup dry red wine
Salt and freshly ground black pepper
1 tablespoon tomato paste, preferably imported Italian

½ cup canned tomatoes, preferably imported Italian, drained and seeded
1½ cups chicken or meat broth plus 5 tablespoons, preferably homemade
1½ packages unflavored gelatin
¼ pound boiled ham, in one piece
1 cup freshly grated Parmigiano
Pinch of freshly grated nutmeg
1 whole chicken (about 4 pounds)
1½ teaspoons rosemary leaves, fresh or preserved in salt or dried and blanched

IN a small saucepan, hard-cook two of the eggs in salted water (10 to 12 minutes). Set aside until needed.

Finely chop the *odori* (onion, celery, parsley, garlic, and carrot).

Heat the olive oil in a large flameproof casserole. When it is hot, add the chopped *odori* and sauté lightly until golden (about 15 minutes), then add the bay leaf, pork chop, ground beef, and chicken breast. Sauté, stirring every so often with a wooden spoon, for 15 minutes more.

Add the wine and let it evaporate slowly (15 to 20 minutes), then

(continued)

POLLO DISOSSATO RIPIENO *(continued)*

taste for salt and pepper. Add the tomato paste and tomatoes and simmer for 4 or 5 minutes more.

Remove the casserole from the heat, discard the bay leaf, and transfer the pork chop and chicken breast to a board. Remove the bones and chop the meat very fine.

Replace the casserole on the heat and add the chopped meat. Simmer for 5 or 6 minutes.

Meanwhile, heat 1½ cups of the broth in a saucepan, then add it to the casserole and simmer very slowly for 10 minutes. Meanwhile dissolve the gelatin in the remaining 5 tablespoons of broth and let rest for 5 minutes. Then add to the casserole, mix very well, and simmer very slowly until all the broth has evaporated and the sauce has become thick (35 to 45 minutes). Season with salt and pepper.

Remove the casserole from the stove and transfer the sauce to a large bowl. Let cool slightly, then refrigerate until chilled, not cold.

When the contents of the bowl are chilled, chop the boiled ham coarsely and add it to the bowl, along with the remaining 2 eggs, grated Parmigiano, and nutmeg to taste. Mix very well with a wooden spoon and let stand until needed.

Shell the hard-cooked eggs and let stand until needed.

Begin boning the chicken by cutting the two tendons at the end of each of the two legs (see illustration on page 385). Free the bone on the inside by hand (there is nothing to cut here) and push out a little bit (see illustration on page 385). Free the thigh bone by cutting the tendon between the leg and thigh. Push the thigh bone from one end and pull from the other (see illustration on page 386).

Starting from cavity end, with a knife, little by little scrape the meat, without breaking it, off the inside of the central carcass (see illustration on page 386). Remove large central bone in one piece (see illustration on page 387).

Cut off the two outer sections of each wing (see illustration on page 387). Remove the bone of the inner section in the same way you did the legs.

Tuck the legs and wings inside and sew up the neck opening.

Preheat the oven to 375 degrees. *(continued)*

Pollo disossato ripieno: Cut the tendon at the end of the chicken leg.

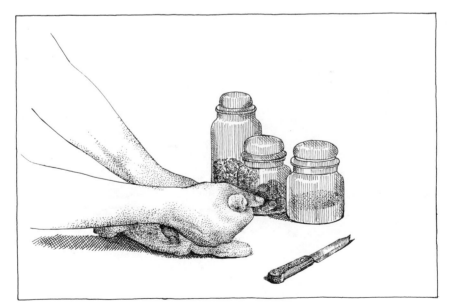

Free the leg bone on the inside.

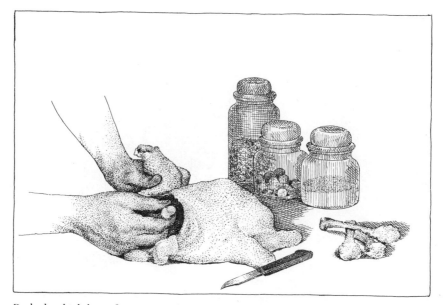

Push the thigh bone from one end and pull from the other.

Scrape the meat from the rib cage.

Remove the carcass.

Cut off the two outer sections of the wings.

Insert one of the hard-boiled eggs when the chicken is half stuffed.

POLLO DISOSSATO RIPIENO *(continued)*

Stuff the chicken from the remaining opening, at the bottom end. When you are halfway through, add the hard-cooked eggs (see illustration on page 388), then continue with the remaining stuffing; sew up the opening. Sprinkle freely with salt, pepper, and rosemary.

Wrap the chicken well in a large sheet of aluminum foil, then place the foil-wrapped chicken in a 13½ × 8¾-inch glass baking dish and bake in the preheated oven for 2 hours, turning the chicken over once, after 1 hour.

Remove the dish from the oven and allow the chicken to cool for 2 hours, first putting a weight on top to flatten it. Then, still with the weight on top, place in the refrigerator until completely cold (about 4 hours).

When cold, unwrap the chicken and transfer to a board. Slice across the width, then place the slices on a serving dish, and serve.

NOTE: It is better to prepare this dish at least one day in advance.

A SUGGESTED DINNER
FOR THANKSGIVING DAY

WINE

Schioppetto Tocai
Avignonesi Vino Nobile di Montepulciano
Brolio Vinsanto

Polpettone di tacchino al tonno
(SEE PAGE 392)

Tortelli di zucca alla modenese
SEE PAGE 202)

Petto di tacchino arrocchiato
(SEE BELOW)

Patate saltate alla salvia
(SEE PAGE 540)

Tartufi di castagne
(SEE PAGE 614)

Petto di tacchino arrocchiato

ROLLED STUFFED TURKEY BREAST

SERVES 6

Turkey started to be used in Italy very soon after the discovery of America. In line with the general confusion about where Columbus and the Florentines, Amerigo Vespucci and Giovanni Verrazzano, had landed, it was at first called "rooster of India" *(gallo d'India)*. (Even the name "turkey" reveals a mistaken geography.) Turkeys were

(continued)

probably adopted so quickly because of their resemblance to the pea-cock, which was a very expensive bird with enormous prestige.

Italians do not generally roast the turkey whole, but rather separate the breast and the remainder and give them different treatments. This is useful, because the dark meat usually takes much more time to become tender, time in which the breast can dry out. In this treatment, the breast is "butterflied," covered with boiled ham and *pancetta* and then rolled, and tied. It is wrapped in foil and baked, and when it is served it is cut into slices like a jelly roll.

1 whole or half turkey breast (about 3 pounds), boned
6 ounces pancetta *or prosciutto, in one piece*
3 ounces boiled ham, in one piece
3 medium cloves garlic, peeled

1 tablespoon plus 2 teaspoons rosemary leaves, fresh or preserved in salt or dried and blanched
Salt and freshly ground black pepper
2 leaves sage (optional), fresh or preserved in salt
4 or 5 whole black peppercorns

PREHEAT the oven to 400 degrees.

Remove the skin from the turkey breast. Place the breast on a board and "butterfly" it, that is, slice it lengthwise through the breast from one side almost to the other, leaving the halves attached only at one side. Open it out into one long thin slice.

Cut the *pancetta* (or prosciutto) and boiled ham into strips and arrange the strips all over breast. Sprinkle the breast with the 1 table-spoon rosemary leaves, salt, pepper, sage, and peppercorns.

Roll up the turkey breast like a *braciola* (or jelly roll) and tie like a salami with thread; place it on aluminum foil shiny-side inside (see illustrations opposite). Sprinkle the outside of the roll with the 2 tea-spoons rosemary leaves, salt, and pepper, then wrap the rolled breast in the aluminum foil and place it in a baking dish. Bake in the preheated oven for 45 to 55 minutes, then remove from the oven and let cool for 20 minutes.

Unwrap the aluminum foil and slice the rolled turkey breast like a loaf. Arrange the slices on a serving dish and serve.

NOTE: This dish is even better when cold. In this case, slice it just a few minutes before serving.

Petto di tacchino arrocchiato: Roll up the turkey breast.

Sprinkle the rolled turkey breast with rosemary, salt, and pepper prior to wrapping it.

A SUGGESTED DINNER

WINE
AVIGNONESI CHARDONNAY

Minestrone di riso
(SEE PAGE 144)

Polpettone di tacchino al tonno
(SEE BELOW)

Fagiolini in fricassea
(SEE PAGE 522)

Castagnaccio
(SEE PAGE 615)

Polpettone di tacchino al tonno

POACHED TURKEY LOAF WITH TUNA FLAVOR

SERVES 8 TO 10

*I*n this treatment boiled dark meat turkey is combined with tuna, ham, and seasonings, then shaped into a loaf, wrapped in cheesecloth, and boiled again. When unwrapped and cold, it emerges almost as a kind of pâté, quite far from its humble origins, and may be eaten as a cold main dish or as an excellent cold antipasto, worthy of a quite festive dinner. It is served cut into slices, with a light sauce of olive oil and lemon.

2 slices white bread, crusts
    removed
1 cup cold milk
5 or 6 sprigs Italian parsley,
    leaves only
1 large clove garlic, peeled
2 ounces boiled ham
1 can (7 ounces) tuna in olive
    oil
1 pound boiled dark meat
    turkey

2 extra-large eggs
4 ounces freshly grated
    Parmigiano
Salt and freshly ground black
    pepper
1/4 cup red wine vinegar
1 large carrot, scraped
1 celery rib
Coarse-grained salt
3/4 cup olive oil
Juice of 1 lemon

SOAK the bread slices in the cold milk for 20 minutes.

Meanwhile, finely chop the parsley, garlic, and ham and transfer to a large bowl.

Drain the tuna to remove the oil, then place on a board with the turkey meat and chop very fine. Transfer the turkey and tuna mixture to the large bowl and mix very well its contents. Add the eggs, Parmigiano, and salt and pepper and incorporate them well with the other ingredients, then squeeze the liquid from the bread slices, add them to the bowl, and mix very well.

On a board, roll the mixture into a large sausage about 3½ inches thick. Spread out a piece of cheesecloth and place the turkey "sausage" on it (see illustration on page 394). Wrap the cheesecloth around several times, and tie like a salami (see illustration on page 394).

Half fill a stockpot with cold water. Add the wine vinegar, carrot, and celery. Put the *polpettone* in the pot (the water should completely cover it), cover, and place over medium heat. When the water reaches a boil, add coarse salt to taste and simmer for 1 hour.

When the *polpettone* has finished cooking, press it by placing it in a baking dish with a weight on top of it. Let the *polpettone* cool this way, then transfer it to the refrigerator with the weight still on it. It should remain in this condition for at least 5 or 6 hours, or better still, overnight.

Unwrap the *polpettone* and cut it into about 20 slices. Place them on

(continued)

POLPETTONE DI TACCHINO AL TONNO *(continued)*

a serving dish and let stand while you prepare the following sauce:

Put the olive oil in a crockery bowl and add the lemon juice little by little, stirring with a wooden spoon. Add salt and freshly ground black pepper, then transfer to a sauceboat and serve with the *polpettone*.

Polpettone di tacchino al tonno: Place the turkey "sausage" on cheesecloth.

The tied *polpettone* before being placed in the pot.

A SUGGESTED DINNER

WINE

SCHIOPPETTO PINOT BIANCO

Ginestrata
(SEE PAGE 135)

Anitra all'arancio
(SEE BELOW)

Spinaci saltati
(SEE PAGE 546)

Pesche ripiene
(SEE PAGE 629)

Anitra all'arancio

DUCK IN ORANGE SAUCE

SERVES 6

I t is difficult for most people to believe that this almost prototyp-ical French dish is really Florentine. One of the dishes that was transported to France through the good offices of Caterina de' Medici, it appears in the earliest fourteenth-century Florentine cookbooks as *paparo o oca o anitra al melarancio* (gander or goose or duck in orange). The original is really closer to the modern French treatment, with its sweetness and glaze, than to the modern Florentine treatment, which has developed the dish away from its original sweetness. Originally, apparently, gander was the preferred bird and duck an acceptable sub-stitute. We all know what happened subsequently.

(continued)

You will notice that this present-day Italian recipe differs from the classical French ones a little. Try it, and don't be too sure that you won't prefer this one once you know it well.

1 fat domestic duck (about 5 pounds)
8 tablespoons (4 ounces) sweet butter
Salt and freshly ground black pepper to taste
1 tablespoon olive oil
1½ cups dry white wine

2 oranges with thick skins
Coarse-grained salt
1 pound raw rice, preferably Italian Arborio
⅛ teaspoon ground saffron
6 or 7 whole black peppercorns
5 sweet, juicy oranges

PREHEAT the oven to 375 degrees.

Clean the duck; remove the liver and set aside for another purpose. Into the cavity of the duck put 4 tablespoons of the butter, salt, and pepper.

Heat the olive oil and the remaining butter in a large casserole. When the butter is melted, put in the duck and sprinkle the outside with salt and pepper. Sauté over low heat until the duck is golden all over (about 30 minutes), then add the wine and let it evaporate very slowly.

When the wine has evaporated, transfer the duck from the casserole to a large roasting pan. Place the pan in the preheated oven for 1½ hours, turning the duck over 2 or 3 times, then remove from the oven. Lift the duck out of the roasting pan and pour the fat into the casserole. Let the casserole stand, with all the juices until needed. Place a grill in the roasting pan, then put the duck back in, on the grill. Return the pan to the oven, still at 375 degrees, for 30 minutes more.

Cut each of the two oranges into quarters and carefully remove the peel, in one piece, from each quarter. Cut the orange peel into very thin strips, cutting away most of the white underside of the peel. Reserve the peeled sections for another use.

Place a saucepan containing 3 cups of cold water on medium heat. When the water reaches the boiling point, add coarse salt to taste, then add the orange strips and blanch them for 5 minutes, then remove from the saucepan and cool under cold running water.

Add 1 cup of cold water to the casserole containing all the duck fat and simmer for 20 minutes.

Meanwhile, heat a large quantity of cold water in a stockpot. When the water reaches the boiling point, add coarse salt to taste, then the rice, saffron, and peppercorns and cook, stirring very frequently with a wooden spoon, until the rice is al dente (about 15 minutes).

While the rice is cooking, discard all but about 1 cup of fat from the casserole. When the duck has baked for 2 hours total, transfer it to the casserole and cook over low heat for 5 minutes; turn it twice. Taste for salt and pepper, then transfer the duck to a large serving dish.

Squeeze 3 of the oranges and add the juice and the orange strips to the fat left in the casserole. Place the casserole back on the heat and warm the sauce to the boiling point, then immediately pour it over the duck.

Drain the rice in a colander and arrange it in a ring around the duck. Cut the remaining two oranges into thin slices and place them as garnish around the outside of the rice ring, and serve.

Anitra in porchetta

DUCK IN THE STYLE OF SUCKLING PIG

SERVES 6

*D*uck as well as chicken is prepared filled with the *pancetta* and generously seasoned stuffing typical of *porchetta,* or suckling pig. This treatment is, if possible, even better than the chicken version, as the duck retains something of the weightiness of pork meat.

1 Italian sweet sausage without fennel seeds or 4 ounces ground pork

3 ounces **pancetta** *or prosciutto, in one piece*

1 large bay leaf

1 heaping tablespoon rosemary leaves, fresh or preserved in salt or dried and blanched

25 leaves sage, fresh or preserved in salt (see page 19)

4 large cloves garlic, peeled

20 whole black peppercorns

Salt and freshly ground black pepper

1 fat domestic duck (about 5 pounds)

2 tablespoons olive oil

REMOVE the skin from sausage and place the meat in a bowl.

Cut the *pancetta* into tiny pieces and coarsely chop the bay leaf, rosemary leaves, 20 of the sage leaves, and garlic, then add to the bowl with the sausage. Add the peppercorns, 4 teaspoons salt, and 1½ teaspoons freshly ground pepper and mix very well with a wooden spoon.

Rinse duck very well and dry it with paper towels. Remove the liver and set aside for another purpose, but do not remove any fat. Stuff the duck with the sausage mixture, then sew up the lower opening with needle and thread. Place the remaining 5 sage leaves in the neck opening and sew it up as well.

Preheat the oven to 375 degrees.

Pour the olive oil in a roasting pan. Put in the duck, sprinkle with salt and pepper, then roast in the preheated oven for 2 hours, turning the duck over twice.

Remove the pan from the oven, take out the duck, and pour off all the fat. Place a grill in the pan and put the duck on the grill. Return to the oven, still at 375 degrees, for 30 minutes more.

Remove the pan from the oven and transfer the duck to a board. Allow it to cool for 10 to 15 minutes before cutting, then cut in half lengthwise and then each half into 4 pieces.

Place the stuffing in the center of a serving dish and the duck pieces around the stuffing. To each diner, serve a piece of duck with a tablespoon of stuffing.

NOTE: This is a dish that is best accompanied by green or mixed salad.

A SUGGESTED DINNER

WINE
CHIANTI CLASSICO ISOLE E OLENA RISERVA

Tortelli della vigilia
(SEE PAGE 198)

Anitra in porchetta
(SEE ABOVE)

Insalata verde
(SEE PAGE 500)

Fragole al vino rosso
(SEE PAGE 631)

Coniglio in agro-dolce

RABBIT IN SWEET AND SOUR SAUCE

SERVES 6

*H*ere the rabbit is cut up and cooked in an elaborate sweet and sour sauce made with *odori* (aromatic vegetables), red wine, wine vinegar, raisins, pignoli, peppercorns, and a little sugar. This sweet and sour rabbit is made all over Italy.

1 rabbit (yields about 3½ pounds with skin and head removed)

2 cups dry red wine

2 red onions, cleaned

1 large bay leaf

5 whole black peppercorns

¼ cup red wine vinegar

1 cup unbleached all-purpose flour

5 tablespoons of olive oil

Salt and freshly ground black pepper to taste

2 ounces raisins, about 5 tablespoons

1 heaping tablespoon granulated sugar

2 ounces pignoli (pine nuts)

RINSE the rabbit well and dry it with paper towels, then cut it into 12 pieces and place them in a large bowl.

Heat the wine, with 1 onion cut in large pieces, bay leaf, peppercorns, and 1 tablespoon of the wine vinegar in a saucepan. When the mixture reaches the boiling point, immediately remove the saucepan from the heat and pour the contents into the bowl with the rabbit. Let the rabbit marinate for 2 hours.

After marinating, remove the rabbit pieces from the bowl and dry them with paper towels, then lightly flour the rabbit by placing the rabbit pieces in a colander and sprinkling the flour over. Gently shake the colander until the pieces are evenly floured. Strain the marinade into a bowl and save it.

Chop the remaining onion coarsely and place it in a large flameproof casserole, preferably terra-cotta, along with the olive oil. Place the casserole on the heat and sauté the onion for 4 or 5 minutes, then add the rabbit pieces and sauté them gently until golden all over (about 15 minutes). Sprinkle with salt and pepper and continue to sauté gently for about 25 minutes more, adding the reserved marinade little by little, as needed, stirring often. During this time, turn over rabbit pieces two or three times.

Meanwhile, soak the raisins in a small bowl of lukewarm water for 20 minutes.

Heat the remaining wine vinegar and the sugar in a small saucepan. When the vinegar is hot and the sugar dissolved, add the soaked raisins and the pignoli and remove from the heat. Cover and let stand until needed. Preheat oven to 375 degrees.

After sautéing for 25 minutes, when the rabbit has absorbed all the wine and is almost cooked, remove the casserole from the heat. Pour in the contents of the small saucepan and stir with a wooden spoon. Cover the casserole and place it in the preheated oven for 15 to 20 minutes. Serve hot.

A SUGGESTED DINNER

WINE

San Felice Il Grigio

Riso forte
(SEE PAGE 102)

Coniglio in agro-dolce
(SEE ABOVE)

Insalata composta
(SEE PAGE 501)

Crema zabaione
(SEE PAGE 565)

A SUGGESTED DINNER

WINE

SAN FELICE POGGIO ROSSO

Pasta e fagioli
(SEE PAGE 152)

Coniglio ripieno con carciofi
(SEE BELOW)

Carciofi fritti
(SEE PAGE 515)

Cenci
(SEE PAGE 592)

Coniglio ripieno con carciofi

TARRAGON RABBIT STUFFED WITH ARTICHOKES

SERVES 4

ere the whole rabbit is cleaned and soaked in wine vinegar to remove any gaminess, stuffed with artichokes and seasonings, including tarragon, and then cooked almost covered with white wine. The wine-tarragon perfume of the rabbit cooking is not easily forgotten. A really delicious dish, this should be the centerpiece of a countrified dinner, and the ideal vegetable to accompany it is artichokes, to go with the artichoke stuffing.

Rabbit is eaten a great deal in Italy and France. Once the most economical of meats, it is now quite expensive in these countries, so that dishes which were once rustic country dishes are now plates for *buongustai*. Rabbits, however, are still plentiful, and are available at many markets, certainly Italian meat markets. Buy the rabbit fresh with the pelt still on and have the butcher skin it for you. The meat is often compared to chicken, but of course it has its own individual, sweet flavor. The meat is light, unlike that of the wild hare, which is dark and gamey.

This recipe is from the until-recently marshy area of Etruscan country in Tuscany, the Maremma, a hunter's paradise.

1 whole rabbit (yields about 3½ pounds with skin and head removed)
1 cup red wine vinegar
1 lemon
3 large artichokes
2 large cloves garlic, peeled
¼ pound **pancetta,** *in one piece, plus 4 long strips* **pancetta** *or* **prosciutto**

Salt and freshly ground black pepper
1 tablespoon fresh tarragon or 1½ teaspoons dried tarragon
5 tablespoons olive oil
2½ cups dry white wine, approximately

RINSE the whole rabbit very carefully and discard the liver, then place the rabbit in a large bowl containing 4 cups of cold water and the wine vinegar. Soak for 1 hour to remove the gamey flavor.

Meanwhile, cut the lemon in half and put in a bowl of cold water. Soak the whole artichokes in this for 30 minutes, then clean (see page 510) and cut into small pieces, using both body and stems. Place the artichoke pieces in a second bowl.

Finely chop the garlic and cut the ¼ pound *pancetta* into tiny pieces and add to the bowl with the artichokes. Add salt and pepper to taste, then the tarragon and mix well.

Preheat the oven to 375 degrees.

When the rabbit has soaked for 1 hour, rinse it in cold running water, making sure all the cavities are clean, then dry with paper towels. Stuff the large cavity of the stomach with the artichoke mixture, then sew up completely with a needle and thread. With a larding needle, lard each leg with a strip of *pancetta*.

Pour the olive oil into a 13½ × 8¾-inch glass baking dish, then

(continued)

CONIGLIO RIPIENO CON CARCIOFI *(continued)*

put in the rabbit. Sprinkle generously with salt and pepper, then pour in the wine; the wine should cover almost two-thirds of the rabbit. Place the baking dish in the preheated oven and bake for 1 to 1½ hours, until all the wine has evaporated. During this time, turn rabbit over twice.

Take the baking dish out of the oven and remove the thread from the rabbit before transferring to a serving dish. Meanwhile, transfer the juices from the rabbit in the baking pan to a saucepan and simmer over low heat for 15 minutes. Slice the rabbit like a loaf and serve with some of the reduced sauce.

NOTE: Only white wine should be drunk with this dish.

Veal, Beef, and Lamb

~

Involtini di vitella

STUFFED LITTLE VEAL "BUNDLES"

SERVES 4

*T*he boneless veal cutlets are pounded very thin, so they can be easily rolled up, and are stuffed with a mozzarella-prosciutto-parsley mixture. The little "bundles" are then tied and sautéed in olive oil and white wine.

Try to find the youngest, whitest veal for this dish, which is suitable for a wide range of occasions, from an ambitious family dinner to a formal entertainment.

**4 thin slices of veal (scaloppine),
    about 4 ounces each**

2 ounces mozzarella

**2 ounces very fat prosciutto or
    pancetta, *in one piece***

**5 sprigs Italian parsley, leaves
    only**

**¼ cup freshly grated
    Parmigiano**

**Salt and freshly ground black
    pepper**

**¼ cup unbleached all-purpose
    flour**

2 tablespoons olive oil

½ cup dry white wine

IF the butcher has not already done so, pound the veal slices thin. (Use an Italian *batticarne,* with the veal between two pieces of wet wax paper.) Coarsely cut the mozzarella, prosciutto, and coarsely chop the parsley. Place the veal slices on a board and place one-fourth of the mixture on top of each slice of veal. Sprinkle with Parmigiano and, if necessary, salt and pepper. (In Italy, mozzarella is unsalted, but in other countries it is sometimes salted. If the cheese is unsalted, then use the salt and pepper.) Roll each slice of veal and tie with thread.

Spread the flour on a board. Roll the *involtini* in the flour to coat them very lightly.

Heat the olive oil in a flameproof casserole. When the oil is warm, place the *involtini* in the casserole and sauté until golden (about 10 minutes). Sprinkle the veal rolls with a little salt and pepper, then add the wine and let it evaporate very slowly (about 10 to 12 minutes), stirring frequently with a wooden spoon.

Remove the casserole from the heat and allow to rest for 5 minutes, then remove the thread with scissors and transfer the *involtini* to a serving dish, pouring a little sauce from the casserole over the top of each one. Serve hot.

A SUGGESTED DINNER

WINE
NIPOZZANO CHIANTI RUFFINA RISERVA

Cannelloni della vigilia
(SEE PAGE 220)

Involtini di vitella
(SEE ABOVE)

Bietole saltate
(SEE PAGE 549)

Bomboloni
(SEE PAGE 588)

A SUGGESTED DINNER

WINE

FELLUGA MERLOT

Denti di cavallo o rigatoni alle salsicce

(SEE PAGE 184)

Braciole di vitella rifatte

(SEE BELOW)

Torta di fagiolini

(SEE PAGE 524)

Meringhe alla panna

(SEE PAGE 598)

Braciole di vitella rifatte

FRIED VEAL CUTLETS, RECOOKED IN TOMATO SAUCE

SERVES 6

*R*ecooking leftovers in a new sauce is a standard procedure of the frugal Tuscans. At the same time, the result is considered a new dish, not mere leftovers, which they hate. However, even the sauces for recooking a specific dish are strictly defined, and you would not redo the cutlets here in any old sauce.

Originally the fried cutlets made the first meal and the recooked ones the dish of a following day. However, the recooked cutlets are so popular, particularly in Florence, that they skip the first step and prepare the fried dish with the sauce immediately. This is probably the most popular version of scaloppine in Florence and is sometimes called *scaloppa alla fiorentina*.

FOR THE SAUCE

2 carrots, scraped
2 celery ribs
10 sprigs Italian parsley, leaves
*   only*
1 small clove garlic, peeled
1 medium red onion, cleaned
1½ pounds ripe fresh tomatoes
*   or 1½ pounds canned*
*   tomatoes, preferably*
*   imported Italian, drained*

4 large basil leaves, fresh or
*   preserved in salt*
Salt and freshly ground black
*   pepper*
2 tablespoons olive oil

FOR THE VEAL

6 veal cutlets, about 4 ounces
*   each*
2 extra-large eggs
Pinch of salt

Vegetable oil for deep-frying
About 1 cup unseasoned bread
*   crumbs, preferably*
*   homemade*

TO SERVE

10 sprigs Italian parsley, leaves
*   only, coarsely chopped*

CUT carrots, celery, parsley, garlic, and onion into large pieces and place them in a medium-sized casserole. If fresh tomatoes are used, cut them into pieces, then add the fresh or canned tomatoes to the casserole along with the basil. Place the casserole over medium heat and cook for ½ hour, stirring every so often with a wooden spoon. Pass contents of casserole through a food mill, using the disc with the smallest holes, into a crockery or glass bowl. Return the strained sauce to casserole, add salt and pepper to taste and the oil, and let reduce over low heat for 15 minutes more, stirring every so often with a wooden spoon.

Meanwhile soak the veal cutlets in the two eggs, lightly beaten with a pinch of salt, for 30 minutes.

When the sauce is ready (sauce may be prepared even one day in advance), heat enough oil to deep-fry the meat in a medium-sized skillet over medium heat. (The oil should be deep enough to submerge the

(continued)

Braciole di Vitella Rifatte *(continued)*

veal in.) When the oil is hot (about 375 degrees), remove the cutlets from the eggs and heavily bread them with the bread crumbs. Cook the cutlets for 30 seconds on each side in the hot oil, until lightly golden; transfer to a serving dish lined with paper towels to absorb the excess fat. Transfer the tomato sauce to a large skillet and reheat it over medium heat. Taste for salt and pepper. When the sauce starts simmering, add the cutlets in one layer, and be sure they are completely covered with the sauce. Simmer for 10 minutes, then remove the skillet from stove and let the meat rest in the sauce for at least 10 minutes before serving. Serve with some of the chopped parsley sprinkled over and some of the sauce.

A SUGGESTED DINNER

WINE

Felluga Sauvignon Bianco

Risotto ai fagioli con l'occhio

(SEE PAGE 258)

Scaloppine ai capperi

(SEE BELOW)

Rape saltate in padella

(SEE PAGE 545)

Bomboloni

(SEE PAGE 588)

Scaloppine ai capperi

VEAL CUTLETS IN A CAPER SAUCE

SERVES 6

*T*hin slices of boneless veal, *scaloppine,* are prepared in a great variety of ways. There are several specifically Tuscan preparations, a sample of which follows. The cutlets should be lightly floured, no bread crumbs. After being seared, they should cook for a short time in the wine and the chopped capers added to the juices after the meat has been removed and the sauce poured over. A quick and delicious dish.

About ½ cup unbleached all-
    purpose flour
6 veal cutlets, about 4 ounces
    each
2 tablespoons (1 ounce) sweet
    butter

4 tablespoons olive oil
¼ cup dry white wine
Salt and freshly ground black
    pepper
6 tablespoons capers, in wine
    vinegar, drained

TO SERVE
15 sprigs Italian parsley, leaves
    only, coarsely chopped

LIGHTLY flour the veal cutlets. Melt the butter with the oil in a medium-sized casserole and when the butter is completely melted, add the scaloppine and cook for 1 minute on each side over low heat. Add the wine, cover, and let simmer for 5 more minutes. Meanwhile coarsely chop the capers on board. Transfer the cooked scaloppine onto a large serving platter, add the chopped capers to casserole with all the juices, season with salt and pepper, and sauté for 3 minutes. Pour the contents of casserole over the scaloppine and serve with the chopped parsley.

A SUGGESTED DINNER

WINE
BARBI BRUNELLO DI MONTALCINO RISERVA

Focaccia al ramerino e aglio
(SEE PAGE 56)

Ossobuco alla fiorentina
(SEE BELOW)

Carciofi all'agro
(SEE PAGE 513)

Macedonia di frutta
(SEE PAGE 559)

Ossobuco alla fiorentina

OSSOBUCO WITH PEAS, FLORENTINE STYLE

SERVES 6

*V*eal shank, cut into horizontal slices, with the piece of bone in the middle, open and revealing a section of marrow, is called *ossobuco* or "hole in the bone." Indeed one of the favorite aspects of this cut is the delicious marrow, which is meant to be eaten with a special small fork. *Ossobuco* is always simmered fairly long in a sauce, though the veal shank meat should still have some bite when cooked.

There are many versions and sauces of *ossobuco,* and generally they are served with rice on the same plate, an exception to the general practice in Italy of serving pasta and rice as a separate course. The Florentine version uses a sauce made with *odori, pancetta,* wine, and some tomato and is always served with peas rather than rice as an accompaniment. The chopped parsley and grated lemon peel combination is a simplified version of the condiment called *gremolada* used with many versions of *ossobuco,* but usually containing chopped sage and garlic in addition.

*4 ounces **pancetta** or*
    prosciutto, in one piece
3 medium carrots, scraped
2 medium ribs celery
1 large red onion, peeled
10 sprigs Italian parsley, leaves
    only
6 ossibuchi (veal shank cut
    into 2-inch to 2½-inch
    slices, with bone and
    marrow)
½ cup olive oil

About ½ cup unbleached all-
    purpose flour
Salt and freshly ground black
    pepper
1 cup dry white wine
1 pound ripe fresh tomatoes or
    1 pound canned tomatoes,
    preferably imported Italian,
    drained
1 to 2 cups chicken or beef
    broth, preferably homemade

FOR THE PEAS
Coarse-grained salt
1 large clove garlic, peeled

*1 pound shelled peas **

TO SERVE
15 sprigs Italian parsley, leaves
    only, finely chopped, mixed
    with grated peel of 1 large
    lemon

CUT *pancetta* into very small pieces. Finely chop carrots, celery, onion, and parsley all together on a board. Tie each *ossibucho* with a string, so the meat remains attached to the bone. Place a medium-sized casserole with the oil over medium heat and when the oil is warm, add the *pancetta* and sauté for 4 minutes. Lightly flour *ossibuchi* on the cut sides,

(continued)

*If frozen peas are used, use the "tender tiny" ones; do not defrost them first. Cooking time should be 2 minutes in the water, then 2 minutes in the sauce. These tiny peas are among the few frozen ingredients I can use, if the fresh peas are too large.

add them to casserole and sauté for 1 minute on each side. Put in the chopped vegetables, stir well with a wooden spoon, and cook for 5 minutes more, turning the meat over once. Season with salt and pepper.

Add the wine and evaporate for 10 minutes. If fresh tomatoes are used, cut them into pieces. Pass fresh or canned tomatoes through a food mill, using the disc with smallest holes, into a crockery or glass bowl. Add tomatoes to casserole, stir, and let cook, covered, for 45 minutes more, adding broth as needed. By that time, the *ossibuchi* should be almost cooked. Remove the meat from casserole and let rest on a platter, covered, until needed.

Meanwhile pass the sauce from the casserole through a food mill, using the disc with smallest holes, into a second casserole.

Bring a medium-sized pot of cold water to a boil, add coarse salt to taste, then the whole clove of garlic and the peas, and simmer for 10 minutes.

Transfer *ossibuchi* to the second casserole, containing the sauce; drain the peas, discarding the garlic, and add them to the casserole with the meat for a final 10 minutes of cooking, with cover on. Taste for salt and pepper. Both meat and peas should emerge properly cooked, with the meat soft.

Transfer meat onto a large platter, remove the strings, and then, with a strainer-skimmer, remove peas from casserole to the platter, arranging them on one side. Spoon the remaining sauce all over the meat and peas, sprinkle with the parsley/lemon, and serve hot.

A SUGGESTED DINNER

WINE
CECCHI VINO NOBILE DI MONTEPULCIANO

Spaghetti al sugo "metà e metà"
(SEE PAGE 186)

Vitella involtata con porcini
(SEE BELOW)

Zucchini trifolati
(SEE PAGE 553)

Torta di ricotta
(SEE PAGE 580)

Vitella involtata con porcini

VEAL WITH WILD MUSHROOMS IN CRUST

SERVES 8

A fancy veal preparation is made with a wild mushroom sauce and a crust covering, usable even for a more formal occasion. The ground veal used is quite affordable and is dressed up. The *bomboloni* pastry is similar to the French brioche and the mushroom sauce both flavors the meat and keeps it from becoming dry, a pitfall for roasted veal.

A not really complicated but most attractive presentation.

(continued)

VITELLA INVOLTATA CON PORCINI *(continued)*

2 medium carrots   Coarse-grained salt

FOR THE CRUST

THE SPONGE

1/2 *ounce (1 cake) fresh*   3/4 *cup plus 1 tablespoon*
  compressed yeast or 1   *unbleached all-purpose*
  package active dry yeast   *flour*
1/2 *cup lukewarm or hot milk,*
  depending on the yeast

THE DOUGH

3 *tablespoons (1 1/2 ounces)*   1/4 *cup lukewarm milk*
  sweet butter   1 1/4 *cups unbleached all-purpose*
2 *extra-large egg yolks*   *flour*
1 *teaspoon granulated sugar*

FOR THE STUFFING AND SAUCE

1 *ounce dried* porcini   4 *tablespoons olive oil*
  mushrooms   *Salt and freshly ground black*
1 *medium carrot, scraped*   *pepper*
1 *small red onion, cleaned*   2 *pounds ground veal shoulder*
1 *small clove garlic, peeled*   1/2 *cup freshly grated*
4 *large leaves sage, fresh or*   *Parmigiano*
  preserved in salt   2 *extra-large eggs*
4 *ounces* pancetta *or*
  prosciutto, in one piece

PLUS

1/4 *cup unbleached all-purpose*   *Salt and freshly ground black*
  flour   *pepper*
                                   1 *extra-large egg, lightly beaten*

CLEAN the carrots, but do not scrape them, and let stand in a bowl of cold water for 30 minutes. Bring a small pot of cold water to a boil, add coarse salt, then the carrots, and let cook for 5 minutes. Peel the carrots under cold running water, pushing off the skin with your fingers. Let stand until needed.

Prepare the sponge, then the dough as for *bomboloni* pastry, using the ingredients and quantities listed above and following instructions on pages 588–590. For further details of making this pastry see pages 423–424 of *Giuliano Bugialli's Classic Techniques of Italian Cooking.*

Prepare the stuffing. Soak the mushrooms in a small bowl with 4 cups of lukewarm water for 30 minutes. Drain the mushrooms, saving the soaking water, and clean them, removing all the sand attached to the stems. Pass the soaking water through several layers of paper towels to remove all the sand and let rest until needed.

Coarsely chop mushrooms, carrot, onion, garlic, and sage, and cut the *pancetta* into small pieces.

Heat the oil in a medium-sized saucepan over medium heat and when the oil is warm, add the chopped ingredients and sauté for 5 minutes. Add ½ cup of the mushroom water, season with salt and pepper, and let cook for 5 minutes more. Use a blender or food processor to coarsely grind the sautéed chopped ingredients. Take 1 cup of the sauce and put it in a large crockery or glass bowl. Return the remaining sauce to pan. Taste for salt and pepper, add 1 cup of the mushroom water, and let reduce over medium heat for 5 minutes. Remove from heat, transfer contents to a crockery or glass bowl and let cool (about 30 minutes). Add veal to the bowl containing 1 cup of the mushroom sauce, then put in the Parmigiano and eggs. Season with salt and pepper and mix very well with a wooden spoon.

When the dough is ready, sprinkle the ¼ cup of flour on a board and put the dough on it. With a rolling pin gently roll out a rectangular sheet about ¼ inch thick. Spread out half of the veal stuffing in the center of the pastry forming a 3 × 14-inch rectangle. Make a line lengthwise down the center with the two carrots and cover with the remaining half of the stuffing, being sure that the carrots remain centered. Wrap dough around everything, then transfer to a buttered jelly-roll pan, with the seam in the pastry facing down. Cover pan with a towel and let rest until the dough has doubled in size (about half an hour). Preheat oven to 375 degrees.

When the dough is ready brush top of pastry with the egg and bake for 45 minutes. Remove from oven, transfer to a board and cut into 1-inch slices. Serve hot accompanied by the sauce, reheated.

Polpette di bistecca in umido

FRESH STEAK "SAUSAGES" IN SAUCE

SERVES 4

*T*hese are sausage-shaped *polpette* of coarsely chopped steak, lightly floured, sautéed in olive oil and then lightly in tomatoes. A simple but quite elegant family dish.

The meat must be of top quality and coarsely ground. With a meat grinder, pass the meat through the disc with medium-sized holes. Already ground supermarket meat should be a last resort.

1 pound coarsely ground round or sirloin

2 tablespoons olive oil plus ½ cup

3 tablespoons freshly grated Parmigiano

Salt and freshly ground black pepper to taste

½ cup, approximately, unbleached all-purpose flour

3 or 4 leaves sage, fresh or preserved in salt

1 cup canned tomatoes, preferably imported Italian, drained and passed through a food mill, using the disc with the smallest holes

1 clove garlic, peeled but left whole

Chicken or meat broth, if necessary, preferably homemade

PLACE the ground meat in a bowl with the 2 tablespoons olive oil, Parmigiano, and salt and pepper to taste. Mix very thoroughly with a wooden spoon, then divide the mixture into 8 parts and roll each into the shape of a sausage. Lightly flour each "sausage." Heat the ½ cup olive oil in a flameproof casserole, preferably terra-cotta, along with the sage leaves. When the oil is hot, add the "sausages" and brown gently, over medium heat, on all sides. Add the tomatoes and the whole garlic clove, then cover and simmer over low heat for 10 minutes. Taste for salt and pepper.

At this point, check the consistency of the sauce. If the tomatoes contain very little liquid, you may need to add a little broth. Be careful, however, not to add too much liquid. There should be very little sauce left unabsorbed at the end. Simmer for 15 minutes more, covered, adding broth as needed.

Remove the garlic clove and serve hot.

A SUGGESTED DINNER

WINE
SAN FELICE VIGORELLO RISERVA

Passato di fagioli
(SEE PAGE 142)

Polpette di bistecca in umido
(SEE ABOVE)

Finocchi al burro
(SEE PAGE 538)

Pesche ripiene di mandorle
(SEE PAGE 630)

Manzo ripieno

ROLLED STUFFED SIRLOIN

SERVES 4 TO 6

*H*ave your butcher butterfly a large, thick, tender slice of sirloin. This is flattened into a very large *braciola,* which is stuffed with a spinach, *pancetta,* egg, and Parmigiano mixture and closed up into one large roll. It is then sautéed. When served, always cold, it is sliced through like a jelly roll, which it does very easily and nicely.

Another dish for a family dinner.

2 pounds fresh spinach	*Salt and freshly ground black*
Coarse-grained salt	*pepper to taste*
3 extra-large eggs	*2 tablespoons freshly grated*
1 medium clove garlic, peeled	*Parmigiano*
5 sprigs Italian parsley, leaves	*4 tablespoons (2 ounces) sweet*
only	*butter*
2 ounces pancetta *or*	*2 tablespoons olive oil*
prosciutto, in one piece	*½ cup dry red wine*
1 large, thick slice of tender	
sirloin (about ¾ pound),	
butterflied (see page 390)	

REMOVE the stems from the spinach and rinse the leaves very well. Heat a large quantity of cold water in a stockpot. When the water is boiling, add coarse salt to taste, then add the spinach and cook it for about 10 minutes; drain and cool under cold running water. Squeeze the spinach very well and chop it fine, then set aside in a bowl until needed.

Fill a saucepan with cold water and the eggs and set on the heat; when the water reaches the boiling point, cook the eggs for 10 minutes until hard-cooked. Remove the eggs and cool under cold running water, then peel and set aside until needed.

Finely chop the garlic and parsley all together; cut the *pancetta* into small pieces.

Place the butterflied slice of meat between two damp sheets of wax paper. Flatten it with a meat pounder *(batticarne),* then place on a board.

Cover the slice of meat with the chopped spinach. On top of the spinach, arrange the *pancetta* pieces and sprinkle with chopped garlic and parsley. Cut the eggs lengthwise into quarters and place them lengthwise on top of the other ingredients. Sprinkle with a little salt, pepper, and Parmigiano.

Pick up one end of meat with both hands and roll it up. Tie up the roll with thread like a salami.

Heat the butter and olive oil in a large flameproof casserole. When the butter is melted, put in the meat roll and sauté very gently, turning it often with a wooden spoon. Cook for about 15 minutes, until golden all over, then add the wine and season with salt and pepper. Cover the casserole and simmer for 15 minutes more, turning the meat roll two or three times. When the wine has evaporated, the meat is ready.

Remove the casserole from the heat and let cool for about 2 hours, then transfer the meat to a board and cut it into ½-inch slices. Arrange the slices on a serving dish and serve.

NOTE: Before serving, you may heat the juice remaining in the casserole and pour it over the slices.

A SUGGESTED DINNER

WINE
SACCARDI CHIANTI CLASSICO

Topini di patate
(SEE PAGE 276)

Manzo ripieno
(SEE ABOVE)

Peperonata
(SEE PAGE 544)

Pan di ramerino
(SEE PAGE 46)

Braciole ripiene

STUFFED MEAT SLICES

SERVES 4

*B*raciola refers to the thin slice of meat itself. The word is used abroad often to refer to what is properly called *braciola ripiena*, or stuffed *braciola*. This filling of artichoke and a thin omelet is one of the classic ways to stuff a *braciola*.

2 small artichokes or 1 large *one*	*5 sprigs Italian parsley, leaves* *only*
1 lemon	*1 medium clove garlic, peeled*
2 extra-large eggs	*2 ounces* pancetta *or*
2 tablespoons freshly grated *Parmigiano*	*prosciutto, in one piece*
2½ tablespoons olive oil	*Salt and freshly ground black* *pepper to taste*
4 bracioline *(very thin slices)* *of boneless sirloin*	*½ cup dry red wine*
	½ cup meat or chicken broth, *preferably homemade*

SOAK the whole artichokes in a large bowl of cold water, along with the lemon cut into halves, for 30 minutes.

Meanwhile, break the eggs into a small bowl and beat them slightly, then mix in the Parmigiano and a pinch of salt. Heat the ½ tablespoon of oil in an 8-inch omelet pan and make a thin omelet from the egg-Parmigiano mixture; place it on a dish to cool.

Remove the outside fat from each meat slice and flatten it between 2 pieces of damp wax paper with a meat pounder *(batticarne)*.

Chop the parsley and garlic, cut the *pancetta,* and place in a bowl.

Remove the outer leaves and inside "choke" from the artichokes, then cut both the bodies and stems into small pieces (see page 510) and add them to the bowl. Mix with the other ingredients and season with salt and pepper.

Cut the cooled omelet into quarters and place one piece on each meat slice. Place one-quarter of the artichoke mixture on top of each piece of omelet. Roll each *braciola* and tie it with thread.

Heat the olive oil in a flameproof casserole and then put in the *braciole*. Sprinkle with salt and pepper and let sauté very slowly until golden (10 to 15 minutes), turning the rolls with a wooden spoon. Add the wine, cover, and simmer until the wine has evaporated (about 15 minutes).

When the wine has evaporated, add the broth and simmer until the *braciole* are cooked (about 12 to 14 minutes), then remove the casserole from the heat and allow to rest for 5 minutes.

Remove the thread from the *braciole* and transfer them to a serving dish. Pour the juice from the casserole over them and serve.

A SUGGESTED DINNER

WINE
CONTE D'ATTIMIS MERLOT

Zuppa di porri
(SEE PAGE 139)

Braciole ripiene
(SEE ABOVE)

Fagioli al forno
(SEE PAGE 520)

Bombe
(SEE PAGE 573)

Stracotto alla fiorentina

POT ROAST, FLORENTINE STYLE

SERVES 6

*T*he Italian pot roast is one large piece. The rump is preferred so it can cook a long time (the word *stracotto* means "very well cooked"). Some fat must be left on, and, so the meat remains juicy on the inside, it is larded by drawing strips of *pancetta* through the inside with a larding needle (in Italian, *ago lardellatore*). The carrot drawn through the center also helps to flavor the inside of the meat and is aesthetically pleasing when the meat is sliced.

Stracotto is cooked with the full red wine of the area where it is made. Barolo is used in Piedmont; in Tuscany, one of the fuller Chiantis.

2 medium red onions, cleaned

3 celery ribs

4 carrots, scraped

5 tablespoons olive oil

Rump roast of beef (about 3½ pounds), with some fat left on

Salt and freshly ground black pepper

4 long strips of pancetta

½ cup dry red wine

1¼ pounds fresh ripe tomatoes or 1¼ pounds canned tomatoes, preferably imported Italian, drained

1 tablespoon tomato paste

1 to 2 cups hot meat broth, preferably homemade

CUT the onions, celery, and 3 of the carrots into ½-inch pieces. Put them in a large flameproof casserole, preferably terra-cotta, along with the olive oil, and set aside until needed.

Put a long, thin knife lengthwise all the way through the meat, in the center. Withdraw the knife and fit the remaining carrot, whole, through the opening made by the knife. Then, with a larding needle, insert 2 4-inch strips of *pancetta* at each end, on either side of the carrot. If you have no larding needle, make 2 punctures with a knife on either end of the carrot, 4 inches deep. Enlarge the holes with your finger and insert a strip of *pancetta* into each puncture.

With thread, tie the meat in the manner of a salami (see page 394), then place in the casserole with the vegetables. Add salt and pepper to taste, then set the casserole over low heat and sauté very gently, stirring the vegetables and turning the meat, until it is golden on all sides (about 20 to 25 minutes). If using fresh tomatoes, cut them into pieces, then pass the fresh or canned tomatoes through a food mill, using the disc with the smallest holes, into a small bowl.

Add the wine and simmer until it evaporates, then add the tomatoes and tomato paste. Cover and simmer very slowly for 2½ hours, adding some hot broth when needed and turning the meat several times. Taste for salt and pepper.

Remove the meat from the casserole and place it on a chopping board for 10 to 12 minutes to rest.

Meanwhile, remove the fat from the top of the sauce and reheat.

Cut meat into slices ½ inch thick. Arrange the slices on a platter and serve, accompanied by the sauce in a sauce boat.

This dish should be served with whole peeled, boiled potatoes. Serve the potatoes in a basket, wrapped in cloth napkins.

A SUGGESTED DINNER

WINE
VITICCIO CHIANTI CLASSICO RISERVA

Taglierini in brodo
(SEE PAGE 132)

Stracotto alla fiorentina
(SEE ABOVE)

Boiled potatoes

Budino di ricotta
(SEE PAGE 627)

A SUGGESTED DINNER

WINE

CHIANTI CLASSICO VILLA ANTINORI

Lasagne

(SEE PAGE 221)

Bistecca alla fiorentina

(SEE BELOW)

Insalata mista

(SEE PAGE 500)

or Insalata composta

(SEE PAGE 501)

Crostata di frutta

(SEE PAGE 576)

Bistecca alla fiorentina

BEEFSTEAK, FLORENTINE STYLE

One doesn't ordinarily think of a good, thick wood- or charcoal-broiled steak as an Italian dish, but nonetheless, centuries before the Alamo and Texas, *bistecca alla fiorentina* was already an established specialty of Florence. A real *fiorentina* requires the special Chianina breed of beef found in the valley of the Chiana near Florence (and justly admired by cattle breeders the world over). However, the Val di Chiana beef is so scarce that it is not available except in Florence, and is becoming less available even there. And so, in Italy, the only place you can get a real *fiorentina* is in Florence.

There is another aspect as well—the cutting of the meat. Like most steaks, this cut comes from the loin *(costata)*. It is the same cut as the American T-bone or Porterhouse, except that only the fillet and contrafillet (also called "shell," "strip," "New York steak," and "entrecôte") are used. The tail is cut off and used for *bollito* (see page 329). For some reason, in Italy only the Florentines cut the meat so that both the fillet and contrafillet are part of the same piece. In the rest of Italy, they are separated.

And so, though Chianina beef is not available abroad, we can more easily get a cut similar to the *fiorentina* there than one can in Italy outside of Florence.

Though the preparation is a simple one, the rules must be very strictly observed to get an authentic *fiorentina*.

BUYING AND PREPARING THE STEAK

Ask your butcher for a T-bone or Porterhouse cut, and ask him to cut off the "tail" third. You may have to buy that piece also. If so, use it for boiling or to make stock.

Have the steaks cut so that each one weighs at least 1¾ pounds after the tail has been removed. Each of these steaks serves 2 people and should be about 3 inches high. Absolutely do not have the steaks cut smaller in order to have individual servings. The meat must be of this size and thickness when cooked.

The meat should be aged for at least six days after the animal is slaughtered. If it seems too fresh to you, or if it was frozen immediately after slaughter, allow it to age in your own refrigerator until it is soft.

Do not wash the steaks; do not marinate the meat or pour any fat over it. And since the correct amount of salt and pepper is just what clings to the steak when it is turned, do not rub the steak with peppercorns or with salt. These will be sprinkled on at a later stage.

Finally, be sure the steaks are at room temperature when it is time to cook them.

COOKING THE STEAK

Prepare the fire with wood or charcoal. Wait until the fire is completely burned out and only hot ash remains; there should be no flames.

Place the grill in a fireplace or on a barbecue well before the steaks (the grill must be very hot before the steaks are placed on it), then place

(continued)

427

BISTECCA ALLA FIORENTINA *(continued)*

the steaks on the grill with your hands or a spatula, *not* a fork. Do not puncture the meat with a fork at any point while cooking.

After 4 or 5 minutes, when the steak is brown and has formed what is almost a crust, turn it with a spatula. Without touching the steak, sprinkle it with salt; do not try to push the salt into the meat. Cook the second side for 4 or 5 minutes and then turn it again with a spatula. Some salt will fall off, and what clings is the right amount for a *fiorentina*.

Cook the first side for 4 or 5 minutes more and immediately remove the steak from the grill and place it on a serving dish. *A real* fiorentina *is always rare inside.* Sprinkle lightly with pepper (a *fiorentina* should not be very peppery) and do not add any oil.

Serve with lemon wedges. (These are not only a garnish, but some people squeeze lemon juice onto the steak. This is optional, according to taste.) Since each steak serves two, cut the steaks into at least 4 pieces each, so that everyone gets some *filetto* and some *controfiletto*.

Enjoy your *fiorentina!*

A SUGGESTED DINNER

WINE
CASTIGLION DEL BOSCO BRUNELLO DI MONTALCINO

Pappa al pomodoro
(SEE PAGE 273)

Spezzatino alla fiorentina
(SEE BELOW)

Broccoli strascicati
(SEE PAGE 526)

Frittelle di riso
(SEE PAGE 622)

Spezzatino alla fiorentina

FLORENTINE BEEF STEW IN CHIANTI

SERVES 4

1 medium red onion, cleaned
1 celery rib
1 carrot, scraped
3 basil leaves, fresh or preserved
    in salt
5 tablespoons olive oil
2 pounds beef chuck, preferably
    eye of chuck, cut into 1½-
    inch cubes

½ cup dry red wine
1 pound canned tomatoes,
    preferably imported Italian,
    drained
Pinch of red hot pepper flakes
Salt and freshly ground black
    pepper to taste

COARSELY chop the onion, celery, carrot, and basil leaves all together.

Heat the oil in a flameproof casserole, preferably terra-cotta, and when it is warm, add the chopped ingredients and sauté on medium heat for 10 minutes. Add the meat, and let sauté for about 15 minutes, stirring every so often with a wooden spoon so the meat does not stick to the pan. Add the wine and lower the heat, to allow the wine to evaporate slowly (about 15 minutes).

Pass the tomatoes through a food mill, using the disc with the smallest holes, into the casserole. Season with salt, pepper, and a pinch of hot pepper flakes, then cover the casserole and simmer very slowly for 2½ hours, adding some cold water if additional liquid is needed.

Taste for salt and pepper and let simmer for 10 to 15 minutes more (at which time the meat should be soft and the sauce rather thick), then remove the casserole from the heat. Transfer the *spezzatino* to a serving dish and serve hot with some of the sauce.

NOTE: In Florence *spezzatino* is served on the same plate with whole boiled potatoes, peeled before serving, or with slices of polenta (see page 476). Sometimes the potatoes are peeled, cut into pieces, and placed in the casserole, about 20 minutes before the *spezzatino* is completely cooked, to allow the potatoes to cook in the meat gravy.

Peposo

PEPPERY BEEF STEW

SERVES 6

*A*nother dish that goes back to the days when freshly ground black pepper was used in some dishes in such quantity that one got beyond the spiciness to the flavor of the pepper itself. The name itself comes from the word for pepper, *pepe.*

The beef shank meat is simmered for a long time in a covered casserole with lots of red wine. There is very little oil and no thickening, but the gelatin from the shank meat itself produces a thick, rich sauce.

Peposo is associated with the little hill town of Impruneta, near Florence, which is famous for making the red tiles that cover the roofs of the city. It is a tradition that, while the tile makers were baking the tiles for Brunelleschi's red dome for the Cathedral, they put the casseroles of *peposo* in the oven to cook at the same time. (The cooking time of tiles and *peposo* are the same.) Michelangelo wrote a little poem when he was departing for Rome to make the dome of St. Peter's, addressed to Brunelleschi's dome: "I go forth to make your sister, larger perhaps, but certainly not more beautiful."

1/4 cup olive oil
4 cups dry red wine
4 large cloves garlic, peeled and
  left whole
3 pounds beef shank, cut into
  pieces 1 inch square
Salt to taste

1 pound fresh ripe tomatoes or
  1 pound canned tomatoes,
  preferably imported Italian,
  drained
1 scant tablespoon freshly
  ground black pepper
2 cups cold water

PUT the olive oil, wine, garlic, and meat in a large casserole, preferably terra-cotta, then set on medium heat and cover. Simmer very slowly for 1 hour. If using fresh tomatoes, cut them into pieces, then pass the fresh or canned tomatoes through a food mill, using the disc with the smallest holes, into a bowl.

Add the tomatoes, cold water, and salt to the casserole and simmer for 2 hours more. Taste for salt and add the freshly ground pepper, then simmer, covered, for 1 hour longer.

By that time the meat should be cooked and tender. If the sauce is too watery, remove the meat and let rest, covered, in a crockery bowl until the sauce is reduced. Transfer the meat to the casserole and let rest for 20 to 25 minutes, covered. Serve from the same casserole.

NOTE: Serve on the same dish with whole boiled potatoes. In this case the *insalata composta* should not contain potatoes. Serve with toasted Tuscan bread rubbed with garlic, or with spinach, boiled and sautéed with garlic and olive oil.

A SUGGESTED DINNER

WINE
FRATELLI ODDERO DOLCETTO D'ALBA

Zuppa di porri
(SEE PAGE 139)

Peposo
(SEE ABOVE)

Insalata composta
(SEE PAGE 501)

Crema zabaione
(SEE PAGE 565)

Crocchette al limone

CROQUETTES BAKED IN LEMON JUICE

SERVES 6

*W*ith the help of abundant lemon juice, the unpromising left-overs from a *bollito* can be transformed into an exciting dish. The meat, combined with *mollica,* garlic, parsley, eggs, and Parmigiano, is coated with high-quality bread crumbs and fried. Then the little croquettes are arranged in a baking dish, topped with lemon juice, and baked for 5 minutes to fully absorb the lemon flavor. Absolutely delicious! I cannot help reiterating that the quality of bread crumbs must be very high; they must be made from first-class bread, unflavored, and slightly toasted to lighten them.

1 cup milk

4 slices white bread

1 pound cold boiled meat or fowl, all fat removed

2 large cloves garlic, peeled

10 sprigs Italian parsley, leaves only

3 extra-large eggs

4 tablespoons freshly grated Parmigiano

Salt and freshly ground black pepper to taste

Freshly grated nutmeg to taste

1 quart vegetable oil (see page 22)

1 cup unseasoned bread crumbs, preferably homemade

PLUS

4 large lemons

Salt

PLACE a small pan over medium heat with the milk and when the milk reaches a boil, add the bread and mix very well until a paste is formed (about 5 minutes). Keep stirring and cook for 2 minutes more. Remove pan from heat and let stand until needed. Using a *mezzaluna* or food processor, finely chop the cold meat together with the garlic and parsley. Transfer the chopped ingredients to a bowl, add the cooled bread, the eggs, and the Parmigiano, and season with salt, pepper, and nutmeg. Mix all the ingredients together using a wooden spoon. Heat the vegetable oil in a fryer over medium heat and when the oil is hot (about 375 degrees), spread out the bread crumbs on a board and take two heaping tablespoons of the croquette mixture and shape it into a round ball. As you bread it, press down gently, flattening the top and bottom. Continue in the same way and when all the croquettes are ready, fry them until lightly golden all over, about 1 minute. Use a strainer-skimmer to remove and transfer them onto a plate lined with paper towels. Heat the oven to 375 degrees. When all the croquettes are on the dish, transfer them to a glass or crockery baking dish and arrange them in a single layer. Squeeze the lemons and pour the juice over all the croquettes, then sprinkle on a little salt and bake for 5 minutes. Serve immediately.

See also The Boiled Course page 325, and The Fried Course page 337, for additional beef dishes.

A SUGGESTED DINNER

WINE
FELLUGA TOCAI FRIULANO

Chiocciole ai gamberi
(SEE PAGE 182)

Crocchette al limone
(SEE ABOVE)

Tortino di carciofi
(SEE PAGE 512)

Crema zabaione with fresh berries
(SEE PAGE 565)

Agnello alla cacciatora

LAMB, HUNTER-STYLE

SERVES 6

*T*he baby or spring lamb—here a boneless leg is used—is cooked in a sauce of olive oil, white wine, and tomatoes and flavored with sage and a pinch of hot red pepper. It is served over slices of Tuscan bread rubbed with garlic.

The sauce descends from the *fricassea,* which goes back to the sixteenth century in Italy. In that preparation, egg yolks are combined with lemon juice. In this latter version, the egg yolks still are associated with the sauce, but are now considered optional, and the late-arriving tomato has replaced the lemon juice. The evolution of this dish gives some insight into the way dishes may have changed in Italy over the centuries.

3 pounds boneless leg of lamb, trimmed
2 medium red onions, peeled
2 medium cloves garlic, cleaned
6 large leaves sage, fresh or preserved in salt
¹/₂ cup olive oil
1 cup dry white wine
2 pounds fresh tomatoes or 2 pounds canned tomatoes, preferably imported Italian, drained

Salt and freshly ground black pepper
Pinch of red hot pepper flakes
6 slices Tuscan bread (5 ✕ 3 ✕ 1), toasted and rubbed on both sides with 2 cloves garlic

OPTIONAL
2 extra-large egg yolks

CUT the meat into 2-inch cubes. Finely chop onion, garlic, and sage together on a board. Place a heavy casserole with the oil over medium heat and when the oil is warm, add the chopped ingredients and sauté lightly for 10 minutes, stirring every so often with a wooden spoon. Add the lamb, raise heat and sauté for 3 minutes, continuing to stir with a wooden spoon. Add wine, lower flame and let wine evaporate for 10 minutes.

If using fresh tomatoes, cut them into pieces. Pass fresh or canned tomatoes through a food mill, using the disc with smallest holes, into a bowl. Add salt and pepper to taste and the pinch of hot red pepper to the casserole, then put in the strained tomatoes. Cover and let simmer for 15 minutes or more depending on the age of the lamb (for baby lamb 10 minutes would be enough).

Warm a large serving dish and line it with the toasted garlic bread. When the meat is cooked and soft, remove casserole from heat, add the egg yolks, and mix very well with a wooden spoon in order to obtain a smooth sauce. Arrange meat over the bread slices, pour the sauce over, and serve immediately.

A SUGGESTED DINNER

WINE
AZIENDA AGRICOLA
ANNUNZIATA PINOT GRIGIO

Pasta e ceci
(SEE PAGE 153)

Agnello alla cacciatora
(SEE ABOVE)

Fagiolini bolliti
(SEE PAGE 521)

Macedonia di frutta
(SEE PAGE 559)

A SUGGESTED DINNER

WINE
GUICCIARDINI STROZZI
VERNACCIA DI SAN GIMIGNANO

Tortelli alla menta
(SEE PAGE 196)

Agnello alla fiorentina
(SEE BELOW)

Piselli alla fiorentina
(SEE PAGE 538)

Pesche ripiene con mandorle
(SEE PAGE 630)

Agnello alla fiorentina

LAMB, FLORENTINE STYLE

SERVES 6

J t is traditional in Florence to eat lamb only in its season, when it is true baby lamb. The preferred preparation is very simple, using the lamb cut into pieces with bone. Garlic, *pancetta,* and white wine are flavorings, but most characteristic is the dominant herb, rosemary, felt to be a crucial ingredient with lamb. Spring lamb, a bit older, may be substituted, the shoulder cut with bone probably working best for this particular dish.

4 pounds (with bone) of baby lamb or lamb shoulder from a spring lamb
2 ounces **pancetta,** *in one piece*
2 medium cloves garlic, peeled but left whole
1 large sprig rosemary or 1 tablespoon rosemary leaves, fresh or preserved in salt or dried and blanched

¹/₄ cup olive oil
1 cup dry white wine
Salt and freshly ground black pepper

CUT lamb into pieces, with bone, not smaller than 2 inches square. Cut *pancetta* into tiny pieces. Heat the oil in a large casserole over medium heat and when the oil is warm, add *pancetta* and sauté for 2 minutes, then add the garlic, rosemary, and the lamb. Sauté for 5 minutes, stirring every so often with a wooden spoon. Add ½ cup of the wine and cook for 5 minutes more. Season with salt and pepper to taste, then cover casserole and cook for 15 minutes more, adding some lukewarm water if more liquid is needed. By that time the lamb should be almost cooked and tender. Raise the flame, add the remaining wine, reduce for 5 minutes, and serve, discarding the clove of garlic. The lamb should be completely cooked and very soft and juicy.

Polpettone alla chiantigiana

MEAT LOAF CHIANTI STYLE

SERVES 8

*T*his special meat loaf of beef and sausage meat flavored with juniper berries, sage, and garlic, moistened with eggs, wine, and olive oil, is wrapped completely in prosciutto and sautéed before baking. The *polpettone* is moist and flavorful, using the herbs associated with game cookery. It may be eaten with one of the sauces suggested or, in a more elaborate alternative, covered with a crust. The Italians are not fond of cold forcemeat dishes, so that these *polpettoni*, unlike many pâtés, are eaten hot, especially when in crust.

3 slices white bread, crust removed

½ cup dry red wine plus 1 tablespoon

2 pounds beef, such as top round or sirloin, in one piece

4 sweet Italian sausages without fennel seeds or 12 ounces pork, in one piece

2 medium cloves of garlic, peeled

4 large sage leaves, fresh or preserved in salt

2 juniper berries

3 extra-large eggs

2 tablespoons olive oil

Salt and freshly ground black pepper

½ pound prosciutto, sliced thin

½ cup unbleached all-purpose flour

TO COOK THE MEAT LOAF

4 tablespoons olive oil

1 large clove garlic, peeled but left whole

2 sage leaves, fresh or preserved in salt

1 cup dry red wine

PUT the bread with the ½ cup wine in a small saucepan over medium heat and keep mixing until a paste is formed (about 5 minutes). Remove from heat and let rest until cool (about 15 minutes). Cut the beef into 1-inch cubes and remove the skin from the sausages. Use a meat grinder, employing the disc with the smallest holes, to grind beef, sausages,

A SUGGESTED DINNER

WINE
BARBI BRUSCO DEI BARBI

Risotto agli spinaci
(SEE PAGE 250)

Polpettone alla chiantigiana
(SEE ABOVE)

Carote in dolce-forte
(SEE PAGE 531)

Frittura mista di frutta
(SEE PAGE 634)

garlic, sage, and juniper berries all together, into a crockery or glass bowl. Add the eggs, olive oil, and remaining tablespoon of wine to the bowl and mix the ingredients together well with a wooden spoon, then add the bread paste. Season with salt and pepper and mix again. Lay out the prosciutto slices on a board, overlapping the slices to form a uniform layer without holes. Oil your hands and shape the prepared meat mixture into a thick cylinder about 11 inches long and 4 to 5 inches wide. Place the meat on and carefully wrap the prosciutto layer around it. Use a thin thread to tie the roll like a salami, then lightly flour it.

Heat the oil in a large skillet over medium heat and when the oil is warm, add the garlic and sage, then the *polpettone;* raise the heat and sauté all over until lightly golden (1 minute each side). Meanwhile preheat the oven to 375 degrees. Transfer the meat loaf to a 13½ × 9¾-inch baking dish, pour the wine over, and bake for 45 minutes, turning the meat twice and basting it several times with its own juices.

(continued)

POLPETTONE ALLA CHIANTIGIANA *(continued)*

Remove from oven. Transfer the meat loaf to a serving dish and let rest, covered, for 5 minutes. When ready, transfer the *polpettone* to a chopping board, untie it, and carefully cut it into slices ½ inch thick.

OPTIONAL

Pommarola (see page 83) or *Sugo scappato* (see page 84) can be served as sauce with the *polpettone*.

NOTE: The *polpettone* may be wrapped in a thin dough crust, prepared with the following ingredients:

FOR THE SPONGE

½ cup unbleached all-purpose flour
½ cup lukewarm water

1 ounce (2 cakes) fresh compressed yeast or 2 packages dry active yeast
Pinch of salt

FOR THE DOUGH

1¾ cups unbleached all-purpose flour

½ cup lukewarm water

PLUS

2 tablespoons olive oil

THE *polpettone* in this case should be baked with the wine for only 10 minutes, then removed and let cool for at least a half hour before wrapping in the dough. Let rest until the wrapping dough has doubled in size, then bake on an oiled cookie sheet for 45 minutes. Brush top with oil after 25 minutes of baking.

Pork
and Sausage

A SUGGESTED DINNER

WINE
CERETTO BARBARESCO BRICCO

Tortelli al gorgonzola
(SEE PAGE 200)

Maiale ubriaco
(SEE BELOW)

Rape saltate in padella
(SEE PAGE 545)

Schiacciata con zibibbo
(SEE PAGE 604)

Maiale ubriaco

"INEBRIATED" PORK CHOPS

SERVES 4

*T*he pork chop in a refreshing treatment, sautéed in wine with fennel seeds among the flavorings. No more difficult or time-consuming than any other simple treatment of pork chops, this is a useful dish for a simple family dinner.

10 sprigs Italian parsley, leaves
*   only*
1 large clove garlic, peeled
2 tablespoons olive oil
Salt and freshly ground black
*   pepper to taste*

1 teaspoon fennel seeds
4 large pork chops, with some
*   fat on them*
1 cup dry red wine

CHOP the parsley and garlic fine, then place in a bowl. Add the olive oil, salt, pepper, and fennel seeds to the bowl and mix all the ingredients together.

Transfer the contents of the bowl to a frying pan and place the pork chops on top. Set the pan over medium heat and sauté the pork for about 5 minutes on each side, then add the wine, lower heat, and cover the pan. Simmer very slowly for 20 minutes, until the wine is evaporated and the pork cooked.

Serve very hot with some of the sauce.

Braciole di maiale con cavolo nero

PORK CHOPS WITH KALE

SERVES 4

*P*ork chops cooked together with kale, again flavored with fennel seeds and also with tomato. Kale is, next to rape, the vegetable that weds best with pork.

After the pork chops and kale are cooked separately, each in its own mode, they are then cooked together to absorb each other's flavors.

2 pounds of kale (cavolo nero)
Coarse-grained salt
5 tablespoons olive oil
1 large clove garlic, peeled and
*   left whole*
4 large pork chops

Salt and freshly ground black
*   pepper to taste*
2 teaspoons fennel seeds
1 cup water
1 tablespoon tomato paste

REMOVE the large stems from the kale. Cut the remaining kale into 2-inch pieces and place them in a large bowl of cold water for 30 minutes. Put a large quantity of cold water into a stockpot and set on the heat. When the water reaches the boiling point, add coarse salt to taste, then the kale, and cook for about 20 minutes.

Meanwhile, heat the olive oil in a large frying pan. When it is warm, add the garlic clove and sauté very gently for 2 or 3 minutes. Add the pork chops and sauté them for 5 minutes on each side, then season with salt, freshly ground pepper, and the fennel seeds.

Heat the 1 cup of water and dissolve the tomato paste in it. Add the watered tomato paste to the frying pan, then cover and let cook for about 30 minutes.

Meanwhile, remove the stockpot containing the kale from the heat. Drain the kale in a colander and cool it under cold running water, then squeeze out excess water and let the kale stand until needed.

Remove the clove of garlic from the pan and transfer the pork chops to a serving dish. Keep warm.

Add the kale to the frying pan and let sauté for about 10 minutes.

Taste for salt and pepper, then replace the pork chops in the pan, putting them on top of the kale. Cover the pan and cook very slowly for 6 or 7 minutes more.

Serve very hot.

A SUGGESTED DINNER

WINE
RENATO RADDI NEBBIOLO

Cannelloni di ricotta
(SEE PAGE 219)

Braciole di maiale con cavolo nero
(SEE ABOVE)

Fresh fruit

A SUGGESTED DINNER

WINE

BIONDI SANTI BRUNELLO DI MONTALCINO

Tortellini alla panna

(SEE PAGE 204)

Arista

(SEE BELOW)

Rape saltate in padella

(SEE PAGE 545)

Pere al vino

(SEE PAGE 632)

with Crema zabaione

(SEE PAGE 565)

Arista

LOIN OF PORK WITH GARLIC, ROSEMARY, AND BLACK PEPPER

SERVES 8 TO 10

Around 1450 the Turks were at the gates of Constantinople, and it seemed that the thousand-year-old Eastern Roman Empire would fall if help did not come from the West. The Emperor and the Patriarch of the Orthodox Church went to Italy to have a conference on the union of that church with that of Rome, a precondition for aid. The Medici were hosts for most of the conference. Benozzo Gozzoli's famous fresco of the journey of the Magi is supposed to depict the personages of that historic event. At one of the feasts (Florence was the culinary center of the West), a roast of pork, a specialty of Florence, was served. One of the Greek dignitaries exclaimed in his own language: *"Arista!"* ("the best"). The Eastern Roman Empire fell, but *arista* has remained to this day.

10 large cloves garlic, peeled

2 heaping tablespoons rosemary leaves, fresh or preserved in salt or dried and blanched

1½ tablespoons salt

1 level tablespoon freshly ground black pepper

4 pounds front part pork loin, boned but untied

10 whole black peppercorns

1 tablespoon olive oil

PREHEAT the oven to 375 degrees.

Cut the garlic cloves into 4 to 6 pieces each lengthwise, then combine, in a bowl, with the rosemary leaves, salt, and ground pepper.

Place the loin on a board and open it out flat, with the inside facing up. Spread half the garlic mixture over the inside surface, then scatter the whole black peppercorns over it. Roll the loin and tie with thread, as follows:

Wrap the thread around the meat, starting at one end, and pull tight. Do not break the thread but bring it down lengthwise 2 inches and wrap it around the meat again. Continue this process until the entire length is tied around, at a distance of every 2 inches or so. (This is the usual way of tying salami in Italy.)

When rolled and tied, make about 12 punctures in the outside of the meat with a thin knife, about ½ inch deep. Fill these holes with most of the remainder of the spice mixture, and if any of the spice mixture is left, sprinkle it over the outside surface of the loin.

Put the olive oil in the bottom of a roasting pan, then set the meat in it. Place the pan in the preheated oven for about 25 minutes to the pound. The pork should not be overcooked; it is advisable to cook the meat completely, but to be careful not to leave it in the oven beyond that point. Not only the weight, but the width of the roll affects cooking time.

After about an hour in the oven, turn the meat over. For the last 5

(continued)

447

ARISTA *(continued)*

to 10 minutes, raise the temperature to 400 degrees, to brown the outside.

Remove the pan from the oven and immediately transfer the *arista* from the pan with its drippings. Let cool for 10 minutes before slicing in thin slices and serving.

NOTE: *Arista* may be eaten cold for several days following, and many Florentines prefer it that way.

The famous painting by Gozzoli of the journey of the Magi, showing the personages of the council to unify the churches and save Constantinople. It was at this council that *arista* got its name.

Salsicce

TUSCAN SAUSAGES

MAKES ABOUT 15

*T*uscan sausages are of pork, the fat of the fresh *pancetta,* and a little veal. Cured with salt, pepper, and whole peppercorns only, they differ from most Italian sausages in that they are not flavored with herbs and spices, nor do they contain preservatives.

Since they are not readily available abroad, the recipe for making them is given. If you do not have the time to make them, use Italian sausages with the least flavoring added, or ground pork. When in Italy, try the sausages of Siena, which are particularly outstanding.

Making your own sausages is, however, worth the trouble. You can, for one thing, avoid artificial preservatives and flavorings. The main thing to remember is not to grind the meat too fine or you will have an uninteresting texture. And be sure to obtain pork casing, not veal or anything else; good pork stores usually have it.

When you see your sausages turn reddish on the third day or so, you won't be able to suppress a feeling of pride. Try them.

2 pounds fresh boneless pork
1 pound fresh **pancetta**
2 ounces boneless veal
1 ½ tablespoons salt

2 teaspoons freshly ground
*   black pepper*
20 whole black peppercorns,
*   approximately*
1 pork casing

CUT the different kinds of meat into small pieces, then grind the pieces coarsely, with a hand or electric grinder, using the disc with medium-sized holes. Add the salt, ground pepper, and peppercorns and mix very thoroughly with a wooden spoon.

Soak the casing in a small bowl of lukewarm water for 10 minutes, then remove from the water and dry with paper towels.

Improvise a syringe by inserting the tube end of a funnel into one end of the casing. Then push the casing up until all of it is rolled onto the funnel tube.

(continued)

SALSICCE *(continued)*

Making sure that your hands are very clean and dry, insert some of the meat into the mouth of the funnel; then, with the handle of a wooden spoon or one of your fingers, push it through the funnel tube into the rolled-up casing, to the end (see illustration below). Gently unroll the casing. The meat pushed through will have opened the entire casing to allow air to rush in. It is now open to stuff.

Little by little, push the meat in until the casing is full, being careful not to leave empty pockets of air. Fill it well, but do not overstuff.

When the casing is full, tie a long string to one end. (At this point, move your hands over casing again to be sure that stuffing is evenly distributed.) Now, 3 inches from the end where it is tied, draw the long string around, pass it through, and knot it tight (see illustration opposite). Every 3 inches, tie the long string around in the same manner, in this way making a long series of sausage links (see illustration opposite).

Let the sausages hang in a cool room with lots of fresh air. About the third day, they should turn a reddish color. Allow them to hang for another 3 or 4 days; the salt will cure the meat in this period. After 6 or 7 days they may be used or refrigerated.

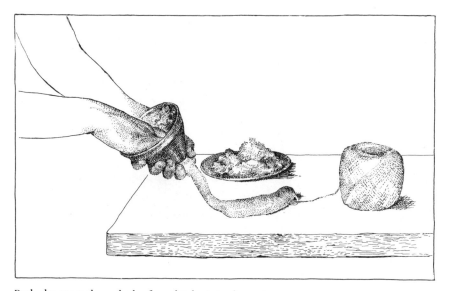

Push the meat through the funnel tube into the casing.

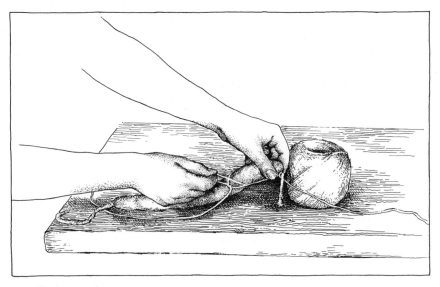

Tie off a link in the sausage.

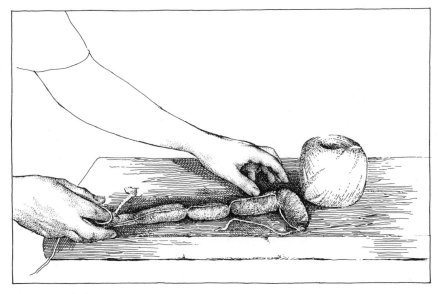

The sausage links.

A SUGGESTED DINNER

WINE
PAGLIARESE CHIANTI CLASSICO

Ribollita
(SEE PAGE 148)

Salsicce con rape
(SEE BELOW)

Frittelle di tondone alla fiorentina
(SEE PAGE 602)

Salsicce con rape

SAUSAGES WITH RAPE

SERVES 4

*T*his is the classic combination, the pork sausage with its ideal complement, wonderful, slightly bitter, green rape.*

2½ pounds broccoli-rab (rape)	**1 clove garlic, peeled but left**
Coarse-grained salt	**whole**
4 Italian sweet sausages	**Salt and freshly ground black**
without fennel seeds	**pepper to taste**
2 tablespoons olive oil	**Lemon wedges**

REMOVE the heavy stalks from the rape, leaving the light stalks and leaves. Cut these into 2-inch pieces and rinse them thoroughly under cold running water, then place in a large bowl of cold water and let soak for 30 minutes.

Bring a large pot of cold water to a boil over medium heat. When the water reaches the boiling point, add coarse salt to taste, then add the rape and cook for about 15 minutes, or until soft. Remove the casserole from the heat, drain the rape in a colander, and cool it under cold running water. Gently squeeze excess water from the rape and let stand until needed.

Puncture the sausages with a fork in two or three places.

Heat the olive oil in a medium-sized flameproof casserole, and when the oil is warm add the garlic and sausages and sauté gently for about 15 minutes.

Remove the garlic clove from the casserole and add the rape. Season with salt and freshly ground pepper and mix thoroughly with a wooden spoon, then cover the casserole and let simmer very slowly, stirring every so often, for about 20 minutes.

Remove the casserole from the heat and transfer the sausages and rape to a serving dish. Serve immediately with lemon wedges.

*See introduction to *Rape saltate,* page 545.

A SUGGESTED DINNER

WINE
BARBI ROSSO DI MONTALCINO

Passato di spinaci
(SEE PAGE 143)

Salsicce e fagioli
(SEE BELOW)

Crostata di ricotta
(SEE PAGE 578)

Salsicce e fagioli

TUSCAN BEANS WITH SAUSAGES

SERVES 4

A filling, satisfying dish for a nice winter night. A rustic family dish that can also be shared with good friends on an informal occasion.

4 Italian sweet sausages without
    fennel seeds
3 tablespoons olive oil
6 large leaves sage, fresh or
    preserved in salt (see page
    19)
4 large cloves garlic, unpeeled
1 pound very ripe fresh
    tomatoes or 1 pound canned
    tomatoes, preferably
    imported Italian, drained

Salt and freshly ground black
    pepper to taste
4 cups boiled cannellini beans
    (see boiled Tuscan beans,
    page 516)

PUNCTURE the sausages with a fork in three or four places.

Heat the oil in a flameproof casserole, preferably terra-cotta. When the oil is hot, add the sausages and sauté over low heat for 15 minutes, turning them over several times. Add the sage and garlic and sauté for 2 or 3 minutes more.

Pass the tomatoes through a food mill, using the disc with the smallest holes, into the casserole and simmer for 3 to 5 minutes more. Season with salt and pepper, then add the boiled cannellini beans and simmer very slowly for 15 minutes more, stirring with a wooden spoon.

Remove the casserole from the heat, and serve hot from the same casserole.

A SUGGESTED DINNER

WINE
FRESCOBALDI POMINO ROSSO

Minestra "povera" di patate
(SEE PAGE 150)

Rospo nel buco
(SEE BELOW)

Fagiolini in umido
(SEE PAGE 523)

Fresh fruit

Rospo nel buco

A more elaborate treatment of the rustic sausage, but still a family dish. The sausage pieces form part of a light batter cake.

8 Italian sweet sausages without fennel seeds
1 tablespoon olive oil
6 extra-large eggs, separated
1 cup milk
6 tablespoons unbleached all-purpose flour

Salt and freshly ground black pepper to taste
1 tablespoon rosemary leaves, fresh or preserved in salt or dried and blanched

PREHEAT the oven to 400 degrees.

Prick each sausage with a fork in two or three places, then place in a 13½ × 8¾-inch baking dish with the olive oil. Put the dish in the preheated oven for 20 to 25 minutes, until all fat has rendered out of the sausages.

Meanwhile, prepare a batter by mixing the egg yolks, milk, flour, salt, pepper, and rosemary leaves in a bowl with a wooden spoon. Let the batter stand for 20 minutes in a cool place, or on the bottom shelf of the refrigerator.

When the sausages are ready, take the baking dish from the oven and remove all but 2 tablespoons of fat.

Use a wire whisk and copper bowl to beat the egg whites until stiff, and quickly fold into the batter. Pour the batter over the sausages in the hot baking dish and put back in the oven, still at 400 degrees. Bake for about 35 minutes.

Remove the "frogs in the holes" from the oven, allow to cool for 5 minutes, and serve.

A SUGGESTED DINNER

WINE

QUINTARELLI GIUSEPPE
AMARONE CLASSICO

Penne ai peperoni
(SEE PAGE 188)

Rocchi di sedano
(SEE BELOW)

Meringhe alla panna
(SEE PAGE 598)

Rocchi di sedano

CELERY CROQUETTES IN MEAT SAUCE

SERVES 6 TO 8

*R*emarkable croquettes made of coarsely chopped celery held to-gether by eggs, Parmigiano, and bread crumbs and flavored with garlic and parsley. Fried, then simmered in a meat sauce of sausage and tomatoes, it is always a smash and a great novelty when I serve it. Rarely has one thought of using celery in such a way. A vegetable course that should be served separately.

When celery was brought by the Byzantines to Italy in the fifteenth century, there was great skepticism about whether it was safe to eat. Now one can't imagine a broth or a sauce requiring *odori* made without it.

2 pounds celery ribs, cleaned
    and with leaves removed
Coarse-grained salt
15 sprigs Italian parsley, leaves
    only
2 medium cloves garlic, peeled
1/3 cup olive oil
Salt and freshly ground black
    pepper

2 extra-large eggs
1/2 cup freshly grated
    Parmigiano
1/2 cup unseasoned bread
    crumbs, preferably
    homemade
1 quart vegetable oil (see page
    22)

FOR THE SAUCE

2 medium cloves garlic, peeled
1/4 cup olive oil
3 Italian sweet sausages without
    fennel seeds, or 9 ounces of
    ground pork

2 pounds canned tomatoes,
    preferably imported Italian,
    drained
Salt and freshly ground black
    pepper to taste

CUT the celery ribs into 2-inch pieces and put them in a bowl of cold water for 30 minutes. Bring a large quantity of cold water to a boil, add coarse-grained salt to taste, then drain the celery, add it to the boiling water, and cook for 15 minutes. Then drain and cool under cold running water. Coarsely chop the celery on a board, then place it in a colander to drain completely for 10 minutes.

Chop the parsley, but not too coarsely, and finely chop the garlic. Heat the oil in a skillet on medium heat, and when the oil is warm, add the chopped ingredients and sauté for 1 minute; then add the drained celery, season with salt and pepper, and sauté for 15 minutes, stirring every so often. Remove from heat and transfer the celery to a bowl to cool for 1 hour.

Meanwhile prepare the sauce. Finely chop the garlic on a board. Place a heavy saucepan with the oil on medium heat, and when the oil is warm add the chopped garlic and sauté for 1 minute. Meanwhile remove the skin from the sausages, add them to the pan, and sauté them for 5 minutes. Pass the tomatoes through a food mill, using the disc with small holes, into the pan with the sautéed garlic. Season with salt

ROCCHI DI SEDANO *(continued)*

and pepper, cover, and simmer for 1 hour, stirring every so often with a wooden spoon.

When the celery has cooled, add the eggs, Parmigiano, and bread crumbs to the bowl, mix very well, and taste for salt and pepper.

Heat the oil in a deep-fat fryer. Prepare a large platter by lining it with paper towels. When the oil is hot (about 375 degrees), shape each heaping tablespoon of the celery mixture into a little ball by rolling it between the palms of your hands. Add these croquettes to the hot oil, one at a time, keeping them separate, and cook them until they are light golden on both sides, then remove them to the prepared platter to drain. Carefully transfer the croquettes to the pan with the sauce (still on medium heat), making a single layer. Lower the heat to minimum and cover the pan. Cook for 2 minutes, then remove pan from heat and let it stand, covered, for 5 minutes before serving.

Variety Meats

❧

A SUGGESTED DINNER

WINE
GRANDUCA BAROLO RISERVA

Pappa al pomodoro
(SEE PAGE 273)

Fegato alla griglia
(SEE BELOW)

Fagioli al fiasco
(SEE PAGE 516)

Ciambella di frutta
(SEE PAGE 620)

Fegato alla griglia

CALF'S LIVER, GRILLED FLORENTINE STYLE

SERVES 4

*T*he simplest of treatments, calf's liver cooked on a *gratella,* the Italian range-top grill. If the liver is fresh and good, all of its own flavor will emerge. Use very thin slices.

Coarse-grained salt
4 large slices calf's liver, sliced
thin
Freshly ground black pepper to
taste

2 tablespoons olive oil
Lemon wedges

PLACE the grill on the heat and sprinkle it with 2 or 3 teaspoons of salt. (If the grill is well seasoned, it should not be necessary to use any oil.) When the grill is very hot, put on one slice of the liver and cook it for about 45 seconds on each side, then remove it to a serving dish; keep warm. Repeat the procedure with the other 3 slices.

Sprinkle the liver with a little freshly ground black pepper and uncooked oil, then serve immediately with lemon wedges.

NOTE: The liver should be light pink inside and very tender and soft. Keep in mind that the longer you cook liver, the tougher it becomes.

A SUGGESTED DINNER

WINE

ROCCA DELLE MACIE CHIANTI CLASSICO RISERVA

Tortelli della vigilia

(SEE PAGE 198)

Fegato alla toscana

(SEE BELOW)

Fagioli all'uccelletto

(SEE PAGE 519)

Latte alla portoghese

(SEE PAGE 568)

Fegato alla toscana

SAUTÉED CALF'S LIVER, TUSCAN STYLE

SERVES 4

*A*nother simple treatment, flavored with olive oil, sage, and very lightly with garlic. If the calf's liver is good, it should be cooked as little as possible. The longer it is cooked, the tougher it gets.

½ cup unbleached all-purpose flour
1½ pounds calf's liver, sliced thin
5 tablespoons olive oil
5 leaves sage, fresh or preserved in salt (see page 19)

1 large clove garlic, unpeeled and left whole
Salt and freshly ground black pepper to taste

FLOUR the liver slices very lightly.

Put the oil, sage, and unpeeled garlic clove in a large frying pan and set over medium heat. When the oil is hot, place the liver slices in the pan and sauté very lightly for about 45 seconds on each side, so the liver remains pink inside. Sprinkle with salt and freshly ground black pepper, then remove the pan from heat.

Transfer the liver to a serving dish and serve hot.

Trippa alla fiorentina

TRIPE, FLORENTINE STYLE

SERVES 4

*T*ripe, cooked first and then simmered with meat broth, tomatoes, and seasonings. It is cut into thin strips almost resembling
pasta, and sprinkled with Parmigiano. A very pleasant introduction to
tripe for those who haven't tried it. (There is no strange aftertaste as in
tripes à la mode de Caen.)

In Florence there are little tripe stands on wheels that sell already
cooked tripe without sauce, as well as sandwiches made with the tripe.
With sly Tuscan humor, these stands poke fun at the Florentine pride
in their long history. Often the wagons have painted on them something
like "This house was founded in 1903."

In Italy the tripe is completely precooked, so it has to be cooked in
sauce only 20 to 35 minutes. In most countries the tripe is precooked
for much less time, and generally requires additional cooking. (Check
with your butcher.)

Coarse-grained salt
2 pounds fresh tripe
10 sprigs Italian parsley, leaves
* only*
1 large clove garlic, peeled
¼ cup olive oil
2 tablespoons tomato paste,
* preferably imported Italian*

Salt and freshly ground black
* pepper to taste*
1 cup meat broth, preferably
* homemade*
¼ cup freshly grated
* Parmigiano*

IF tripe is not completely precooked, bring a large amount of cold water
to a boil in a stockpot. When it is boiling, add coarse salt to taste, then
the tripe and simmer (in most countries from 2 to 4 hours, depending
on the amount of precooking it has undergone).

When the tripe is cooked, cool it under cold running water, then
slice it into strips ⅓ inch wide.

Chop the parsley and garlic coarsely. Heat the olive oil in a flameproof casserole. When it is warm, add the chopped ingredients and sauté very gently for about 10 minutes. Add the tripe to the casserole and cook for 5 minutes more.

Add the tomato paste and broth. Simmer until the broth is almost completely evaporated (about 25 minutes) and the tripe is soft, then taste for salt and pepper and cook for 5 minutes more.

Remove the casserole from the heat. Transfer the tripe to a serving dish and allow it to cool for 2 minutes, then sprinkle with the Parmigiano and serve.

A SUGGESTED DINNER

WINE
PRUNOTTO BARBARESCO

Minestrone alla contadina
(SEE PAGE 146)

Trippa alla fiorentina
(SEE ABOVE)

Insalata di peperoni alla griglia
(SEE PAGE 505)

Budino di riso
(SEE PAGE 626)

Ciambella con cibreo

POTATO-RICOTTA RING WITH CHICKEN-LIVER SAUCE

SERVES 4

*C*ibreo sauce should be made not only with chicken livers, but also with the crests and wattles of the rooster. Another touch of a generation ago was to use as well the little yellow eggs that were still inside the hen when slaughtered. These combs and eggs have disappeared from most markets recently enough perhaps to arouse some nostalgia. If you can get them, by all means include them in the recipe.

14 ounces potatoes for boiling, but not new potatoes	*Salt and freshly ground black pepper to taste*
15 ounces ricotta, drained	*½ cup unseasoned bread crumbs, preferably homemade (see page 58), approximately*
5 extra-large eggs, one of them separated	
3 tablespoons freshly grated Parmigiano	*Cibreo sauce (see page 88)*

PUT the potatoes in a large saucepan of boiling salted water and cook for about 30 minutes, then peel and pass them through a potato ricer into a large bowl.

Add the ricotta to the bowl and mix well with the potatoes. Add the whole eggs, the egg yolk, Parmigiano, salt, and pepper and mix thoroughly, until homogenous.

Butter a ring mold (8½ inches in diameter) and coat it with the bread crumbs; preheat the oven to 400 degrees.

Using a wire whisk and a copper bowl, beat the egg white until stiff, then fold it very gently into the contents of the bowl. Transfer the potato mixture from the bowl to the ring mold and place in the preheated oven for 20 to 25 minutes.

Remove the mold from the oven and allow to cool for 15 to 20 minutes before unmolding.

Meanwhile, prepare the *cibreo* sauce using 1 pound of chicken livers and veal kidneys if the crests and unlaid eggs are not available.

Unmold the ring on a serving dish; then, with a slotted spoon, transfer the solids in the sauce to the center of the ring. Pour remaining sauce from pan into sauceboat. Serve each person a slice of *ciambella,* or ring, with some of the solids and sauce on the side.

A SUGGESTED DINNER

WINE
CONTI SERRISTORI CHIANTI CLASSICO

Passato di spinaci
(SEE PAGE 143)

Ciambella con cibreo
(SEE ABOVE)

Meringhe alla panna
(SEE PAGE 598)

Torta manfreda

ANTIQUE CHICKEN LIVER PÂTE

SERVES 6

*H*ere, coarsely chopped chicken livers are sautéed with wine, *pancetta,* and other ingredients. *Mollica* (crustless bread), eggs, and Parmigiano are added, and then all is transferred to a pie-plate mold, the top coated with bread crumbs, and baked.

A great favorite of the Renaissance, the dish appears in almost all cookbooks of those early centuries.

Usually served hot, *torta manfreda* makes a good appetizer or first dish for an important dinner, as well as a good light second dish after a heavier first one, still for a rather formal type of dinner. A very versatile dish indeed.

6 ounces **pancetta** *or*
    prosciutto, *in one piece*
2 tablespoons olive oil
1 pound chicken livers, cleaned
½ cup dry red wine
2 slices white bread, crusts
    removed
4 extra-large eggs
8 ounces freshly grated
    Parmigiano

5 tablespoons unseasoned bread
    crumbs, preferably
    homemade (see page 58)
Salt and freshly ground black
    pepper to taste
2 tablespoons (1 ounce) sweet
    butter, approximately

PREHEAT the oven to 375 degrees.

Cut the *pancetta* into tiny pieces. Set a saucepan containing the olive oil over low heat. When the oil is hot, add the *pancetta* and sauté gently until lightly golden.

Chop the chicken livers coarsely and add them to the saucepan. Sauté gently for 4 or 5 minutes, then add the red wine and let it evaporate.

Remove the pan from the heat, transfer the solid contents to a board, and chop them fine. Return the chopped ingredients to the saucepan and put the pan back on the heat. Taste for salt and pepper and cook slowly for 3 or 4 minutes, then remove the pan from the heat again.

Put the crustless bread slices in a crockery bowl. Pour the contents of the saucepan over the bread and let cool, then mix well with a wooden spoon, incorporating the bread into the other ingredients. Stirring constantly, add the eggs, one at a time, then the Parmigiano and 1 tablespoon of the bread crumbs. Taste for salt and pepper.

Coat a pie plate with the butter and some of the remaining bread crumbs. Transfer the contents of the bowl to the pie plate, pressing the mixture down well so the top is level. Sprinkle the top with the last of the bread crumbs.

Place the pie plate in the preheated oven and bake for 30 to 35 minutes, then remove from the oven and let cool for 10 to 15 minutes.

Unmold onto a serving dish and serve.

NOTE: *Torta manfreda* can be eaten as an appetizer, in place of pasta as a first course, or as a second course.

A SUGGESTED DINNER

WINE
BANFI CHIANTI CLASSICO

Timballo di riso
(SEE PAGE 260)

Torta manfreda
(SEE ABOVE)

Piselli alla fiorentina
(SEE PAGE 538)

Frittura mista di frutta
(SEE PAGE 634)

A SUGGESTED DINNER

WINE

FATTORIA DI ARTIMINO CARMIGNANO

Pasta e ceci

(SEE PAGE 153)

Fegatelli alla fiorentina

(SEE BELOW)

Rape saltate in padella

(SEE PAGE 545)

or Insalata verde

(SEE PAGE 500)

Pane co' santi

(SEE PAGE 608)

Fegatelli alla fiorentina

PORK LIVER, FLORENTINE STYLE

SERVES 6

resh pork liver cut into pieces, rolled in a mixture of good bread crumbs, fennel seeds, salt, pepper, and crushed bay leaf, and then wrapped in caul fat. Sautéed in olive oil and then simmered in wine, a flavor is achieved that would not be possible with any other kind of liver. The caul fat cooks away, but the liver has absorbed the flavors of all the ingredients. Pork liver is often very cheap because it is unjustly neglected.

½ pound pork caul fat
1½ pounds pork liver
¾ cup unseasoned bread
   crumbs, preferably
   homemade (see page 58)
2 tablespoons fennel seeds

Salt and freshly ground black
   pepper to taste
6 medium bay leaves
6 tablespoons olive oil
½ cup dry red wine

SOAK the caul fat in a small bowl of lukewarm water for 10 minutes. Meanwhile, cut the pork liver into 12 pieces and set aside. Combine the bread crumbs, fennel seeds, salt, and pepper in a large bowl and mix well with a wooden spoon.

Carefully open the caul fat and spread it out on a board. Cut the caul fat into 12 pieces.

Put the liver pieces in the large bowl and mix well with the bread crumb mixture, then place each piece of liver on top of a piece of caul fat. Add ½ bay leaf to each piece and wrap the liver and bay leaf completely in fat (see the illustrations below and on page 474). Fasten the caul fat to the liver with a toothpick.

(continued)

Fegatelli alla fiorentina: Place a piece of liver and half a bay leaf on a piece of caul fat.

Wrap the pork liver completely in caul fat.

Fegatelli alla fiorentina *(continued)*

Heat the olive oil in a large frying pan and add all the wrapped liver pieces. Sauté very gently, over medium heat, for 10 minutes, turning the liver pieces once or twice, then sprinkle with salt and pepper. Add the wine, cover, and simmer for 20 minutes, turning the *fegatelli* once more.

Remove the pan from the heat; the caul fat will have dissolved. Transfer the *fegatelli* to a serving dish, sprinkle over one or two tablespoons of the juices, and serve immediately.

Polenta

*P*olenta is made from corn meal, cooked in a special way, and serves as the basis for hundreds of dishes. It is a staple of the diet of the Veneto region and some of the other far northern parts of Italy. There is no doubt that polenta is the descendant of the staple food of the ancient Roman Empire, *puls*. Remember that bread made from wheat flour was only eaten by the rich in those days. The *puls* was not yet made from corn meal, because there were still many centuries to wait before corn was brought to Europe from America. But corn meal replaced other grains, and polenta is still very much with us. Unfortunately, there is only space for a few recipes, those with sausage and with herring, and for a more complicated dish in which the polenta is cooked and cut into strips that serve as the pastry for a *timballo* filled with quails and sauce.

In addition, there is a polentalike recipe, *gnocchi di farina gialla* (see page 266), that is used as a first course.

The main danger to avoid in cooking polenta is the formation of lumps. For this reason it must be stirred constantly while it cooks over low heat. The technique of first pouring the meal into the boiling liquid must also be mastered to avoid the meal's bunching together. Follow the instructions carefully and all will be well.

2¼ quarts cold water	*1 pound Italian coarse yellow*
Coarse-grained salt	*corn meal*

HEAT the water in a stockpot. When the water reaches the boiling point, add coarse salt to taste, then begin adding corn meal. Pour it in a very slow stream, simultaneously stirring with a wooden spoon or a simple nonrotary rolling pin. (It is important to pour slowly and steadily and to keep stirring because otherwise the polenta can easily become lumpy.) Stir slowly, without stopping, for about 55 minutes. If some lumps form, push them against the side of the pot to dissolve them.

Prepare a smooth wooden surface (preferably a round board about 18 inches in diameter, or substitute a pasta board) by wetting it with cold water.

When the polenta has cooked for about 55 minutes, leave it on the heat for about 3 minutes more without stirring. Shake the pot a little; in this way, some steam will form under the polenta and it will completely detach from the bottom of the pot. After the 3 minutes are up, quickly reverse the pot of polenta onto the wooden surface.

Polenta is best cut with a string. Fit a string under the polenta layer and draw it through to the top surface (see below). Continue slicing the polenta this way, then place the slices on individual dishes.

Cover with whichever sauce you have prepared and serve hot.

How to slice polenta with a string.

Polenta con salsicce

POLENTA WITH SAUSAGES

SERVES 6

*S*ausages cooked in a wonderful sauce made with wild mushrooms and all poured over slices of polenta. It makes one look forward to the cold weather.

4 ounces dried **porcini** **mushrooms**

6 Italian sweet sausages, without fennel seeds

1 red onion, cleaned

5 tablespoons olive oil

¼ cup tomato paste, preferably imported Italian

Salt and freshly ground black pepper to taste

2 cups meat or chicken broth, preferably homemade

FOR THE POLENTA

2½ quarts cold water

Coarse-grained salt

1 pound coarse Italian yellow corn meal

SOAK the dried mushrooms in a bowl of lukewarm water for 30 minutes. Meanwhile, cut the sausages in half; chop the onion fine.

Heat the olive oil in a saucepan over medium heat. When it is warm, add the chopped onion and sauté until golden (about 12 minutes), stirring every so often with a wooden spoon. Add the sausage pieces and sauté very lightly for 10 minutes, then add the tomato paste and simmer for 5 minutes more. Clean the mushrooms, removing all the sand attached to the stems. (If the soaking water is saved for another dish, strain it through several layers of paper towels to remove sand. The water may be frozen in ice cube trays.) Add the soaked mushrooms and season with salt and pepper.

In a second saucepan, heat the broth to boiling. When it is hot, pour it into the saucepan containing the sausages. Let simmer very slowly until a large quantity of broth has evaporated (about 25 minutes).

While the sauce is reducing, make the polenta, with quantities listed, according to the directions on page 476. When the polenta is ready and on its round board (or pasta board), cut it into slices with a string.

Pour the sauce into a large sauceboat and serve hot, along with the polenta. Place several slices of polenta on each individual dish and cover them with the sausage sauce.

A SUGGESTED DINNER

WINE
MONTEVERTINE CHIANTI SODACCIO

Crostini al ginepro
(SEE PAGE 107)

Polenta con salsicce
(SEE BELOW)

Buccellato alle fragole
(SEE PAGE 603)

A SUGGESTED DINNER

WINE
VOLPAIA CHIANTI CLASSICO

Passato di spinaci
(SEE PAGE 143)

Aringhe e polenta
(SEE BELOW)

Fresh fruit

Aringhe e polenta

HERRING WITH POLENTA

SERVES 4

*P*erhaps herring does not leap to mind as an Italian dish. But it is widely eaten in the Tuscan Appenines. The salted smoked herring is not soaked, so it remains potently salty. Cooked on the Italian range-top grill, the *gratella,* and eaten in a small quantity with polenta, on a cold winter night, it can be a very satisfying, hearty country dinner. Often, as a joke, the friends of a bridegroom would give him a bachelor party in the country the night before his wedding. They would have this dish made, with the humorous intent that the following day the groom would be incapable of opening his mouth to say "I do."

Polenta
2 herrings, with milt or roe
½ cup olive oil

Freshly ground black pepper to taste

PREPARE the polenta using ingredients listed and directions on page 476. Place it on a wooden surface and cover with a cotton dishtowel to keep warm. Take herrings directly from the barrel. Do not wash, soak, or fillet; leave whole, with the milt or roe.

Heat the *gratella* until very hot; put no fat on it, or salt. Place the herrings on the hot grill and cook them on both sides until quite golden (about 8 minutes each side). Those lucky enough to have a fireplace for cooking should roast them instead over the open fire until each side is brown.

Place the herrings in a large soup bowl and pour over the uncooked olive oil. Sprinkle with freshly ground black pepper.

Slice polenta with string and place several slices on each individual dish. Cut herrings in half widthwise and place a half herring with some of its sauce on each dish.

Timballo di polenta con quaglie

PASTRY DRUM OF POLENTA FILLED WITH QUAIL

SERVES 4

*T*his dish is the ennoblement of polenta. Made into an elegant *timballo* filled with quail, at this point polenta may be served at the fanciest of tables. (Two small squabs may be substituted for the 4 quails, but the result is definitely a compromise.)

Making the *timballo* with polenta is even more difficult than making the normal *timballo,* so practice making it for the family before you try it for an important dinner. The steps that require extreme care are pointed out in the recipe. Be sure that the polenta is extra smooth, with no lumps, before beginning.

FOR THE POLENTA

2 quarts water
Coarse-grained salt

¾ pound very fine Italian yellow corn meal

FOR THE FILLING

¼ pound pancetta or prosciutto, in one piece
1 large clove garlic, peeled
8 leaves sage, fresh or preserved in salt (see page 19)
¼ cup olive oil
Salt and freshly ground black pepper
4 quails or 2 small squab
1 tablespoon tomato paste, preferably imported Italian

½ pound canned tomatoes, preferably imported Italian, drained
1½ cups hot chicken or meat broth, preferably homemade
1 bay leaf
3 or 4 tablespoons (1½ or 2 ounces) of sweet butter
2 cups freshly grated Parmigiano

To make the polenta, put 2 quarts of water in a stockpot and set on the heat. (The *timballo* polenta requires a larger proportion of water than the classic polenta.) When the water reaches the boiling point, add coarse salt; then add the corn meal, pouring in a continuous stream and

A SUGGESTED DINNER

WINE
MONTEVERTINE LE PERGOLE TORTE

Passato di verdura
(SEE PAGE 140)

Timballo di polenta con quaglie
(SEE ABOVE)

Bietole all'agro
(SEE PAGE 548)

Fragole al vino rosso
(SEE PAGE 631)

stirring constantly with a wooden spoon. Keep stirring until the polenta is completely cooked (at least 50 minutes).

Stop stirring and let the polenta rest on the flame for about 3 minutes. Shake the pot a little. In this way a little steam will form at the bottom of the pot, which will help to unmold the polenta.

Unmold the polenta onto a wet, smooth surface of marble, wood, or Formica, then spread it out with a wet spatula until it is uniformly ¼ inch thick. Let the polenta cool for 2 hours. Meanwhile, begin to make the sauce.

Cut the *pancetta* into tiny pieces and coarsely chop the garlic and sage together.

Heat the olive oil in a saucepan, preferably terra-cotta, and when it is hot, add the chopped ingredients and *pancetta* and sauté on medium heat until golden (about 15 minutes). Put a pinch of salt and pepper inside each quail and add them to the saucepan. Sauté for 5 to 7 minutes. Add the tomato paste and allow 2 or 3 minutes for it to incorporate.

(continued)

TIMBALLO DI POLENTA CON QUAGLIE *(continued)*

Pass the tomatoes through a food mill, using the disc with the smallest holes, into a small bowl.

Add the tomatoes, enough hot broth to cover the quails completely (1 to 1½ cups of broth) and the bay leaf, then taste for salt and pepper and simmer very gently for 20 to 25 minutes. Remove from the heat and let cool for 30 minutes. Remove and discard the bay leaf.

Meanwhile, start to put the *timballo* together.

To make the circular top of the *timballo,* place the removable bottom of an 8-inch springform pan on the polenta layer and cut around it. The circular bottom of the *timballo* must be a little larger than the top. Place the bottom of the springform pan on the polenta layer again, but this time cut the circle ½ inch larger all around.

Put the springform pan together and butter it generously, then carefully place the bottom layer of the *timballo* inside. Since it has a larger diameter than the springform pan, the edges will curl up and overlap the sides.

To make the sides of the *timballo,* cut long strips of polenta as wide as the pan is high (about 2¾ inches). Fit the strips along the inside of the pan, being careful to place them inside the overlap of the circular *timballo* bottom. For the sides, try to use as few separate pieces as possible, and be sure to allow ½ inch overlap in the connection of 2 separate polenta strips.

Remove the quails from the saucepan and place them inside the *timballo.* Sprinkle 2 tablespoons of the Parmigiano and 2 tablespoons of the sauce over them.

Cut the leftover polenta into 1-inch squares; preheat the oven to 400 degrees. Fit polenta squares between and around the quails, filling in empty spaces. Again sprinkle with Parmigiano and sauce.

Using additional polenta squares, completely fill in the *timballo,* using up the remaining Parmigiano and sauce as well. Top with the pats of butter and cover with the *timballo* top.

Bake for 50 minutes, then allow to cool for 15 minutes.

Say a prayer and open the springform. Place the *timballo* on a serving dish and serve hot, cutting through like a cake, being careful to leave the quails whole.

Composite Main Courses

∾

Sformato di prosciutto cotto

HAM "SOUFFLÉ"

SERVES 6

Sformati, meaning literally "unmolded," are, along with certain types of *budini,* the Italian soufflés. (See the discussion of the dessert *budino* on page 625.) This *sformato* of ham is a main dish employing the same technique that is used more often for an elaborate vegetable treatment appropriate for a *piatto di mezzo.* It is a very light and delicate second course, useful for a formal light meal, or as a relief to a heavier first course.

FOR THE BALSAMELLA

6 tablespoons (3 ounces) sweet butter
½ cup unbleached all-purpose flour

2 cups milk
Pinch of salt

FOR THE SFORMATO

10 ounces boiled ham, in one piece
½ cup brandy
1 tablespoon (½ ounce) sweet butter
1 tablespoon unbleached all-purpose flour

2 tablespoons freshly grated Parmigiano
4 extra-large eggs, separated
Salt and freshly ground black pepper
Pinch of freshly grated nugmeg

MAKE a thick *balsamella,* using the ingredients in the quantities listed, according to the directions on page 62. Transfer the *balsamella* to a bowl, cover with buttered wax paper, and let cool for about 25 minutes.

Cut 6 ounces of the boiled ham into small pieces and marinate in the brandy for 30 minutes; melt the butter in a small saucepan and let cool for 10 minutes.

When the *balsamella* is cool, very finely chop the remaining 4 ounces of boiled ham and add to the sauce. Mix together well until thoroughly combined, then add the flour, Parmigiano, egg yolks, marinated ham, and melted butter and mix very well. Taste for salt and pepper; add a pinch of nutmeg.

Preheat the oven to 400 degrees.

Use a wire whisk and copper bowl to beat the 4 egg whites until very stiff; then fold them gently into the ham mix. Transfer the ham mix to a buttered 8½-inch soufflé dish.

Place the dish in a large casserole of lukewarm water, making an improvised *bagno maria* (bain-marie). Place the *bagno maria* in the pre-heated oven for about 45 minutes, then remove the dish from the oven and allow to cool for 10 minutes.

Unmold the *sformato* onto a serving dish and serve hot, slicing it.

A SUGGESTED DINNER

WINE

ANTINORI ROSÉ DI BOLGHERI
ANTONIOLO GATTINARA GRAN
CRU ROSSO

Ravioli nudi
(SEE PAGE 268)

Sformato di prosciutto cotto
(SEE ABOVE)

Cardi dorati
(SEE PAGE 528)

Tartufi di castagne
(SEE PAGE 614)

A SUGGESTED DINNER

WINE

ANTINORI CHIANTI CLASSICO

Timballo di tortellini

(SEE PAGE 241)

Arrosto girato alla fiorentina

(SEE BELOW)

Insalata mista

(SEE PAGE 500)

Zuppa inglese

(SEE PAGE 586)

Arrosto girato alla fiorentina

MIXED MEAT AND FOWL ROASTED ON THE SPIT

SERVES 12

A huge spit over a roaring fire of wood or charcoal is one of the trademarks of the Italian country villas and even of the country restaurants. The spit has given its name, *girarrosto,* to a kind of restaurant in which these specialties are served. If you have a wood and charcoal grill with a spit, you can make these dishes with no problem. But even if you do not, it is possible to get something very close indeed to the original in your own kitchen. As a matter of fact, this recipe not only tells you how to prepare a variety of meat and fowl for a mixed broil on the spit, it tells you how to improvise a spit in your own kitchen.

This is a wonderfully festive countrified Sunday or holiday dinner, the kind that can be enjoyed by everyone from *buongustaio* to those of the simplest tastes.

1 chicken (about 3½ pounds)
1¾ pounds loin of pork
18 to 24 leaves sage, fresh or
preserved in salt
(see page 19)
Salt and freshly ground black
pepper to taste
12 quails
3 squabs
12 Italian sweet sausages,
without fennel seeds

1 pound pork liver, prepared for
cooking as **fegatelli alla**
fiorentina *(see page 472)*
(optional)
1 pound **pane in bianco** *(see*
note)
12 to 14 bay leaves
Coarse-grained salt
1 cup olive oil, approximately

PREPARE the meat and fowl as follows:

Cut the chicken and pork loin each into 12 pieces; place ½ sage leaf, salt, and pepper in cavity of each quail; cut the squabs in quarters; puncture the sausages with a fork. If you also want to use pork liver, prepare it, using caul fat, bread crumbs, and fennel seeds, according to the directions on page 473.

Cut the bread in pieces about 1 inch wide and ½ inch thick.

Before you put the meat on the spit, either start the fire in your hearth or improvise an open-air grill for your oven by putting 4 cups of cold water in a very large stockpot or casserole, along with 1 tablespoon olive oil and 1 tablespoon coarse salt; preheat the oven to 375 degrees. You will rest the skewer on the stockpot. In this way the steam coming from the water will keep the meat soft and moist, and the result will be almost the same as open-air cooking; see the illustration on page 490.

Hold a long spit or skewer vertically and push each piece of meat onto it, drawing the first piece to the other end of the spit to make room for the others. Place the meat on the spit according to the following pattern:*

Chicken piece, ½ bay leaf, bread; pork loin piece, ½ sage leaf, bread; squab quarter, ½ bay leaf, bread; sausage, ½ sage leaf, bread;

(continued)

---

*With these quantities it is necessary to use several skewers over a nonautomatic grill or the stockpot in the oven. For smaller quantities using a single skewer, the automatic spit could be used.

Arrosto girato alla fiorentina: How to improvise an open-air spit in an oven.

ARROSTO GIRATO ALLA FIORENTINA *(continued)*

quail, ½ bay leaf, bread; optional pork liver piece, ½ sage leaf, bread.

Continue this pattern until the spit is full. The bay leaf and sage should alternate, but it doesn't matter which is next to which meat.

When all the ingredients are on the spit, sprinkle freely with salt and pepper, then place the spit either over your wood fire (be sure the ash is very hot and there are no flames) or rest it on the stockpot, which should then be placed in the preheated oven. Cook the *arrosto* very slowly (turning it either electrically or by hand) for about 1 hour (1 hour 15 minutes in the oven), sprinkling the meat every so often with salt and brushing with olive oil (using a feather brush). In oven, turn about every 5 minutes.

Remove the *arrosto* from the spit to a serving dish and serve immediately.

NOTE: The bread commonly used for this dish is a Tuscan bread that is shaped in the form of a very long loaf, 1½ inches thick, and baked only for 35 minutes. Because of its short baking time, the bread does not form a crust and retains a whitish color, even if the dough is made with whole wheat flour. If you prefer, you can substitute ordinary Tuscan bread (see page 39).

In Italy, under the skewer itself we put a special pan called a *ghiotta*. Potatoes are placed in the *ghiotta* to cook so they can collect the delicious drippings from the meat cooking above on the spit. These *patate alla ghiotta* accompany the dish when made on the open-air spit.

A SUGGESTED DINNER
FOR NEW YEAR'S EVE

WINES
FONTODI CLASSICO RISERVA
FATTORIA CALCINAIA CHIANTI CLASSICO
SAN FELICE VINSANTO

Crostini al ginepro
(SEE PAGE 107)

Timballo di tortellini
(SEE PAGE 241)

Gran bollito misto
(SEE PAGE 332)

with Savore di noci
(SEE PAGE 70)

and Maionese
(SEE PAGE 64)

Arrosto girato alla fiorentina
(SEE ABOVE)

Insalata verde
(SEE PAGE 500)

Timballo di pere
(SEE PAGE 582)

A SUGGESTED DINNER

WINE
ROCCHE COSTAMAGNA BARBERA D'ALBA

Tortellini alla panna
(SEE PAGE 204)

Budino di carne
(SEE BELOW)

Melanzane alla parmigiana
(SEE PAGE 535)

Pasticcini ripieni
(SEE PAGE 574)

Budino di carne

"PUDDING" OF VEAL, CHICKEN BREAST,
AND PROSCIUTTO

SERVES 6

*T*his is a light second dish for a more formal dinner, but is easy enough also to do for the family. The *balsamella* is prepared, then the three kinds of meats are ground. These are mixed with the remaining ingredients and slowly baked in a soufflé dish placed in a *bagno maria* (bain-marie). The *budino* is unmolded onto a dish before serving. Cut like a cake, it is served warm. There is an optional sauce often used with it, but I prefer it without.

FOR THE BALSAMELLA

3 tablespoons (1 1/2 ounces)
sweet butter

1/4 cup unbleached all-purpose
flour
1 cup milk

FOR THE BUDINO

2 tablespoons (1 ounce) sweet
butter
4 slices white bread, crusts
removed
1 cup cold milk
1/4 pound veal
1 small whole chicken breast,
boned and skinned

6 ounces prosciutto, in one piece
3 extra-large eggs
1/4 cup freshly grated
Parmigiano
Salt, freshly ground black
pepper, and freshly grated
nutmeg to taste
5 sprigs Italian parsley, leaves
only

FOR THE SAUCE (OPTIONAL)

1 chicken liver, cleaned
2 tablespoons olive oil
1/2 pound canned tomatoes,
preferably imported Italian,
drained and seeded

Salt and freshly ground black
pepper to taste

MAKE the *balsamella,* using the ingredients and quantities listed, according to the directions on page 62, then transfer to a glass or crockery bowl and press a piece of buttered wax paper on top and let cool for 1 hour.

Melt the butter for the *budino* in a small saucepan and let it cool for 20 minutes; soak the bread slices in the cold milk for 20 minutes.

Grind the veal, chicken breast, and 4 ounces of the prosciutto in a meat grinder. Place the meat in a large bowl and add the eggs, Parmigiano, and melted butter. Mix well with a wooden spoon until all the ingredients are well amalgamated.

Squeeze the bread dry and add it to the bowl, along with the *balsamella,* salt, pepper, and nutmeg. Mix thoroughly, then coarsely chop the remaining prosciutto and the parsley and add them to the bowl. Gently mix them in. (continued)

BUDINO DI CARNE *(continued)*

Preheat the oven to 400 degrees.

Butter and flour a soufflé dish 8½ inches in diameter, then improvise a *bagno maria* (bain-marie) by placing the soufflé dish in a 13½ × 8¾-inch baking dish containing 5 cups of lukewarm water. Transfer the mixture from the bowl into the soufflé dish and place the improvised double boiler in the preheated oven for 55 to 60 minutes.

Remove the soufflé dish and allow to rest for 10 to 15 minutes, then unmold onto a serving dish. Slice the *budino di carne* like a cake and serve, if desired, with the optional sauce, prepared as follows.

Chop the chicken liver fine. Heat the olive oil in a small saucepan, and when the oil is warm, add the chopped liver and sauté gently for 2 minutes. Add the tomatoes, salt, and pepper and simmer for about 20 minutes, stirring every so often with a wooden spoon.

A SUGGESTED DINNER

WINE
ANTINORI–TIGNANELLO

Torta manfreda
(SEE PAGE 470)

Pastello di caccia
(SEE BELOW)

Insalata mista
(SEE PAGE 500)

or Insalata composta
(SEE PAGE 501)

Pesche al vino
(SEE PAGE 632)

Pastello di caccia

GREAT PIE OF QUAIL, SQUAB, CHICKEN,
SAUSAGE, AND TORTELLI

SERVES 10 TO 12

A huge pie of many layers, filled with whole quails, chickens, squabs, sausages, and *tortelli* of chicken breast. It must be made in a very large casserole with two handles, preferably of tin-lined copper. I usually make it in a large antique copper one, 15 inches in diameter and 6 inches high. This fourteenth-century recipe is reminiscent of "four and twenty blackbirds baked in a pie," and it was indeed such a dish to which the rhyme referred. A fifteenth-century English adaptation of it was called "grete pye." In those days it could be made in a huge cauldron in the big stone fireplace, with dozens of birds and even a whole beast in it.

This recipe will serve about 12 people. In an old pot, when brought in whole, it can make a stunning effect. Each person is served a quail, a squab quarter, some *tortelli,* a sausage and a piece of chicken with some crust. For a large party, naturally it is possible to make more than one, but the pies must be served hot. *Pastello di caccia* is a *piatto unico,* a single dish that includes both first and second course. It should be preceded only by something light, if by anything. Save it for your fanciest party.

FOR THE CRUST

3 cups unbleached all-purpose flour
1 tablespoon olive oil

Pinch of salt
1 cup very cold water

FOR THE TORTELLI FILLING

1 tablespoon olive oil
2 tablespoons (1 ounce) sweet butter
1 whole chicken breast, from a 3½-pound chicken
1 bay leaf
Salt and freshly ground black pepper to taste

¼ pound prosciutto or pancetta, in one piece
2 extra-large egg yolks
¼ cup freshly grated Parmigiano
Freshly grated nutmeg to taste

(continued)

495

PASTELLO DI CACCIA *(continued)*

FOR THE TORTELLI

**2 cups unbleached all-purpose
    flour**
2 extra-large eggs

Pinch of salt
**2 teaspoons olive or other
    vegetable oil**

PLUS

2 tablespoons olive oil

Coarse-grained salt

FOR THE PASTELLO FILLING

1 chicken (about 3½ pounds)
**Salt and freshly ground
    black pepper**
3 squabs
12 quails
**20 leaves sage, fresh or
    preserved in salt (see page
    19), approximately**
**12 Italian sweet sausages
    without fennel seeds
    (preferably Tuscan
    sausages; see page 449)**

2 tablespoons olive oil
1½ bay leaves
**12 thin slices pancetta or
    prosciutto**
**1 tablespoon rosemary leaves,
    fresh or preserved in salt or
    dried and blanched**

PREPARE the crust first.

Place the flour on a pasta board and make a well in it. Put the olive oil, salt, and water in the well, then incorporate with half of the flour, mixing with a metal fork.

Start kneading, gently but steadily, until all but 3 or 4 tablespoons of the flour is incorporated. From this point knead for 20 minutes more, incorporating 1 more tablespoon of flour.

Wrap the dough in a dampened cotton dishtowel and let rest in a cool place for 3 hours; do not refrigerate.

To make the *tortelli* filling, heat the oil and butter in a small casserole, over low heat. When the butter is melted, add the chicken breast and bay leaf and sauté over low heat for 20 minutes, turning the chicken breast over several times. Sprinkle with salt and pepper, then remove the casserole from the heat.

Place the chicken breast on a chopping board, discarding the bay leaf, skin and bone the chicken breast and chop it coarsely. Add the prosciutto to the chicken meat and continue to chop until quite fine.

Transfer the chopped ingredients to a bowl. Add the egg yolks, Parmigiano, and 1 tablespoon of fat from the casserole. Season with salt, pepper, and nutmeg, then mix thoroughly with a wooden spoon. Cover the bowl and place in the refrigerator until needed.

Make fresh pasta, using the ingredients in the proportions listed above, according to the directions on page 159, then form into *tortelli* as directed on page 194, using the filling you have just prepared.

Place a stockpot containing a large quantity of cold water on the heat. While the water is coming to a boil, fill a large bowl full of cold water and add the 2 tablespoons of oil; wet a cotton dishtowel with cold water and spread it out on a board.

When the water reaches the boiling point, add coarse salt to taste, then place 10 *tortelli* at a time in the boiling water and let them cook for 20 seconds. Remove from the stockpot with a strainer-skimmer and place in the bowl of cold water. Let the *tortelli* cool for 3 or 4 minutes, then transfer them from the bowl to the wet towel and spread them out.

Repeat the procedure until all the *tortelli* are on the towel, then wet a second cotton dishtowel and place it on top of the *tortelli*. Let stand while you prepare the rest of the *pastello* filling.

Open the chicken, cutting it through the breast, then place it, open side down, between two sheets of wet wax paper and flatten it by pounding it with your fist. Transfer the chicken to a dish, sprinkle with salt and pepper, and let stand until needed.

Rinse the squabs and quails very well, removing and discarding the livers. Place a leaf of sage and a pinch of salt and pepper inside each bird.

Puncture the sausages with a fork in two or three places. If using ground pork, form into several small balls.

Heat the olive oil in a very large casserole, over medium heat. When

(continued)

497

PASTELLO DI CACCIA *(continued)*

the oil is warm, add the sausages or pork balls, squabs, and quails and sauté gently for about 30 minutes, gently moving the birds around every so often with a wooden spoon.

Remove the casserole from the heat and let cool for 1 hour.

When you are ready to put the *pastello di caccia* together, oil a very large two-handled casserole, preferably of tin-lined copper; preheat the oven to 375 degrees.

Divide the ball of dough in half and roll out one half into a paper-thin sheet, large enough to completely line the casserole. Lower the pastry sheet into the casserole, letting the extra pastry hang out over the sides.

Place the flattened chicken on the bottom of the casserole, then scatter over 3 or 4 leaves of sage and ½ bay leaf cut in pieces. Wrap each quail in a slice of *pancetta* or prosciutto and place on top of the chicken. Fill in the cracks with about 15 *tortelli,* then sprinkle with a little salt and pepper. Place squabs on top.

Make a layer of quail. Place more *tortelli* over them, sprinkle with salt and pepper, and add 1 more bay leaf cut in pieces.

Next make a layer of sausages and the remaining *tortelli,* then make a layer of the remaining *pancetta* or prosciutto. Sprinkle with rosemary leaves.

Roll out the other half of the dough into a sheet about ¼ inch thick. Cover the top of the casserole with this sheet of pastry, pressing the edges of the two pastry layers together all around the casserole. Make sure the edges are closed, then cut off any overlapping pasta with a knife.

With a toothpick, make 3 or 4 holes in the top pastry layer, then place the casserole in the preheated oven for about 45 minutes. Place a sheet of aluminum foil over the casserole and raise the oven temperature to 400 degrees for about 35 minutes more.

Remove the pie from the oven and serve directly from the casserole. Break the top layer of pastry and prepare each plate with some *tortelli,* sausage, quail, squab, and crust. (The chicken at the bottom is usually finished by those who return for second helpings.)

Salads

Insalata verde and Insalata mista

GREEN SALAD AND MIXED SALAD

*F*or a simple salad, Italians use a single green, dressed with olive oil, salt, and wine vinegar or lemon juice. This is referred to as *insalata verde.*

When green salad is the only vegetable for the dinner, generally Italians prefer to have the more elaborate *insalata mista,* which is a mixture of different kinds of greens with the addition of some vegetable, which gives a different flavor and color. For this reason, the name "mixed salad."

The greens used in Tuscany are delicate leafed lettuce (not iceberg) and romaine lettuce. In addition, there are two kinds of leaf salad, one green type with many variants and the other red, and called appropriately *radicchio verde e rosso.* The red radicchio (which comes from Treviso or Chioggia near Venice) is now widely exported. Wild field salad greens have returned to popularity.

Dandelion leaves and watercress (*crescione*) are not used a lot in Tuscany, but both also make good additions to these salads. Arugola (*ruchetta*) has recently become popular in Tuscany.

The other vegetables that can be used in the salad, in moderation, are carrots, celery, fennel bulbs (all in small pieces), and tomato. Italians prefer tomato still a little green for salad. (In Italy do not expect ripe tomatoes in salad unless requested.)

So an *insalata mista* could consist of any combination of the following: Lettuce, romaine lettuce, dandelion, arugola, watercress, carrots, celery, fennel, tomato. The dressing is always olive oil (the best available) and vinegar made from good red wine, or lemon juice. Salt is added but no pepper. And Italians never add cheese, croutons, or anything else to a salad.

DRESSING THE SALAD

First pour olive oil into a large spoon that will distribute it evenly over the salad and mix it through. (This coats the leaves so the vinegar or lemon juice will not make them wilt.) Then place salt in the tablespoon and pour vinegar or lemon juice onto it. With a fork, stir hard to dissolve the salt in the vinegar, and as it dissolves, let the vinegar run off the spoon throughout the salad. Finally, with two tablespoons toss the salad lightly but thoroughly to distribute the dressing evenly. Then serve.

Insalata composta

"COMPOSED" SALAD

*I*nsalata composta, meaning "composed" salad, is made up of several boiled vegetables. Used a lot in summer when fresh vegetables and fresh basil are in season, it is dressed with olive oil like a green salad and served with lemon wedges, which may be used or not, according to taste. (Vinegar is not used for *insalata composta*.)

Boil a variety of vegetables which are in season and cook them separately (see methods under individual vegetables). When all the vegetables are cold, place them in a large serving dish in rings or in rows, each vegetable to one ring or row. Freely sprinkle with salt and pepper, and pour on olive oil, then tear several basil leaves into 2 or 3 pieces and place them over the vegetables.

Serve cold.

Pomodori e mozzarella

TOMATO AND MOZZARELLA SALAD

SERVES 4

A salad of mixed fresh tomato squares and little squares of mozzarella, seasoned with olive oil. This salad is also known as
Insalata caprese.

4 fresh medium tomatoes, ripe	**¼ cup olive oil**
but not overripe	**Salt and freshly ground black**
4 ounces mozzarella	**pepper to taste**
6 fresh basil leaves	

RINSE the tomatoes very carefully, remove the tough part where the
stem was, then cut in half horizontally and remove the seeds. Cut the
tomato halves into ½-inch squares and place in a serving dish.

Cut the mozzarella into slightly smaller squares and add pieces to
the serving dish, then tear the basil leaves into 2 or 3 pieces and sprinkle
them over the tomatoes and mozzarella.

Season with olive oil and pepper (tasting for salt, because frequently
non-Italian mozzarella is salty), then mix very well and serve cold.

Pomodori in insalata

TOMATO SALAD

SERVES 4

*P*omodori in insalata is perhaps the summer vegetable course that
is most used. I would say that almost every Italian family has its
own style of preparing this dish, but the base is always the same: ripe
(never overripe) tomatoes, good olive oil, fresh basil, salt, and pepper.
Basil is the natural spouse of tomatoes.

*4 medium fresh tomatoes, ripe
    but not overripe*
*Salt and freshly ground black
    pepper to taste*

¼ cup olive oil
6 fresh basil leaves

RINSE the tomatoes very carefully, remove the tough part where the stem was, then cut them into slices about ⅓ inch thick. Remove the seeds from each slice and place the slices on a serving dish, in one layer.

Sprinkle the tomatoes with salt, pepper, and olive oil, then tear the basil leaves into 3 or 4 pieces and sprinkle them over the tomato slices.

NOTE: You can vary the salad by placing half an anchovy fillet and 2 or 3 capers in wine vinegar over each tomato slice.

Pomodori e capperi

TOMATO AND CAPER SALAD

SERVES 4

A salad of tomato halves, with a dressing of chopped capers in wine vinegar and olive oil.

*4 medium fresh tomatoes, ripe
    but not overripe*
*3 heaping tablespoons capers in
    wine vinegar, drained*

¼ cup olive oil
*Salt and freshly ground black
    pepper to taste*
6 fresh basil leaves

RINSE the tomatoes very carefully, remove the tough part where the stem was, then cut them in half horizontally and remove the seeds. Place tomatoes on a serving dish.

Chop the capers fine and place them in a small bowl. Add the olive oil, salt, and pepper and mix well with the capers.

Pour some caper mixture on each tomato half, then tear the basil leaves into 3 or 4 pieces and sprinkle over the tomatoes. Serve cold.

Carote all' agro

MARINATED RAW SHREDDED CARROTS

SERVES 6

*T*he tender part of the raw carrot, shredded and marinated in olive oil and lemon juice, used both as a salad and as an antipasto, but not as a vegetable to accompany the second course. This classic treatment is widely used.

6 large carrots, scraped
Juice of 2 lemons
Salt and freshly ground black
  pepper to taste

¼ cup olive oil
10 sprigs Italian parsley, leaves
  only

RINSE the carrots, then cut off top and bottom ends. The outer ring of the carrot is darker in color and more tender than the inner core. With a swivel-action peeler, shred only the tender, darker part of the carrot into a bowl; discard the tougher, lighter-colored inner core.

Add the lemon juice to the bowl, along with the salt, pepper, and olive oil. Mix everything together well, then cover the bowl and place in the refrigerator for at least 1 hour.

When ready to serve, coarsely chop the parsley. Remove the bowl from the refrigerator, transfer its contents to a serving dish, sprinkle with the chopped parsley, and serve.

Insalata di peperoni alla griglia

GRILLED PEPPER SALAD

SERVES 4

A special technique of roasting peppers right on the burner of a kitchen stove, while keeping the surrounding air moist with steam. The skin is peeled off, and the pepper that remains is still crunchy, with all the flavor of a fresh pepper. The peppers are then cut into strips and dressed as a cold salad. A versatile accompanying vegetable, also useful for buffets.

4 large sweet bell peppers, green, yellow, or red

Salt and freshly ground black pepper to taste
¼ cup olive oil

HEAT a large quantity of water in a stockpot, over high heat. When the water reaches boiling point and a lot of steam is rising, place the peppers, whole, on the burner next to the steaming stockpot, to roast on the high flame. Turn peppers frequently so the skin will be evenly roasted all over, and keep the stockpot on the flame until the peppers are completely roasted (about 20 minutes), so that while the skin blisters the inside part of the peppers does not dry out.

Remove the peppers from the stove and place them in bowl of cold water. Let them soak for 15 minutes, then peel under cold running water, removing stems and seeds.

Cut the peppers into thin strips and place them in a serving dish. Season with salt, pepper, and oil, mix together well, and serve.

Insalata di patate alla fiorentina

POTATO SALAD, FLORENTINE STYLE

SERVES 4

A cold potato salad, seasoned with olive oil, anchovies, fresh parsley, and pepper. Lighter than potato salads made with *maionese,* this is a useful dish to accompany lightly flavored main dishes, and for buffets and snacks.

2 pounds potatoes for boiling, but not new potatoes
Coarse-grained salt
4 whole anchovies in salt or 8 anchovy fillets in oil, drained

¼ cup olive oil
Freshly ground black pepper
10 sprigs Italian parsley, leaves only

PUT a large quantity of cold water in a stockpot and set on the heat. When the water reaches the boiling point, add coarse salt to taste, then the potatoes, and let them cook for about 25 minutes. (If the potatoes are large, they may require 5 minutes more.) The potatoes should be completely cooked but still firm. Remove the pot from the heat, transfer the potatoes to a board, and peel them. Let rest until cold (about 25 minutes).

Meanwhile, if using whole anchovies, clean them under cold running water, removing the bones and excess salt. Coarsely chop the anchovies.

Cut the potatoes into pieces about 1 inch square and place in a serving bowl. Add the chopped anchovies, olive oil, and freshly ground pepper, then mix all the ingredients together.

Sprinkle parsley leaves over and serve.

Pomodori e tonno

TOMATO AND TUNA SALAD

SERVES 4

*F*resh tomato halves covered with chopped tuna and capers in wine vinegar, held together by homemade *maionese*. This may be used both as an antipasto and as a salad, but is not eaten together with the main course.

Maionese *(see page 64)*
Salt and freshly ground black
    pepper to taste
4 fresh medium tomatoes, ripe
    but not overripe

1 3½-ounce can tuna, drained
1 heaping tablespoon capers in
    wine vinegar, drained
8 fresh basil leaves

MAKE the *maionese,* seasoning it with salt and pepper to taste, and set aside until needed.

Rinse the tomatoes very carefully, remove the tough part where the stem was, then cut them in half horizontally and remove the seeds. Chop the tuna and capers fine and place in a small bowl. Add 3 tablespoons of the *maionese* to the bowl and mix thoroughly, then fill the tomato halves with the contents of the bowl.

Place the filled tomatoes on a serving dish and spread a layer of the remaining *maionese* on each stuffed tomato half. Top each with a whole basil leaf and serve cold.

Vegetables

ARTICHOKES

*I*taly has many celebrated artichoke dishes, some of the best known being from Rome. The seasons for artichokes in Italy are fall and winter. Nowadays they can be found for more of the year because of the variety of growing seasons all over the world.

The larger Italian artichokes are called *"mamme,"* or "mothers," and come from Empoli, the famous center of Tuscan glassmaking. These are usually stuffed as *carciofi ritti* (see page 514). The smaller ones come from all over Italy.

Non-European artichokes are of a slightly different species, and have tough inner leaves and a purple "choke," both of which must be removed. In addition, they are less tender than Italian artichokes. By way of illustration, it is perhaps inconceivable to those who know only non-European artichokes that in Florence the favorite way of eating artichokes is raw, *in pinzimonio* (see page 98). The small Italian ones are indeed tender enough to be eaten that way.

Cleaning the Non-European Artichoke

1. Trim off all of the darker outer ring. The inner core is the best part because it has the real taste of the artichoke.

2. Remove as many rows of the outer leaves as necessary to arrive at those tender inner rows where you can clearly see the separation between the green at the top and the light yellow at the bottom. Then remove the top green part. Press your thumb on the bottom of each leaf, the light part, to hold it in place, and with the other hand, tear off the top green part. As each new row is uncovered the tender yellow part of the leaves will be bigger. When you reach the rows in which only the very tips of the leaves are green, cut off all the tips together with a knife.

Scoop out the choke. Notice the gradation in the trimmed leaves.

3. It is best to cut the artichoke into quarters lengthwise, in order to remove the choke. Draw the tip of the knife blade across just below the choke to draw it out. Or if artichoke is left whole for stuffing, scoop out the choke.

Carciofi bolliti

BOILED ARTICHOKES

CLEAN the number of artichokes you plan to use as described above. Cut lengthwise into slices about ½ inch thick and place in a bowl of cold water with half a lemon.

Fill a saucepan with cold water and place on the heat. When the water reaches the boiling point, add coarse salt to taste, then the artichoke pieces and a small piece of the lemon, and boil for about 15 minutes; at that time they should be cooked but still firm.

Drain the artichokes, discarding the lemon piece, and place in a dish to cool. They are now ready to be used for such dishes as *carciofi all' agro* or *sformato di carciofi* (see page 554).

Tortino di carciofi

ARTICHOKE TORTINO

SERVES 4 AS MAIN COURSE OR 6 TO 8 AS APPETIZER

*N*ot a frittata because it is very flat, these sautéed artichoke slices covered with egg form one of the most popular of all Tuscan dishes. It is used as appetizer, vegetable, and perhaps most of all as a light main dish.

When the wonderful artichokes from the Roman region or the large *"mamme"* from Empoli are in season, there is scarcely a *trattoria* in Florence that does not have this dish even on the most limited menu.

2 large artichokes
1 lemon
½ cup olive oil
About ½ cup unbleached all-
  purpose flour

5 extra-large eggs
Salt and freshly ground black
  pepper

PLACE the artichokes in a bowl of cold water with the lemon, cut in half, for 30 minutes. Clean the artichokes according to the directions on pages 510–511 and cut into quarters. Cut each quarter into slices less than ½ inch thick. Place the artichoke slices back in the cold water with the lemon. Heat the oil in a large skillet over medium heat. When the oil is warm, drain the artichokes and pat them dry with paper towels; then lightly flour them, add a few at a time to the skillet, and sauté until lightly golden and tender (about 4 minutes). Transfer the cooked artichokes to a serving platter lined with paper towels to absorb all the extra fat. When all the artichoke pieces are cooked, break the eggs in a crockery or glass bowl, add a pinch of salt and pepper, and lightly beat them with a fork. Lightly oil a 12-inch omelet pan with the oil from the skillet and place it over low heat. When the oil and the pan are warm, add the artichokes and arrange them all over the pan. Pour over the eggs and swirl the pan in order to have the eggs cover it evenly. Prick the eggs all over so that the still uncooked egg runs underneath the artichokes. The *tortino* will be ready when all the eggs are incorporated by the artichokes. Unmold the *tortino* onto a serving dish and serve, slicing it like a pie.

Carciofi all' agro

ARTICHOKES WITH OLIVE OIL AND LEMON JUICE

SERVES 4

*S*imple boiled artichokes, cleaned down to their tender leaves, cut into eighths, and dressed with oil and abundant lemon juice. Lemon has a special affinity for artichokes; it is used to keep their green color from turning dark while soaking and while cooking, and it does most to bring out the flavor of the vegetable. *Carciofi all' agro* is probably the most frequent treatment of artichokes in Florence.

4 large artichokes
2 lemons
4 tablespoons olive oil

Salt and freshly ground black
pepper to taste

TO COOK THE ARTICHOKES
Coarse-grained salt

CLEAN artichokes according to directions on pages 510–511, and cut them lengthwise into eighths. Place them in a bowl of cold water with half a lemon squeezed. Place a saucepan of cold water over medium heat and when the water reaches a boil, add coarse-grained salt, then the artichoke pieces and the squeezed lemon half, and cook for about 20 minutes or until artichokes are soft. Meanwhile squeeze the remaining 1½ lemons. When the artichokes are ready, drain them. Spoon the olive oil over them, pour over the lemon juice, and season with salt and pepper.

Carciofi ritti

STUFFED ARTICHOKES

SERVES 4

4 large artichokes	**1 lemon**

FOR THE STUFFING

2 medium cloves garlic, peeled	**¼ pound pancetta or**
10 sprigs Italian parsley, leaves	**prosciutto, in one piece**
only	**Salt and freshly ground black**
	pepper to taste

FOR COOKING THE ARTICHOKES

1 small clove garlic, peeled	**2 cups chicken or meat broth,**
10 sprigs Italian parsley, leaves	**preferably homemade**
only	**Salt and freshly ground black**
2 ounces pancetta or	**pepper to taste**
prosciutto, in one piece	**2 tablespoons olive oil**

SOAK the artichokes for 30 minutes in a large bowl of cold water with the lemon, cut in half. Clean the artichokes according to the directions on page 510–511, then cut off the stems and save for the stuffing. Replace the stemless artichokes in water with lemon and let stand while you make the stuffing.

To make the stuffing, coarsely chop the 2 cloves garlic and the parsley, and cut the *pancetta* as well as the artichoke stems into small pieces. Place in a small bowl, add salt and pepper, and mix well.

Drain the artichokes, dry off the outsides, and stuff them with the mixture in the bowl.

To cook the artichokes, finely chop the clove of garlic and the parsley together, cut the *pancetta* into small pieces, then place in a flameproof casserole, preferably terra-cotta, along with the olive oil. Stand artichokes in the casserole, on top of the chopped ingredients and oil, then place the casserole over medium heat and sauté its contents for 5 minutes, moving the artichokes around slightly so they don't stick.

Add 1 cup of broth to the casserole, cover, and simmer slowly for

15 to 20 minutes, then sprinkle with a little salt and pepper and add the remaining broth. Lower the heat and simmer very slowly for 20 minutes or longer; by that time the artichokes should become tender but remain whole.

Carefully transfer the whole artichokes to a serving dish. Pour some juice from the casserole over each artichoke and serve either immediately or cold.

Carciofi fritti

FRIED ARTICHOKES

SERVES 4

4 large artichokes
Juice of 1 lemon
4 extra-large eggs
Salt to taste

1 cup unbleached all-purpose
flour, approximately
1 quart vegetable oil (see page
22)
Lemon wedges

CLEAN the artichokes according to the directions on pages 510–511 and cut them vertically, including the stem in the central part, into slices about ½ inch thick. Place the artichoke pieces in a large bowl of cold water and the lemon juice and let stand for 30 minutes.

Meanwhile, beat the eggs with a pinch of salt in a small bowl. Drain the artichoke pieces and dry them with paper towels. In order to flour the pieces, place them in a colander, sprinkle the flour over them, then shake them around. The pieces will be lightly floured and the excess flour will drop on the counter.

Heat the oil in a frying pan. When it is hot (about 375 degrees), dip each artichoke piece in beaten egg and place in the hot oil. Deep-fry the artichoke pieces for about 2 minutes on each side, until golden.

Prepare a serving dish by lining it with paper towels. Remove the cooked artichokes from the frying pan with a strainer-skimmer and place them on the serving dish to drain. Repeat the procedure until all artichoke pieces are on the serving dish, then remove the paper towels.

Sprinkle with salt and serve hot with lemon wedges.

BEANS

Fagioli bolliti

BOILED TUSCAN BEANS

SOAK the amount of dried cannellini beans you wish to use in a large bowl of cold water, with 1 tablespoon of flour, overnight. See note on page 29.

Rinse the beans in cold water and place the beans in large stockpot containing cold water and coarse salt. (The amount of water depends on the quantity of beans. In Italy we say that the amount of cold water should be 6 times the weight of the beans, so, since a quart of water weighs about 2 pounds, 1 pound of beans would require 3 quarts of water.) Add 4 or 5 leaves of sage, fresh (or preserved in salt; see page 19), and about 1 tablespoon of olive oil.

Place the stockpot over very low heat and simmer very slowly for about 1 to 1½ hours. (The beans must be cooked very slowly to stay whole and to retain their shape. When beans are used for soups, they may be boiled more quickly.) The beans may be served with olive oil and with or without lemon juice.

Fagioli al fiasco

TUSCAN BEANS COOKED IN A FLASK

SERVES 6 TO 8

*I*n this, one of the scenic Florentine dishes, white beans are placed inside a wine flask or another flask of thick Italian glass, which in turn is placed in a pan of water. The technique is basically *bagno maria* (bain-marie). Very little liquid is added to the flask, so the beans retain all of their own flavor and that of the *pancetta,* sage, and other seasonings.

The main precaution to take to ensure that the flask does not crack is to begin with cold water, both inside and outside the flask. Then, if additional water must be added to the pan because of evaporation, be sure that the added water is boiling. In other words, if the temperatures inside and outside the flask are the same, there should be no problem about the glass, so do not be afraid to try it. In any case, the worst that can happen is that a simple crack will appear in the flask, the flask remaining in one piece, so it is not dangerous. But if you follow instructions, there is really very little probability of it cracking. And when it succeeds, the effect is quite attractive when the pan (particularly if it is a beautiful one of antique copper) containing the bean-filled flask is brought to the table. The beans may be served with a spoon, or if the mouth of the flask is large enough, with a ladle.

Fagioli al fiasco may be used to accompany a variety of hearty dishes, both simple and more formal, and the leftover beans may be used to make *zuppa lombarda* (see page 154).

1 pound dried cannellini beans
1 tablespoon unbleached all-purpose flour
2 ounces pancetta *or prosciutto, in one piece*
¼ cup olive oil
2 large cloves garlic, peeled but left whole

10 leaves sage, fresh or preserved in salt (see page 19)
Salt and freshly ground black pepper to taste
5 whole black peppercorns

SOAK the beans in a bowl of cold water, with 1 tablespoon of flour, overnight.

The next day, drain and rinse the beans under cold running water, then put them into the flask you have chosen. (A wine flask is adequate. One of the larger green Italian ones with a wide mouth is even better for this purpose, as it takes less time to put the beans into the flask and to remove them when cooked.) Add only enough cold water to reach about 1 inch above the beans.

Dice the *pancetta,* then add to the flask, along with the olive oil, whole garlic cloves, and sage. Season with salt, pepper, and peppercorns.

(continued)

517

Fagioli al fiasco: The beans, in their flask, simmering in a water bath.

FAGIOLI AL FIASCO *(continued)*

Place the flask in a stockpot or a large, decorative copper pan containing a large quantity of cold water. Set over medium heat and simmer very slowly for 3 to 4 hours (see above), with the following precautions:

Keep a saucepan of boiling water ready over low heat, so you can add boiling water, little by little, to the stockpot when the water evaporates to about half. Do not add cold water to stockpot, otherwise the flask will break. Do not add any liquid to the beans inside the flask while they are cooking.

Remove the stockpot from the heat and let cool for 10 minutes, then remove the flask from the stockpot and transfer beans to serving dish. Or, if you have used the flask with large mouth, you can serve from the flask itself.

Fagioli all'uccelletto

TUSCAN BEANS COOKED IN THE MANNER
OF LITTLE BIRDS

SERVES 4

*B*oiled beans simmered in tomatoes, olive oil, sage, and whole unpeeled garlic cloves. The name comes from the manner of cooking *uccelli,* little songbirds.

¼ cup olive oil
6 large leaves sage, fresh or
    preserved in salt (see page
    19)
4 large cloves garlic, unpeeled
    and left whole
1 pound very ripe fresh
    tomatoes or 1 pound canned
    tomatoes, preferably
    imported Italian, drained

Salt and freshly ground black
    pepper to taste
4 cups boiled cannellini beans
    (see page 516)

HEAT the olive oil in a flameproof casserole, preferably terra-cotta. Add the sage and unpeeled garlic cloves and sauté, over medium heat, for 4 or 5 minutes.

If using fresh tomatoes, cut them into pieces. Pass the fresh or canned tomatoes through a food mill, using the disc with the smallest holes, into a bowl, then transfer to the casserole. Taste for salt and pepper and simmer very gently for about 10 minutes. Add the beans to the casserole, mix very well with a wooden spoon, and simmer for 10 minutes more.

Serve hot.

Fagioli al forno

BAKED TUSCAN BEANS

SERVES 6

*B*aked beans, Tuscan style. Again the beans are the white cannellini. They are baked in a closed terra-cotta casserole, with *pancetta,* whole garlic cloves, sage, and tomatoes and olive oil. A very Mediterranean version, and one you are sure to add to your repertoire.

3 cups dried cannellini beans	*6 sage leaves, fresh or preserved*
1 tablespoon unbleached all-	*in salt (see page 19)*
purpose flour	*¹/₄ cup olive oil*
¹/₄ pound **pancetta** *or*	*1 large ripe fresh tomato or 2*
prosciutto, in one piece	*canned tomatoes, preferably*
2 large cloves garlic, peeled but	*imported Italian, drained*
left whole	*Salt and freshly ground black*
	pepper

SOAK the beans overnight in a bowl of cold water with the flour. The next day, drain and rinse the beans and place them in a casserole, preferably terra-cotta.

Preheat the oven to 375 degrees.

Cut the *pancetta* into small pieces, then add to the casserole along with the garlic cloves, sage, olive oil, and tomatoes. Pour in enough fresh cold water to cover the beans completely, then sprinkle with salt and freshly ground black pepper.

Cover the casserole and place it in the preheated oven for 2 to 3 hours. (Cooking time of beans varies because older beans are drier and must cook longer.) Every half hour check the beans and stir gently.

Remove the casserole from the oven and allow to cool, still covered, for 15 minutes. Serve from the same casserole.

STRINGBEANS

I talian stringbeans are used very young, thin, and tender for most dishes. Since stringbeans in other countries are picked when they are more mature and larger, they are not suitable for many Italian recipes. (Can't we prevail upon our growers to let us also have some of the small, young ones?)

The three recipes included here, following the recipe for boiled stringbeans, work well with larger stringbeans. The second, *fagiolini in umido,* is often made with the special variety of long stringbeans called *"serpenti,"* which incidentally are sometimes found in Chinese and other East Asian markets abroad. But large stringbeans may also be used.

Fagiolini in erba bolliti

BOILED STRINGBEANS

To boil, remove the ends of the stringbeans as well as the coarse thread that runs along the side. Soak the beans in a bowl of cold water for 30 minutes.

Heat a large amount of cold water in a stockpot. When the water reaches the boiling point, add coarse salt to taste, then the stringbeans, and let them cook for about 15 minutes. By that time they should be cooked but still firm.

Drain the stringbeans and cool them under cold running water. They are now ready to be used in such dishes as *sformato di fagiolini* (see page 554), *insalata composta* (see page 501), and *fagiolini in fricassea* (see below). Or they can be served with olive oil and with or without lemon juice.

Fagiolini in fricassea

FRICASSEE OF STRINGBEANS

SERVES 4 TO 6

A fricassee of stringbeans, with the usual egg-lemon sauce. It makes a good accompaniment to most main dishes that do not have a sauce of their own.

2 pounds stringbeans	*1 lemon*
4 tablespoon (2 ounces) sweet	*2 extra-large egg yolks*
butter	
Salt and freshly ground black	
pepper	

BOIL the stringbeans according to the directions above, but for about 12 minutes. When the stringbeans are cooked and cold, heat the butter in a large flameproof casserole. When the butter is melted, add the stringbeans. Season with salt and pepper and let the beans sauté very lightly for 2 minutes.

Meanwhile, squeeze the lemon into a small bowl. Add the egg yolks to the bowl and mix very well until thoroughly combined.

When the stringbeans are ready, remove the casserole from the heat and add the egg-lemon mixture, little by little, mixing thoroughly with a wooden spoon until the egg yolk is homogeneously incorporated. Serve hot.

Fagiolini in umido

STRINGBEANS WITH TOMATOES AND BASIL

SERVES 4 TO 6

*T*he *odori* (aromatic vegetables) are lightly sautéed and then the stringbeans are added, along with tomato and basil, and simmered for a long time. This dish may be used with a variety of main dishes, but do not use it with those that already have a tomato sauce.

2 pounds stringbeans
1 small carrot, scraped
1 small red onion, cleaned
¼ cup olive oil
2 cloves garlic, peeled but left
   whole

1 pound fresh ripe tomatoes,
   blanched and seeded, or 1
   pound canned tomatoes,
   preferably imported Italian,
   drained and seeded
4 leaves basil, fresh or preserved
   in salt (see page 18)
Salt and freshly ground black
   pepper to taste

REMOVE the ends of the stringbeans as well as the coarse thread, then soak the beans in a large bowl of cold water for 30 minutes. Chop the carrot and onion coarsely. Heat the olive oil in a casserole, preferably terra-cotta, then add the chopped ingredients and whole garlic cloves. Sauté very gently until lightly golden (about 10 minutes), then remove the garlic.

Add the stringbeans to the casserole. Place the tomatoes and basil leaves on top, then season with salt and pepper, cover, and simmer for 30 minutes. (No liquid should be needed because stringbeans shed a lot of water.) By that time the stringbeans should be almost cooked, but still firm.

Stir the stringbeans well and taste for salt and pepper. Cook for 1 or 2 minutes more, without the lid, and then transfer the stringbeans to a serving dish. Serve very hot.

Torta di fagiolini

STRINGBEAN TORTE

*T*his attractive vegetable preparation mixes chopped stringbeans with some cut into pieces and is held together by egg and cheese. Its round form gives it the name *torta* in Italian. It is less elaborate than a *sformato* as it does not contain *balsamella* and the eggs are not separated. Without the beaten whites, it does not rise. Covered with good bread crumbs, it comes out flat and crisp. It is a good treatment even for larger stringbeans that are not tender.

*2 pounds stringbeans,
    preferably thin ones*
Coarse-grained salt
*2 tablespoons (1 ounce) sweet
    butter*
1 tablespoon olive oil
*1 large clove garlic, peeled but
    left whole*
*Salt and freshly ground black
    pepper*

Pinch of freshly grated nutmeg
4 extra-large eggs
2 extra-large egg yolks
*¼ cup freshly grated
    Parmigiano*
*10 sprigs Italian parsley, leaves
    only*
15 large fresh mint leaves

PLUS
*1 tablespoon (½ ounce) sweet
    butter*

*5 tablespoons unseasoned bread
    crumbs, preferably
    homemade*

CLEAN stringbeans, removing the ends and the coarse thread, and let stand in a bowl of cold water for 30 minutes. Meanwhile bring a large pot of cold water to a boil, add coarse salt to taste; then add the beans and cook for 15 minutes or longer if the beans are thick. Beans should be fully cooked but still retain some bite. Drain and cool beans under cold running water. Finely chop half of them on a board and cut the remaining ones into ½-inch pieces. Place both in a crockery or glass bowl and mix very well with a wooden spoon.

Place the butter and the oil over medium heat and when the butter is melted, add the whole clove of garlic and sauté for 2 minutes. Discard garlic and add stringbeans; season with salt, pepper, and nutmeg, mix well, and sauté for 5 minutes more. Transfer beans to a crockery or glass bowl to cool for about an hour.

Preheat oven to 375 degrees.

When stringbeans are cool, taste again for salt, pepper, and nutmeg, then add the eggs, egg yolks, and Parmigiano. Coarsely chop parsley on a board and add it to the stringbean mixture along with the mint leaves, left whole. Mix all ingredients together well with a wooden spoon.

Heavily butter a pie plate and coat it with bread crumbs, saving the leftover crumbs. Pour in the contents of the bowl, level the top without pressing, using a spatula, and sprinkle the remaining bread crumbs over. Bake for 45 minutes. Remove from oven, let cool for a few minutes, then transfer to a serving platter and serve immediately, slicing torte like a pie.

BROCCOLI

Broccoli strascicati

"STIR-SAUTÉED" BROCCOLI

SERVES 4

ou might describe making a dish *strascicato* as "stir-sautéing." Here the raw broccoli is cut into small pieces. The toughest parts of the stems are discarded and only the tender parts kept. The stem pieces require more cooking than the flower pieces, so they should be placed on the bottom and then the whole stirred gently, so as not to disturb the arrangement with the stem pieces on the bottom. The broccoli pieces, which should be crunchy and retain the flavor of fresh broccoli, are seasoned very simply, with garlic, olive oil, and a little hot pepper.

1 large bunch broccoli
5 tablespoons olive oil
1 large clove garlic, peeled but left whole

Salt and freshly ground black pepper
Pinch of red hot pepper flakes

REMOVE the large stems from the broccoli and cut the remainder into approximately 1½-inch pieces and put in a large bowl of water for 30 minutes.

Heat the olive oil in a flameproof casserole, preferably terra-cotta, and add the whole garlic clove. Sauté the garlic very lightly, on medium heat, for 2 minutes, then remove it. Drain the broccoli and immediately add the broccoli stem pieces to the casserole, then the flowerettes. Season with salt, pepper, and a pinch of pepper flakes, then cover and sauté very lightly, stirring with a wooden spoon every so often.

Adding a little bit of cold water if needed, cook the broccoli for about 20 minutes. At that time it should be completely cooked but still firm. Serve very hot.

CARDOONS

*C*ardoons are the stems of the young thistle artichoke plant, picked before the artichokes or flowers themselves appear. The species is slightly different from the artichoke, and its flowers are less interesting than its stems.

Cardi bolliti

BOILED CARDOONS

1 bunch cardoons (about 2½ pounds)
1 lemon

2 tablespoons unbleached all-purpose flour
1 cup cold water
Coarse-grained salt

REMOVE the outer stalks and stringy top part from the cardoons, then cut the remaining stalks into pieces 2 inches long. Rub each piece with half a cut lemon and place it in a large bowl of cold water. Squeeze the remaining half lemon into the water with the cardoons and let soak for 30 minutes.

Dissolve the flour in the 1 cup of cold water and pour into a large stockpot, preferably terra-cotta. Add 3 quarts of cold water and place on the heat. When the water reaches a boil, add coarse salt to taste, then drain the cardoons and add to the stockpot. Simmer for about 30 minutes or more, until they are cooked but still firm.

Remove the stockpot from the heat and let the cardoons cool in the pot for 20 minutes, then remove them from the pot with a strainer-skimmer and dry them on paper towels. They are now ready to be used in such dishes as *cardi trippati* (see below) or *gobbi (cardi) dorati* (see page 528). Or they can be served with olive oil and with or without lemon juice.

Gobbi (cardi) dorati

DEEP-FRIED CARDOONS

SERVES 4

*T*he cardoons are boiled with flour, then they are lightly floured, dipped in beaten egg, and deep-fried in vegetable oil and a little olive oil.

1 bunch cardoons (about 2½ pounds)	1½ cups unbleached all-purpose flour
1 lemon	1 quart vegetable oil
3 extra-large eggs	½ cup olive oil
Coarse-grained salt	Lemon wedges

BOIL the cardoons according to the directions on page 527. Dry on paper towels and let stand until completely cooled.

Meanwhile, beat the eggs in small bowl with a pinch of salt; spread the flour out on a board.

When the cardoons are cool and dry, lightly flour them.

Heat the vegetable oil and olive oil in a large frying pan. When the oil is hot (about 375 degrees), quickly dip the cardoons in the beaten egg and place them in the pan. (Don't put in too many cardoons at a time because they must float in the oil.) Deep-fry them for 3 or 4 minutes on each side.

Meanwhile, prepare a serving dish by lining it with paper towels.

When the cardoons are cooked and golden brown all over, remove them with a strainer-skimmer to the prepared serving dish. When all the cardoons are on the serving dish, remove the paper towels. Serve very hot with lemon wedges.

Cardi trippati

CARDOONS CUT IN THE FORM OF TRIPE

SERVES 4

*T*his is one of the most elaborate vegetable dishes in the Italian repertory, used more often as an in-between course, a *piatto di mezzo,* than as an accompanying vegetable. The cardoons are cooked four ways to make the dish, so it is time-consuming—but well worth the trouble.

1 bunch cardoons (about 2½ pounds)
1 large clove garlic, peeled
½ small red onion, cleaned
28 tablespoons (14 ounces) sweet butter
1 cup freshly grated Parmigiano

Salt and freshly ground black pepper to taste
1 ¼ cups unseasoned bread crumbs, preferably homemade (see page 58), approximately

BOIL the cardoons as described on page 527.

Chop the garlic and onion coarsely, then place in a large skillet, along with 8 tablespoons (4 ounces) of the butter, and sauté for 5 minutes, until golden. Add the cardoon pieces to the pan and sauté for 5 minutes, stirring carefully to avoid breaking up the pieces.

Sprinkle the contents of the pan with ½ cup of the grated Parmigiano. Taste for salt and pepper and sauté for 2 minutes more, stirring to mix in the cheese, then remove the pan from the heat and let the cardoons stand until completely cooled (about 1 hour).

Prepare a serving dish by lining it with paper towels; preheat the oven to 375 degrees.

Spread out about 1 cup of the bread crumbs on a surface. Remove the cold cardoon pieces from the pan and roll them lightly in the crumbs. Heat 12 tablespoons (6 ounces) of the butter in a frying pan. When the butter is completely melted and very hot, quickly deep-fry

(continued)

CARDI TRIPPATI *(continued)*

the cardoon pieces until golden all over (about 3 minutes), then remove from the frying pan with a strainer-skimmer and place on the prepared serving dish.

When all the cardoons are on the serving dish, butter a baking dish and line the bottom with a layer of cardoons. Sprinkle with some of the remaining grated Parmigiano and dot with 2 or 3 tablespoons of the remaining butter. Then make a second layer of cardoons. Keep alternating layers of cardoons with Parmigiano and butter until you have used up all ingredients; the top layer should be of cardoons.

Sprinkle the top with the remaining ¼ cup bread crumbs, then bake in the preheated oven for 20 minutes. Remove from the oven and serve hot.

CARROTS

Carote bollite

BOILED CARROTS

CUT off the tips of the carrots on both ends. Do not scrape or peel them; carrots retain more flavor when cooked with their skins. Place the carrots in a large bowl of cold water and let them soak for about 30 minutes.

Heat a large quantity of water in a flameproof casserole. When the water reaches the boiling point, add coarse salt to taste, then put the whole carrots into the casserole and let them boil until cooked but still firm (about 15 minutes), then drain and place them in a large bowl of cold water to cool (about 15 minutes).

When the carrots are cooled, peel them. This is best done by gently pushing off the outer skin; it will come off easily and whole.

At this point, carrots are ready to be used for different dishes, such as *sformato di carote* (see page 554) or *insalata composta* (see page 501). Or they can be served with olive oil and with or without lemon juice.

Carote in dolce-forte

SWEET AND SOUR CARROTS

SERVES 6 TO 8

*B*oiling the carrots with this method retains their full flavor. They are then sautéed in butter with wine vinegar and a touch of sugar, resulting in a full-flavored vegetable dish, which can be used with many main courses.

1 ½ pounds medium-sized
   carrots
Coarse-grained salt
8 tablespoons (4 ounces) sweet
   butter
1 tablespoon unbleached
   all-purpose flour

1 tablespoon granulated sugar
3 tablespoons red wine vinegar
Salt and freshly ground black
   pepper to taste

SOAK the carrots, whole, in a bowl of cold water for a half hour. Bring a large pot of cold water to a boil, add coarse-grained salt to taste, then add the carrots and let cook for 15 minutes, until they are cooked but still firm. Cool carrots under cold running water, then remove their skins by gently pushing them off. Cut carrots vertically into fourths, then cut each fourth into 2-inch pieces.

Place a medium-sized skillet with the butter over medium heat and when the butter is melted, add the flour, mix well with a wooden spoon, add the sugar and when it is completely incorporated, add the vinegar, stir and put in the carrots. Gently shake the skillet until the carrots become coated with the sauce. Taste for salt and pepper and serve very hot.

CAULIFLOWER

*I*n Italian cooking, the outer leaves of the cauliflower are removed, but often the tender inner ones are left on. The whole
cauliflower is soaked for about 30 minutes in abundant cold water to
minimize its strong cabbage-family smell. Some Italians go even further
and place a teaspoon of white wine vinegar in the water when boiling.

Cavolfiore bollito

BOILED CAULIFLOWER

To boil, leave the cauliflower whole. Remove the outer leaves but leave
the tender inner leaves on. Soak the cauliflower in a bowl of cold water
for 30 minutes. Heat a large quantity of cold water in a flameproof
casserole. When it reaches the boiling point, add coarse salt to taste,
then place the whole cauliflower in the casserole and let boil, covered,
for 15 to 20 minutes. (Turn cauliflower over once to be sure that it is
evenly cooked, but cook a bit longer right side up, as the bottom is less
tender than the top.) By that time the cauliflower should be cooked but
still firm.

With a large strainer-skimmer, transfer the whole cauliflower to a
serving dish. It is now ready to be used for different dishes, such as
cavolfiore all'olio (see page 533), *sformato di cavolfiore* (see page 554), or
cavolfiore con acciugata (see page 534). Or it can be served with olive oil
and with or without lemon juice.

NOTE: We do not include *cavolfiore gratinato,* as do some Italian
cookbooks outside of Italy, as we feel *gratinée* dishes to be completely
French.

Cavolfiore fritto

DEEP-FRIED CAULIFLOWER

WHEN all the leaves are removed from the head of cauliflower, turn it bottom side up. You can see that the cauliflower has a solid central piece with a myriad of little flowerets attached to it each by a delicate stem. Detach the flowers at the stem from the central piece. You should have a large number of pieces, each in the shape of a flower. Leave the smaller flowers whole, not exceeding 1 inch thick and 2 inches long, and cut the larger ones into pieces the same size. Discard the central stalk.

Cauliflower is deep-fried in the same way as artichokes (see page 515), and the cooking time is about the same.

Cavolfiore all'olio

CAULIFLOWER WITH OLIVE OIL

SERVES 4 TO 6

*T*he simplest of treatments of boiled cauliflower. Leaving the vegetable whole, with a few tender leaves left on, is not only better for the taste, but makes a nicer presentation as well.

1 head cauliflower
Coarse-grained salt

Salt and freshly ground black pepper
¼ cup olive oil, approximately

BOIL the cauliflower according to the directions on page 532. Place the boiled whole cauliflower on a serving dish, sprinkle with salt and freshly ground black pepper, and pour the olive oil over it. Serve either hot or cold.

Cavolfiore con acciugata

CAULIFLOWER WITH ANCHOVY SAUCE

SERVES 4 TO 6

*B*oiled whole cauliflower blends extremely well with anchovy sauce. However, because it has a strong flavor, it should be served separately, after the second dish, or perhaps in lieu of the first dish if you want a very light dinner.

1 cauliflower **Acciugata** *(see page 73)*
Coarse-grained salt

BOIL the cauliflower according to the directions on page 532. While it is cooking, prepare the *acciugata*.

Place the whole boiled cauliflower on a serving dish, pour the hot anchovy sauce over it, and serve immediately.

EGGPLANT

Melanzane alla parmigiana

EGGPLANT IN THE STYLE OF PARMA

SERVES 6

*W*hen selecting eggplants at the market, choose either large or small ones, but feel them to be sure they are firm. If they feel very soft, it means they are full of seeds, which is not desirable.

Italians generally use eggplants unpeeled. The slices should be sprinkled with coarse salt and allowed to stand for 30 minutes to an hour. The eggplants shed some dark liquid, and with it a good bit of the bitterness of the vegetable. Instructions for doing this are included in the recipe.

Here the eggplant slices are first deep-fried without flouring and arranged in layers, alternating with a lightly simmered tomato sauce, coarsely grated mozzarella and "Swiss" cheese (Groviera), and a sprinkling of Parmigiano with a pat of butter. When baked, this dish should be considerably lighter than many recipes with the same name.

6 small or 2 large eggplants
Coarse-grained salt
1 pound very ripe fresh
  tomatoes or 1 pound canned
  tomatoes, preferably
  imported Italian, drained
1 tablespoon tomato paste,
  preferably imported Italian
1 tablespoon olive oil
6 leaves basil, fresh or preserved
  in salt (see page 18)

Salt and freshly ground black
  pepper
4 ounces mozzarella
4 ounces Groviera (Swiss cheese)
1 quart vegetable oil (see page
  22)
5 or 6 tablespoons (2½ or 3
  ounces) sweet butter
½ cup freshly grated
  Parmigiano

CUT the eggplants lengthwise into slices ⅓ inch thick; do not peel. Sprinkle the eggplant slices with coarse salt, place them in a dish, place a second dish containing a weight over, and let stand for 30 minutes. Meanwhile, prepare the sauce.

Pass the tomatoes through a food mill, using the disc with the smallest holes, into a saucepan. Add the tomato paste, olive oil, and basil leaves to the saucepan, then place on the heat. Season with salt and pepper and simmer for 15 minutes.

Coarsely grate the mozzarella and Groviera into a bowl; rinse the eggplant slices in cold water and wipe with paper towels; prepare a serving dish by lining it with paper towels.

Heat the oil in a frying pan. When it is very hot (about 375 degrees), deep-fry the eggplant slices, a few at a time, until golden on both sides (about 3 minutes). Remove the fried slices from the pan and place on the prepared serving dish to drain. When all eggplant slices are transferred to the serving dish, sprinkle them with a little salt.

Preheat the oven to 375 degrees.

(continued)

MELANZANE ALLA PARMIGIANA *(continued)*

Spread 1 tablespoon of the sauce over the bottom of a 13½ × 8¾-inch baking dish. On top of the sauce put a layer of eggplant slices. Then add a layer of mozzarella and Groviera, sprinkled with Parmigiano. In this and every subsequent layer, also add a pat of butter. Make one more layer of eggplant and on top a layer of sauce. Alternate layers of eggplant and cheese and sauce, finishing with sauce on top.

Bake in the preheated oven for 25 minutes.

NOTE: This may also be eaten well chilled. If serving hot, let rest for 15 minutes before serving.

FENNEL (Finocchio)

*F*ennel, both raw and cooked, is used much more as a vegetable in Italy than abroad, though it grows in most places and is easily found at many specialty vegetable markets and Italian markets. It has a light flavor, similar to that of the fennel seeds that are used as a spice.

Of the many ways that fennel is cooked in Italy, we include two recipes here, besides a basic one for boiling. Cultivated "bulb" or Florence fennel is called for here, not wild fennel, whose leaves and stalks are used for flavoring mainly in southern Italy.

Finocchi bolliti

BOILED FENNEL

IF the fennel stalks are medium-sized, cut them into quarters vertically. Discard the outer leaves. Cut off the small knob at the bottom and cut out the hard inner part at the bottom, which is a continuation of the knob. Place the fennel quarters in a large bowl of cold water and let them soak for about 30 minutes.

Heat a large quantity of cold water, with coarse salt added, in a flameproof casserole. When the water reaches boiling point, add coarse salt to taste, then add the fennel and let it boil until cooked but still firm (about 10 minutes, varying a bit depending on size).

Drain the fennel, then place it on paper towels to absorb all excess liquid. The fennel is now ready to be used in such dishes as *sformato di finocchi* (see page 554), *insalata composta* (see page 501), or *finocchi al burro* (see below). Or it can be served with olive oil and with or without lemon juice.

Finocchi in sugo finto

FENNEL IN WINTER TOMATO SAUCE

SERVES 4

*H*ere the fennel pieces are floured and browned in olive oil, and then simmered in the sauce.

4 medium fennel "bulbs"
1 cup unbleached all-purpose
    flour, approximately
5 tablespoons olive oil
Salt and freshly ground black
    pepper to taste

¾ pound ripe fresh tomatoes or
    ¾ pound canned tomatoes,
    preferably imported Italian,
    drained

REMOVE the outside leaves from the fennel, then cut the stalks into lengthwise slices, ½ inch thick. Place the slices in a bowl of cold water for 30 minutes, then remove from the water and dry on paper towels.

Spread out the flour on a counter and lightly flour the fennel pieces.

Heat the olive oil in a large frying pan. When it is hot, put in the fennel pieces and sauté them, turning them, until golden all over (about 2 minutes on each side). Sprinkle with salt and pepper.

Pass the tomatoes through a food mill, using the disc with the smallest holes, into the frying pan. Simmer very slowly for 15 minutes, loosening the fennel pieces every so often with a spatula so they do not stick.

Remove the pan from the heat and serve very hot.

Finocchi al burro

FENNEL SAUTÉED IN BUTTER

SERVES 4

*T*he fennel is cut into pieces and then boiled, after which it is sautéed in butter and oil and seasoned with nutmeg and Parmigiano.

4 fennel "bulbs"
Coarse-grained salt
6 tablespoons (3 ounces) sweet
*   butter*
1/2 tablespoon olive oil

Salt, freshly ground black
*   pepper, and freshly grated*
*   nutmeg to taste*
1/4 cup freshly grated
*   Parmigiano*

BOIL the fennel as described on page 536, but for 3 or 4 minutes less. After draining it, let it cool.

Heat the butter and oil in a flameproof casserole. When they are hot, add the fennel. Sprinkle with salt, pepper, and nutmeg, then mix very well and sauté for about 5 minutes. Sprinkle with the Parmigiano and mix thoroughly.

Cook for 2 minutes more, then remove the casserole from the heat. Transfer the fennel to a serving dish and serve hot.

PEAS

Piselli alla fiorentina

PEAS IN THE FLORENTINE MANNER

SERVES 4

*T*he small peas, *piselli novelli,* were developed in Florence in the early sixteenth century. When they arrived in France they were called there *petits pois.* However, if one uses the larger fresh peas that are found for much of the year, the shelled peas must be soaked for an hour in cold water with a little flour to cause fermentation, which tenderizes them. After this, when cooked, they should be as tender as the real *piselli.*

1 1/2 pounds of shelled fresh peas, preferably very small

1 tablespoon unbleached all-purpose flour

4 ounces pancetta *or* prosciutto, *in one piece*

10 sprigs Italian parsley, leaves only

1 large clove garlic, peeled

4 tablespoons olive oil

Salt and freshly ground black pepper to taste

3/4 to 1 cup hot meat broth, preferably homemade

1 1/2 tablespoons granulated sugar

UNLESS they are very small, soak the peas in a large bowl of cold water with the flour for 1 hour.

Cut the *pancetta* into tiny pieces and coarsely chop the parsley and garlic. Heat the olive oil in a flameproof casserole, then add the chopped ingredients and sauté very gently for about 5 minutes. Drain and rinse the peas in cold running water.

Add the peas to the casserole. Season with salt and pepper, then stir the peas thoroughly and add 1/2 cup of hot broth. Simmer very slowly until broth has evaporated (about 15 minutes). At that time, if the peas are small and tender, they should be cooked; if not, add more broth and simmer till it evaporates (about 8 minutes) or until the peas are cooked. Add the sugar and simmer for 1 minute more, until the sugar has dissolved.

Remove the casserole from the heat, transfer the peas to a serving dish, and serve immediately.

NOTE: This is the typical *contorno* (accompaniment) for the Easter season.

POTATOES

Patate saltate alla salvia

POTATOES SAUTÉED WITH SAGE

SERVES 6

*P*otatoes, cut into small pieces and "stir-sautéed" with olive oil, sage, and the light garlic flavor that comes from using the whole clove with the skin left on. Easy to prepare and a delicious way to make potatoes, one that goes with almost any main dish.

2 pounds potatoes for boiling,
but not new potatoes
6 tablespoons olive oil
6 leaves sage, fresh or preserved
in salt (see page 19)

1 clove garlic, unpeeled and left
whole
Salt and freshly ground black
pepper to taste

PEEL the potatoes and cut them into 1-inch pieces.

Heat the olive oil in a flameproof casserole, preferably terra-cotta, then add the sage leaves and unpeeled garlic clove. Sauté very lightly for 2 minutes, then add the potato pieces and stir with a wooden spoon. Cover and cook for 2 minutes over low heat, then stir the potatoes again. Season with salt and cover the casserole again. The potatoes should be stirred about every 2 minutes, but must be kept covered in between. After 20 minutes, they should be cooked.

Remove the clove of garlic and transfer the potatoes to a serving dish. Serve immediately, sprinkling with freshly ground pepper.

Patate con pesto

POTATOES WITH PESTO

SERVES 6

*P*otatoes have a special affinity for pesto. Even when pasta is prepared with this sauce, it is boiled with a potato. Here the potatoes are boiled, cut up, and tossed very gently with a little olive oil. Then the pesto is added. This is a very strong-flavored vegetable, which should accompany only dishes that do not have their own sauce.

Coarse-grained salt
2 pounds potatoes for boiling,
but not new potatoes

1 tablespoon olive oil
5 heaping tablespoons pesto (see
page 92), approximately

PUT a large quantity of cold water in a stockpot and set on the heat. When the water reaches the boiling point, add coarse salt to taste, then add the potatoes, whole, in their skins; the potatoes must be completely covered with water. Let the potatoes boil until cooked but firm (about 35 minutes for medium potatoes).

Remove the potatoes from the pot and transfer them to a board, using a strainer-skimmer in order not to puncture them. Peel the potatoes while still very hot, then cut into pieces about 1 inch square.

Place the potatoes in a serving dish, pour the olive oil over them, and mix very gently. Let stand until cooled.

When the potatoes are cool, place the pesto sauce on top and serve.

Patate alla contadina

COUNTRY STYLE POTATOES

SERVES 3

*B*oiled potatoes, cut up and flavored with olive oil, coarsely chopped fresh parsley and garlic. A simple dish of extraordinary flavor; you will use it often once you try it.

Coarse-grained salt
1 pound potatoes for boiling,
    but not new potatoes
1 large clove garlic, peeled

10 sprigs Italian parsley, leaves
    only
1/4 cup olive oil
Salt and freshly ground black
    pepper to taste

PLACE a flameproof casserole with cold water over medium heat. When the water reaches a boil, add coarse salt to taste; then add the potatoes and simmer until the potatoes are soft (about 35 minutes for medium potatoes).

Meanwhile, finely chop first the garlic, then the parsley. Place them in a serving bowl, along with the olive oil and salt and freshly ground pepper to taste.

When the potatoes are ready, peel them while still very hot and cut them into pieces about 1 inch square. Add the potato pieces to the bowl and mix with the other ingredients, using a wooden spoon.

Serve warm or cold, to accompany boiled meat.

PEPPERS

Peperoni e melanzane

PEPPERS AND EGGPLANT

SERVES 6

*P*eppers, eggplant, onions, and tomato all simmered together with just a little olive oil produce the most marvelous vegetable dish. May be used to accompany a large range of main dishes. Do not use it with main dishes that have a tomato sauce.

*4 sweet bell peppers, yellow,
  orange, red, green or mixed*
4 tablespoons olive oil
1 medium red onion, cleaned
2 medium eggplants
*1 pound fresh ripe tomatoes,
  blanched and seeded, or 1
  pound canned tomatoes,
  preferably imported Italian,
  drained and seeded*

*Salt and freshly ground black
  pepper to taste*

SOAK the peppers in a bowl of cold water for 30 minutes. Put olive oil in a casserole. Then cut onion into ½-inch pieces and add to the casserole. Remove stems and inside parts of the peppers and cut into rings. Make a layer on top of the onions in the casserole. Cut the eggplants into 1-inch cubes and place on top of the peppers. Add the tomatoes, and sprinkle with salt and pepper. Do not mix.

Cover the casserole with a lid and place it over medium heat. Simmer for 20 minutes without mixing. Then mix thoroughly and taste for salt and pepper.

Simmer for 10 minutes more, without lid, mixing every so often with a wooden spoon. Transfer to serving dish and serve.

This dish may accompany boiled or roasted meat.

Peperonata

PEPPERS SAUTÉED IN TOMATOES

SERVES 4

*P*eppers simmered in tomatoes, cooked just long enough to retain some of the crispness of the peppers and keep the sweet, light quality of the tomatoes, without the acidity produced by cooking them too long. The large number of Mediterranean dishes that combine peppers with tomatoes suggests their affinity.

6 sweet bell peppers, yellow, orange, red, or green, or mixed
1 medium red onion, cleaned
2 large cloves garlic, peeled

1½ pounds very ripe fresh tomatoes, blanched and seeded, or 1½ pounds canned tomatoes, preferably imported Italian, drained and seeded
3 tablespoons olive oil
Salt and freshly ground black pepper to taste

SOAK the peppers in a bowl of cold water for 30 minutes. Remove the stems and seeds from the peppers, then cut them into pieces about 2 inches square (see note below). Cut the onion and garlic into small pieces.

Heat the olive oil in a large casserole, then add the onion and garlic and sauté very gently for 4 minutes. Add the peppers to the casserole and place the tomatoes over them; do not mix. Add salt and pepper.

Cover the casserole and cook for 10 minutes, then mix the ingredients with a wooden spoon. Taste for salt and pepper and cook, uncovered, for 15 minutes more, until the peppers are soft.

Remove the casserole from the heat, transfer the *peperonata* to a serving dish, and serve either hot or cold.

NOTE: In Florence it is not usual to peel the peppers. For those who prefer to do so, see technique of peeling them on page 505.

RAPE

Rape saltate in padella

SAUTÉED RAPE

SERVES 4

*T*he pleasantly bitter turnip green called *"rape"* in Italian is sometimes known abroad by its southern Italian dialect name, *broccoli-rab*. Because of its strong flavor, it ideally accompanies roast meats, especially pork (see *arista,* page 446). However, it is quite versatile.

Recipes for rape appear in the first cookbooks of the fourteenth century. Spinach aside, there is probably no vegetable more typically Tuscan. Therefore it is strange that Janet Ross, an Englishwoman of the late nineteenth century, does not even mention it in her well-known Tuscan vegetable cookery book.

2 pounds rape	*4 tablespoons olive oil*
Coarse-grained salt	*Salt and freshly ground black*
1 large clove garlic, peeled	*pepper to taste*

REMOVE the heavy stalks from the rape, leaving the light stalks and leaves. Cut these into 2-inch pieces, then rinse them very well in cold running water. Place the cut rape in a large bowl of cold water and let soak for 30 minutes.

Heat cold water in a large flameproof casserole. When the water reaches the boiling point, add coarse salt to taste, then drain the rape and add to the casserole. Cook 15 minutes until soft. Drain the rape in a colander and cool under cold running water, then gently squeeze out excess water.

Cut the garlic clove coarsely. Place it in a large saucepan, along with the olive oil, and sauté until lightly golden (about 2 minutes). Add the rape to the saucepan. Taste for salt and pepper and mix thoroughly with

(continued)

a wooden spoon, then cover the saucepan and let simmer very slowly for about 5 minutes, stirring every so often. At that time all the liquid should be absorbed and the rape ready to be served.

Remove the saucepan from the heat, transfer the rape to a serving dish, and serve immediately.

SPINACH

Spinaci saltati

"STIR-SAUTÉED" SPINACH

SERVES 4

*H*ere, boiled spinach is "stir-sautéed" with a little olive oil and garlic. In Florence it is probably the most frequently used accompanying vegetable. Indeed, it can be used to accompany almost anything.

3 pounds fresh spinach
Coarse-grained salt
1 large clove garlic, peeled

3 tablespoons olive oil
Salt and freshly ground black
* pepper*

CLEAN the spinach well, removing the heavier stems, and soak in a bowl of cold water for 30 minutes. Place a large pot of cold water over medium heat, and when the water reaches a boil, add coarse salt to taste, then drain spinach and add to pot and cook it for 5 minutes. Drain, then place under cold running water to cool. When the spinach is cold, lightly squeeze it and chop it coarsely.

Cut the garlic clove into small pieces and place them in a frying pan, along with the olive oil. Place the pan over medium heat and let the garlic sauté very slowly, until golden (about 2 minutes).

Add the chopped spinach to pan and season with salt and freshly ground pepper. Mix the spinach thoroughly with the other ingredients, using a fork, then let cook over medium heat for 2 minutes.

Transfer the spinach to serving dish and serve hot.

Spinaci alla fiorentina

SPINACH, FLORENTINE STYLE

SERVES 4 TO 6

*H*ere, after boiled spinach is "stir-sautéed" with a little olive oil and garlic, it is mixed with *balsamella* with Parmigiano and arranged in a baking dish with a layer of the same sauce on top. After baking, it is served hot. It may be used with a wide variety of main dishes, but avoid those that already have a *balsamella* sauce. It may also be used as a light first course.

FOR BALSAMELLA WITH PARMIGIANO

6 tablespoons (3 ounces) sweet butter

6 tablespoons unbleached all-purpose flour

2½ cups milk

4 tablespoons freshly grated Parmigiano

Salt and freshly ground white pepper to taste

Pinch of freshly grated nutmeg

FOR THE SPINACH

3 pounds fresh spinach

Coarse-grained salt

1 large clove garlic, peeled

3 tablespoons olive oil

Salt, freshly ground black pepper, and freshly grated nutmeg to taste

MAKE the *balsamella* with Parmigiano according to the directions on page 62, using quantities listed here. Let the sauce cool in the covered pan.

Prepare the spinach as directed in the recipe for *spinaci saltati* (see page 546), up to the point where the chopped spinach is added to the

(continued)

547

pan with the garlic. Season with salt and pepper and sauté the spinach, stirring constantly, for 5 minutes. Transfer to a bowl to cool.

Preheat the oven to 375 degrees.

Place half the *balsamella* in the bowl with the spinach. Add nutmeg and mix very well, until the *balsamella* is incorporated into the spinach.

Butter the bottom and sides of a 13½ × 8¾-inch baking dish. Place the spinach in the dish, making a smooth, even top surface, then pour on the remaining *balsamella* as a top layer. Put the pan in the preheated oven and bake for about 25 minutes; the top layer should be lightly golden.

Serve hot, right from the baking dish.

SWISS CHARD

Bietole all'agro

BOILED SWISS CHARD WITH OLIVE OIL AND LEMON

SERVES 4

*S*o-called Swiss chard is used in Italy almost as much as spinach, and is sometimes substituted for it or mixed with it. It has a milder, sweeter taste. Use boiled Swiss chard dressed *all'agro* to accompany a great many dishes that do not have specific vegetables associated with them. Indeed, Swiss chard is almost always a safe accompanying vegetable.

3 pounds fresh Swiss chard
Coarse-grained salt
Salt and freshly ground black
*   pepper*

3 tablespoons olive oil
1 lemon

CLEAN the Swiss chard very carefully. Remove the stems and place the leaves in a bowl of cold water; let soak for 30 minutes.

Heat a stockpot of cold water over medium heat. When the water reaches the boiling point, add coarse salt to taste, then drain the Swiss chard and add it to the pot. Cook for 10 minutes or until soft.

Drain the Swiss chard and cool it under cold running water, then gently squeeze it to remove excess water and chop it very coarsely. Place it in a serving dish.

Sprinkle the Swiss chard with salt and a pinch of pepper and pour the olive oil over it. Squeeze half of the lemon over the Swiss chard and serve with the other lemon half, cut into wedges. Serve cold.

Bietole saltate

"STIR-SAUTÉED" SWISS CHARD

FOLLOW recipe for *spinaci saltati* (see page 546) substituting 3 pounds of Swiss chard for the spinach.

TOMATOES

Pomodori fritti

DEEP-FRIED GREEN TOMATOES

TOMATOES are deep-fried in the same way as artichokes (see page 515). The tomatoes, which must still be green, are first cut horizontally into slices ½ inch thick and then dried very carefully with paper towels.

The cooking time is about 2 minutes on each side.

Pomodori al forno

BAKED TOMATOES

SERVES 6

*F*resh tomato halves, lightly baked, with a little basil, parsley, garlic, and olive oil to bring out their flavor. Some bread crumbs are sprinkled over to make a crisp top. This dish may accompany almost anything.

6 large ripe fresh tomatoes
Coarse-grained salt
1 large clove garlic, peeled
1 ½ cups fresh basil leaves
1 ½ cups Italian parsley, leaves
  only

Salt and freshly ground black
  pepper to taste
4 tablespoons unseasoned bread
  crumbs, preferably
  homemade (see page 58)
¾ cup olive oil

RINSE the tomatoes and wipe them with a paper towel, then cut in half horizontally and remove all the seeds. Sprinkle the inside of the tomato halves with coarse salt and let them stand for 20 to 25 minutes.

Meanwhile, chop the garlic very fine, then chop the basil and parsley leaves coarsely. Mix the chopped garlic with the chopped basil and parsley and season with salt and pepper.

Preheat the oven to 400 degrees.

Place the salted tomato halves face down on paper towel for a few minutes, then wipe them off with a paper towel and fill the cavities with the chopped herb mixture. Sprinkle the tops with bread crumbs, then place the stuffed tomatoes in a baking dish containing 2 tablespoons of the olive oil.

Sprinkle remaining olive oil over tomatoes and bake in the preheated oven until the tomato halves are still whole but soft (about 25 minutes).

Serve hot.

ZUCCHINI

Zucchini bolliti

BOILED ZUCCHINI

*I*n selecting zucchini, try to find them as small and young as possible. The very large zucchini pay a large price in taste for their size. Zucchini should be very firm and the skin light green.

To boil, cut off both ends of the zucchini, top and bottom, and put into a large bowl of cold water for about 30 minutes, then slice lengthwise in quarters, if zucchini are very thin into halves. Cut slices into 1-inch pieces.

Soak the zucchini pieces in more cold water for 30 minutes more.

Heat a large quantity of water in a large flameproof casserole. When the water reaches the boiling point, add coarse-grained salt to taste, then drain and add the zucchini pieces and let them simmer until they are cooked but firm (about 8 minutes). (Cooking time of zucchini varies a lot because it depends on how fresh they are, if they grew in a sunny or shady place, and if they have been in the refrigerator for a long period.)

Drain the zucchini and place in a dish to cool. It is now ready to be used in such dishes as *sformato di zucchini* (see page 554) or *insalata composta* (see page 501). Or it can be served with olive oil with or without lemon juice.

Fiori di zucca fritti

FRIED ZUCCHINI BLOSSOMS

SERVES 4

*Z*ucchini have female and male flowers or blossoms. The vegetable we eat is the stem of the female flower, and those flowers attached to the female are less good for eating. The male has a thin stem that never grows into the zucchini vegetable but puts all its force into its orange blossom, which is delicious when fried with a light batter.

Batter as for **pollo fritto** *(see page 340)*
16 zucchini blossoms

1 quart vegetable oil
Salt
1 lemon cut into wedges

PREPARE the batter. Set aside in a cool place (not the refrigerator) for 2 hours.

Cut off the stems of the blossoms and remove the pistils from inside. Rinse the blossoms very gently in cold water and dry them with paper towels.

Heat the vegetable oil in a deep-fat fryer. While it is heating, prepare a serving dish by lining it with paper towels.

Dip each blossom into the batter and place in the hot oil (about 375 degrees). Cook for about 1 minute on each side, until golden, then remove with a strainer-skimmer and place on the prepared serving dish.

Repeat the procedure until all the blossoms are cooked and on the serving dish, then remove the paper towels from the serving dish, sprinkle the blossoms with a little salt, and serve immediately with lemon wedges.

Zucchini fritti

FRIED ZUCCHINI

CUT the zucchini into strips 2 inches long by 1½ inches wide and fry in batter as for fried zucchini blossoms above.

Zucchini trifolati

SAUTÉED ZUCCHINI

SERVES 4

*S*autéed zucchini cooked without tomatoes in an olive oil, garlic, and parsley base, with white wine. *Trifolati* refers to the shape into which the zucchini are cut. The vegetable is not cut into discs when sautéed in Italy, but rather the shape described in this recipe. The disc shape is usually reserved for frying. The other vegetable often cut into the *trifolati* shape is fresh wild mushrooms such as *porcini*.

*1 pound zucchini, preferably
    very thin
1 medium clove garlic, peeled
10 sprigs Italian parsley, leaves
    only*

*¼ cup olive oil
Salt and freshly ground black
    pepper to taste
¼ to ½ cup dry white wine*

IF using very thin zucchini, cut them lengthwise into halves, otherwise into quarters, then cut each strip into 1½-inch pieces. Place the zucchini in a bowl of cold water and let soak for a few minutes. Meanwhile coarsely chop garlic and parsley together on a board. Heat the oil in a small saucepan over medium heat. When the oil is warm, add the chopped ingredients and sauté for 30 seconds, then drain the zucchini, add it to pan, and sauté for 2 minutes. Season with salt and pepper, cover, and cook for 2 minutes more. Add ¼ cup of the wine, cover again, and finish cooking for 5 minutes longer. By that time the zucchini should be cooked but not overcooked; if not cooked enough, add a little more wine and cook for 2 minutes more. Mix very well, transfer to a serving dish, and serve.

Sformati di verdura

BAKED VEGETABLES IN MOLD

SERVES 6

This molded dish represents the most elaborate treatment of vegetables. A variety of vegetables may be used, boiled first and then treated in the same manner as *sformati* of meat or pasta or dessert. As usual with Italian *sformati*, the dish is unmolded when served.

Because of the special treatment of the vegetables, the dish is often used as a *piatto di mezzo*, the course in between the *primo piatto* and *secondo piatto*, in an important dinner.

1 pound of a fresh vegetable such as artichokes, asparagus, carrots, fennel, or cardoons, boiled (see the individual vegetables for procedure on boiling)
10 tablespoons (5 ounces) sweet butter
Salt and freshly ground black pepper to taste

½ cup unbleached all-purpose flour
2 cups milk
4 extra-large egg yolks
3 tablespoons freshly grated Parmigiano
Freshly grated nutmeg to taste
3 tablespoons unseasoned bread crumbs, preferably homemade (see page 58)

WHEN the boiled vegetable is cool, cut it into pieces smaller than ½ inch. Heat 4 tablespoons of the butter in a saucepan. When the butter is warm, add the vegetable pieces and sauté for about 5 minutes. Taste for salt and pepper, then remove the saucepan from the heat and let the vegetable cool completely (about 30 minutes).

Make *balsamella*, using the remaining 6 tablespoons of the butter, the flour, and the milk, according to the directions on page 62. When the *balsamella* is done, cover the saucepan and let the sauce cool completely (about 30 minutes).

Preheat oven to 400 degrees.

When *balsamella* is cool, transfer it to a large bowl. Add the egg yolks and grated Parmigiano to the bowl and mix thoroughly with a

Sformati di verdura: The loaf pan containing the *sformato* mixture in a water bath.

wooden spoon. Add the vegetable pieces and salt, pepper, and nutmeg to taste, then gently mix all the ingredients together.

Butter a 9 × 5 × 3-inch loaf pan and coat it with the bread crumbs, then pour the contents of the bowl into the pan.

Prepare a *bagno maria* (bain-marie) (see page 33 and illustration above) and place it in the preheated oven for about 1 hour and 15 minutes. (If during baking the top of the *sformato* begins to darken too much, place a sheet of aluminum foil over it.)

When the *sformato* is done, remove the loaf pan from the oven and let cool for 20 minutes. As the *sformato* cools, it will detach itself from the bottom and sides of the pan. Carefully unmold the *sformato* on a serving dish and serve immediately.

Desserts

❦

*A*t this point it is common knowledge that the end of a usual Italian meal is not a dessert, but rather fresh fruit. A dessert is served at the end of a family meal about once a week, perhaps on Sunday.

But nonetheless there is an unsurpassed number and variety of Italian desserts. When are they served, besides at that once-a-week family meal? At a formal dinner or when there are guests; on traditional feast days; at the café (in Italy called "bar"); at home for guests who call between meals. The variety of any area of Italian cooking is generally apparent only over the course of the entire year, since many dishes are meant to be made only once a year, for a particular day. This is true of desserts as well.

Italian desserts run the gamut of complicated pastries; creams and custards; sweet breads and *schiacciate;* nut biscuits; specialties with chestnuts and chestnut flour; *crespelle* (crêpes); rice desserts; fruit fried in batter; *budini* (most using the principle that the French called "soufflé" when they adopted it); meringues; fruit in pastry drums; stuffed fruit; special seasonal fruits, such as *fragoline di bosco* (wild strawberries) adorned simply with wine or whipped cream; etc., etc.

In short, the Italians have an enormous repertoire of desserts, and have through the centuries developed the most sophisticated techniques for producing them, but this sophistication is balanced by native good sense, which since the sixteenth century has run side by side with the sophistication, creating a balance to it. The repertoire is there, but rich desserts are not eaten with every meal nor even every day.

Macedonia di frutta

FRESH FRUIT MACEDONIA

SERVES 6

*W*hile it is unadorned fresh fruit which most often forms the sweet end of an Italian repast, the *macedonia* of fresh fruit comes next in popularity. Large fruits such as apples, pears, peaches, and apricots are diced, bananas are sliced, and grapes and berries are left whole. The ideal combination occurs in the season when fresh fruits are all available, but *macedonia* is made also off season, omitting the peaches, apricots, and cherries, and increasing the percentage of orange pieces. A minimum of sugar is added as the sweet raisins do the job better and in a more healthy way. Lemon and orange juice used together with the wine produce the special flavor that separates a *macedonia* from an ordinary fruit salad. Melons of any kind are not used as a rule in a *macedonia* and pineapple is only recently available in Italy and does not enter into the traditional selection. While varying combinations occur and are legitimate, the dessert is not an improvisation and does have limits on the choice of fruit employed. Easy to make and healthy, this is a dessert to be used often.

4 tablespoons raisins	*1 banana*
2 tablespoons light rum	*1 bunch of grapes*
3 large oranges	*2 peaches, ripe but not overripe,*
1 lemon	*either freestone or cling*
2 Delicious apples, yellow or	*2 apricots*
red, ripe but not overripe	*1 pint strawberries*
2 pears, preferably Bosc, ripe	*8 ounces cherries*
but not overripe	

PLUS

2 cups dry red or white wine   *2 tablespoons granulated sugar*

PLACE the raisins in a large crockery or glass bowl and add the rum. Squeeze two of the oranges and the lemon and add the juice to the

(continued)

bowl. Peel the other orange and cut it into slices less than ½ inch thick and add to bowl. All the remaining fruit must be peeled and cut into cubes of less than ½ inch, discarding the cores. Grapes, strawberries, and cherries must be cleaned, but left whole. Sometimes the cherries are pitted, but not always. As the fruit is ready it is added to the bowl but not mixed. When all the fruit is used, add the wine and sprinkle the sugar all over. Cover the bowl and refrigerate for at least 1 hour before serving. Mix everything together when ready to be served.

CUSTARDS AND CREAMS

Crema

CUSTARD CREAM

SERVES 4

*C*rema is an independent dessert; it is not used to fill anything. Made in a double boiler, with the same technique as we will see in the pastry creams, it is not difficult if instructions are followed carefully. Watch for the change in color of the eggs, add the milk lukewarm, then place the mixture over the heat and absolutely do not let it boil.

Crema is a nice old-fashioned dessert that was eaten most at teatime at the turn of the century. When served with tea, it was put into cups rather than dessert bowls.

4 extra-large egg yolks
⅓ cup granulated sugar
1 cup lukewarm milk

Small piece of lemon or orange
peel or 2 or 3 drops of
vanilla extract

PUT water in the bottom part of a double boiler and set on the heat.

Place the egg yolks in a crockery or glass bowl and add the sugar. Stir with a wooden spoon, always in the same direction, until the sugar is completely incorporated and the egg yolks turn a lighter color. Add the lukewarm milk, mixing slowly and steadily, then transfer the contents of the bowl to the top part of the double boiler along with the lemon or orange peel or vanilla.

When the water in the bottom of the double boiler is boiling, put on the top part. Stir constantly with a wooden spoon, always in the same direction. Just at the moment before it boils, the cream should be thick enough to stick to the wooden spoon. That is the moment it is ready. *Absolutely do not allow it to boil.*

Immediately remove the top part of the double boiler, and continue to stir the contents for 2 or 3 minutes more. Remove the lemon or orange peel, if present, and transfer the *crema* to individual dessert bowls to cool.

Crema may be eaten at room temperature after 1 hour; it may also be eaten chilled. After it reaches room temperature, cover the bowls and refrigerate until needed.

NOTE: Crema retains optimum flavor for about 24 hours.

Crema pasticcera

PASTRY CREAM

MAKES ABOUT 1½ CUPS

*T*he techniques of pastry cream and the following chocolate pastry cream are similar to that of *crema* (see above). If the same care is taken in its preparation, it will not be difficult to make.

Crema pasticcera is used to fill cream puffs (see page 574) and *bomboloni* (see page 588) and as a layer on such pastries as *crostata di frutta* (see page 576).

4 extra-large egg yolks	**1 cup lukewarm milk**
3 tablespoons granulated sugar	**Small piece of lemon or orange**
2 tablespoons potato starch or	**peel or 2 drops of vanilla**
unbleached all-purpose	**extract**
flour	

PUT water in the bottom part of a double boiler and set on the heat.

Place the egg yolks in a crockery or glass bowl and add the sugar and potato starch or flour. Stir with wooden spoon, always in the same direction, until the sugar and starch are completely incorporated and the egg yolks turn a lighter color. Add the lukewarm milk slowly, mixing steadily, then transfer the contents of the bowl to the top part of the double boiler, along with the lemon or orange peel or vanilla.

When the water in the bottom part of the double boiler is boiling, insert the top part. Stir constantly with a wooden spoon, always in the same direction. Just at the moment before it boils, the cream should be thick enough to stick to the wooden spoon. That is the moment it is ready. *Absolutely do not allow it to boil.*

Immediately remove the top part of the double boiler from the heat, and continue to stir the contents for 2 or 3 minutes more, then remove the lemon or orange peel, if present, and transfer the *crema pasticcera* to a crockery bowl to cool (about 1 hour).

The *crema* may be used in other recipes after cooling for 1 hour, or may be prepared some hours in advance and kept, covered, in the refrigerator until needed.

Cioccolata pasticcera

CHOCOLATE PASTRY CREAM

MAKES ABOUT 2 CUPS

*C*hocolate pastry cream is exactly like pastry cream, except that the melted chocolate is added when the pastry-cream ingredients in the top of the double boiler have become warm.

Though chocolate cream and glaze are widely used in Italy, there is no such thing as chocolate cake. (Think of nearby Austria and Germany!) But for the Italians, chocolate would make the cake itself too heavy. They prefer to add the chocolate only as filling or decoration.

(Chocolate as a drink, hot, with whipped cream, is another matter. Florentines are mad about it and make some of the best hot chocolate there is.)

4 extra-large egg yolks
⅓ cup plus 1 tablespoon granulated sugar
1½ tablespoons potato starch or unbleached all-purpose flour

1 cup plus 2 tablespoons lukewarm milk
2 or 3 drops vanilla extract
2 tablespoons unsweetened cocoa powder

PUT water in the bottom part of a double boiler and set on the heat.

Place the egg yolks in a crockery or glass bowl and add the ⅓ cup sugar and the starch. Stir with a wooden spoon, always in the same direction, until the sugar is completely incorporated and the egg yolks turn a lighter color. Slowly add the 1 cup of lukewarm milk and drops of vanilla, mixing thoroughly.

In a small saucepan, dissolve the cocoa powder and the tablespoon of sugar with the 2 tablespoons of milk. Keep the saucepan near the heat but not on the flame.

Transfer the contents of the bowl to top of the double boiler.

When the water in the bottom part of the double boiler boils, put on the top part. Stir steadily with wooden spoon, without stopping, always in the same direction. When the ingredients in the top of the double boiler are warm, add the chocolate mixture. *(continued)*

CIOCCOLATA PASTICCERA *(continued)*

Just at the moment before boiling, the *cioccolata pasticcera* should be thick enough to stick to the wooden spoon. That is the moment it is ready. *Absolutely do not allow it to boil.* Immediately remove the top part of the double boiler from the heat, and continue to stir the contents for 2 or 3 minutes more.

Transfer the *cioccolata pasticcera* to a crockery bowl. After about 15 minutes, cover the bowl and allow the cream to cool for about 1 hour more before using.

Zabaione

ZABAGLIONE

MAKES ABOUT 1 CUP

*T*he technique of making *zabaione* is similar to that for pastry cream, except that it uses Marsala wine in place of milk.

Zabaione is used as a filling for sweets or as an accompaniment to fruit and pastry desserts. It is often mixed with whipped cream to make *crema zabaione* (see page 565), and in that form can also be eaten independently. Pure *zabaione* would be overly rich to eat by itself.

Marsala flavoring has come to replace almost all the sweet wines that were used for cooking in Italy: Malvasia (Malmsey), Greco, the old sweet Vernaccia, and so on. The fine dessert wines that still exist in Tuscany, Vin Santo and Aleatico, are only occasionally used in cooking. (They are perfect accompaniments to desserts not made with wine.)

3 extra-large egg yolks
3 tablespoons granulated sugar
½ cup dry Marsala

PUT water in the bottom of a double boiler and set on the heat.

Place the egg yolks in a crockery or glass bowl and add the sugar. Stir with a wooden spoon, always in the same direction, until sugar is completely incorporated and the egg yolks turn a lighter color. Add the

Marsala slowly, mixing steadily, then transfer the contents of the bowl to the top part of the double boiler.

When the water in the bottom part is boiling, insert the top part. Stir constantly with wooden spoon, always in the same direction. Just at the moment before boiling, *zabaione* should be thick enough to stick to the wooden spoon. That is the moment it is ready. *Absolutely do not allow it to boil.*

Immediately remove top part of the double boiler from the heat, stir the contents for 2 or 3 minutes more, then transfer the *zabaione* to a crockery bowl to cool (about 1 hour). It is ready to be used when called for.

Crema zabaione

WHIPPED CREAM WITH ZABAGLIONE

SERVES 6 TO ACCOMPANY FRUIT DESSERT

*C*rema zabaione is made by mixing whipped cream and *zabaione* to a homogenous texture.

It is used to accompany the stuffed peaches on page 629 and as an alternative to pastry cream for filling in *pasticcini ripieni* (see page 574) and with *bocca di dama* (see page 585).

It is also served as an independent dessert in small bowls.

Zabaione (see page 564)　　　**2 tablespoons granulated sugar**
2 cups heavy cream　　　**1 teaspoon confectioners' sugar**

MAKE the *zabaione*. When it has been transferred to the crockery bowl, cover it and let stand until completely cold (about 1 hour).

When the *zabaione* is cold, make *panna montata,* using the heavy cream and sugar, according to the directions on page 566. When the whipped cream is ready and very stiff, gently fold in the cold *zabaione.* Mix very carefully but thoroughly with a whisk.

Cover the bowl and place it in the refrigerator until needed.

Panna montata

WHIPPED CREAM, FLORENTINE STYLE

MAKES 2 TO 2½ CUPS

*T*he critical condition for making whipped cream is that all utensils and the cream itself must be cold. Also, the fresher the cream, the easier it usually is to whip. Indeed, if the cream is very fresh, it often whips easily without all of the precautions. A stainless steel bowl is preferred for beating cream. Prepare by placing the bowl and wire whisk in the refrigerator, then place the cold bowl in ice.

Whipped cream is used a great deal in Italy, especially in Florence. But it is usually the only "rich" ingredient in the dish. It is used to mix with fresh fruit or to fill an otherwise unadorned pastry. You will not find it used to "gild the lily" in an already rich dessert, such as one using *crema* (see page 560), or in *zuppa inglese* (see page 586). It is always part of the dish, not an adornment.

Italian whipped cream is sweetened a little with both granulated and confectioners' sugar.

1 cup heavy cream   *1 teaspoon confectioners' sugar*
2 tablespoons granulated sugar

PLACE the heavy cream, beating bowl, and wire whisk in refrigerator for a minimum of an hour.

Improvise a cold double boiler by placing a stainless steel bowl in a larger bowl of ice cubes. Pour the heavy cream into the chilled bowl and then, with the whisk, start whipping, with a continuous rotary motion from bottom to top. Continue to whip until cream is no longer liquid (about 1 minute). At this point, to avoid any danger of the heavy cream turning to butter, add 1 teaspoon of the granulated sugar. Then continue whipping until the cream is solid but soft (about 2 minutes for this amount).

When the cream is almost ready, sprinkle with the remaining granulated sugar and confectioners' sugar and mix gently.

NOTE: Whipped cream may be kept in the refrigerator, covered, for several hours.

Lattaiolo

OLD-FASHIONED CINNAMON CUSTARD

SERVES 6

*A*n older type of custard dessert, unfortunately disappearing even in its native land. Unlike *latte alla portoghese* (see page 568), it is not made with sugar, but is lightly sprinkled with confectioners' sugar before it is served. Its subtle flavor of cinnamon, nutmeg, and vanilla bean is well worth preserving.

Mixing milk and eggs with a little thickening and then baking it is the main procedure in custard-type dishes. Encased in a bottom crust, this procedure appears in the fourteenth-century Florentine *torta di latte* and is the basis for the category of dishes generally known by the French name "quiche." When sweetened and used without crust, custard is the basis of a number of well-known desserts.

5 cups milk
Pinch of salt
1 small piece lemon peel
1 piece vanilla bean (about 2 inches)
2 extra-large eggs plus 6 extra-large egg yolks

2 tablespoons unbleached all-purpose flour
Pinch of freshly grated nutmeg
½ teaspoon ground cinnamon
1 tablespoon cold butter to butter the mold
½ cup confectioners' sugar

PUT the milk in a saucepan, along with the salt, lemon peel, and the piece of vanilla bean, then set the saucepan over medium heat. When the mixture reaches the boiling point, simmer very slowly for 30 minutes. With a wooden spoon keep removing the skin that forms on top of the milk.

Remove the saucepan from the heat and let the milk cool for 1 hour.

Preheat the oven to 300 degrees.

Place the eggs and egg yolks in a crockery or glass bowl, then add the flour and mix very well. Add the nutmeg and cinnamon, and then, when the milk is cool, pour it into the bowl and mix thoroughly. Pass

(continued)

LATTAIOLO *(continued)*

the contents of the bowl through a piece of cheesecloth into another bowl. Prepare a water bath *(bagno maria)* by placing a few layers of paper towels or a dishtowel in a baking pan and adding enough lukewarm water to reach almost the level of the ingredients in the mold.

Butter a loaf pan (9 × 5 × 2¾ inches) and pour in contents of the bowl. Place the pan in the prepared baking pan and bake in the preheated oven for 1 hour, then remove from the oven and let cool for 1 hour.

Cover the loaf pan and place in refrigerator for at least 4 hours, then unmold the *lattaiolo* onto serving dish, sift the confectioners' sugar over the top, and serve.

Latte alla portoghese

CARAMEL CUSTARD

SERVES 6

*L*atte alla portoghese is the same as *crème caramel*. The name suggests an origin in the Iberian peninsula, and perhaps the flan is the original of all these dishes. As previously mentioned, however, the principle is already present in a fourteenth-century Florentine manuscript.

Sugar replaces the cinnamon and nutmeg flavoring of *lattaiolo* (see above); the dish is coated with caramelized sugar, the process for which is explained below.

5 cups cold milk
Pinch of salt
Small piece vanilla bean

1¼ cups granulated sugar
2 extra-large eggs plus 6 extra-large egg yolks

HEAT the cold milk in a saucepan, along with salt, the small piece of vanilla bean, and ¼ cup of the sugar. When the mixture reaches the boiling point, simmer very slowly for 30 minutes. With a wooden spoon, keep removing the skin that forms on top of the milk.

Remove the saucepan from the heat and let the milk cool for 1 hour.

Meanwhile, place ¾ cup of the sugar in a small saucepan, preferably of copper, and set over low heat until the sugar dissolves into a brown syrup. (Italians generally do not add water to the sugar when caramelizing it and usually melt the sugar in a copper pan, as here, not in the mold itself.) Immediately and completely, coat a 9 × 5 × 2¾-inch loaf pan with the caramelized sugar by pouring the syrup into the loaf pan and moving it around until the pan is completely lined. Let the loaf pan stand until cool (about 40 minutes).

Preheat the oven to 275 degrees.

Place the eggs, egg yolks, and the remaining ¼ cup of sugar in a large bowl. Stir continuously until eggs become lighter in color, then strain the milk through a piece of cheesecloth into the bowl. Mix very well with a wooden spoon and pour the mixture into the prepared loaf pan.

Place the loaf in the preheated oven and bake for 60 to 75 minutes, until firm, then remove the pan from the oven and let rest until cool (about 1 hour).

Cover the pan and place it in refrigerator for at least 4 hours, then unmold on a serving dish and slice, as a loaf, to serve.

NOTE: *Latte alla portoghese* can also be made in the oven in a *bagno maria* (bain-marie). Cooking time will be about 15 minutes longer.

PASTRY AND PASTRY DESSERTS

*J*t is impossible to speak about Italian pastry techniques without discussing the debt of French pastries to Italy. Almost all of the basic types of pastry listed in *Larousse Gastronomique* went to France from Italy.

Pasta Soffiata (Cream puff pastry/pâte à chou)

In 1533 Pantanelli, one of the Florentine cooks of the court of Caterina de' Medici, brought *pasta soffiata* to France. The name *"pâte à chou"* is supposed to be a corruption of *pâte à chaud,* using a hot technique as opposed to the cold technique of puff pastry. The technique is described on page 572.

Pasta Sfoglia (Puff pastry/pâte feuilletée)

Larousse has a long discussion, justly refuting the derivation of the name from the pastry cook Feuillet, and taking its history back long before his time. The history of "flaky" pastry without butter need not concern us here, but the early use of puff pastry with butter by the Dukes of Tuscany is well documented* and accepted by *Larousse*. Strangely, *Larousse* does not seem to realize, however, that the name *"pâte feuilletée"* is simply a translation of *"pasta sfoglia."* Its use seems to have become widespread in France under Henry IV, married to Maria de' Medici. (It is amusing to think that Henry of Navarre, leader of the Protestant cause, became King of France largely with the financial backing of his

---

*The fourteenth-century *torta frescha* used puff pastry.

in-laws, the Medici, even though two members of the family had recently been pope.)

Although puff pastry plays a big part in many Italian recipes, in "salted" antipasti, snacks, and desserts, I have made the reluctant decision not to include it in this book, since there is not space to deal with it properly.*

Pasta Frolla (Short pastry/pâte sucrée)

Again of Italian origin. There are a number of types of *pasta frolla*, but the basic ingredients are flour, shortening (butter, lard, or both), sugar, and eggs, flavored with lemon, orange, or vanilla. All four recipes that we use here (pages 576–583) are slightly different from one another, the variations being in the butter and/or lard, the flavoring, and the proportions of ingredients. The *pasta frolla* used in Genoa, without eggs, is not given here.

Bomboloni

Bomboloni pastry is fundamentally the same as brioche pastry, though *bomboloni* are deep-fried rather than baked. The recipe is included on page 588.

Bocca di Dama (Italian spongecake/pâte à biscuit Italien)

This light basic cake utilizes the Florentine technique of separating egg whites and yolks, and folding in the stiffly beaten whites. The recipe is given on page 585.

*Note: See my *Classic Techniques of Italian Cooking* pages 451–459. See also page 487 for Pasta Genovese *(genoise)*, another Italo-French pastry from Genoa.

Pasta soffiata

CREAM PUFF PASTRY

MAKES ABOUT 3½ CUPS

1½ cups cold water
Pinch of salt
1 heaping tablespoon
*   granulated sugar*
8 tablespoons (4 ounces) sweet
*   butter*

1¼ cups unbleached all-purpose
*   flour*
4 extra-large eggs

PUT the water and salt in a saucepan and set over low heat. Add the sugar, and when the water reaches the boiling point add the butter.

When the butter is completely dissolved, remove the pan from the heat and immediately add all the flour at once. Mix very well with a wooden spoon until all flour is well incorporated and the dough is smooth (about 10 minutes).

Place the pan back on the heat and cook for 7 or 8 minutes more, stirring constantly with wooden spoon.

Remove the pan from stove. Add one of the eggs to the dough, and working very fast, mix until completely absorbed. (If you do not work fast enough, the egg may cook and curdle.) Repeat the procedure with, one by one, the second, third, and fourth eggs.

When eggs are completely incorporated, the dough should be very smooth and completely detached from the bottom and sides of the pan. It is then ready to be used.

Bombe

DEEP-FRIED PASTRY "NUGGETS"

SERVES 6 TO 8

*L*ittle balls of *pasta soffiata* flavored with orange are deep-fried and then sprinkled with confectioners' sugar.

Pasta soffiata *(see page 572)*   *1 quart vegetable oil (see page*
Grated peel of 1 orange   *22)*
                                          ¾ cup confectioners' sugar

MAKE the *pasta soffiata.* Add the orange peel to the dough, mixing thoroughly.

Heat the vegetable oil in a deep-fat fryer; prepare a serving dish by lining it with paper towels.

When the oil is hot (about 375 degrees), make separate little *bombe* by dropping individual tablespoons of dough into the deep-fryer, each one well separated from the others. Leave enough room, because the *bombe* will swell up a lot.

Fry the *bombe* until golden all over, then remove with a strainer-skimmer and place on the prepared serving dish.

When all the *bombe* are on the serving dish, remove the paper towels and sprinkle the confectioners' sugar over them. Serve immediately.

Pasticcini ripieni (bignè)

CREAM PUFFS

MAKES ABOUT 24

*C*ream puffs filled with *crema zabaione* or whipped cream. The pastry is *pasta soffiata*.

A pastry syringe is necessary to form the pastry puffs. An illustration of the pastry syringe and the technique of making the puffs is shown below.

Pasta soffiata *(see page 572)*

Crema pasticcera *(see page 562),* **cioccolata pasticcera** *(see page 563),* **crema zabaione** *(see page 565),* or **panna montata** *(see page 566)*

MAKE the *pasta soffiata*.

Butter a cookie sheet; preheat the oven to 350 degrees.

Fill a pastry syringe with the *pasta soffiata* batter; do not put on a tip. Press down on the end of the syringe, making two circular move-

Pasticcini ripieni (bigne): Form the puffs using a pastry syringe.

ments and causing the exiting string of batter to form an outer ring (2 inches in diameter) connected to an inner one on the pastry sheet (see illustration opposite). Continue until all the batter is used up.

Place the cookie sheet in the preheated oven for about 30 minutes; do not open the oven for at least 15 minutes. Raise the heat to 375 degrees and bake 15 minutes more. Remove the cookie sheet from the oven and let the *pasticcini* cool (about 1 hour).

Meanwhile, prepare the filling you have chosen, following the appropriate recipe for procedure. (If you make *panna montata,* however, make it when the pastries are already cold.) Let the filling stand until cool.

Place the finest tip on your pastry syringe and fill it with the selected filling. Insert the syringe inside each *bignè* and fill it with about 2 teaspoons of the cream. Then, still using the syringe, place a little of the filling on top of the *bignè* (see illustration below). (Leave the glazed topping to the commercial pastry shops.)

Place all the *pasticcini ripieni* in a serving dish. If you do not plan to serve the pastries immediately, cover the serving dish and place it in the refrigerator.

With a pastry syringe, fill the puffs.

Crostata di frutta

FRUIT "SHORTCAKE"

SERVES 6

*P*asta frolla, baked and covered with a layer of pastry cream topped by an eye-catching arrangement of fresh fruit. The fruit —which can include half or sliced peaches or apricots, whole strawberries, raspberries, grapes—makes a color design in which you can use your own eye and imagination (see illustration opposite).

FOR THE PASTA FROLLA

8 tablespoons (4 ounces) sweet butter

4 tablespoons lard or additional sweet butter

3 cups unbleached all-purpose flour

½ cup granulated sugar

1 lemon or 1 thick-skinned orange

1 extra-large egg plus 2 extra-large egg yolks

Crema pasticcera (see page 562)

FOR THE FRESH FRUIT TOPPING

1½ pounds assorted fresh fruit such as peaches, apricots, strawberries, raspberries, grapes, blueberries, blackberries (but not apples or pears)

Juice of 1 lemon

2 tablespoons granulated sugar

FIRST make the *pasta frolla*.

Melt the butter and lard over a double boiler and let stand until cool (about 20 minutes).

Put the flour on a pasta board in a mound, then make a well in it. Place sugar in the well. Grate the lemon or orange skin into the well, then put in the egg, egg yolks, and melted butter and lard. Using a fork, quickly mix all ingredients in the well together with the flour.

Knead the dough for a very short time, just long enough to form a large ball, then wrap the *pasta frolla* in a cotton dishtowel and let rest in a cool place, or on the bottom shelf of the refrigerator, for 30 minutes.

576

Thoroughly butter a cookie sheet; preheat the oven to 375 degrees.

With a rolling pin, roll out the *pasta frolla* into a circle a little over 12 inches in diameter. If the pastry is very breakable, roll it out between two pieces of plastic wrap. Place the pastry on cookie sheet and cut all around with a pastry wheel to make a perfect circle 12 inches in diameter, by placing the bottom part of a springform pan over it. Bake in the preheated oven for about 30 minutes. Remove cookie sheet from the oven and let stand until cold (about 1 hour).

Meanwhile, make the *crema pasticcera.* Cover the pan and let stand until cool (about 40 minutes).

Rinse the fruit you have selected for the topping very carefully, removing possible pits and stems. If using large strawberries, cut them in half lengthwise; for large grapes, cut in half lengthwise and remove the seeds; for peaches or apricots, halve them, remove the pits, and then cut them in slices less than ¼ inch thick.

Sprinkle the lemon juice and sugar over the fruit and set aside until needed.

Transfer the pastry from the sheet to a large serving dish. Place the *crema pasticcera* on top and spread it out evenly with a long spatula, then arrange the fruit pieces in whatever design you like, and serve.

NOTE: Generally I arrange fruit in rings of contrasting colors and place a whole large strawberry or half a peach or apricot in the center. Some place a glaze over the fruit, but I dislike it because it detracts from the naturalness of the fruit.

A finished *Crostata di frutta,* with the fruit arranged in a design.

Crostata di ricotta

ITALIAN CHEESECAKE

SERVES 6

*T*his is close to what is known abroad as "Italian cheesecake." The crust of *pasta frolla* covers the bottom and sides. The ricotta is mixed with eggs and flavored with ground almonds held together with egg white, and with glacéed fruit and raisins soaked in rum. The filling is quite light, and the crisscross of pastry strips on top is attractive and traditional.

FOR THE CRUST

*1½ cups unbleached all-purpose
    flour*
⅓ cup granulated sugar
*6 tablespoons (3 ounces) sweet
    butter*

*1 extra-large egg plus 1 extra-
    large egg yolk*

FOR THE FILLING

2 ounces mixed glacéed fruit
*2 ounces raisins, about 5
    tablespoons*
½ cup white rum
*2 ounces blanched almonds,
    with 2 or 3 almonds
    unblanched*
3 extra-large eggs

15 ounces ricotta
Grated peel of 1 small lemon
Grated peel of 1 small orange
7 tablespoons granulated sugar
*3 tablespoons unbleached
    all-purpose flour*

MAKE the dough for the crust, using the ingredients in the proportions listed, according to the directions on page 576. While the dough is resting, make the filling.

Put the glacéed fruit, raisins, and rum in a small bowl and let soak 20 to 25 minutes. Meanwhile, grind all the almonds very fine with mortar and pestle or blender or food processor. Separate one of the eggs and add the egg white to the almonds, mixing thoroughly.

Drain the ricotta in a piece of cheesecloth, then place it in a large bowl, along with the eggs and the egg yolk, and mix very well with a wooden spoon. Add the orange and lemon peel to the ricotta mixture, then drain the glacéed fruit and raisins, discard the rum, and add the fruit mixture, along with the almond and egg white mixture and the sugar, to the bowl. Mix thoroughly.

When the mixture is homogenous, add the flour and keep stirring until it is uniformly incorporated. Set aside until needed.

Butter a 9-inch layer cake pan with a removable bottom; preheat the oven to 375 degrees.

With a rolling pin, roll the dough out to a sheet ⅜ inch thick. If the pastry is very breakable roll it out between two pieces of plastic wrap. Place the sheet of dough over the prepared layer cake pan and gently fit it to the shape of the pan, letting the excess dough hang over the sides.

Transfer the filling from the bowl to the dough-lined pan and distribute it evenly with a wooden spoon. Cut around the perimeter of the pan top to remove excess dough, and use the leftover dough to make ½-inch strips; place these crisscross on top.

Bake in the preheated oven for 40 minutes. Let the *crostata* cool for about ½ hour before removing it from the pan. The *crostata* may be eaten warm or cold.

Torta di ricotta

RICOTTA "TORTE"

SERVES 6

$\mathcal{A}$ nother Italian cheesecake, but flavored with anisette, topped with a layer of ground almonds, and then covered with meringue and baked a second time.

The pastry is again *pasta frolla.*

FOR THE CRUST

*1 ½ cups unbleached all-purpose
   flour*
⅓ cup granulated sugar
*6 tablespoons (3 ounces) sweet
   butter*
*1 extra-large egg plus 1 extra-
   large egg yolk*

Pinch of salt
1 drop vanilla extract
*Grated peel of 1 orange or
   lemon*

FOR THE FILLING

3 ounces glacéed mixed fruit
2 ounces glacéed cherries
1 cup lukewarm milk
15 ounces ricotta
4 extra-large egg yolks

*4 ounces semisweet chocolate,
   cut into pieces smaller than
   ½ inch*
⅔ cup granulated sugar
2 tablespoons anisette liqueur
3 ounces almonds, blanched

FOR THE MERINGUE

2 extra-large egg whites

2 tablespoons granulated sugar

MAKE the dough for the crust, using the ingredients in the proportions listed, according to the directions on page 576, adding salt and vanilla with the eggs. While the dough is resting, make the filling.

Soak the glacéed fruit in a bowl containing the lukewarm miilk for 20 minutes.

Meanwhile, drain the ricotta in a piece of cheesecloth and place it in a bowl, along with the egg yolks, chocolate, sugar, and anisette. Mix very well with a wooden spoon, then drain the glacéed fruit and add to the bowl. Combine thoroughly and let rest for 10 to 15 minutes in a cool place, or on the bottom shelf of the refrigerator.

Butter a 9-inch cake pan with removable bottom; preheat the oven to 375 degrees.

With a rolling pin, roll out a sheet of dough ⅜ inch thick. If the pastry is very breakable, roll it out between two pieces of plastic wrap. Place the sheet of dough over the prepared layer cake pan and gently fit it to the shape of the pan, letting the excess dough hang over the sides.

Transfer the filling from the bowl to the dough-lined pan and distribute it evenly with a wooden spoon. Cut around the perimeter of the pan top to remove excess dough, then bake in the preheated oven for 45 to 50 minutes. Let cool for 10 minutes.

Meanwhile, grind the almonds, then sprinkle them over the cooked ricotta layer.

Use a wire whisk and copper bowl to whip the 2 egg whites very stiff with the 2 tablespoons of sugar. Spread the egg whites over the *torta,* making sure you touch the crust all around, then replace the *torta* in the oven for 10 minutes more. Turn off the heat in the oven and let the *torta* remain inside for 10 minutes more, then remove from the oven and cool for about ½ hour before removing it from the pan. Remove and serve, or wait and serve cold.

Timballo di pere

SERVES 6

A combination of elegance and simplicity. Whole pears are poached in good dry red Italian wine and port and then placed in a pastry drum made of *pasta frolla*. Whipped cream is spooned into the spaces between the pears, and the pastry lid sits lightly on it like a little hat.

The whole ensemble, sitting on a large serving dish, is brought in. Each serving should consist of a whole, wine-colored pear with some sauce spooned over and some whipped cream on the side. The *timballo*, or pastry drum, is supposed to be for presentation. But the temptation is always too great, and everyone ends up by eating some of it. And why not? But the little game is always played first.

It is particularly important for presentation that the pears used have nice full stems. This is a dish for special occasions.

18 tablespoons (9 ounces) sweet butter
4 cups unbleached all-purpose flour
1 extra-large egg plus 4 extra-large egg yolks
1 cup plus 2 tablespoons granulated sugar

Pinch of salt
¼ cup dry white wine or dry Marsala, if necessary
Pere al vino (see page 632)
Panna montata (see page 566)

To make the pastry, melt butter in a double boiler and let cool for about 30 minutes.

Put the flour in a mound on a pasta board and make a well in it. Put the melted butter, egg, egg yolks, sugar, and salt into the well and mix well with a metal fork, then incorporate the adjacent flour until only 3 or 4 tablespoons of flour remain.

Knead for only about 1 minute, just enough to make dough into a ball, then place the dough in plastic wrap and let rest in a cool place or on the bottom shelf of the refrigerator for 2 hours.

This sweet dough for *timballo* is unpredictable. Sometimes after resting, especially when it is hot and dry, the dough becomes tough and impossible to roll properly. If so, after the dough has rested, add ¼ cup dry white wine or dry Marsala to make it elastic. Flour the dough again and knead for 1 minute more. Roll out the dough, make a lid, line the springform pan, and bake according to procedure on pages 237–241. If the pastry is very breakable, roll it out between two pieces of plastic wrap.

Prepare *pere al vino* according to the directions on page 632, up to the point where the sauce is refrigerated.

Open the springform pan and place the baked *timballo* on a serving dish. Remove the pears from refrigerator and place them in *timballo,* then sprinkle cold sauce over them.

Prepare the whipped cream, according to the directions on page 566, then spoon into the spaces between the pears.

Put the *timballo* lid in place for presentation and serve immediately.

Alkermes di Firenze

ALKERMES OF FLORENCE

*T*he red liqueur Alkermes is essential for a genuine *zuppa inglese.* Not only is its taste important to the dish, but also the particular red color, which contributes to the alternating yellow and red of the outer layer of *bocca di dama.*

Alkermes di Firenze (of Florence) was long a secret formula of the Medici family, and was also called the "Elixir of the Medici." (Maria de' Medici and her alchemist Ruggieri took it to France, where it was called "Liquore de' Medici").

(continued)

ALKERMES DI FIRENZE *(continued)*

Where pure grain alcohol is not sold freely as it is in Italy, substitute an 80 proof vodka, which is all but tasteless and gives just about the same result as pure grain alcohol. If you cannot obtain cochineal, there is an essence of Alkermes sold by Milan Laboratories on Spring Street in New York City, U.S.A., which can be ordered by mail.

12 grams cinnamon (about 2 tablespoons)

10 grams coriander seeds (about 2 scant tablespoons)

7 grams cochineal (about 1 heaping tablespoon)

3 grams mace (about ½ tablespoon)

2.5 grams cloves (about a scant ½ tablespoon)

5 grams dried orange peel (about 1 scant tablespoon)

3 grams aniseed (about ½ tablespoon)

10 pods cardamom

½ vanilla bean

3 cups unflavored 80 proof vodka

3½ cups cold water

1¾ pounds granulated sugar

½ cup rose water

PUT all the spices except the vanilla bean in a spice grinder or a mortar and grind them very well with the pestle; cut the vanilla bean into 4 or 5 pieces.

Place the ground spices and vanilla pieces in a 2-quart jar with a screw top. Add the vodka and 1½ cups of the cold water, then close the jar and let it stand for 1 week, shaking the jar once a day.

After a week, dissolve the sugar in the remaining 2 cups of cold water. Add the water with the dissolved sugar to the jar and let it rest for 1 more day, shaking the jar twice during this time.

Strain the contents of the jar through a coffee filter into a large bowl. Add the rose water to bowl, then transfer the contents to 2 bottles. Close the bottles and let them rest for 1 day more. Then the Alkermes is ready to use.

NOTE: Left in closed bottles, Alkermes will last indefinitely. Use it as needed.

Bocca di dama

ITALIAN SPONGECAKE

MAKES 1 TEN-INCH CAKE

*T*his is the basic Italian cake, which is never eaten as is but is used to make many other desserts. It is a light cake, flavored with a bit of lemon or orange rind. This cake, as a matter of fact, is never made in a heavier form in Italy. It would not be mixed with chocolate, ground nuts, or the other ingredients that make for the varieties of heavier cake with which we are familiar in other countries. It is not even really sweet enough to satisfy our idea of cake. As in *zuppa inglese,* which follows this recipe, the *bocca di dama* is adorned and made into a complete dessert.

In Italy, *bocca di dama* can often be bought commercially made and used to make the dessert. This, of course, produces a result inferior to that which comes from making your own fresh cake.

The French call it *"biscuit italien"* and use it in the same way as the Italians. Its "spongy" quality comes from separation of whites and yolks of egg, the whites then being beaten stiff and folded into the batter, causing the dough to rise a little when baked and to be very light and full of air. This is the same principle used to make the soufflé-type dishes, such as *budini* and *sformati.* The French adoption of *biscuits italiens* is proof that this technique went from Florence to France, and not vice versa.

6 extra-large eggs, separated
6 ounces granulated sugar
1½ cups unbleached all-purpose
    flour

Grated peel of 1 lemon or
    1 orange

PLACE the egg yolks in a large crockery bowl, along with the sugar, and stir continuously with wooden spoon for about 20 minutes, until the sugar is completely incorporated and the color of the egg yolks lightens. Pour in the flour, little by little, in a light shower, mixing continuously with the wooden spoon. Finally, add the lemon or orange peel.

(continued)

BOCCA DI DAMA *(continued)*

Butter a 10-inch tube pan; preheat the oven to 375 degrees.

Beat the egg whites until stiff, then fold them gently into the egg-yolk mixture.

Pour the contents of the bowl into the tube pan and bake in the preheated oven for 45 minutes; do not open the oven for 30 minutes after you put in the pan.

Remove the tube pan from the oven and let cool for 2 hours, then remove the *bocca di dama* from the pan and place on a serving dish. Use as needed.

Zuppa inglese

THE ORIGINAL ITALIAN RUM CAKE

SERVES 8

Zuppa inglese, meaning, literally, "English soup," is a dessert made with Italian spongecake, *bocca di dama,* and pastry cream and is the authentic original for the type of pastry sometimes called "Italian rum cake." However, though some rum is used in *zuppa inglese,* the critical ingredient is another liqueur called *Alkermes di Firenze.* The name of the dessert is sometimes said to derive from its supposed relation to the English trifle. This is incorrect. The name derives instead from the color of the Alkermes, which is the same red used in the British flag (and which, incidentally, is made from cochineal, a substance produced by an insect).

Because it has become very difficult to find Alkermes even in Italy nowadays, the true *zuppa inglese* is disappearing. Of Florentine origin, it was a favorite *dolce* all over Italy, copied in Bologna and Ferrara as well as the south. See the recipe for Alkermes on page 583, as it is not possible to buy it outside of Italy, and be sure to have it ready several days in advance of making the *zuppa inglese.*

Bocca di dama *(see page 585)*
8 *extra-large egg yolks*
¾ *cup granulated sugar*
4 *teaspoons potato starch or*
    unbleached all-purpose
    flour

2 *cups lukewarm milk*
2 *small pieces orange peel*
1½ *cups rum*
1 *cup Alkermes (see page 583)*
1 *tablespoon (½ ounce) sweet*
    butter

PREPARE the *bocca di dama,* then let cool for at least 3 hours. (It would be much better if the *bocca di dama* could be done one day in advance.)

Using the egg yolks, sugar, potato starch or flour, milk, and orange peel, make a *crema pasticcera* according to the directions on page 562. When it is done, transfer from the top part of the double boiler to a crockery or glass bowl. Cover and let cool for 30 minutes, then place the bowl in the refrigerator until completely cold.

Cut the *bocca di dama* into slices less than ½ inch thick and set out two large serving dishes; lay half of the slices flat on one serving dish and the other half on the second. Soak the *bocca di dama* slices on the first serving dish with 1 cup of the rum and those on the other with the Alkermes.

Butter a 9 × 5 × 2¾-inch loaf pan and place it in refrigerator for about 10 minutes; meanwhile, preheat the oven to 375 degrees.

Remove the loaf pan from the refrigerator and line it completely, bottom and sides, with soaked slices of *bocca di dama,* alternating rum slices with Alkermes slices. Make a thin layer of *crema pasticcera* over the cake lining the bottom of pan, then make another layer of cake slices and cover it with *crema pasticcera.* Repeat the procedure until the pan is completely filled; the top layer must be of cake slices.

Cover the top of the pan and place in preheated oven for 25 minutes. Remove from the oven and let cool for 30 minutes, then place in the refrigerator until completely cold (about 3 hours).

Remove the pan from the refrigerator and unmold the *zuppa inglese* onto a large serving dish. Pour the remaining ½ cup rum over and serve, slicing it like a loaf of bread.

Bomboloni

FLORENTINE CUSTARD DOUGHNUTS

MAKES ABOUT 14

*B*omboloni are made with a yeast dough, which is cut out in discs and filled with pastry cream and deep-fried rather than baked.

As a variant, *bomboloni* are sometimes filled with fruit preserves or a combination of pastry cream and preserves.

Crema pasticcera *(see page 562)*

FOR THE "SPONGE"

1 ounce (2 cakes) compressed fresh yeast or 2 packages active dry yeast

½ cup of lukewarm or hot milk, depending on the yeast

¾ cup unbleached all-purpose flour

Pinch of salt

FOR THE DOUGH

8 tablespoons (4 ounces) sweet butter

3 extra-large egg yolks

1½ tablespoons granulated sugar

½ cup warm milk

2¼ cups unbleached all-purpose flour

PLUS

1 quart vegetable oil (see page 22)

8 tablespoons lard

¾ cup granulated sugar

MAKE the pastry cream. Let stand until needed.

To make the "sponge," dissolve the yeast in ½ cup lukewarm or hot milk. Place the flour in bowl and make a small well in it, then put in the dissolved yeast and a pinch of salt. Keep mixing with wooden spoon until all the flour is incorporated, then cover the bowl with a cotton dishtowel and let stand in a warm place, out of drafts, until doubled in size (about 60 minutes).

Improvise an oversized double boiler by bringing a large quantity of water to boil in a stockpot and placing a large metal bowl over it. Put the butter into the metal bowl and let melt very slowly, then remove the bowl from the stockpot and let butter cool in the bowl (about 15 to 20 minutes). When the "sponge" is ready, and the butter is cool, start adding egg yolks, one at a time, into the butter with a wooden spoon.

Place the sponge in the bowl with the butter and eggs. Mix very well, with a rotary motion for 10 to 15 minutes, then add the sugar and warm milk, stirring continuously. When all the ingredients are well amalgamated, add 2 cups of the flour, a little at a time, stirring continuously.

When all the flour is incorporated, keep stirring for 10 minutes more, until the dough is completely detached from bowl, then cover with a cotton dishtowel and let stand in a warm place until doubled in size (about 1 to 1½ hours).

Sprinkle the remaining ½ cup of flour over a pasta board and place the dough on it. Roll out gently with rolling pin to make a sheet about ¼ inch high, then cut out 28 discs with a cookie cutter 2 inches in diameter.

Bomboloni: Forming the bomboloni.

BOMBOLONI *(continued)*

On each of 14 circles, place 1 heaping teaspoon of the *crema pastic-cera.* Moisten the edges of the discs with water, then cover with the other 14 circles. Press the edges to be sure they are sealed firmly.

Cover the *bomboloni* with a cotton dishtowel and let rest for about 1 hour, until doubled in size.

Heat the vegetable oil and lard in a deep-fryer; prepare a serving dish by lining it with paper towels. When the lard is melted and hot (about 375 degrees), carefully transfer 4 *bomboloni* to the deep-fryer with a spatula. Let fry for about 30 seconds on each side, turning them with a strainer-skimmer. (In that time, they should rise and become a golden color.) With the strainer-skimmer, transfer the fried *bomboloni* to the prepared serving dish.

Repeat the procedure until all are cooked, then remove the paper towels from the bottom of the serving dish, coat the *bomboloni* with the sugar, and serve hot.

NOTE: *Cioccolata pasticcera* (see page 563) or jam may be substituted for the pastry cream.

Tortelli dolci

DESSERT TORTELLI

SERVES 6

*L*ike *cenci* (see page 592), *tortelli dolci* are made with pasta dough and deep-fried. They are now eaten as a dessert, but centuries ago, before the distinction was made between "salted" and "sweet" dishes, many kinds of pasta, even lasagne, were eaten sweet, first with honey, later with sugar. Many so-called "sweet and sour" dishes are holdovers from that time.

These are real *tortelli,* filled with a ricotta sweetened and flavored with rum. They are flamed using rum, then lightly sprinkled with sugar.

FOR THE FILLING

1 ½ ounces raisins (about 4 tablespoons)

½ cup white rum

8 ounces ricotta, drained

2 extra-large egg yolks

1 ½ tablespoons granulated sugar

FOR THE PASTA

2 cups unbleached all-purpose flour

2 extra-large eggs

2 teaspoons olive or vegetable oil

Pinch of salt

PLUS

1 quart vegetable oil (see page 22)

½ cup granulated sugar

½ cup white rum

MAKE the filling first. In a small bowl, soak the raisins in the rum for 20 minutes.

Meanwhile, place the ricotta in a large bowl and add the egg yolks and sugar. Mix thoroughly with a wooden spoon, then drain the raisins and add to the ricotta and combine thoroughly.

Make fresh pasta, using the ingredients and the quantities listed, according to the directions on page 157, then form into *tortelli* as directed on page 194, using the stuffing you have just made.

Heat the vegetable oil in a deep-fat fryer; prepare a serving dish by lining it with paper towels.

When the oil is hot (about 375 degrees), put in the *tortelli,* a few at a time, and cook until golden on both sides (about 1 minute a side), then remove the *tortelli* with a strainer-skimmer and place them on the prepared serving dish to drain.

Repeat the procedure until all the *tortelli* are cooked and on the dish, then remove the paper towels from the bottom of the dish and sprinkle the *tortelli* with the ½ cup of sugar.

In small saucepan, warm the rum over very low heat for 30 seconds. Pour over the *tortelli,* immediately light with a match to flame, and serve.

Cenci

"RAGS," DEEP-FRIED PASTRY SNACKS

SERVES 6

*T*he dough for *cenci* is fundamentally like that for making pasta, except that it is flavored with rum. After resting an hour, the little squares of pasta are deep-fried and sprinkled with sugar. These little snack cookies are eaten widely.

3 cups unbleached all-purpose flour	*Pinch of salt*
	½ cup granulated sugar
2 extra-large eggs	*1 quart vegetable oil (see page 22)*
3 tablespoons olive oil	
2 tablespoons white rum	*½ cup confectioners' sugar*

PLACE the flour in a mound on a pasta board and make a well in it. Put the eggs, oil, rum, salt, and sugar in the well, then mix the ingredients in the well together with a fork, working outward little by little to absorb almost all the flour.

Knead the dough until very smooth (15 to 20 minutes), then cover with a cotton dishtowel for 1 hour.

With a rolling pin, roll the dough out to a sheet about ⅛ inch thick, then cut into rectangles, 1 inch wide and 2 inches long, with a pastry wheel.

Heat the vegetable oil in a deep-fryer; prepare a serving dish by lining it with paper towels.

When the oil is very hot (about 375 degrees), place the rectangles, a few at a time, in it to fry. When golden on both sides (about 1 minute), place them on the prepared serving dish to drain.

When all the *cenci* are cooked and placed on the dish, remove the paper towels and sprinkle confectioners' sugar over them generously. Serve hot.

Brigidini

*T*he traditional Florentine fairs are held in the great piazzas. Each piazza has its own fair once a year, called by such picturesque names as "fair of the jealous ones," "fair of those in love," "fair of the birds," and so on. The stands that are set up sell many things, among them always the wafers called *"brigidini,"* made with a *schiaccia,* a type of waffle iron. The villagers of a little place called Lamporecchio make the most celebrated *brigidini,* and they set up stands at every fair to sell them.

The *schiaccia* must be well seasoned with oil, and after use, oiled again and wiped clean with paper towels. It may be placed on an ordinary stove for cooking. Directions are also given for preparing *brigidini* without the *schiaccia.*

1 tablespoon aniseed	*2 extra-large eggs*
1 tablespoon olive oil	*10 tablespoons granulated*
2 cups unbleached all-purpose	*sugar*
flour	*Pinch of salt*

GRIND the aniseed coarsely with mortar and pestle, blender, or spice grinder. If the blender requires liquid, put in the olive oil now and be careful not to grind the aniseed too fine.

Place the flour in a mound on a pasta board and make a well in it, then place in it the eggs, sugar, salt, ground aniseed, and oil if not already used. Using a wooden spoon, mix all ingredients together with the flour until they are completely amalgamated.

Knead the dough for 2 or 3 minutes, then divide into balls of about ½ inch in diameter.

Place the *schiaccia* over the heat for 5 minutes. Then open the *schiaccia,* place one ball of dough in the center, and close tightly.

Place the *schiaccia,* with the piece of dough inside, on the heat and

(continued)

let stand for about 30 seconds on each side, then remove the *schiaccia* from the flame, open it, and remove the *brigidino*. Put the wafer into a bowl or serving dish.

Repeat the procedure for all the balls of dough.

If you don't have a *schiaccia,* roll out each ball of dough into a thin layer with rolling pin. Cut out the dough, using a cookie cutter of any desired shape. Oil a cookie sheet; preheat the oven to 375 degrees. Place the cookie shapes on the cookie sheet and place it in the preheated oven for about 15 minutes, until golden brown and crisp, then remove from oven and transfer the *brigidini* into bowl or serving dish. Let them cool for about 2 hours.

NOTE: If kept in a closed jar, *brigidini* may last as long as two weeks without losing any flavor.

Amaretti

BITTER ALMOND COOKIES

MAKES ABOUT 30

*A*lready packaged *amaretti* are widely available, imported from Italy. However, any packaged commercial product cannot be as authentic as the real thing, freshly made at home. Try to find bitter almonds (see page 26; you will probably have the best luck at a Hungarian store); a very small quantity goes a long way. And try these homemade *amaretti,* made almost totally from ground almonds, both sweet and bitter, and then you will know the difference.

10 ounces sweet almonds, blanched
1 ounce bitter almonds, blanched, or sweet almonds, unblanched

1½ cups granulated sugar
1 heaping tablespoon confectioners' sugar
5 extra-large egg whites

MIX the sweet and bitter or unblanched almonds together; preheat the oven to 375 degrees.

Place a cookie sheet containing all the almonds in preheated oven for 2 minutes, then remove from the oven and let cool for about 15 minutes.

Place the almonds, 1¼ cups granulated sugar, and confectioners' sugar in a mortar (or blender or food processor) and grind everything fine, then transfer to bowl. Add the egg whites to the bowl and mix very well with a wooden spoon until a homogenous paste results.

Lightly oil and flour a cookie sheet.

Fill a pastry bag with a round tip with the paste, and make ball, 1 inch in diameter, on the cookie sheet. Sprinkle a little of the remaining sugar on top of each ball and place the cookie sheet in the 375° oven for 20 minutes.

Remove the sheet from the oven and carefully detach the *amaretti.* Transfer the *amaretti* to a serving platter and let them cool completely (about 1 hour).

NOTE: *Amaretti* can keep for months in a closed jar. However, do not place them in the jar until they are completely cold.

Biscotti di Prato

LITTLE ALMOND COOKIES

SERVES 8 TO 10

*T*he favorite "cookie" of Tuscany, and very well known through-out Italy. It is an almond cookie, with the nuts both ground up in the dough and left in large pieces throughout. The best ones are made in the lively commercial town of Prato, ten miles from Florence. It was Prato's Datini who is reputed to have invented the invoice in the fourteenth century. His letters also reveal him to have been a great *buongustaio* (gourmand).

Biscotti di Prato are almost always served with one of the two sweet wines of Tuscany, Vin Santo or Aleatico. They are most often dipped into the wine. This combination may be dessert after a very rustic meal, but is most often served to guests who come in the afternoon or after dinner.

2 ounces almonds, blanched	*3 extra-large eggs*
6 ounces almonds, unblanched	*Pinch of salt*
4 cups unbleached all-purpose flour	*Pinch of ground saffron*
	Scant teaspoon baking soda
1¾ cups granulated sugar	*1 extra-large egg white*

PREHEAT the oven to 375 degrees.

Place both the blanched and unblanched almonds on a cookie sheet and toast in the preheated oven for 15 minutes, until lightly golden.

Grind 4 ounces of mixed blanched and unblanched toasted almonds very fine, then cut the remaining toasted almonds in two or three pieces.

Place the flour on a pasta board in a mound and make a well in the center. Put the sugar and eggs in the well. Mix together well, then add the salt, saffron, and baking soda. Mix thoroughly and when all the ingredients in the well are well integrated, incorporate the flour little by little, until all but about 2 tablespoons is incorporated. Set the leftover flour aside.

Knead the dough for 10 to 15 minutes, then add the very finely ground almonds and the almond pieces. Knead for 2 or 3 minutes more, incorporating the remaining flour.

Preheat the oven to 375 degrees.

Divide the dough into 8 pieces. With your hands, shape each piece into a long, thin roll about ¾ inch in diameter, then place, widely apart, on a buttered and floured cookie sheet. Beat the egg white slightly in a small bowl and lightly coat the tops of the 8 rolls with it, using a pastry brush, then put the baking sheet in the preheated oven for 18 to 20 minutes.

Remove the rolls from oven (they will have expanded in size sideways) and cut with a long slicing knife at a 45-degree angle every ¾ inch (see illustration below) to get the shape required for this type of little cookie, or *biscotto*. Place the *biscotti* back in the oven, this time at 275 degrees, for 35 to 45 minutes. They will be very dry.

Remove from the oven and let cool.

NOTE: These cookies are much better eaten after 2 or 3 days, when they have softened a little; keep them in a paper bag. If you wish to keep them indefinitely, transfer after a week to a jar or can.

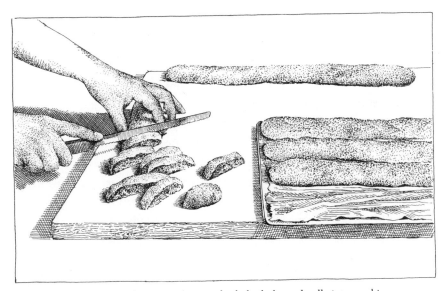

Biscotti di Prato: At a 45-degree angle, cut the baked almond rolls into cookies.

Meringhe alla panna

MERINGUES WITH WHIPPED CREAM

SERVES 6

*M*eringues appear in the fourteenth-century dish *pinocchiati,* in which they are baked, flavored with a few pignoli and an orange or lemon. The principle is almost certainly a Florentine discovery.

In this more modern dish, the baked meringues are filled with a light whipped cream. A versatile dessert, and easier to make than the finished product might seem.

3 very fresh extra-large egg whites, at room temperature	**1 cup heavy cream**
7 tablespoons granulated sugar	**3 tablespoons confectioners' sugar**

BEAT the egg whites in a copper bowl with a wire whisk until stiff. Add 5 tablespoons of the sugar and keep beating until very firm.

Butter and flour a baking sheet; preheat the oven to 375 degrees.

Place the whipped egg whites in a pastry bag. Squeeze at the top to form 12 to 14 individual half-balls, 2 inches in diameter, on the baking sheet. Sprinkle over 1 more tablespoon of sugar and let rest for 10 or 12 minutes. Place the baking sheet in the preheated oven for 4 or 5 minutes, then lower the oven heat to minimum and leave meringues in for 40 minutes more.

Remove the baking sheet from the oven and carefully detach the meringues with a spatula. Replace the baking sheet with the meringues detached in the oven at minimum heat or just the pilot light for about 15 minutes or more, until very crisp. Remove the meringues from the oven and let them cool (about 20 minutes).

Whip the cream with a whisk, in a chilled metal bowl, adding the remaining tablespoon of sugar and the confectioners' sugar.

When the meringues are cold, fit 2 half-balls together to make a ball. Put some whipped cream in the center between the halves, then place on a serving dish. Continue until all the meringues and whipped cream are used up, then serve.

Ricotta fritta

FRIED RICOTTA

SERVES 8

*R*icotta, sweetened and orange-flavored, formed into little balls held together with a few egg yolks and deep-fried. Unusual, imaginative, and very good. Not difficult to make if you are sure to squeeze out the excess water from the ricotta so the balls don't fall apart.

15 ounces ricotta

2 extra-large eggs plus 3 extra-large egg yolks

2 cups unbleached all-purpose flour, approximately

1 large orange, with thick skin

1 quart vegetable oil (see page 22)

1 cup granulated sugar, approximately

DRAIN ricotta very well in cheesecloth to remove all excess water. Place the drained ricotta in a bowl, along with the egg yolks and 3 tablespoons of the flour. Grate the orange peel into the bowl and mix all ingredients well with wooden spoon.

Spread the remaining flour on a large platter. On the floured platter, roll the ricotta into balls 1 inch in diameter. In rolling, lightly coat the balls with flour.

In a second bowl, beat the eggs with a pinch of salt; prepare a serving dish by lining it with paper towels.

Heat the vegetable oil in a deep-fat fryer. When it is hot (about 375 degrees), quickly dip the balls in the beaten eggs and then drop them into the fryer. Cook the balls until lightly golden all over (about 2 minutes), then remove from the fryer with a strainer-skimmer and place them on the prepared serving dish.

When all the balls are cooked and on the serving dish, remove the paper towels and sprinkle with the sugar. Serve hot.

Ritortelli pieni alla fiorentina

RENAISSANCE EGG CRESPELLE

MAKES 10

*C*respelle or *crespe* appear in Renaissance cookbooks in many forms. Some batters use more flour, others more eggs. Ths favorite type of the sixteenth century uses mainly eggs and is flavored with orange, like the later French crêpes Suzettes. Italians are not as fond of cooking with distilled liqueurs as the French, though in the period of this recipe no one was doing it yet. Instead the dried grapes are soaked in an orange sauce, which thickens naturally. After the *ritortelli* are stuffed, the orange sauce is put over them and they are briefly baked.

Crêpes have their counterpart in a number of countries. Whether the French ones did indeed come from the simple folk of Brittany or whether the French court imported them from Italy, we leave for you to ponder.

4 large sweet oranges
4 ounces raisins, about a scant
 ⅔ cup
¼ cup granulated sugar
1 scant teaspoon ground
 cinnamon

4 tablespoons (2 ounces) sweet
 butter
4 extra-large eggs
2 tablespoons milk
Pinch of salt
1 tablespoon unbleached all-
 purpose flour

SQUEEZE the oranges into a bowl. Add the raisins to the juice, along with the sugar and cinnamon, and let soak for 1 hour. Meanwhile, melt the butter in a double boiler and let cool for 20 minutes.

Place eggs, milk, and salt in a second bowl and beat well with fork. Mix in the flour slowly, being careful to prevent lumps from forming. Let rest for 10 to 15 minutes in a cool place.

Lay out several pieces of paper towels or wax paper; preheat the oven to 375 degrees.

When you are ready to make the *crespelle,* brush an omelet pan 8½ inches in diameter with melted butter and prepare to work quickly.

Place the pan over low heat. Put about 3 tablespoons of the batter in a ladle, and when the pan is hot, pour batter into the pan and very quickly swirl it around until the bottom of the pan is covered. As the batter sets, shake the pan vigorously to keep the bottom of the *crespella* detached from the pan. All this happens very quickly, and after 40 seconds it should be firm enough to turn. Shake the *crespella* over the edge of the pan so, with finger and thumb of both hands, you can quickly turn it over. Cook other side for only 5 seconds, then slip the *crespella* out onto the aluminum foil.

In a similar manner, make the remaining 9 *crespelle* and stack them on top of the first.

Butter a 13½ × 8¾-inch glass baking dish. Place one *crespella* on a plate. At one end put a tablespoon of the orange-raisin mixture, then roll the *crespella* up around the filling and put it in the baking dish. Repeat the procedure until all the *crespelle* are in baking dish.

Pour the remaining orange-raisin mixture over the *crespelle* and place the dish in the preheated oven for about 18 minutes. Remove the dish from the oven and serve immediately from the same dish.

Frittelle di tondone alla fiorentina

PANCAKE FRITTERS

SERVES 6

*U*nusual "fritters" made by first cooking a large pancake, and then making a batter by crushing the cooked pancake. The *frittelle* that result are light and fluffy on the inside and really very good.

6 ounces raisins, about 1 cup
1 ½ cups unbleached all-purpose
    flour
1 cup of cold water
Pinch of salt
2 tablespoons (1 ounce) sweet
    butter

Grated peel of 1 lemon
8 extra-large eggs
1 quart vegetable oil (see page
    22)
1 cup granulated sugar

SOAK the raisins in lukewarm water for 20 minutes.

Meanwhile, make a batter by placing the flour in a bowl and making a well in it. Pour in the cold water little by little, stirring constantly with a wooden spoon, then stir until the batter is smooth, without lumps. Add a pinch of salt.

Melt the butter in a 12½-inch omelet pan over medium heat. When the melted butter is hot, pour in the batter all at once. A high pancake will form; turn it over when still a very light color and cook other side only for 30 seconds.

Place the pancake *(tondone)* in a mortar, blender, or food processor and grind it up until it becomes a soft and homogeneous dough. Remove the dough and place it in a large bowl.

Sprinkle the lemon peel over the dough in the bowl, then add 3 of the eggs and mix them in very well with a wooden spoon, until they are completely incorporated. Drain the raisins and dry them with paper towels. Add them to the bowl and mix them into the dough, then let the dough rest for 15 to 20 minutes.

Separate the remaining 5 eggs. Place the egg yolks over the dough and put the egg whites in a copper bowl and beat them stiff with a wire whisk. With a wooden spoon, incorporate the egg yolks very carefully into the dough; then, very gently, fold in the egg whites.

Heat the vegetable oil in a deep-fat fryer; prepare a serving dish by lining it with paper towels to absorb excess grease. When the oil is hot (about 375 degrees), make separate little *frittelle* by placing a tablespoon at a time of dough in the pan, each one well separated from the others. Cook the *frittelle* until golden on both sides, then remove to the prepared serving dish to drain.

When all *frittelle* are cooked and transferred to the serving dish, remove the paper towels. Sprinkle the *frittelle* with sugar and serve hot.

BREAD AND CAKE DESSERTS

Buccellato alle fragole

BUCCELLATO WITH STRAWBERRIES

SERVES 8 TO 10

*T*his recipe is not simply a way of using leftover *buccellato* in Lucca. It is such an important dessert in that town that often the *buccellato* is made just in order to make this dessert. Try it, the combination is preordained.

A different fruit would never be substituted, since strawberries are the one that blends ideally—an aspect of the Tuscan point of view that is perhaps the most difficult for foreigners to understand.

Buccellato *(see page 48)*
1½ pounds fresh strawberries
6 heaping tablespoons
   granulated sugar

5 cups dry red wine

(continued)

MAKE the *buccellato*. When it is ready and cold (and it is better made a day in advance), cut it into ¼-inch slices. Let the slices stand until needed.

Carefully clean the strawberries, then place them in a large bowl, along with the sugar. Mash the strawberries with a fork, amalgamating them with the sugar, then add the wine to strawberry-sugar mixture and combine thoroughly. Place the bowl in the refrigerator and let stand for 2 hours.

Make a layer of *buccellato* slices on the bottom of a large tureen, then pour over some of the strawberry mixture. Alternate layers of *buccellato* slices and strawberries until the last slice of *buccellato* is used; the top layer should be of strawberries.

Cover the tureen and allow to stand for a minimum of 2 hours in a cool place or on the bottom shelf of the refrigerator. Serve carefully with a spatula, keeping slices whole.

Schiacciata con zibibbo

SCHIACCIATA WITH RAISINS

SERVES 6 TO 8

*T*his is a winter version of the *schiacciata* made with the fresh grapes of the Chianti harvest. In season, use wine grapes.* The large Muscat raisins are close enough to the *zibibbo,* the raisin made from a type of large grape in Italy, to successfully reproduce this winter version.

It is also like a distant dessert relative of *pan di ramerino* (see page 46), because of the olive oil and rosemary.

6 ounces large seedless raisins, about 1 cup

1 ounce (2 cakes) compressed fresh yeast or 2 packages active dry yeast

*See note: *Foods of Italy,* page 230.

¾ cup lukewarm or hot water,
  depending on the yeast
3½ cups unbleached all-purpose
  flour
½ cup olive oil
4 tablespoons (2 ounces) lard or
  sweet butter

2 tablespoons rosemary leaves,
  fresh or preserved in salt or
  dried and blanched
⅔ cup granulated sugar
1 extra-large egg

SOAK the raisins in lukewarm water for 20 minutes. Meanwhile, dissolve the yeast in the ¾ cup lukewarm or hot water.

Place the flour in a large bowl and make a well in it. Pour the dissolved yeast into the well and mix with a wooden spoon until about one-third of the flour is incorporated into the yeast mixture. Cover the bowl with a cotton dishtowel and let stand until the "sponge" has doubled in size (about 1 hour).

Meanwhile, drain the raisins and pat them dry with paper towels. Place the olive oil and lard in a saucepan, along with the rosemary leaves, and sauté very gently for 5 minutes, then remove the pan from the heat and let cool for 10 minutes.

When the sponge is doubled in size, pour half the contents of the saucepan, still lukewarm, over the sponge; then add ⅓ cup of the sugar, the egg, and all of the raisins. Stir everything into the sponge with a wooden spoon, then incorporate all the flour but 2 or 3 tablespoons.

Transfer the dough to a pasta board and knead until the remaining flour is incorporated and the dough is smooth (about 15 minutes).

Oil a jelly-roll pan. Place the dough on pan and spread it out with your fingers to cover the surface. Pour the remaining contents of the saucepan over dough and sprinkle with the remaining sugar.

Cover the pan with plastic wrap and let rest until the dough has doubled in size (about 1½ hours).

Preheat the oven to 400 degrees.

When the dough has risen, bake in the preheated oven for 35 or 40 minutes, until the top is golden.

Remove from oven and serve, hot or cold, from the same jelly-roll pan.

Schiacciata unta di Berlingaccio

SWEET CARNIVAL SCHIACCIATA

SERVES 6

*L*ow like a *schiacciata,* this dessert pastry has shortening (lard) and is flavored with orange, vanilla, nutmeg, and saffron. It is this last, combined with the lard, that gives it its antique flavor. A dessert for the Carnival season, it takes the name of one of the Commedia dell'Arte masks, *Berlingaccio.* It is also eaten at the big parties given on Thursday of Easter week.

1 ounce (2 cakes) compressed fresh yeast or 2 packages active dry yeast	*1 large, thick-skinned orange*
	½ teaspoon ground saffron
	2 or 3 drops vanilla extract
1 cup lukewarm or hot water, depending on the yeast	*Pinch of freshly grated nutmeg*
	2 extra-large eggs
2 cups plus 5 tablespoons unbleached all-purpose flour	*⅔ cup granulated sugar*
	6 tablespoons (3 ounces) lard or sweet butter
Pinch of salt	

PLUS

¼ cup confectioners' sugar

IN a small bowl, dissolve the yeast in the lukewarm or hot water. Put the 2 cups of flour in a large bowl. Make a well in the center and put in the dissolved yeast, along with a pinch of salt. Stir the yeast mixture with a wooden spoon, gradually incorporating half of the surrounding flour.

Cover the bowl with a cotton dishtowel and let rest in a warm place, until the "sponge" is doubled in size (about 1 hour). While the sponge is rising, grate the orange peel into another small bowl. Add the saffron, vanilla, nutmeg, eggs, and sugar and mix very well with a wooden spoon.

Melt all but 1 tablespoon of the lard in a double boiler, then remove from the heat and let stand for 10 to 12 minutes, until lukewarm.

When the sponge has risen, add the orange-peel-saffron mixture to it and stir with a wooden spoon until well amalgamated. Add the lukewarm lard and keep stirring, using a motion pushing up from the bottom rather than a rotary one. Incorporate all the flour remaining in the bowl.

Add the 5 tablespoons of additional flour, one by one, incorporating each before adding the next. Continue to mix, using the motion described above, for 10 minutes more. The "dough" will have the consistency of a very thick batter.

Grease a jelly-roll pan with remaining tablespoon of lard. Pour the thick batter into the pan, cover with plastic wrap and let rise until almost doubled in size (about 1 hour).

Preheat the oven to 400 degrees.

When the dough has risen, place the pan in preheated oven for 35 to 40 minutes, then remove from the oven and allow to cool. Sprinkle with confectioners' sugar and serve.

Pane co' Santi

MAKES 1 LOAF

*T*he sweet version of the nut bread. See the discussion of bread for All Saints' Day on page 50.

FOR THE "SPONGE"

2 ounces (4 cakes) compressed fresh yeast or 4 packages active dry yeast

1 cup lukewarm or hot water, depending on the yeast

1 1/2 cups unbleached all-purpose flour

FOR THE DOUGH

4 ounces raisins, about a scant 2/3 cup

4 ounces shelled, blanched walnuts

1 cup olive oil

2 tablespoons (1 ounce) lard or sweet butter

2 ounces blanched almonds

6 cups unbleached all-purpose flour

Pinch of salt

1/2 cup granulated sugar

Grated peel of 1 lemon

Grated peel of 1/2 orange

1 teaspoon aniseed

1 teaspoon freshly ground black pepper

3/4 cup lukewarm water

To make the "sponge," dissolve the yeast in the lukewarm or hot water. Place the flour in a bowl and make a well in center. Pour in the thoroughly dissolved yeast and stir very well with a wooden spoon to incorporate all the flour. Cover the bowl with a cotton dishtowel and place it in a warm place, away from drafts. Let the "sponge" rise until doubled in size (almost 1 hour). Meanwhile, soak the raisins in lukewarm water for 20 minutes; chop the blanched walnuts coarsely.

Heat the olive oil and lard in a saucepan, over low heat. Add the chopped walnuts and sauté very gently, then remove the pan from the heat and add the soaked, drained raisins. Allow to cool for 10 minutes.

While the walnut-raisin mixture is cooling, chop the blanched almonds coarsely.

When the "sponge" is ready, place the 6 cups of flour on a pasta board. Make a well in the center and place the sponge in it. To the sponge, add the lukewarm walnut-raisin mixture and stir carefully with a wooden spoon, in order to integrate the sponge and olive oil. Then mix into the sponge one by one: a pinch of salt, the sugar, grated lemon and orange peel, aniseed, coarsely chopped almonds, and pepper. Add the ¾ cup lukewarm water and incorporate it with the other ingredients in the well.

Start kneading, little by little absorbing the flour. After almost all the flour is absorbed, keep kneading until the dough is elastic and smooth (about 15 to 20 minutes). Place dough on a buttered and floured baking sheet. Cover the dough with a cotton dishtowel and move the baking sheet and dough to a warm place, without drafts, to rise.

Preheat the oven to 400 degrees.

When the dough has doubled in size (1 to 2 hours), place it in the preheated oven for 50 to 55 minutes.

Remove from the oven and allow to cool for about 2 hours before eating.

Torta di mele

APPLE CAKE

SERVES 6

*A*n apple cake, with half of the apples incorporated into the dough and the other half thinly sliced and arranged on top, a cake for family occasions, not very difficult to make. (A more complicated version, with pastry, called *crostata di mele* is served on more formal occasions.)

Generally in Italy, Delicious- and Golden Delicious–type apples are used.

½ cup raisins
4 tablespoons (2 ounces) lard or
 sweet butter
5 medium Delicious apples
Juice of ½ lemon
1½ cups unbleached all-purpose
 flour

1 ounce (2 cakes) compressed
 fresh yeast or 2 packages
 active dry yeast
¼ cup lukewarm or hot water,
 depending on the yeast
⅔ cup granulated sugar
Grated rind of 1 lemon
2 extra-large eggs

SOAK raisins in lukewarm water for 20 minutes; melt the lard in a double boiler and let cool.

Cut the apples in quarters and remove the cores and skin, then cut them into thin slices. Place the apple slices in a bowl and sprinkle the lemon juice over them.

Place 1 cup of the flour in a bowl and make a well in it. Dissolve the yeast in the ¼ cup of lukewarm or hot water and pour it into the well; stir with a wooden spoon. Add the sugar, melted lard, grated lemon peel, and eggs, and when these ingredients are all well incorporated, sprinkle the remaining ½ cup of flour over. Stir very well until dough is homogeneous and very soft, then add the soaked raisins and half of the apple slices to the dough, incorporating them well.

Oil a cake mold or 12-inch springform pan. Place the dough in the mold and arrange the remaining apple slices on top. Cover with a cotton

DESSERTS

dishtowel and leave to rise until the dough is almost doubled in size.
Preheat the oven to 400 degrees.
When the dough has risen, place the mold in the preheated oven
for 35 to 40 minutes, until the top is golden brown. Let cool for 30
minutes, then unmold and serve.

Dolce di polenta

CORN-MEAL CAKE

SERVES 6

A sweet cake of corn meal, lightly flavored with saffron and white
wine, the outside covered with confectioners' sugar. It has the
shape of a long, serrated jelly mold. Appropriate for the cooler season.

*8 tablespoons (4 ounces) sweet
 butter
1 cup unbleached all-purpose
 flour
¾ cup coarse Italian yellow
 corn meal
½ cup granulated sugar*

*1 extra-large egg yolk
Pinch of ground saffron
1 cup dry white wine
½ cup unseasoned bread
 crumbs, preferably
 homemade (see page 58)
½ cup confectioners' sugar*

MELT 6 tablespoons of the butter in a double boiler and let cool for 15
minutes.
Mix the flour and corn meal in a bowl with a wooden spoon. Make
a well in the center, then place the sugar and melted butter in it and
stir very well, incorporating the sugar into the butter but not the flour
mixture. Add the egg yolk and saffron to the sugar and butter, then
begin incorporating the flour mixture little by little, at the same time
adding the wine, a little at a time.
When all the ingredients are well combined, stir for 10 minutes
more in order to have a very soft dough.

(continued)

DOLCE DI POLENTA (continued)

Coat a serrated 4 × 7 × 2½-inch jelly mold with the remaining butter and the bread crumbs; preheat the oven to 375 degrees. Pour the dough mixture in the prepared mold and bake in the preheated oven for about 1 hour 20 minutes. (If the top of the cake appears to be browning too quickly, place a piece of aluminum foil over the top.) Remove from the oven, let rest for 10 minutes, then unmold on a serving dish.

Let the cake rest until completely cold, sprinkle the confectioners' sugar over it, and serve.

NOTE: This cake is even better eaten the following day.

CHESTNUT AND CHESTNUT-FLOUR DESSERTS

*I*taly is a great land for chestnuts. Indeed, many of the chestnuts we find outside of Italy are imported from there. Even the particular excellence of the wild mushrooms found in Tuscany comes from their growing under chestnut trees. The mountainous area known as the Garfagnana uses the flour of chestnuts for many dishes, including those which would ordinarily use polenta or other flours. Naturally, many chestnut and chestnut-flour desserts come from Tuscany and the Garfagnana.

The fall is the best period for chestnuts, and that is when they are exported from Italy. The shipment of chestnut flour arrives in the Italian markets a little before the Christmas holidays. There is usually only one shipment a year, so it is best to buy enough for the entire winter and spring. The flour keeps until the summer.

The desserts made from chestnuts or chestnut flour *(farina dolce)* are hearty ones, and are most appropriate to cooler weather.

Following are recipes for flamed roasted chestnuts, chestnut "truffles," a low cake of chestnut flour, and *crespelle,* or crêpes, of chestnut flour.

NOTE: Be sure to obtain Italian flour, made from fresh chestnuts.

Some countries, such as Hungary, make flour from dried chestnuts, and the result is very different. To keep fresh, store the flour in the freezer for up to 6 months.

Bruciate ubriache

BURNED, DRUNKEN CHESTNUTS

SERVES 4

ruciate ubriache, "burned, drunken chestnuts," describes the dish with Tuscan humor. The chestnuts are roasted in a special pan, then peeled and flamed with sugar and rum. They could be served as dessert for a hearty dinner, either simple or elegant. They would go well after a good roast.

1 pound large fresh Italian chestnuts (**marroni**)

¼ cup granulated sugar
½ cup light rum

MAKE a small cut, lengthwise, on each individual chestnut, then place them in a perforated pan. Set the pan over low heat, and shaking the pan frequently by the handle, roast the chestnuts. This will take about 40 minutes; the chestnuts should be soft inside and the outside shell lightly burned all over.

Remove the shells from chestnuts and place them in an ovenproof serving dish. Add the sugar to the chestnuts and mix together. (If you do not use them immediately, cover the chestnuts with a cotton dish-towel and a woolen cloth—in Italy, a piece of bedspread is used—to keep the chestnuts warm. This will prevent them from drying out.)

At the moment you are ready to serve the *bruciate,* warm rum for 30 seconds over low heat. Remove the cover from the chestnuts and bring the serving dish to the table.

Pour the rum over the chestnuts and flame it. While the rum is burning, stir the chestnuts so that all the sugar is flamed, and as soon as the flame burns out, serve immediately.

Tartufi di castagne

CHESTNUT "TRUFFLES"

SERVES 12

*A*dessert of much fantasy, useful also for a dinner of some elegance. The chestnuts are cooked and then made into a shape resembling a truffle. When rolled in chocolate powder, the resemblance is intensified. These may also be eaten as a snack.

Coarse-grained salt
2 pounds large fresh Italian
    chestnuts (**marroni**)
5 tablespoons light rum
2 tablespoons plus 1 cup
    unsweetened cocoa powder

¼ cup granulated sugar
2 tablespoons confectioners'
    sugar
4 tablespoons (2 ounces) sweet
    butter
½ cup cold milk, approximately

PLACE a stockpot three-quarters full of cold water on the heat. When the water is boiling, add coarse salt to taste, then the unshelled chestnuts, and let boil for about 1½ hours, or until soft.

Remove the pot from the heat. Take the chestnuts out of the hot water, a few at a time, and peel them, making sure you remove both shell and inner skin.

When all the chestnuts are shelled, pass them through the ricer (or mash them in a blender or food processor) and transfer to a crockery bowl. Add the rum, 2 tablespoons cocoa powder, granulated sugar, and confectioners' sugar and mix very well.

Melt the butter in a double boiler and add it, hot, to the mashed chestnuts. Mix very well until all the ingredients are well incorporated. The consistency should be firm, but smooth. If not smooth enough, add some cold milk—the quantity necessary may vary from 2 tablespoons to ½ cup—and mix very well.

Spread the remaining cup of cocoa powder in a thin layer on a piece of wax paper. Take 1 tablespoon at a time of mashed chestnuts and roll it into a ball on the cocoa powder. The outer coating of cocoa powder and the shape will suggest the form of a truffle.

Place "truffles" in serving dish and let rest for 1 hour before serving.

Castagnaccio o Migliaccio

FLAT CHESTNUT CAKE

SERVES 6

A low cake made of chestnut flour, this most typical Florentine sweet is found in the earliest cookbooks, those of the fourteenth century. Flavored with olive oil, rosemary, raisins, and nuts, it makes a perfect hearty snack or the ending to a rustic meal. To this day it is one of the most widely appreciated Florentine specialties. Until recently, *castagnaccio* slices were sold on street corners, from a large copper pan.

3 tablespoons raisins
½ cup lukewarm milk
2 cups plus 2 tablespoons
 Italian chestnut flour
1 tablespoon granulated sugar
Pinch of salt
2 tablespoons pignoli (pine
 nuts) or walnuts

2 cups cold milk
3 tablespoons olive oil
1 tablespoon rosemary leaves,
 fresh or preserved in salt or
 dried and blanched

IN small bowl, soak the raisins in the lukewarm milk for 20 minutes. Sift all but 1 tablespoon of the chestnut flour into a large bowl. Add the sugar, a pinch of salt, and the pignoli or walnuts. (If you use walnuts, cut them into pieces.) Mix very well with a wooden spoon, then add the 2 cups of cold milk little by little, stirring constantly and being careful to avoid lumps.

Drain the raisins and flour them with the remaining tablespoon chestnut flour. Add the raisins to bowl, along with 1 tablespoon of the olive oil, and mix very well until smooth.

Oil a round baking pan, preferably tin-lined copper, 9½ inches in diameter and 3 inches high, with the entire second tablespoon of olive oil (do not remove the excess oil from the pan); preheat the oven to 400 degrees.

Pour the contents of the bowl into the prepared pan and sprinkle

(continued)

CASTAGNACCIO O MIGLIACCIO *(continued)*

the remaining tablespoon of olive oil and the rosemary leaves over. Place the pan in the preheated oven for 40 to 50 minutes. (If you are not using a copper pan, the cooking time will be about 10 minutes less.)

Remove the cake from the oven and let rest for 15 to 20 minutes before serving. Serve from the same pan, sliced in the manner of a pie.

NOTE: *Castagnaccio* can also be eaten cold, but do not keep it in the refrigerator.

Recipe from an early fourteenth-century Florentine manuscript, for *crespelle* or *crespe* (crêpes). There were many kinds of early Florentine crêpes. Included in this book are recipes for *crespelle* of chestnut flour and egg *crespe* flavored with orange, called *ritortelli alla fiorentina*.

Crespelle di farina dolce

CHESTNUT-FLOUR CRÊPES

MAKES 18

*C*respelle, or crêpes, made from chestnut flour are very good indeed, and may be served filled with a ricotta-rum filling or, for extra lightness, with just whipped cream (see note below).

4 ounces raisins, about a scant
    ²/₃ cup
¹/₂ cup light rum
2 cups plus 1 tablespoon Italian
    chestnut flour
2 extra-large eggs plus 1 extra-
    large egg yolk
Pinch of salt

2¹/₂ cups cold milk
15 ounces ricotta, drained
4 ounces bittersweet chocolate,
    coarsely chopped
3 tablespoons granulated sugar
4 tablespoons (2 ounces) sweet
    butter

IN a small bowl, soak the raisins in the rum for about 30 minutes.

Meanwhile, sift the flour into a bowl and make a well in it. Place the eggs and egg yolk in the well and start mixing with a wooden spoon very slowly, incorporating a little bit of flour. (Be sure that no lumps form, because it is very difficult to remove them afterward.) Add a pinch of salt and then, still mixing continuously, add the cold milk, little by little, until all the milk and flour are incorporated.

Let the batter stand for 30 minutes in a cool place or on the bottom shelf of the refrigerator.

Place the ricotta in a large bowl and add the chocolate and sugar. Mix very well with a wooden spoon until thoroughly combined, then drain the raisins and add them to the ricotta mixture. Mix gently until the raisins are well distributed.

Cover the bowl and place it in the refrigerator until needed.

Melt the butter in a double boiler, then remove from the heat.

Using the batter and the melted butter, make the *crespelle,* according to the directions on page 601. Place the *crespelle* stacked one on top of the other, with paper towels between them, to cool. (You can prepare

(continued)

crespelle even one day in advance, keeping them in the refrigerator.) After cooling, they should be wrapped completely with wax paper or parchment paper.

Butter 2 13½ × 8¾-inch glass baking dishes; preheat the oven to 375 degrees.

Place 2 tablespoons of the ricotta mixture on each *crespella,* then roll it up and place it in one of the baking dishes with the seam side up. Repeat the procedure with all the *crespelle.*

Place the baking dishes in the preheated oven for about 10 minutes, then remove and serve immediately.

NOTE: You can substitute a whipped-cream and coarsely chopped chocolate filling for the ricotta mixture. In this case, do not place the *crespelle* in oven.

Using 2 cups heavy cream, ¼ cup granulated sugar, and 2 teaspoons confectioners' sugar, make *panna montata* as described on page 566, then mix 4 ounces coarsely chopped bittersweet chocolate throughout the whipped cream. Place 2 heaping tablespoons of the whipped cream mixture on each *crespella* and roll it up. Do not heat, but place the filled *crespelle* on a serving dish and serve.

RICE DESSERTS

*W*e include two simpler, but extremely characteristic rice desserts, *frittelle,* or rice fritters, and *budini,* or little rice cakes. The large rice custard cake is appropriate for an elaborate dinner and the *ciambella,* the large rice ring stuffed with fruit and covered with a fruit-wine sauce, is even more so. Among the soufflé-type dishes, you will also find a type of rice soufflé, the *budino di riso* (see page 619).

Budini di riso

MAKES 16 TO 18

*L*ittle baked rice cakes, eaten mainly for breakfast or the eleven o'clock morning coffee break. In the cafés, they are delivered still warm, as that is the best way to eat them. At home, they would go very well for a brunch or ambitious breakfast, made shortly in advance so that they remain warm but not hot. Florentines I know who are resident abroad miss most, along with Brunelleschi's dome of the Cathedral and the many bells of Florence, the *budini di riso.*

When in Florence, have a *cappuccino* with *budini* at a café in the central Piazza della Repubblica.

3 cups whole milk
¾ cup raw rice, preferably Italian Arborio
Pinch of salt
½ cup granulated sugar
4 tablespoons (2 ounces) sweet butter
½ cup mixed glacéed fruit

1 thick-skinned orange or 1 lemon
2 extra-large eggs, separated
2 tablespoons light rum
1 cup unseasoned bread crumbs, preferably homemade
½ cup confectioners' sugar

HEAT the milk to the boiling point in a flameproof casserole. Add the rice and salt and stir with a wooden spoon until the milk reaches boiling point again. Simmer for about 10 minutes, stirring every so often, then add the sugar and butter and let simmer until the rice is almost cooked (about 7 or 8 minutes more). Add the glacéed fruit and simmer for 1 minute longer, stirring with a wooden spoon.

Remove the casserole from the heat and transfer the rice to a bowl with a strainer-skimmer. Allow the rice to cool for 1 hour. When the rice is cool, grate the orange or lemon peel into the bowl. Add the egg yolks and rum and mix very well.

Butter a 12-muffin pan (10 × 7½ inches) and coat it with the bread crumbs; preheat the oven to 375 degrees.

(continued)

Use a wire whisk and copper bowl to beat egg whites until stiff, then gently fold them into the rice mixture. Place a heaping tablespoon of mixture in each cup of the muffin pan, then place the muffin pan in the preheated oven for about 25 or 30 minutes. Remove the muffin pan from the oven, allow to cool for 10 minutes, then gently uncup the *budini* with a knife.

Transfer the *budini* to a serving dish, sprinkle the tops with the confectioners' sugar, and serve hot.

Ciambella di frutta

RICE RING STUFFED WITH FRUIT

SERVES 8

A beautiful presentation with its rice crust, the sauce making a rich color, the drama of flaming when serving it. It is also a versatile dish, because with fresh fruit it is a fine dish for summer, and with dried fruit it works well for winter.

It is also useful as a strong dessert course for dinners that have elaborate but light first and second courses.

FOR THE RICE RING

1 quart whole milk
1½ cups raw rice, preferably Italian Arborio
1 small piece vanilla bean
Pinch of salt
1 tablespoon (½ ounce) sweet butter

1 large, thick-skinned orange
2 extra-large eggs plus 1 extra-large egg yolk
3 tablespoons granulated sugar

FOR THE FILLING

6 medium ripe plums	**4 tablespoons granulated sugar**
3 large, ripe peaches, either	**4 or 5 small pieces lemon peel**
freestone or cling	**¼ cup dry red wine**
2 ounces raisins, about 5	**1 medium orange**
tablespoons	

PLUS

¼ cup granulated sugar	**¼ cup light rum**

PUT the milk and rice in a flameproof casserole, along with the vanilla bean and salt. Place the casserole over medium heat and stir with wooden spoon until it reaches the boiling point. Add the butter, stir for 1 minute more, and then simmer very slowly until the rice is half cooked stirring every so often (about 10 or 12 minutes). Remove the casserole from the heat, let rest for 10 minutes, then drain rice in a colander. Leave rice in colander until cool (about 30 to 35 minutes).

Start the stuffing. Remove the stones from the plums and peaches and cut them into quarters. Place the fruit pieces in a second flameproof casserole with the raisins, sugar, lemon peel, and wine. Place the casserole on medium heat and simmer very gently for 15 minutes.

Cut the orange into very thin slices (with the peel) and add to the casserole. Simmer for 15 minutes more, then remove the casserole from the heat and let rest until cool (about 20 minutes).

Butter a tube pan and coat it with about ¼ cup sugar; preheat the oven to 400 degrees.

Transfer the rice to a large bowl, removing the vanilla bean. Grate the orange peel into the bowl, then add the eggs, egg yolk, and sugar. Mix very well with a wooden spoon until all ingredients are well amalgamated, then arrange three-quarters of the rice mixture around the bottom and sides of the prepared tube pan. Fill the cavity with fruit, but no juice.

Cover the fruit completely with the remaining rice and smooth with a small spatula. Sprinkle with a little sugar, then place the tube pan in a large roasting pan. Pour 4 or 5 cups of lukewarm water into the roasting pan in order to improvise an oversized *bagno maria* (bain-marie).

(continued)

CIAMBELLA DI FRUTTA (continued)

Place the *bagno maria* in the preheated oven for 45 to 50 minutes, then remove the tube pan from the *bagno maria* and let cool for 15 minutes. Unmold on a large ovenproof serving dish.

Warm the rum in a small saucepan (for 30 seconds over low heat) and pour over the *ciambella*. Flame it and serve immediately, with the leftover fruit sauce in a sauceboat.

NOTE: The stuffing for this *ciambella* can be done with dried fruit in winter. The technique will be the same.

FOR THE DRIED FRUIT STUFFING

6 dried peach halves
10 dried apricots
2 ounces raisins, about 5
    tablespoons

4 or 5 small pieces lemon peel
4 tablespoons granulated sugar
1½ cups dry red wine
2 fresh oranges

SOAK the dried fruit in lukewarm water for 20 minutes, then place in a flameproof casserole with the raisins, lemon peel, sugar, and wine. Simmer very slowly for 40 minutes or until soft. Cut the oranges into thin slices (with peel), place them in casserole and simmer for 10 minutes more.

Then proceed with the rest of the recipe.

Frittelle di riso

RICE FRITTERS

SERVES 6

On March 19, the feast of San Giuseppe, every family in Florence makes *frittelle di riso,* these characteristic rice fritters. Every family has its own slight variation, and it is the custom for families to exchange their *frittelle* with others. My aunt used to exchange *frittelle* with twenty to twenty-five families and ate nothing else for all of the day of San Giuseppe. In my family, they fold in egg whites to make the *frittelle* lighter, and flavor with orange and vanilla.

FOR THE FIRST STAGE

3 cups whole milk

1 cup water

1 cup raw rice, preferably

    Italian Arborio

Pinch of salt

2 tablespoons (1 ounce) sweet

    butter

2 or 3 drops vanilla extract

Scant ½ cup granulated sugar

FOR THE SECOND STAGE (NEXT MORNING OR 5 OR 6 HOURS LATER)

4 extra-large egg yolks

1 thick-skinned orange

2 extra-large egg whites

2 quarts vegetable oil (see

    page 22)

¾ cup confectioners' sugar

PUT the milk and water in a flameproof casserole. Add the rice and salt and set the casserole on the heat. Stir continuously with a wooden spoon until the contents reach the boiling point, then add the butter, vanilla, and sugar. Let simmer very slowly, until the rice is soft and has absorbed almost all the liquid (about 15 minutes).

Remove the casserole from the heat and let rest for 10 to 15 minutes, then transfer the contents of the casserole to a colander and let stand overnight (or a minimum of 5 to 6 hours) to drain completely and to thicken.

The next day (or 5 to 6 hours later), transfer the rice to large bowl, add the egg yolks, and mix very well. Grate the orange peel into the bowl and mix thoroughly, then use a wire whisk and a copper bowl to beat the egg whites until stiff and fold into the rice. Prepare a serving dish by lining it with paper towels.

Heat the vegetable oil in a deep-fryer.

When the oil is hot (about 375 degrees), make separate little *frittelle* by placing heaping tablespoons of the rice mixture in the pan, each one well separated from the others. Cook the *frittelle* until golden on both sides, then remove with a strainer-skinner to the prepared serving dish to drain.

When all the *frittelle* are cooked and on the serving dish, remove the paper towels and sprinkle over with the confectioners' sugar. Serve hot.

Torta di riso uso Garfagnana

RICE CUSTARD CAKE

SERVES 6 TO 8

*O*ne of the ambitious rice desserts. A large rice cake, incorporating the technique for *latte alla portoghese* (see page 568) and flavored with Marsala. It is a specialty of the area of the marble quarries near Carrara, where white marble has been quarried since Roman times, scarcely making a dent in the huge marble mountains. These white mountains are among the great sights of Italy; the stone of Michelangelo's sculpture comes from there. Did Michelangelo eat this dessert while he was collecting stone for the monument of Julius II?

1 cup raw rice, preferably
*   Italian Arborio*
Pinch of coarse-grained salt
5 extra-large eggs
9 tablespoons plus 1 cup
*   granulated sugar*
½ cup dry Marsala

1 tablespoon confectioners'
*   sugar*
1½ cups cold milk
Grated peel of a medium orange
*   or lemon*
3 or 4 drops vanilla extract

PUT the rice in a saucepan containing 6 cups of cold water and a pinch of salt. Place the pan over medium heat and keep stirring with a wooden spoon until the water reaches the boiling point, then stop stirring and let the rice half cook (about 10 or 12 minutes). Remove the saucepan from the heat, drain the rice, and cool it under cold running water. Leave the rice in the colander.

Place the eggs in a bowl with the 9 tablespoons sugar and stir with a wooden spoon. When the eggs change color, turning almost white, add the Marsala, confectioners' sugar, cold milk, grated orange or lemon peel, and vanilla. Stir very well until all ingredients are well combined.

Put the 1 cup sugar in a heavy saucepan and place on a very low flame. Let the sugar caramelize very slowly. (See page 569 for procedure.) When golden, quickly pour it into a 9 × 5 × 2¾-inch loaf pan and move it around so the pan is lined completely. Let rest until cool (about 15 minutes).

Preheat the oven to 350 degrees and prepare a water-bath (*bagno maria,* see page 33).

Transfer the rice from the colander to the bowl containing the other ingredients. Mix thoroughly, then pour all the contents of the bowl into the prepared pan. Place pan in the prepared *bagno maria* and bake for 1½ hours.

Remove the pan from the oven and let rest until cool (about 30 minutes), then unmold the *torta* onto a serving dish, leaving the mold on the rice mixture, and refrigerate for at least 5 hours.

Remove the mold, slice the *torta* with a spatula, and serve.

THE DESSERT BUDINO

*T*hese *budini* share with *sformati* the soufflélike principle of folding in egg whites to make the mixture rise when baked. They are, of course, extremely light. Both types are completely Italian, and evidence points to this principle having traveled from Italy to France and not vice versa. Unlike the French, however, the Italians often prefer to unmold these *budini* and *sformati,* causing them to fall slightly. If you are careful, they do not fall very much. Or, if you prefer, serve them in the baking dish.

(Though the word *budino* probably derives from the same root word as the English "pudding," it usually does not connote a similar dish.)

Budino di riso

RICE CAKE WITH AMARETTI

SERVES 6 TO 8

*T*his is related to the *budino di ricotta,* and should not be confused with the little pastries called *budini di riso.*

The rice is cooked in milk and flavored with orange and the bitter-almond taste of *amaretti.* Stiffly beaten egg whites are folded in, and when baked the dessert rises to a fine lightness.

2½ cups whole milk
Pinch of salt
¾ cup raw rice, preferably Italian Arborio
1 tablespoon (½ ounce) sweet butter
10 large amaretti cookies, imported or homemade (see page 595)

1 large, thick-skinned orange
4 extra-large eggs, separated
4½ tablespoons plus ¼ cup granulated sugar
3 tablespoons unbleached all-purpose flour

HEAT the milk to the boiling point in a saucepan. Add the salt and rice and stir continuously for 3 or 4 minutes with a wooden spoon. Let simmer until the rice is half cooked (10 to 12 minutes), then, stirring continuously, add the butter and let simmer until all the milk is absorbed by the rice. Place the contents of the saucepan in a large bowl and let cool (about 1 hour).

Grind the *amaretti* into crumbs in a blender or food processor and place them in a small bowl. Grate in the orange peel and mix through.

When the rice is cold, add the *amaretti* and orange peel to the rice; then mix in the egg yolks and 4½ tablespoons of sugar and stir until all ingredients are very well amalgamated. Add the flour, little by little, stirring constantly for 10 minutes.

Take a soufflé dish 8½ inches in diameter and coat it with butter and the ¼ cup sugar; preheat the oven to 400 degrees.

Use a wire whisk and copper bowl to beat the egg whites until stiff, and fold them very gently into the rice mixture. Pour the rice mixture into the prepared soufflé dish and bake in the preheated oven for 35 to 40 minutes.

Remove from the oven, allow to cool for 10 minutes, then unmold onto a serving dish. Serve hot or cold.

Budino di ricotta

RICOTTA SOUFFLÉ

SERVES 6

*T*he egg whites folded into the ricotta make this dish beautifully light. If unmolded, the *budino* may remain for several days, gradually falling a bit when cold, but turning into one of the lightest of cheesecakes.

3 tablespoons mixed glacéed
   fruit or raisins
1 cup lukewarm milk
15 ounces ricotta, drained
1 large, thick-skinned orange

4 extra-large eggs
2 tablespoons unbleached all-
   purpose flour
11 tablespoons granulated
   sugar

SOAK the glacéed fruit in a bowl containing the lukewarm milk for 20 minutes. Drain the ricotta in a piece of cheesecloth to remove excess liquid, then place in a bowl. Grate the orange peel into the ricotta. Separate 3 of the eggs and add the yolks and the remaining whole egg and mix thoroughly. When the mixture is homogeneous, add the flour, 7 tablespoons of the sugar, and the drained glacéed fruit. Mix very well with a wooden spoon for 3 to 4 minutes.

Butter a soufflé dish 8½ inches in diameter, and coat it with the ¼ cup sugar; preheat the oven to 375 degrees.

Use a wire whisk and copper bowl to beat the egg whites until stiff, then very gently fold into the ricotta mixture. Pour the mixture into the prepared dish and place in the preheated oven for 45 minutes.

Remove from the oven, unmold onto a serving dish, and serve hot.

FRUIT DESSERTS

*T*wo very elaborate treatments of fruit for dessert have already been given: *timballo* of pears poached in wine with whipped cream and *ciambella di frutta,* the rice ring stuffed with fruit and covered with a wine sauce. These two are for the most elaborate, most formal dinners.

A second stage, less elaborate but still fancy, is represented by three recipes: peaches filled with an *amaretti* stuffing, accompanied by *crema zabaione* or whipped cream; peaches filled with a stuffing of *savoiardi* (crushed, toasted ladyfingers), almonds, and bitter almonds, also possibly accompanied by one of the two creams mentioned above; pears poached in wine, preferably Chianti with a little port (this time without the *timballo*), possibly accompanied by one of the two creams.

Thirdly, we have fresh fruit in some special treatment: strawberries in red wine; fresh peaches in red wine; raspberries with whipped cream. These are probably the most favored treatments of these fruits.

In its own category is the Florentine favorite, fruit dipped in batter and deep-fried. The recipe included suggests apples, pears, and strawberries. Deep-fried apple slices is another Florentine specialty adopted by the French as *beignet des pommes.*

And finally, though there is no recipe necessary, let us not forget that the most frequent way to complete a meal in Italy is with simple unadorned fresh fruit of the season. Though this would not be served at a formal dinner, it is very frequently served to family and close friends.

Pesche ripiene

STUFFED PEACHES

SERVES 6

*T*he peaches are baked just enough so they don't lose their fresh taste. The natural flavor is also enhanced by the stuffing, which has an apricot flavor, complementing the peach taste without covering it.

6 large freestone peaches, ripe but not overripe

3 ounces amaretti cookies, imported or homemade (see page 595)

6 tablespoons (3 ounces) sweet butter

¼ cup granulated sugar

¼ cup brandy

PREHEAT the oven to 375 degrees.

Divide the peaches in half and remove the pits. (To halve a peach and remove the pit without breaking the peach, find the line that girdles the peach and follow it in cutting through with a knife. Place one hand firmly on each of the peach halves. To loosen both halves from the pit, gently turn the two halves in opposite directions until they are free of the pit.) With a teaspoon, enlarge the holes left by the pit a little.

Butter a 13½ × 8¾-inch glass baking dish and place all 12 peach halves in it. Crush the *amaretti* into crumbs with mortar and pestle or blender, then fill the peach holes with the *amaretti* crumbs. Put half a tablespoon of butter, then a teaspoon of sugar, over each peach half.

Place the baking dish in the preheated oven for 20 minutes, then remove the dish from oven, add 1 teaspoon of brandy to each peach half, and bake for 15 to 20 minutes more.

Remove the dish from the oven and transfer the peaches to a serving dish. Let stand until completely cooled; do not refrigerate.

NOTE: The dish may be eaten as is or with *panna montata* (see page 566) or *crema zabaione* (see page 564) or *crema pasticcera* (see page 562).

Pesche ripiene con mandorle

PEACHES STUFFED WITH ALMONDS

SERVES 6

*S*imilar to the previous treatment but with a more elaborate stuffing. Almonds and bitter almonds work extremely well in complementing the still-fresh taste of the peaches.

⅔ cup mixed glacéed fruit

1 cup dry white wine

6 large freestone peaches, ripe
    but not overripe

1 lemon

18 **savoiardi** *(ladyfingers)*

4 ounces almonds

1 ounce bitter almonds or
    unblanched almonds

10 tablespoons granulated
    sugar

1 extra-large egg yolk

PREHEAT the oven to 375 degrees.

In a small bowl, soak the glacéed fruit in the wine for 1 hour; place the peaches in a large bowl of cold water with the lemon, cut into halves, and let soak until needed.

Toast the ladyfingers in the preheated oven for about 15 minutes. (Italian ladyfingers are crisp. When the softer ones are toasted, they have a similar texture.) Meanwhile, mix the sweet and bitter almonds together and blanch them, if bitter almonds are available. Otherwise blanch only the 4 ounces sweet almonds.

Remove the ladyfingers from oven and let them cool (about ½ hour). While they cool, place the blanched almonds in the 375-degree oven to toast for about 15 minutes. Remove the almonds from the oven and let them cool (about 15 minutes).

Place the ladyfingers in a mortar (or food processor) and grind them very fine. Transfer them to a large bowl.

Place the cooled toasted almonds in the mortar (or food processor) and grind them very fine as well. Add the ground almonds to the bowl with the ladyfingers. Add 6 tablespoons of the sugar, the glacéed fruit, and its wine to the bowl, then mix all the ingredients together with a wooden spoon. Add the egg yolk to the bowl and mix thoroughly.

Remove the peaches from the water and dry with paper towels. Cut the peaches in half, removing the pits, then enlarge the holes left by the pits slightly with a teaspoon. Fill each peach half with some of the mixture in the bowl, then place the peaches in a buttered 13½ × 8¾-inch glass baking dish. Sprinkle each peach half with 1 teaspoon of the remaining sugar.

Place the baking dish in the 375-degree oven for 35 to 40 minutes, then remove the baking dish from oven and let cool for 30 minutes. Transfer to serving dish to cool completely. Serve at room temperature; do not refrigerate.

NOTE: This dish may be accompanied by *panna montata* (see page 566) or *crema zabaione* (see page 565).

Fragole al vino rosso

STRAWBERRIES IN WINE

SERVES 4

*I*talians choose a "setting" for a special fruit that will best bring out the quality of that fruit. Good red wine is made for strawberries. Good Chiantis generally absorb the fragrance of flower or fruit growing nearby. Perhaps that is why they wed so well with strawberries.

1 pound strawberries
1 lemon

4 cups good-quality dry red wine
½ cup granulated sugar

CLEAN the strawberries and rinse them carefully, then dry with paper towels. Cutting the large strawberries in half, place the strawberries in a large bowl. Squeeze the lemon over the strawberries, then add the wine and sugar to the bowl. Mix the contents of bowl very well and let rest, covered, in the refrigerator for several hours.

Serve a portion of strawberries with some of the wine in each individual bowl.

Pesche al vino

PEACHES IN WINE

SERVES 6

*O*f the nonberry fruits, it is fragrant fresh peaches that respond best to wine. The peaches should not be overly ripe, and should be allowed to live with the wine for some hours, to wed with it.

6 peaches, ripe but not overripe, either freestone or cling
1 lemon

6 heaping tablespoons granulated sugar
3 cups good-quality dry red wine

CAREFULLY rinse the peaches; do not peel them. Cut the peaches in half, removing the pits, then cut the peach halves into 6 square pieces.

Place the pieces in a crockery bowl. Squeeze the lemon into the bowl, over the peaches, then sprinkle on the sugar.

Add the wine to the bowl, cover, and place in the refrigerator for at least 4 hours.

Remove the bowl from the refrigerator, mix the contents well, and transfer them to a serving bowl. (Generally, the bowl is then placed in an improvised oversized *bagno maria* (bain-marie) prepared with ice, because *pesche al vino* should be served very cold.)

Pere al vino

PEARS POACHED IN WINE

SERVES 6

*T*hese whole pears, carefully peeled and with their long stems intact, if cooked according to the directions given will acquire a beautiful wine-red color. They make a fine presentation, simply accompanied by whipped cream or *crema zabaione* or as the contents of an elaborate *timballo* (see page 582). They should be cooked in a typically Italian wine, the finer the quality, the better. A good Chianti or Chianti Riserva will produce a really fine result.

6 large, firm pears, preferably Bosc, with stems

4 cups good-quality dry red wine

1 cup tawny port

1 cup cold water

½ lemon

6 tablespoons granulated sugar

PEEL the pears with a peeler rather than a knife, then flatten the bottoms by cutting off a thin slice. Stand the pears up in a large metal casserole. (The casserole should be large enough to fit pears closely together without crowding, but not large enough to allow them to fall over.)

Add the wine, port, and water to the pears. Squeeze the half lemon and cut off a slice of peel. Add the juice and peel to the casserole, then sprinkle over with 4 tablespoons of the sugar.

Cover the casserole tightly and let simmer slowly for about 25 minutes. Test with a toothpick to be sure the pears are well cooked before removing from the heat, then leave the cooked pears in the casserole for 10 to 15 minutes to cool.

Stand cooled pears up on a serving dish. Cover the dish, being careful not to bruise the pears. Place the dish in the refrigerator for an hour.

Remove the lemon peel from the casserole and transfer the sauce to a small saucepan. Add the remaining sugar and simmer again until the sauce is reduced to the consistency of a light syrup (30 to 40 minutes). Let the sauce cool for 20 to 30 minutes, then remove the pears from the refrigerator and pour the sauce over. Return the pears to the refrigerator for at least 3 hours more before serving.

Lamponi alla panna

RASPBERRIES WITH WHIPPED CREAM

SERVES 4

*I*n Italy, June is the chief month for the incomparable wild straw-berries, *fragoline di bosco,* and for soft, sweet raspberries. These delicacies should be accompanied by the soft unobtrusiveness of a light whipped cream. Fortunately, raspberries are now available for this dessert for much of the year.

1 pound raspberries **Panna montata *(see page 566)***
¼ cup granulated sugar

CLEAN and rinse the raspberries very carefully, then dry with paper towels and let them stand on some more paper towels. Sprinkle the raspberries with a little sugar.

Make the *panna montata.* When the whipped cream is ready, transfer it to a serving bowl. Add the raspberries a few at a time, mixing very gently. Serve immediately.

NOTE: You can prepare this dessert in advance, but combine the *panna montata* and raspberries only at the very last moment before serving.

Frittura mista di frutta

DEEP-FRIED FRUIT IN BATTER

SERVES 8

*T*he fruit is used absolutely natural and fresh, and not marinated. It is dipped in a batter similar to that used for deep-frying chicken, except that brandy replaces the wine. The folded-in egg whites lighten the batter, and keep it full of air when fried. But the nicest aspect of the dish is that the fruit tastes almost fresh after cooking. The apple version is best known, but pears are equally good. The strawberries work marvelously, and usually create a little sensation.

1 ½ cups unbleached all-purpose flour	*2 large Bosc pears, ripe but firm*
Pinch of salt	*Lemon juice*
1 ½ tablespoons olive oil	*16 large strawberries*
2 extra-large eggs, separated	*2 quarts vegetable oil (see page 22)*
¾ cup cold water	*1 cup granulated sugar*
3 tablespoons brandy	
2 large Delicious apples, ripe but firm	

FIRST prepare the batter.

Place the flour in large bowl; add the salt and mix thoroughly. Make a well in the flour and put in the oil and egg yolks, then begin stirring, adding the cold water little by little and incorporating the flour. When all the water is added and the flour incorporated, put in the brandy and stir very well for 10 minutes more.

Let the batter rest, covered, for at least 2 hours in a cool place; do not refrigerate.

Meanwhile, prepare the fruit.

Core apples and pears with an apple corer, then peel carefully and cut horizontally into slices almost ½ inch thick. Place the slices of fruit on a dish. (If you do not use fruit immediately, sprinkle it with some lemon juice to keep it from turning brown.)

Remove the stems from the strawberries and rinse very carefully. Dry with paper towels and let stand on the towel until needed.

When the batter is ready (after at least 2 hours of resting), use a wire whisk and copper bowl to beat the egg whites until stiff. Gently fold the beaten egg whites into the batter and mix carefully. Heat the vegetable oil in a deep-fat fryer; prepare a large serving dish by lining it with paper towels.

When the oil is hot (about 375 degrees), dip each piece of fruit in the batter, making sure that the fruit is completely coated with batter

(continued)

FRITTURA MISTA DI FRUTTA *(continued)*

but that excess is removed. Place the coated fruit pieces in the pan and fry until golden all over (about 1 minute on each side for apples and pears and 1 minute in all for strawberries). Remove the fruit from the pan with a strainer-skimmer and place it on the prepared serving dish.

Place the sugar in a small dish. When all the fruit is cooked and placed on the serving dish, remove the paper towels and then coat the fruit pieces on both sides with sugar. Arrange them on the serving dish in the shape of a ring and serve very hot.

COFFEE

*C*offee is always served at the end of a dinner in Italy, and it is always served black. In the north of Italy it is not accompanied by lemon peel. As previously mentioned, it is served in another room, not at the dinner table.

Anyone who has traveled in Italy has probably noticed that there is a great difference in the taste of the coffee there and what is called "espresso" in some other places. This has to do with both the kind of bean used and the way of roasting it.

The chief bean used in Italy is from the species called *coffea robusta,* and it is found in Africa, Madagascar, India, Southeast Asia, and Java. It is roasted very slowly, at low temperatures. It acquires a color and flavor very different from what is often called "Italian roast" abroad. It is brown rather than black in color. From the taste I would guess that it is roasted both longer and at lower temperatures than the black "Italian roast," and is a mixture of beans of different origin. Certainly it should not have the bitterness one often finds in espresso abroad.

If you have access to a store that sells a variety of coffee beans, I would suggest a mixture of 50 percent Java beans and 50 percent another bean, brown rather than black roast, if you can't find the *coffea robusta* types.

The best espresso is made with a large machine that has strong steam pressure, so that the water passing through the coffee always remains boiling. The closest home machine to this is the Moka type of pot because it also uses the same technique. The reason I do not recommend the Neapolitan type of pot is that when it is turned, though the first water passing through is boiling, it cools down considerably by the time the last water passes through. And it is only boiling water that can draw the essence, the *crema,* out of the coffee to produce the best possible flavor. Of course if you have a small real espresso maker at home, that is best.

Coffee originated in Ethiopia, where it grows wild at high altitudes. It was introduced into Europe by the Venetians in the fifteenth century and into South America, where it is not native, in 1723. It was in the eighteenth century that the real coffee rage started; the first café in Paris was founded around 1700 by the Florentine Procopio.

Making Coffee with the Moka Machine

Fill the detachable bottom half with cold water up to the level of what looks like a little screw on the outside of the pot.

After the beans have been freshly ground, fill the coffee holder loosely without pressing down on the coffee.

From the very beginning, keep the pot over low heat. The pressure will force the water up through the coffee into the upper half. Because the water must travel up, it requires a consistently high temperature to produce the pressure, keeping the water boiling hot even at the end. When the machine begins to gurgle, all the water has passed through and the coffee is ready.

The instructions that come with the machine give some additional tips.

A little sugar brings out the flavor of the coffee. Do not drink the coffee too hot, or you will not taste it.

Afterword: The Aesthetic of Florentine Cooking

*A*t the center remains the Renaissance concept of balance and linearity. One should be able to taste all ingredients. It is the correct proportions of a few ingredients that yields the oft-mentioned "whole greater than the sum of the parts."

The simplicity of Florentine cooking is the conscious simplification of very complex cooking. Waverley Root* has written, "[it is] subtle in its deliberate eschewing of sophistication, which is perhaps the highest sophistication of all."

The reverberations of this simplicity go on and on.

*Waverley Root, *The Food of Italy,* Atheneum, New York, 1971.

639

Measurements Used in This Book

U.S. Measurement*	Conversion to Metric System (1 kilogram = 1000 grams)
1 cup all-purpose flour (do not sift) = about 4 ounces	about 112 grams
1 cup granulated sugar = about 8 ounces	about 224 grams
16 tablespoons = 1 cup	
3 teaspoons = 1 tablespoon	
1 ounce (solid)	about 28 grams
1 pound (solid)	about 448 grams
4 cups = 2 pints = 1 quart (liquid)	almost 1 liter

*Cup measurements are based on U.S. standard measuring cups such as Foley.

Index

INDEX

For information on how you can have **Better Homes and Gardens** delivered to your door, write to Mr. Robert Austin, P.O. Box 4536, Des Moines, IA 50336.